HOLLYWOOD'S HAWAII

War Culture

Edited by Daniel Leonard Bernardi

Books in this new series address the myriad ways in which warfare informs diverse cultural practices, as well as the way cultural practices—from cinema to social media—inform the practice of warfare. They illuminate the insights and limitations of critical theories that describe, explain and politicize the phenomena of war culture. Traversing both national and intellectual borders, authors from a wide range of fields and disciplines collectively examine the articulation of war, its everyday practices, and its impact on individuals and societies throughout modern history.

HOLLYWOOD'S HAWAII

Race, Nation, and War

DELIA MALIA CAPAROSO KONZETT

R

RUTGERS UNIVERSITY PRESS

New Brunswick, Camden, and Newark, New Jersey, and London

Library of Congress Cataloging-in-Publication Data

Names: Konzett, Delia Caparoso, author.

Title: Hollywood's Hawaii : race, nation, and war / Delia Malia Caparoso Konzett.
Description: New Brunswick, New Jersey : Rutgers University Press, [2017] | Series:
War culture | Includes bibliographical references and index.
Identifiers: LCCN 2016024605| ISBN 9780813587448 (hardcover : alk. paper) | ISBN
9780813587431 (pbk. : alk. paper) | ISBN 9780813587455 (e-book (epub)) | ISBN
9780813587462 (e-book (web pdf))
Subjects: LCSH: Hawaii—In motion pictures. | Oceania—In motion pictures. |
Motion picture locations—Hawaii. | Motion picture locations—Oceania. | Motion
pictures—Social aspects—United States—20th century. | Motion pictures—United
States—History—20th century. | Race relations in motion pictures.
Classification: LCC PN1995.9.H38 K66 2017 | DDC 791.4309961—dc23
LC record available at https://lccn.loc.gov/2016024605A British Cataloging-in-
Publication record for this book is available from the British Library.

∞   The paper used in this publication meets the requirements of the American
National Standard for Information Sciences—Permanence of Paper for Printed
Library Materials, ANSI Z39.48-1992.

www.rutgersuniversitypress.org

Manufactured in the United States of America

For my mother
And in memory of my father, native of Honolulu,
Korean and Vietnam War veteran, and recipient of the
Bronze Star Medal, who spent happy childhood days
diving off Pier 16

CONTENTS

ACKNOWLEDGMENTS

This book owes its intellectual debt to my key mentors during my graduate education, namely Spanish philosopher Angel Medina and German film studies scholar Miriam Hansen. I have also benefited greatly from the valuable insights of Charles Musser, specialist extraordinaire of early cinema studies, and his continued sponsorship of my research project. My original research was made possible with the help of a grant from the National Endowment for the Humanities that allowed me to visit the University of Hawai'i at Manoa and consult its archives of military history, particularly the Hawai'i War Records Depository, where I was kindly assisted by James Cartwright and the ever helpful Sherman Seki. Additional visits to the Bernice Pauahi Bishop Museum (Honolulu) and its vast collection of Pacific cultural artifacts and the James Jones literary estate at Beinecke Library (New Haven, Connecticut) provided further helpful background. Cinema scholar Glenn Man has also supported my research over the years. At the University of New Hampshire, I would like to acknowledge the generous support of the English Department, the Women's Studies Program, and the Center for Humanities that made this research project possible with various grants and awards. Janet Aikins Yount, Andrew Merton, Rachel Trubowitz, and Marla Brettschneider in their function as chairs have lent encouragement and help. My colleagues have likewise supported me with their interest, advice, and steady backing of my research. I would further like to thank *Quarterly Review of Film and Video* and the *Contemporary West* for their early interest in my work. This work would not have found its ideal publisher without the invitation of series editor Daniel Bernardi to submit my manuscript for review at Rutgers University Press. I would like to thank especially editor-in-chief Leslie Mitchner and assistant editor Lisa Boyajian for their enthusiastic professionalism in guiding this work through the publishing process, Carrie Hudak for overseeing the entire production process, and Joseph Dahm for a superb job of copyediting. Finally, I owe deep gratitude to my extended Hawaiian *ohana* on the mainland and in the islands for their love and care as well as my patient partner who joined me in long late-night hours of watching many of the discussed films.

HOLLYWOOD'S HAWAII

INTRODUCTION

The American Empire in the South Pacific and Its Representation in Hollywood Cinema, 1898–Present

> To most Americans, then, Hawai'i is theirs: to use, to take, and, above all, to fantasize about long after the experience.
>
> —Haunani-Kay Trask

> We were on the island of Hawaii. I think I was there three months. It was fantastic. It is not much different than films.
>
> —Bo Derek

When celebrated Hollywood director King Vidor decided to film *Bird of Paradise* (1932), he made several key decisions about set and location. Given that the majority of South Seas dramas were shot on studio back lots or Catalina Island off the shore of Los Angeles, Vidor nevertheless aimed for some authenticity when he finally chose Hawaii and its South Pacific vicinity as the film's location. However, his search for an authentic set quickly gave way to more radical construction when he discovered that his chosen location, a Hawaiian lagoon originally gleaned from a travel brochure, revealed in fact intrusive elements such as modern residences and a country club. Moving the film location to another lagoon that unfortunately lacked the necessary palm trees, Vidor set out to remake the idyllic South Pacific on his own terms: "I decided to employ the telephone company's large trucks, built for installing telephone poles, to move cocoanut palm trees from an inland grove to a selected beach near which the yacht could maneuver and subsequently anchor. With their derricks the linesmen transplanted about twenty impressive trees. By now the natives were beginning to wonder about my sanity."[1] This seemingly harmless and humorous anecdote reveals the willful articulation of a reality removed from the original, a practice that is the hallmark of Hollywood melodrama. Vidor's casting of ethnic characters similarly betrayed a disregard for authenticity but suited Hollywood's prevalent Jim Crow practices by not offending the sensibilities of its mainstream audiences and their apartheid codes of social interaction. Vidor settled for the common practice of casting roles of nonwhite characters with stand-in performances of fetishized and more acceptable ethnic actors. He chose the Mexican actress Dolores del Rio, the first popular crossover Latina celebrity in Hollywood, for the role as the native Polynesian girl Luana, love interest of the film's white lead and star Joel McCrea. A pre-code film, *Bird of Paradise* created a scandal when del Rio appeared nude in a lengthy, erotic underwater scene as well as topless with only leis to hide her breasts in a frenzied hula performance. In the context of US geopolitical interests in the South Pacific after its 1893 overthrow and 1898 annexation of Hawaii's kingdom, the anecdote and film further point to practices of imperialism that Hollywood all too readily incorporates into its cinematic rhetoric, thereby aestheticizing the national political agenda of overseas expansion. Polynesian culture is cinematically constructed and fetishized within the symbolic imagination of the United States, itself a fluid concept of a nation actualizing itself in repeated acts of cinematic inauguration.

Unlike traditional European nationalisms built on literature and the arts, twentieth-century American nationalism is most significantly promoted in the medium of cinema. The narration of nation becomes the main function of Hollywood cinema, an institution that in its vertical integration of production, distribution, and exhibition mirrors US capitalist enterprise and in its narrative codes replicates the nation's major social markers of race, gender, class, religion, and sexual orientation. The first major founding narrative of nation is offered by D. W. Griffith's infamous *The Birth of a Nation* (1915). This testament film revisits the Civil War, the founding moment of the modern unified nation, and does so with a racist and revisionist perspective, showing empathy for southern slave owners, contempt for the liberated slaves, and heroic worship of the Ku Klux Klan. These reactionary claims are couched within a melodramatic plot of white male chivalry with its restoration of plantation culture. As French philosopher and film scholar Gilles Deleuze claims, "The American cinema constantly shoots and reshoots a single fundamental film, which is the birth of a nation-civilisation, whose first version was provided by Griffith."[2] American cinema, according to Deleuze, is based on a "belief in the finality of universal of history . . . the blossoming of the American nation."[3] Subsequent nation birthing films become even more ambitious as Hollywood achieves global economic dominance in the 1920s. The teleology of Manifest Destiny, represented by expanding Christian capitalism and its growing claim as the new legitimate world leader of commerce and democratic freedom, was to produce the highest achievement of nation building in history, namely America's exceptionalism as the greatest nation on earth. Major Hollywood directors following Griffith, namely Raoul Walsh, W. S. Van Dyke, King Vidor, Victor Fleming, John Ford, John Huston, Howard Hawks, Edward Dmytryk, Fred Zinnemann, Otto Preminger, and many others, similarly give birth to the American nation in repeated acts of cinematic inauguration, turning especially to the South Pacific as a gateway to the world. As Wheeler Winston Dixon notes, "the lure of the tropics is the same as the lure of Manifest Destiny, the desire to escape beyond existing frontiers into newer ones."[4]

The remote and highly imaginary South Pacific and Hawaii provide a convenient narrative that cements a nation internally torn and divided. The South Pacific was increasingly brought under the scopic regime of Hollywood, allowing studios to concoct narratives of cultural/civilizational superiority and benevolent territorial administration, spreading thereby the influence of Eurocentric Judeo-Christian belief systems. Griffith would repeat his inaugurating act of birthing the nation in *The Idol Dancer* (1920), a film set in the Pacific to reinforce his views of US exceptionalism and its mission to convert minstrel-like heathens and exoticized cannibals. Pacific island fetishism, with its fantasy return to an imagined utopian paradise, so vividly displayed in Hollywood's South Seas films, can be attributed to the intertwined logic of colonial desire and domination. As Slavoj Žižek explains, "The notional background for fetishism thus lies in evolutionist universalism: 'fetishism' has a place within the notions of a universal history progressing from the lower stage (the veneration of natural objects) to the abstract spiritual stage (the purely spiritual God); it allows us to grasp the unity of human species, to recognize the Other, while none the less asserting our superiority. The fetishized Other is always 'lower'—that is to say, the notion of fetishism is strictly correlative to the gaze of the observer who approaches the 'primitive' community from the outside."[5] The regime of looking at foreign Pacific territories, suitably framed as the locale of lower civilizations refracted by the lenses of US colonial fantasy and cinema, promotes the narrative of global expansion and the nation's rise to world leader as the existential narrative of the American Dream. In an endless series of films about the South Pacific, Western expansion is shown as a necessary export of higher civilizational standards to less productive pagan cultures in need of modern Western practices of free-market capitalism and moral uplift. The films' melodramatic and escapist fantasies of colonial desire mirror and reinforce the legitimacy of the actual colonial and imperialist expansion into the Pacific that the United States has pursued aggressively since the 1890s, after its westward expansion was concluded and consolidated during the last major Indian Wars and the surrender of their territories.

The Mexican-American War gave a first indication that US territorial expansion was not to stop at foreign borders. With its militarily imposed Treaty of Guadalupe Hidalgo, the United States secured in 1848 large land gains such as California, half of New Mexico, and most of Arizona, Nevada, and Utah as well as the remaining parts of Wyoming and Colorado. Similarly, overseas in Hawaii, when arguments of cultural superiority failed to convince, military power was brought to bear as in the Bayonet Constitution of Hawaii in 1887, rewritten with US economic interests and enforced by a hired militia. In 1893, this assertion of military power ended in the overthrow of the Hawaiian Kingdom with the help of three hundred Marines from the US cruiser *Boston*. Finally, during the Spanish-American War of 1898, the United States expanded its secured continental borders to the overseas territories of Hawaii, the Philippines, Puerto Rico, and Cuba. In contrast to the earlier land conflict with Mexico, this war involved for the first time the extensive use of the US Navy and the Asiatic Squadron in the Battle of Manila Bay. Following in the tradition of the British Empire, the United States realized that naval power was absolutely essential for global domination. As early as 1873, General Schofield on a secret mission to check the defenses of US ports recommended the establishment of a US naval port at Pearl Harbor twenty years prior to the kingdom's overthrow. This gateway to the Pacific and the eventual seat of the Pacific Fleet would ultimately draw the not so surprising Japanese "sneak" military attack on Hawaii as a strategic outpost of major US naval forces.

In addition to military control, the scopic range of newly acquired overseas territories needed appropriate lenses to size up the new possessions and bring them under visual control. Hollywood, with its various scenarios of Westerns, border films, and South Seas fantasies, would fulfill this function of national consolidation at the level of symbolic representation. While films are generally viewed as harmless entertainment products, their suggestive and coercive power for mass consensus cannot be ignored. The connection between modern military power and cinema, as philosopher Paul Virilio has argued, is not merely coincidental. In Virilio's notion of the logistics of perception, which undergirds contemporary warfare, the field of battle also exists as a "field of perception": "Alongside the 'war machine,' there has always existed an ocular . . . 'watching machine' capable of providing soldiers, and particularly commanders, with a visual perspective on military action under way."[6] The extensive use of cameras during World War I for air reconnaissance of the battlefield offers a simple example that superior vision translates into military superiority. On the battlefield of competing symbolic and cultural representation, Hollywood cinema provides a similar superior angle from which territories can be brought under its scopic regime and recast in the vision and the language of the conqueror. It is one thing to conquer the world but another to make the citizens of one's country grasp and realize this newly attained global dominance. A war drama and spy film such as Henry Hathaway's *The House on*

92nd Street (1945), telling the story of counterespionage against the Nazis, curiously includes initial references to December 7 and the dropping of the atom bomb on Japan, even though the plotline is entirely focused on Germany. By means of these references, the film establishes a global map extending from the Pacific to Western Europe with the United States as its guardian of democracy. Routinely subjected to Hollywood's colonial lenses, Hawaii and the Pacific thus operate as the synecdochal stand-in for US world domination, a vision that is repeatedly celebrated in numerous South Seas films and transmitted to its audiences as a form of national pedagogy on world citizenship.

Cinema had barely learned to walk during the late 1890s when it was able to convey direct images of US expansion in the Pacific to home audiences, thereby naturalizing these new acquisitions. Since the South Pacific is essentially a non-Western territory, it requires violent acts of translation via cinema that distort the representation of its depicted region. Apart from an initial pragmatic stocktaking of the new territories and their economic potential seen in early shorts by Thomas Edison (shot on Hawaii between 1898 and 1906), Hollywood soon began adding fiction to fact (starting around 1914 in early South Pacific films), embarking on a fantasy ride of national imaginings. This function of cinema becomes especially apparent during moments of national crisis as seen in World War II, where it is intentionally enlisted as a propaganda tool for military effort. However, cinema as a tool of national surveillance and expansion is not entirely the product of warfare but also permits during times of peace for the visual assimilation of newly acquired territories. Such is the case with Hawaii, which after being forcefully incorporated as a territory has since taken on the life of a culture of military occupation. This colonial and military annexation, however, is not immediately visible due to the overwhelming presence of Hawaii's tourist industry and its reputation as an island paradise, one firmly established in Hollywood's pre- and postwar cinema. As Kathy E. Ferguson and Phyllis Turnbull argue, the military in Hawaii "is hidden in plain sight" and its terrain is marked by the "paradox of visibility and invisibility."[7]

In its trajectory, this book traces Hollywood's representation of the major historical upheavals that have affected Hawaii since its annexation, beginning with Edison's 1898 shorts and spanning from South Seas fantasy films (1915–1933) to military and mass ornament musicals (1934–1941), often with plantation culture values as their background. The attack on Pearl Harbor causes a rupture in this tradition and advances new genres such as World War II combat films and war/propaganda documentaries (1941–1945). Post–World War II films combine military and tourist leisure aspects in various genres of war films, romantic comedies, and social problem films (1946–1963). Since then films have variously revisited the Pacific with clichéd scenarios of tourism, romance, escape, or heroic military history, with only a few addressing the history of Hawaii's colonization by New England missionaries and its subsequent subordination to US interests, be they military or commercial in nature. While the majority of films are not direct historical documents and are fictive in nature, they address, refract, and recast indirectly the following historical moments: (1) colonization, occupation, and annexation of Hawaii beginning in 1898 and its subsequent stages of the revival of southern plantation culture in a post–Civil War United States during the first three decades of the twentieth century; (2) militarization during the 1930s as the United States felt increasingly challenged by Japanese imperial expansion in the Pacific; (3) escalation of this rivalry into war and the attack on Pearl Harbor as a result of having turned Hawaii into a major naval base and military fortress; and (4) post–World War II conversion of plantation culture into a modern-day leisure/entertainment industry and the accompanying birth and development of the military-industrial complex. Hollywood films about Hawaii and the Pacific thus serve a double function of consolidating the nation's racial and cultural hierarchy from within while also laying claim to US leadership in the world, particularly in their emphasis on military and geopolitical interests. As instructive scenarios, they turn the midwesterner, as Henry Luce argued in his *Life* magazine essay "The American Century," published in February 1941, into a cosmopolitan: "Midwestern Americans are today the least provincial people in the world."[8]

Hawaii's statehood, granted in 1959, is often construed as a major turning point in its history, but it does little to change the conditions of ownership on the islands (one-fourth of Oahu's land is in military possession) and its dominant military culture (one-fifth of the population serves in the military); nor does it change Hawaii's ideological representation in cinema. Hawaiian sovereignty movements, a powerful voice in the 1990s, likewise could not reverse Hawaii's forceful incorporation into US military and commercial interests. President Clinton's apology for the US takeover of Hawaii, ratified by Congress as a joint resolution in 1993, appears as a first step in the right direction with its frank admission of the violation of Hawaii's sovereignty: "To acknowledge the 100th anniversary of the January 17, 1893 overthrow of the Kingdom of Hawaii, and to offer an apology to Native Hawaiians on behalf of the United States for the overthrow of the Kingdom of Hawaii."[9] However, this apology remains purely formal in nature and comes with no responsibility on the part of the US government. The more recent Akaka Bill (Native Hawaiian Government Reorganization Act) demands federal recognition of native Hawaiians as indigenous people in the manner of Native Americans. This bill was originally introduced in 2000 and frequently amended but failed to achieve legislation in 2011. In the meantime, the state of Hawaii signed the Native Hawaiian Recognition Bill into law in 2011, granting indigenous rights to native Hawaiians and their descendants. In the current registration process for electing a native governing body, however, native Hawaiians share conflicting views whether their fate resembles those of Native Americans. Some call instead for the outright restoration of sovereignty rather than mere protected rights from within US administrative structures. International legal scholars similarly argue that Hawaii is still presently under occupation, since no treaty was ever signed between the abolished Hawaiian Kingdom and the United States, agreeing to this hostile takeover.[10]

The political status of Hawaii presents itself as an ongoing and complex question that cannot be addressed within the scope of this more limited and specialized study, which focuses solely on Hollywood's representation of Hawaii and the South Pacific. Hollywood aggressively participated in nation building and the expansion of markets and territories both in practice and on screen, where it helped rewrite US history in the view of its victors for mass audiences and popular consumption. During World War II, Hollywood directly worked in tandem with the government in order to spread and defend its interests. Hollywood's cinematic apparatus was and is instrumental in construing the mythology of contemporary Hawaii and its incorporation into the United States. As such, it makes artificial and externally imposed changes appear as natural and self-evident, with Hawaii appearing as a legitimate new space representing US interests. In order to implement this mythology, powerful cinematic tropes of containment, substitution, and appropriation are deployed and represent natives as undeserving of their land, feature colonial settlers at home in the cultural traditions of the Pacific, and transform Pacific traditions into phantom mirages of Hollywood fantasies. By extension, Hawaii and the Pacific with its majority nonwhite population of Hawaiians and Asians become "the first strange place," as Bailey and Farber argue, the gateway and access route to US global dominance.[11]

The most important discourse in helping to accomplish this representational makeover of Hawaii in terms of Hollywood fantasy is that of an idealized whiteness subsuming nonwhite ethnicities under its rule. Noted film scholars such as Miriam Hansen, Thomas Cripps, Richard Dyer, Michael Rogin, Daniel Bernardi, and Charles Musser have stressed how the construction of modern whiteness emerges in the nascent stages of Hollywood cinema as part of its reflection of the national and social formation of race discourse in the United States. Diverse European immigrant cultures were taught by Hollywood and other cultural institutions to adopt a perspective of whiteness that eradicated their difference and ensured their successful assimilation into an imagined white mainstream structured around core values of Anglo-American culture. Representations of idealized whiteness disseminated in film not only were intended for perpetuating an internal hierarchy of race but also served the additional purpose of instructing the nation in new entitlements that articulated its exceptionalism on the global stage.

Given these strong biases in Hollywood, it is necessary to analyze and understand the national cinematic imagination in the Pacific in relation to the cultural landscape on the continent and its prevalent discourses on race, global governance, and military culture. In analogy to Gary Okihiro's study *Island World* (2008), Hollywood's imaginary Hawaii and the Pacific are presented not as peripheral to the nation but as central to the formation of its narrative. Okihiro focuses particularly on the intense exchanges between Hawaii and New England in the nineteenth century. However, my research here, which is mainly concerned with Hollywood's construction of Hawaii, says very little about the actual histories of the Pacific and Hawaii, already covered in many excellent historical and critical works by Ronald Takaki, Gary Okihiro, Noenoe K. Silva, Haunani-Kay Trask, Jane Desmond, Beth Bailey, David Farber, Kathy Ferguson, and Phyllis Turnbull, to name just a few. Instead, my work explores the cinematic rhetoric of Hollywood's expansionist, military, and Orientalist imagination and its performance of the narration of US nationhood. For this reason, I have retained the spelling of "Hawaii" in its traditional colonized form ("Hawaii" rather than "Hawai'i") to indicate that we are dealing with an imagined product erected on the colonial fantasy surrounding this formerly sovereign kingdom. The goal is to understand the inner workings of the US colonial perspective and its system of representation as conveyed via Hollywood melodrama and narrative. Robert Schmitt, Houston Wood, Glenn Man, Luis Reyes, and Jeffrey Geiger have laid first foundations for this type of inquiry. The scope of these earlier works is extended here through an analysis of South Pacific cinema from 1898 to the present with the use of contemporary critical methodologies.

My analysis seeks to turn the traditional white investigative and ethnographic gaze upside down by placing the entertainment products of Hollywood themselves under scrutiny. In line with W.E.B. Du Bois's charge that minorities, particularly African Americans, are falsely and conveniently represented as "problem groups," problematic practices of white majority culture as given in Hollywood's Pacific cinema are examined instead with a critical lens. This work benefits especially from the groundbreaking inquiries of film historian and critic Richard Dyer in his study *White: Essays on Race and Culture* (1997); from Michael Rogin and Daniel Bernardi's work on whiteness in cinema; and perhaps in a more indirect way from the subversive exposure of white exhibition practices and museum culture in the installations of Fred Wilson as given especially in *Mining the Museum* (1992). Wilson's installation "[examines] the ideological apparatus of the museum in general and [explores] how one museum in particular has ignored the histories of people of color."[12] As Lisa G. Corrin summarizes Wilson's strategy, "It is one thing to talk about race and museums in an alternative space or hip commercial gallery, but it is quite another to address it in an established museum by using its own collection and its own history."[13] Similarly, *Hollywood's Hawaii* places this powerful national and global institution into a long overdue dialogue concerning its exclusionary and ethnographic practices, thereby foregrounding and reversing the colonial politics of the gaze to which Hawaii and the South Pacific have long been subjected in Hollywood films.

1 ❊ THE SOUTH PACIFIC AND HAWAII ON SCREEN

Territorial Expansion and Cinematic Colonialism

It is perhaps no mere coincidence that the end of the Hawaiian Kingdom falls into the same time period when Thomas Edison, a founding figure in the modern invention of cinema, designed and developed the Kinetoscope.[1] Around the same time, the anti-monarchist Bayonet Constitution of 1887, imposed upon King Kalakaua and enforced by the US Navy, triggered a transfer of Hawaii's sovereignty in 1893 with a coup d'état by the US military. Sanford B. Dole, a relative of the Big Five family oligarchy that controlled Hawaii's economic affairs, led the provisional government that paved the way for Hawaii's full annexation by the United States in 1898.[2] Thomas Edison premiered and exhibited his first film, *Fred Ott's Sneeze*, one year after the kingdom's overthrow in 1894, producing thereafter numerous film shorts depicting daily and mundane events of American life. The advent of cinema coincided with American territorial expansion via military force in the Spanish-American War of 1898, which brought the United States into the possession of Puerto Rico, Cuba, the Philippines, and Guam, along with its territorial annexation of Hawaii. Edison's film crew captured and restaged this war in more than sixty film shorts for an American audience that had yet to catch up to the new reality of the country's overseas imperialism. French philosopher and cultural theorist Paul Virilio, a specialist in military technology and logistics, links the new technology of cinema directly to the birth of modern warfare with its improved abilities of surveillance and battlefield reconnaissance: "Just as the nitrocellulose that went into film stock was also used for the production of explosives, so the artilleryman's motto was the same as the cameraman's: lighting reveals everything."[3] The logistics of perception, one can argue, extends beyond the battlefield to the enterprise of colonial and territorial expansion, since it delivers the geological contours, topography, and socioeconomic outlines of new territorial possessions. As we will see, Thomas Edison's first shorts depicting Hawaii are far from innocent local portrayals of the islands but pursue a strategic goal that parallels US expansionism at the beginning of the twentieth century.

Cinema ushered in the modern era for the United States since it developed a unique art form with a photographic realism unmatched by earlier arts, one that would allow American culture to document, reassure, and replicate itself simply by the act of narrative self-observation in motion pictures. In the context of this new medium of mass entertainment, Miriam Hansen speaks of the simultaneous emergence of a new public sphere with a much wider range of social inclusiveness and participatory democratic access to the medium. For example, this new inclusiveness of cinema extended to the working classes and newly settled immigrants: "The nickelodeons offered easy access and a space apart, an escape from overcrowded tenements and sweatshop labor."[4] Cinema's introspective national gaze marketed for mass consumption would quickly become the dominant mode of symbolic cultural discourse and in some ways dislocate reality as such. In the much quoted words of Judith Mayne, "movie houses and nickelodeons were the back rooms of the Statue of Liberty."[5] American acculturation and norms would, so to speak, begin in cinema, before they would find their way into the real world.

This reversal of cause and effect in which cinematic reality would appear to have preceded reality also applies to the perception of modern Hawaii, which can be roughly dated to the end of its monarchy and the rise of cinema. The perception of this remote and newly acquired territory by a wider mass audience on the mainland occurred predominantly through the illusion of cinema.[6] Not surprisingly, the earliest existing film footage of Hawaii dates to its annexation in 1898 and was shot by James H. White and W. Bleckyrden of the Edison Manufacturing Company on their trip to the Philippines, which entailed a stopover in the harbor of Honolulu. From this point on, Hawaii would slowly insert itself into the national imaginary on the US mainland via the dissemination of cinema, reaching its culmination during World War II and the attack on Pearl Harbor. Paralleling its development of increasing significance in the national imaginary, one can also see an evolution as the cinematic depiction of Hawaii traversed various film genres. After Hawaii and the Pacific's initial portrayals within the scope of realism and mundane actualities, a second stage of idealization shaped its cinematic expression around fantasy and romance with an emphasis on the exotic, primitive, and mythical Hawaii and the South Seas. Increased realism in the late 1930s with a focus on modern Hawaii gave way to the World War II combat genre, highlighting geopolitical concerns and Hawaii's multicultural society. Eventually low mimetic forms such as comedy highlighting mass tourism and leisure (e.g., Elvis Presley as the returning soldier in *Blue Hawaii*) emerged in the postwar era.

This lapse from exotic fantasy into war and postwar realism would also confront American viewers increasingly with troubling questions pertaining to race, territory, and democracy that had been buried and repressed in the initial depiction of Hawaii and the Pacific's exotic islands. In fact, the escapist fantasies found in films depicting Hawaii and the Pacific in the 1920s and 1930s should not be disconnected from war film altogether, as they tacitly continued an act of war and territorial annexation—namely completing Hawaii's annexation from 1898—through an imperialist visual assimilation of Hawaii as a Pacific outpost for the US Navy into the cultural and cinematic imaginary of the United States. As Miriam Hansen points out, the "universal-language metaphor," implying that cinema's visual language could communicate across cultural, linguistic, and national divides, "had harbored totalitarian and imperialist tendencies to begin with."[7] From an economic point of view, one could also argue that the selling of imperialist fantasies via cinematic illusions of Hawaii and the adjoining South Pacific proved just as lucrative as the actual economic exploitation of Hawaii. This study, concerned with the representation of Hawaii and the South Pacific in US cinema, will pay specific attention to this secondary symbolic structure through which Hawaii and the South Pacific are disseminated, traded, and eventually incorporated into the national imaginary. In the modern era, cinema superseded the mostly written accounts of US forays into the Pacific in the nineteenth century (e.g., novellas by Herman Melville; letters and essays by Mark Twain; travelogues and seafaring journals) since now, as a twentieth-century mass medium, it reached a much wider audience and was no longer restricted to a smaller audience composed of educated and elite readers.

HAWAII: A TERRITORIAL ACQUISITION IN FILM

The development of cinema or the photoplay as a theatrical form of visual entertainment projected onto a screen for a seated audience is generally attributed to the Lumière brothers, who premiered their *cinématographe* in 1895 as a combined camera, printer, and on-screen projector. Edison's Kinetoscope, a more individualized viewing or peeping box, was quickly adapted and updated to accommodate the more collectively engaging medium of screen projection and used for the first time in its American version as the Vitascope projector in 1896. As Charles Musser notes in *The Emergence of Cinema*, "In late April 1896 the vitascope was showing films in only one American theater, Koster & Bial's Music Hall in New York City, but the subsequent diffusion was remarkable. By May 1897, only one year later, several hundred projectors were in use across the country. Honolulu had its first picture show in early February 1897."[8] This rapid transition to public screenings across the United States and its territories would eventually prove crucial for the dissemination of cinema as a powerful mass medium. It is remarkable to note that Honolulu was already included early on in the distribution of this new technology, one year prior to Hawaii's official annexation. This new national imaginary carried via the medium of cinema was extended to the outer borders of the newly emerging American empire and played a crucial role in its consolidation. The inclusion of Honolulu serves a further purpose than the mere extension of cinema's US markets, making use of the imperialist annexation of Hawaii's territory. America's latest technology was meant to be marketed worldwide, and Honolulu can in this sense be understood as one of the nation's significant gateways to the world.

As Richard Abel notes in his *Encyclopedia of Early Cinema*, Hawaii was in a vanguard position in the global expansion of its industry, particularly pertaining to the South Pacific: "Moving pictures also prospered on other islands in the Pacific, and again Hawaii was in the vanguard. As early as 1908 there were five nickelodeons in Honolulu, and five or six more on other islands of the group by the following year. In 1915 *Photoplay* reported that there were no fewer than 35 moving picture theaters in Honolulu alone. . . . Generally the audience who attended Hawaiian shows were mixed—American (white), Hawaiian, Chinese, Japanese."[9] In contrast to later mystifications and clichés of Hawaii as a leisurely island paradise, the United States pursued clearly pragmatic economic goals in its newly annexed territory. In line with this market expansionist ideology, Edison's company and their offshoots produced film footage of the Spanish-American War in 1898 and also documentary shorts of daily life in Hawaii as early as 1898. Much like those of the Lumière brothers, Edison's recordings produced actualities, slices of mundane reality, to be consumed by audiences as mirror images of themselves and their modernizing nations.

Edison Manufacturing Company produced the earliest example of Hawaii on film with its cameramen James H. White and W. Bleckyrden. The recently restored film short, titled *Kanakas Diving for Money, no. 2* (June 22, 1898), shows a number of Hawaiian boys and young adults diving for money thrown from a boat or pier on which a stationary camera is filming their activity.[10] The image, with its deep focus, is thoroughly structured into distinct planes of foreground (young divers), middle ground (an outrigger canoe slowly traversing the screen), background (a large merchant ship on a dock), and remote background (multiple large merchant vessels lining the horizon). This screen image evokes hardly an island paradise but rather a busy commercial harbor. Even leisurely activities such as diving involve the pursuit of money and are placed into the foreground. The middle ground, which shows Hawaii's traditional outrigger canoe, is fully encircled and framed by commercial activities.

This subject was reshot in 1901 by Robert Bonine in the film short *Boys Diving, Honolulu*,[11] displaying again young Hawaiian boys diving for coins. A former cameraman for Edison Studios, Bonine would deliver further film footage of Hawaii in 1902 while working for Edison's competitor American Mutoscope and Biograph

Company. This company, founded by Edison's former coworker William Kennedy Dixon, challenged Edison's Vitascope projection technology and would eventually win out as the dominant film company, signing America's film pioneer D. W. Griffith in 1908. American Mutoscope and Biograph Company not only surpassed the quality of Vitascope but also was linked to subsidiaries of the British Mutoscope Company, ensuring wider global distribution.

Along with *Boys Diving, Honolulu*, Bonine shot two shorts in 1901 documenting the harvesting of sugar cane that emphasize a commercially exploitative use of Hawaii's islands. *Cutting Sugar Cane* (1902),[12] a short of approximately twenty-five seconds, opens with a wide shot of a Hawaiian cane field populated with multiple workers who look to be of Filipino descent given their darker skin complexions. Near the center of the frame in the middle ground, a foreman (possibly white) on a white horse is shown pointing and directing workers who occupy the foreground. The foreman turns in a circle and eventually disappears into the field in the remote background. His riding trajectory measures out the large enterprise of harvesting that the audience witnesses, revealing further workers in the background. In the foreground, a similarly busy and industrious atmosphere prevails with workers loading the harvested cane onto a horse carriage seen on the right side of the frame with another white horse behind it. The entire frame is densely populated and highly kinetic, depicting an ambience of industriousness and tireless work. Cinematically, the filmmaker displays excellent skills in the use of deep space composition with the structuring of the fore-, middle-, and background that highlights a mobile kinetic frame as well as off-screen space, which extends the busy activity beyond the screen with workers moving in and out of the frame.

Loading Sugar Cane (1902) completes the documentation of the commercial enterprise of harvest sugar cane.[13] In this short, the audience is placed into the midst of the loading activity. It opens with local field workers with head covers for protection against heat, carrying bundled cane across several loading planks onto what appears to be a freight vehicle, possibly a train. A foreman occupies the center of the frame, supervising the workers. Suddenly, several white men, distinguished by their business suits and straw hats, walk into the frame from behind the camera and begin assisting the workers. As in the previous shorts, the American empire is shown hard at work and provides viewer identification via the use of off-screen space that connects the reality outside the frame to the one witnessed on-screen. An intimate over-the-shoulder perspective links the viewer directly to the harvest activity. In addition, the footage, with its unusual inclusion of businessmen assisting in the loading, stresses the financial, commercial, and administrative aspects of the American empire. The ultimate subject of the short is not the local workers but the commercial enterprise owned by white businessmen who are actively performing the work of nation and empire building, making proper capitalist use of the recently annexed Hawaiian land. The short moreover depicts the proper racial hierarchy, relegating Asians to the background as an anonymous group of field laborers framed by white individual businessmen in the foreground. This perspective differs sharply from the famous Lumière short *Workers Leaving the Factory* (1895) that looks more empathetically at the labor force being released into leisure time at the end of their day's work.

In 1906, Robert Bonine would return to the islands and shoot twenty-six shorts (of which only a few are extant) for Edison Studios. Whereas Bonine's earlier 1902 footage shows a clear pragmatic economic focus of exploiting Hawaii's resources, the footage filmed in 1906 relaxes into a broader perspective of the islands and introduces an early version of the imperial ethnographic gaze that separates modern white subjects from premodern nonwhite natives. In a revision of the busy commercial harbor atmosphere seen in *Kanakas Diving* (1898), *Native Canoes* (1906) distinguishes between modern and traditional Hawaii. Against a static horizon lined by merchant vessels, the audience now sees multiple outrigger canoes entering the frame from off-screen space, moving toward the foreground and center. The suggestion here is that of an idyllic coexistence between ancient Hawaii, associated with natives, and modern Hawaii, associated with white American colonizers and capitalism.

However, this claim to a peaceful coexistence denies any tensions between the people of Hawaii and US colonizers and when examined reveals itself as a colonial rhetoric of containment. Similarly, *Pa-u Riders* (1906) displays a ceremonial mass ornament of Hawaiian women horseback riders wearing leis and long traditional skirts (*pa'u*) flowing majestically in the wind, representing the queen and the princesses of Hawaii's eight major islands. White spectators can be seen on the side in suits and Victorian fashion, watching this parade reviving ancient traditions with the film emphasizing a nostalgic tone toward the empty exhibition of the now abolished monarchy. In fact, *Pa'u* parades were revived only in 1900 after the annexation of Hawaii. In Bonine's short, this shift in history is acknowledged as US cavalry on horseback ride behind the ceremonial riders, suggesting once again a distinction between traditional Hawaii and its new modern identity as an American-administered territory. In addition, the shift marks a clear transition from ritual and ceremonial functions toward exhibition, thereby marketing Hawaii as a fetish for the gaze of white spectators.

The colonial gaze that defines Hawaii, as Kathy Ferguson and Phyllis Turnbull point out, takes on a threefold dimension: "The missionaries found a people they define as dark, mysterious, lacking civilization but capable of being domesticated. Entrepreneurs and sugar planters found the people lacking industry, the land uncultivated but a promising venue for profit once an appropriate labor force could be secured. The military saw/sees Hawai'i as strategically important and in need of defense, which imported American soldiers can supply."[14] From these early shorts it appears that the main emphasis in film is economic exploitation and development and domestication of the island, albeit in more secular terms. However, the military development, which would play a dominant role after the attack on Pearl Harbor, should not be overlooked in these early years of annexation. As Ferguson and Turnbull state, "Military inscription on Hawai'i's spaces was deep, extensive, and immediate following Annexation. The military buildup began four days after Annexation with an initial company of soldiers garrisoned near Diamond Head. The construction of a naval base at Pearl Harbor began with dredging in 1900; the first warship entered in 1905."[15] Thus, while the discussed film shorts, with the exception of *Pa-u Riders*, do not feature the military directly, the many shots of Hawaii's harbors lined with ships point to its economic, geopolitical, and military importance. In fact, Major General Schofield conducted secret surveillance of Pearl Harbor as early as 1873 and "decided it would make an ideal naval base, and in a report kept top secret for the next twenty years recommended that it be acquired in whatever manner possible."[16]

The rhetoric of acquisition in early cinema depicting Hawaii informs all aspects of social, economic, and military use projected for the islands. Further shorts from Bonine's film expedition of 1906 highlight diversely a modern railway traversing Hawaii's rural landscape, Japanese wrestlers with both Hawaiian and Asian locals as well as white businessmen in attendance, the pounding of the traditional poi dish, and local customs such as Hawaiian cowboys departing for a luau and various Waikiki Beach scenes. Footage of Waikiki Beach is of particular interest, since it shows once again traditional outrigger canoes entering the frame coming toward the camera. The camera shoots from water level, providing tangible medium close-ups of the canoe riders. These canoe riders, interestingly, are not locals but all white males going local, so to speak. Thus, white visitors or settlers, appropriating a legacy of Polynesian nautical skills developed over many centuries, transform canoeing into a leisure activity divorced from any practical function such as fishing or traveling between the islands. In an act of symbolic annexation, white males become the new natives and mingle on Waikiki's beaches. Only two years after this short was filmed, "In May, 1908, the Outrigger Canoe Club came into being on an acre and a half of choice beachfront land located between the Moana and Seaside Hotels (site of today's famous Royal Hawaiian Hotel) leased from the Estate of Queen Emma for $10 per year."[17] The Outrigger Canoe Club's membership requirements were highly exclusionary financially and racially and resembled all-white country clubs on the mainland. With its location on Waikiki Beach near Diamond Head and one of the prime properties on Oahu, white US business interest once again asserts itself, converting economic gain into leisure and entertainment.

Early film shorts of Hawaii document not only the economic exploitation and development of the islands but also the wholesale appropriation and fetishizing of

Hawaiian customs, its symbolic and cultural capital. For viewers on the mainland, these shorts do not explain the history of Hawaii and its annexation but represent it as an already established fact. Stephen Greenblatt similarly explains the early colonization of the New World as a set of inaugural linguistic acts: "For Columbus taking possessions principally meant the performance of a set of linguistic acts: declaring, witnessing, recording."[18] Likewise, film executes the illegitimate appropriation of Hawaii's kingdom and dissolution of its sovereignty for a second time, presenting the results of its own inaugural acts as documentary footage to the mainland audiences. Since only a minority of financial elites, military officials, and missionaries visited Hawaii during the early 1900s, the filmic images of Hawaii carry a quasi-reality status on the mainland that cannot be challenged or disputed. These images, focusing on the interests of sugar cane, commerce, and appropriated customs and land, complete the annexation of Hawaii and raise it to a secondary symbolic order of America's national imaginary.

In distinction to print colonialism as discussed by Greenblatt, the modern visual or screen imperialism of cinema proves even more powerful as it establishes objective visual evidence rather than subjective claims by individual authors. No longer is the process of verification dependent upon reading skills and one's interpretation of what authors describe as the marvelous possessions of newly acquired territories; rather, it is immediately verifiable in the directness and reality of an image that can be understood even by illiterate mass audiences. The camera's seemingly objective and unbiased eye invites its viewers to see the world through its screen reality. The Biograph Company, as Charles Musser points out, quickly discovered its own political relevance, apart from its initial entertainment value, when its production was utilized during the presidential campaign of William McKinley. The verisimilitude of cinema supplanted the powers of print and delivered the candidate "in the flesh" in a direct fashion to the people: "Republicans poured into Hammerstein's Olympia, wanting a glimpse of their candidate 'in the flesh'—a rare opportunity since McKinley's front-porch campaign kept him in Canton."[19] Similarly, cinematic impressions of a remote Hawaii were understood as reality and consolidated the kingdom's incorporation as a possession of the United States, delivering Hawaii in the flesh.

SOUTH SEAS FANTASIES: SETTLER COLONIALISM, RACE, AND THE NATIONAL IMAGINARY

Once the incorporation of Hawaii into the national imaginary had been accomplished, its visual culture became more open to manipulation and fantasy production. Whereas early film shorts delivered quasi-documentary footage of Hawaii, a second phase of screen imperialism enlarges the scope of these images, moving into the realm of fantasy. Roughly beginning around 1915 with the film

Aloha Oe,[20] which borrows its title from Queen Liliuokalani's famous Hawaiian farewell song, South Seas fantasy films emerged on the American screen, presenting the contact of civilization with Polynesian culture with a strong emphasis on fiction rather than fact. In doing so, these films retreated from contemporary history into an earlier era of first cultural contact and expansion and frequently presented this encounter with considerable romantic nostalgia, not unlike that of the Western film genre. The South Pacific and its last remnants of ancient Polynesian cultural tradition are about to be obliterated by the grasp of the modern world. First-encounter romanticism, including its tragedy-tinged nostalgia for disappearing civilizations, rewrites a history that was in reality extremely violent in its subjection of the Pacific through the use of Western military advantages in weaponry and brutal domination of explorer and settler colonialism. As direct and indirect reports from early South Seas explorations show, most forays by the British, French, and American explorers such as Captain Samuel Wallis, Louis Antoine de Bougainville, Captain James Cook, and the notorious American David Porter resulted in immediate violent retaliation for any perceived minor transgressions on the part of Pacific Islanders, leading to significant casualties as superior military technology was instantly brought to bear. As Jeffrey Geiger notes, David Porter, called "the first American imperialist," for example, "adopted a shock and awe strategy" in his territorial conflict with the Taipi and launched a "pre-emptive strike," setting fire to forests and villages and killing inhabitants: "The Taipi, he states, brought the destruction upon themselves, it was a slaughter he was obliged to commit."[21]

Apart from its rhetoric that euphemistically belittles the usual violence that accompanied the so-called discovery and settlement of the Pacific by Europeans and Americans, these films also begin to address issues of race in America's post–Civil War society, with the United States still developing and refining its own national hierarchies of race on the continent. Hawaii's social reality of a growing multicultural coexistence of native Hawaiians and various Asian settler groups (Japanese, Filipinos, Korean, and Chinese) is eclipsed in these films as the national imaginary cannot yet begin to conceive of such a multicultural landscape. Instead, this diversity of race and heritage is reduced to binary encounters between civilization and natives, depicted in the reimagined Pacific islands of the Marquesas, Tahiti, and Samoa during the mid-nineteenth century, reflecting the United States' own simplistic black/white Jim Crow binaries. This trend of depicting Pacific islands in their early encounter with Western colonialism was particularly strong during the 1920s and early 1930s. Eventually, films such as *Flirtation Walk* (1934), *Waikiki Wedding* (1937), and *Honolulu* (1939) returned to a contemporary setting of Hawaii, albeit largely distorted by the established conventions of the South Seas genre and the southern plantation genre borrowed from the mainland.

Early feature films such as *Aloha Oe* (Thomas Ince-Triangle Film Corporations, 1915) and *The Bottle Imp* (Lasky-Paramount, 1917) demonstrate both the imaginary liberty taken by filmmakers concerning the topic of Hawaii as well as the less systematic and censored racial representation of the Pacific that would become more firmly established in the 1920s. A poster advertising *Aloha Oe* at Honolulu's Bijou Theater, located on Hotel Street, would warn its audience in advance about the discrepancy between the representation of Hawaii for mainland viewers and the actual reality of Hawaii familiar to its local population: "This picture created a sensation on the mainland. Although not taken in Hawaii yet a great deal of the plot is supposed to be laid about our wonderful Volcano. The photography is perfect. Those who know Hawaii will notice that it is not the genuine article, but the great majority are deceived. However, the story, the thrills, the scenic effects and above all the sentiment of a real Hawaiian love story is there."[22] *Aloha Oe* was filmed on the mainland with white actress Enid Markey cast as the Hawaiian girl Kalaniweo, something that must have looked rather odd to the local audience in Honolulu. *The Bottle Imp*, shot on location in Hawaii, strove for more fidelity in its depiction of an island romance, casting as its lead Japanese American screen star Sessue Hayakawa in the role of Lopaka and Hawaiian Lehua Waipahu, a descendant of the royal family, as Kokua. Thus, in a rare instance, Hawaiian film characters are cast more or less authentically with Asian and Pacific Island actors, taking center stage in this melodrama. Subsequent productions, however, featuring Hawaii or the Pacific Islands would begin to establish clear racial hierarchies that would limit representations of Hawaiians, Asians, and Pacific Islanders in their various narratives. Casting would resort to various strategies of substitution such as blackface, brownface, or yellowface and increasingly limit and ultimately ban interracial relationships.

McVeagh of the South Seas (also known as *Brute Island*; Cyril Bruce, Harry Carey, 1914) offers an early instance of a South Seas film in which the idealization of the genre has not yet taken place. The main character, Captain Cyril Bruce McVeagh (Harry Carey), "Harvard 05—self exiled to the South Seas for the age old cause, the scorn of a woman" is shipwrecked in the Pacific during a typhoon. Subsequently, he is shown to be a brutal and ruthless colonizer of the Solomon Islands where he hunts for pearls, indulges in excessive drinking, and tortures natives on a cross, a visual indictment of Christianity and the missionaries' work in the South Seas. An African American actor chained to a cross portrays a native in the first torture scene, shot in an unstable frame of canted angles, and thereby also invokes the brutal legacy of slavery. McVeagh, said to be a "gent once," has turned into a "hound o' hell." The film uses variously African American, Latino, and white actors in costume and Afro wigs for its portrayal of natives and does not rely on strict blackface performances, as also given in D. W. Griffith's *The Idol Dancer* (1920). McVeagh further engages in an interracial romance with Liani, the daughter of a native chief, whom he acquires via trade for liquor. Natives are shown not in any idealized fashion but rather as morally deficient. As Tanarka, Liani's native betrothed, tries to win back his fiancée, he is overpowered by McVeagh and his shipmate Gates and sentenced to be chained to the cross, suggesting a continuity between slavery and the colonial subjection of the Pacific. Before the sentence is executed, however, Liani manages to set Tanarka free. Gates, who has witnessed her secret intervention and likewise succumbs to the corruption of the tropical climate, uses blackmail and tries to assault Liani, but McVeagh rescues her. Exacting revenge, Gates plots with the natives a rebellion against the captain's rule. In contrast to later South Seas fantasies, which often characterize Polynesians as remnants of an Edenic culture, this early example of the genre suggests that a treacherous climate inevitably induces its indigenous tribes and Western visitors to immoral behavior, debauchery, scheming, and corruption. Hence, it is understood that McVeagh's desire to escape from civilization is an illusion from which he must be cured. Miraculously, McVeagh's former girlfriend, Nancy Darrell, is marooned around the same time on his island "as if by fate." However, deaf to the pleas of Nancy, McVeagh orders his shipmate to kill two pearl divers on a canoe and rob them of their wealth. "I expected to find a man at least," protests Nancy, "not a savage amongst savages!" Another shipmate eventually tips off McVeagh about the impending rebellion by natives, now cast exclusively with African Americans wielding guns and thereby invoking the feared image of a slave rebellion. Liani sees the natives burning down McVeagh's home, presumes him dead, and weeps over her loss. McVeagh, however, escapes with his scheming shipmate who has suddenly come to his senses and makes it aboard a ship where Nancy waits. They set course for San Francisco and are rejoined with civilization and happily reunited: "A ship sailing toward the sunlit sea, toward civilization—and happiness."

Were it not for the racist and unsympathetic portrayal of the natives, one could see this film offering a critique of American expansionism in the Pacific. Harry Carey wrote, produced, and co-directed the film independently. It also features Carey's celebrated minimal acting style, which he would later use in John Ford's Westerns and exert a tremendous influence on John Wayne. The overall message of the film is perhaps that of American continental insularity, warning viewers of the destructive effects of the South Seas and its corrupting nontemperate climate, a myth held by many geographers and cultural anthropologists at the time in their effort to construct an evolutionary ladder of civilization based on climate zones. Gary Okihiro cites "Yale geographer and president of the board of the American Eugenics Society" Ellsworth Huntington, who in his pseudo-scientific work *Civilization and Climate* (1915) complains that apart from race and social institution the crucial role of "climate in the rise of civilization" is overlooked.[23] While the film ultimately resorts to a similar rationalization of climate zones to account for the white man's erratic barbaric behavior, it does not yet hide, like subsequent South Seas fantasies, the systematic violence needed to support an expansionist and colonial enterprise in the Pacific. With its cross-referencing of the South Pacific with African American slavery and rebellion, *McVeagh of the South Seas* further evokes racial fears of a Jim Crow society ambivalent about overseas expansion into areas inhabited by nonwhite races. In contrast, *Aloha Oe* (1915), a film that no longer exists other than in the American Film Institute's plot description, does not contain this partial critique of imperialism or evoke racial angst, providing instead civilizational escapist fantasy. Its hero David Harmon, suffering from a nervous disorder, is sent for recovery to the South Seas, where he leads the life of a beachcomber and saves the chief's daughter Kalaniweo from impending human sacrifice, dates her, and eventually has a child with her. After a brief return to his mainland home, the song "Aloha Oe" triggers the happy memories of Polynesian island life, prompting him to return for good to the Pacific paradise and live with his family and racially mixed child.

D. W. Griffith's *The Idol Dancer* (1920) can be seen as a first important example in the systematic cinematic construction of South Seas fantasies. As a romantic comedy and adventure tale, the film features a double narrative of a romance ending in marriage alongside a tale of adventure. This type of double narrative, facilitated by Griffith's skillful parallel editing, would eventually become one of the stock formulas of Hollywood filmmaking and had already been established in earlier films by Griffith. As Miriam Hansen points out, "Griffith's work for the Biograph Company (1908–1913) has been seen as an attempt to translate the heritage of the bourgeois novel into cinematic forms—in its development of complex forms of narration, especially parallel editing."[24] In contrast to the prenarrative documentary shorts produced around the turn of the century, the focus in these early proto-Hollywood feature films shifts away from realism toward a stronger fantasy engagement with the film narrative and the characters' psychology achieved through "closer camera ranges for connotations of intimacy, interiority, and individuality."[25] In addition, classic Hollywood narrative structure as developed in its rudimentary form by Griffith now begins to cover up its cinematic apparatus, inserting the spectator more directly into the cinematic illusion via POV identification and editing techniques that serve the ready-made narrative in self-explanatory manner: "Transitional films sought more consistently to ensure the spectator's perceptual placement *within the narrative space*, by means of different camera set-ups and editing devices such as shot-reverse shot, the 180-degree rule, eyeline match, and point of view. Such devices were not just attempts to position the spectator in relation to particular aspects of the scene, they were part of a system that assumed the very notion of the spectator as an implicit reference point, functionally comparable to the vanishing point in Renaissance perspective."[26] The direct imbrication of the spectator into the film narrative in this systematic manner would eventually turn Hollywood into a pedagogical institution where audiences would both experience and acquire the social norms of its represented cultural realities.

The South Seas genre represents in this ideological sense an exotic backdrop onto which the national imaginary projects itself beyond depicted individualized story lines. As Michael Rogin observes in connection with Griffith's *Birth of a Nation*, "Griffith's fundamental contribution to the full-length motion pictures was to join the 'intimate and the epic'; he linked the personal and the historical through racial fantasy."[27] Not only does the South Seas genre provide melodramatic entertainment via its fantasy plot but it also embeds within these fantasies the social norms that regulate the cultural perception of the Other. The audience absorbs these norms and codes in distracted and unconscious fashion, mistaking them for a quasi-reality, and internalizes its embedded ideologies. Griffith's *Idol Dancer* begins innocently enough, since it shows none of the historical specificity of early cinema's actualities but centers instead its melodramatic plot upon the reluctant religious conversion of two disbelievers, a derelict white beachcomber and an idol-worshipping girl of mixed French-Polynesian ancestry. The film's promotional poster (see Figure 1) curiously misrepresents the mixed-race heroine as white and claims that the film was shot in the South Seas, when, in fact, it was shot in Florida and the Bahamas. By the end of the film, both protagonists firmly embrace the Christian values advocated by the missionary Donald Blythe, a belief system they had scorned and challenged earlier. This narrative trajectory allows Griffith to vent some of his own reservations about New England Puritanism that inform the religious and cultural values of the missionary and his nephew Kincaid, while also highlighting in stereotypical fashion the exoticism and unrestrained vitality of the islands offering an escape from civilization. Kincaid, on a visit to the islands, is depicted as sickly and falls under the spell of the vibrant Mary, the Polynesian island girl. It is his near fatal illness that eventually leads Mary, the island girl, and Dan, the white beachcomber, to reconsider their atheism and join in Christian matrimony, with Kincaid stepping aside and repressing his own love interest.

To ensure that the romantic plot does not transgress the American standards of religion and race, Griffith puts certain restraints in place. In a prominent scene toward the end of the film, we see Mary casting her tiki idol into the ocean, therefore legitimizing the missionary expansion and Christianization of the Pacific. For further contrast, Griffith inserts a pirate-like white trader, who with a gang of native cannibals, most prominently embodied by Chief Wando, attempts to pillage the missionary station as well as rape and steal the local women. In a final woman-in-distress rescue scenario typical of Griffith's films, the reformed beachcomber Dan and his fellow fishermen overcome the intruders, free the captive women, and restore normalcy on the islands. It is interesting to note that the film disavows commercial interests by placing the white trader alongside cannibals, extolling instead the more lasting spiritual values of the missionary. The film similarly glorifies America's Manifest Destiny with its westward expansion into the Pacific and paints it with idealistic overtones. The commercial conquest of the Pacific, the

FIGURE 1. Poster of D. W. Griffith's *The Idol Dancer* (1920) falsely claiming that the film was shot in the South Seas and advertising the mixed-race heroine as white.

main impetus for America's interest in the South Seas as a trading route to China, is completely obscured. In the typical Hollywood binaries of good versus evil, good American Christian values ultimately prevail in this moral melodrama, a cleverly disguised commercial entertainment product that disavows any monetary interests.

Since his highly problematic and controversial film *The Birth of a Nation* (1915) that helped revive the Ku Klux Klan, Griffith had made some weak attempts to distance himself from charges of racism. For instance, *The Idol Dancer* features a heroine of mixed French, Javanese, and Samoan ancestry who is warmly welcomed into the Christian fold by Reverend Blythe and subsequently marries a white man. In the United States, existing laws against miscegenation forbade such racial mixing and interracial marriage until the 1960s. To contain this type of interracial utopia, Griffith's film stresses in many scenes the inassimilable nature of the racial Other. Chief Wando, a cannibal caricatured in blackface performance, is shown with two shrunken heads dangling around his chest and a bone pierced through his nose (see Figure 2). Watching the island girl Mary, he begins to salivate and betrays his cannibalistic primitivism. Further blackface performances establish the characters of Peter and Pansy. Whereas Peter, a convert who assists Reverend Blyth, is said to "enjoy his religion—particularly in a long coat," Pansy is described as "a savage flower, who yields to missionary clothes, but wriggles from all other conventions." Both Peter and Pansy are also parodied as naïve and silly house servants, shown gesticulating wildly (Pansy) or being cowardly inefficient (Peter), relegating them to the traditional infantilized view of natives via comical routines of minstrelsy.

Classical Hollywood editing with its more toned-down acting performances based on the close-up and subtle facial gestures appears to have left the theatrical histrionics of early silent film behind. Yet when it concerns race and the legacy of minstrelsy, Hollywood's films remain steeped in this tradition and carry it forward. As Rogin observes, "Griffith, however, did not banish histrionics forever from film. . . . Blackface was the legacy of vaudeville entertainment and silent film."[28] Peter, Pansy, and Chief Wando establish via blackface routines a sharp dividing line of race that cannot be crossed, upholding American binaries of black and white that inform Jim Crow and placing the racial Other outside modern Hollywood conventions. Whereas white characters are developed with the use of subtle cinematographic techniques that give them a human psychology, racial Others are built on caricature and remain flat without any interiority. Rogin's insight is crucial, demonstrating that the birth of American cinema is perversely connected to a tradition of minstrelsy and carried forward into classical Hollywood narrative. What Hansen discusses in classical Hollywood editing as a "system that assumed the very notion of the spectator as an implicit reference point,"[29] also points in its obverse sense to a systemically maintained exclusion of the racial Other. The casting of whites in blackface as natives in *Idol Dancer* established and consolidated

FIGURE 2. Chief Wando, blackface Polynesian native, depicted as cannibalistic in Griffith's *Idol Dancer* (1920).

discriminatory industry practices of Hollywood for years to come. Likewise, the film's clichéd images of tropical palm settings and half-naked natives in grass skirts with bones in their noses established the industry's lack of interest in any fidelity to reality concerning the representation of the cultural or racial Other.

Griffith's *The Idol Dancer* would also bring a certain A-list prestige to the South Seas genre, heightening the impact of its ideology, and would eventually inspire renowned American filmmakers such as Raoul Walsh (*Lost and Found on a South Sea Island*, 1923; *Sadie Thompson*, 1928; *The Revolt of Mamie Stover*, 1956), Victor Fleming (*Hula*, 1927), W. S. Van Dyke and Robert Flaherty (*White Shadows in the South Seas*, 1928), Lewis Milestone (*Rain*, 1932; *Mutiny on the Bounty*, 1962), King Vidor (*Bird of Paradise*, 1932), and Frank Lloyd (*Mutiny on the Bounty*, 1935) to try their hand in this genre. American audiences were already familiar with the main male lead in *The Idol Dancer*, the beachcomber played by David Barthelmes, from Griffith's highly acclaimed *Broken Blossoms* (1919), which features another interracial romance in London. In the latter film, Barthelmes plays the character of the Yellow Man in a yellowface performance of a Chinese Buddhist missionary who befriends a young domestically abused girl played by silent screen star Lillian Gish. It is interesting to note that interracial romances in both films have to occur offshore in either the utopian space of the South Seas or a distant Charles Dickensian London and its seedy Limehouse District, thereby depriving these romances of any reality on the US continent. Also, all actors in these interracial romances are white and impersonate the racial Other, thereby not offending the prevailing race etiquette of the time. Interracial relationships ultimately remain a product of pure fantasy with little bearing on American reality. Griffith's *The Love Flower* (1920), a South Seas fantasy shot immediately after *The Idol Dancer*, deracializes the narrative even more radically by using the South Seas as a mere backdrop for a melodrama involving a fugitive white father and his devoted daughter. Once again the racial binaries are solidly maintained with Griffith casting actual black actors in sequences shot on the West Indies but relying on blackface performances for representing Polynesian culture in the film. In addition to their blackface treatment, the natives from the South Seas are endowed with exaggerated racial markers, such as oversized Afros, that mark them as African. Whereas the narrative of *The Idol Dancer* culminated in miscegenation with a mixed-race heroine of French, Javanese, and Samoan ancestry marrying a white man and desired by another, *The Love Flower* ensures that Polynesian culture does not in any manner challenge the established American black-and-white binary, placing Polynesians firmly into the taboo category.

W. S. Van Dyke and Robert Flaherty's *White Shadows in the South Seas* (1928) offers a significant departure from Griffith's films but still relies on many conventional features of the South Seas genre. Co-director Robert Flaherty, known for his documentary *Nanook of the North* (1922) depicting the daily lives of Inuit natives, adds a stronger realism to this fantasy genre, although not without his own ethnographic restaging of indigenous culture. In *Nanook*, Flaherty's nostalgic and ethnographic documentary required some restaging and editing as the Inuits were already modern, using rifles and guns for hunting as opposed to spears. Nevertheless, the inclusion of the native population performing a lifestyle prior to contact with Western civilization gave the film the appearance of documentary authenticity. Similarly, in *White Shadows*, Tahiti's natives were asked while filming the middle sequence of the film to restage their culture before its contact with white civilization. As Raymond F. Betts, notes, however, the ethnographic approach to Tahiti was entirely fictive, since primitive tribal life had disappeared long ago and Hollywood's modern studio apparatus itself had invaded the location of the illusionary idyllic island: "The film stock itself was processed and projected on site in a special studio that had been built 'entirely with native labor and was located within 50 feet of the shores of the South Sea on a strange little isle of the south Pacific,' as the program for the premiere proclaimed."[30]

This intentionally staged documentary appeal, however, had already met with increasing disinterest among American movie audiences by the mid-1920s, as their tastes sided more with melodrama and escape fantasies. As Betts states, "Nothing original is to be found in this canned ecology."[31] Flaherty's *Moana* (1926), documenting the natives of Samoa, also no longer found favor with American audiences and performed poorly at the box office.[32] As Wheeler Winston Dixon notes, "Flaherty depicts Samoan life as virtually Utopian, in sharp contrast to Flaherty's initial foray into 'ethnographic filmmaking,' the equally transparently staged and manipulated *Nanook of the North*."[33] To prevent a further flop at the box office, MGM paired up Flaherty with the more experienced commercial filmmaker Van Dyke, who was supposed to contain and soften Flaherty's documentary drive and turn his utopian vision into melodrama. The film cornered additional production value, since it was MGM's first sound picture, using mostly a music score that included native chanting and a single spoken "hello" when the hero chances upon a flock of bathing maidens.

In *White Shadows*, Flaherty again brings his typical documentary emphasis to the film. The film was shot entirely in Tahiti, much like Raoul Walsh's *Lost and Found on a South Sea Island* (1923).[34] To ensure a wider commercial appeal, Van Dyke used Walsh's experienced Hollywood cinematographer Clyde de Vinna, who would eventually win an Oscar for *White Shadows*. In stark contrast to Griffith's work, the film does away with blackface performance, using instead a large segment of Tahiti's native population. The film radically opens and ends with an explicit indictment of white colonialism, heretofore not seen on American cinema screens. After initial idyllic and prelapsarian aerial and wide shots of an island paradise, the intertitles abruptly break with this romanticized illusion: "But the white man, in his greedy trek across the planet, cast his withering shadow over these islands. . . . And the business of 'civilizing' them to his interests began." Two remarkable sweeping tracking shots follow with the first going from left to right, moving along a typical shore setting from a distance. After the first tracking shot, another intertitle appears alerting us to the change brought about by the contact with Western civilization: "Today—the results of 'civilization.'" Erasing the earlier shot, so to speak, the camera now tracks in the reverse direction, from right to left, suggesting a regression rather than progress, and focuses with greater close-up detail on fragmented modern life.

In a stunning uninterrupted tracking shot lasting roughly forty seconds, the film offers us a series of images such as a sickly native with swollen legs due to elephantiasis leaning against a palm tree, local workers gathering coconuts, free-range chickens, fishing nets, livestock, a barbershop with a barber shaving a local customer, children playing, a local worker pulling a cart, basket weavers, a woman chasing a pig out of a hut, and a man carrying a chicken. The scene finally wraps with a white man entering the commercial premises, the trading post and bar owned by the white villain and pearl trader Sebastian. The initial image of the sickly man evokes fears about health and sanitary conditions and subsequently shows a local rural culture subverted by the practices of modern commerce. Also, none of the island's activities are interrelated or show any organic cohesion, suggesting the fragmentation of a formerly unified culture. The shot ends on the trading post location and emphasizes that the island has totally succumbed to modern commerce.

The commercial exploitation is further highlighted in the pearl-diving business run by the ruthless trader Sebastian. In addition to producing visually stunning underwater photography, this plot sequence also shows many local divers risking their lives or dying in the treacherous pursuit of wealth. The white hero, Dr. Matthew Lloyd, a derelict and medical doctor, rails against Sebastian's exploitative practices but is eventually tricked to board a plague-infected ship, and thereby neutralized. After surviving a typhoon, Lloyd is marooned on a yet untouched island, allowing once again for South Seas fantasies to take up the center of the film. As Lloyd secretly spies upon numerous native women swimming nude in a pond and showering under a waterfall, the soundtrack sets in with organ music reminiscent of that played at carnivals. The viewer is treated to a voyeuristic view from behind thick tropical leaves, revealing the physical contours of women in soft focus. In a reverse long shot, the intruder is seen comically belittled in scale and hiding among large leaves. The shot cuts back to a nude woman seen from the back and then to a soft lens close-up of a reclining female adorned with a tropical gardenia in her hair. In a further reverse shot, Lloyd is heard over the music for the first time uttering "hello" and then met with a panicked stare by the discovered young female who alerts her companions. The Edenic illusion is destroyed as the white man enters this untouched world visually and moreover sonically with MGM's new sound technology transitioning from the music soundtrack to the first audible word. Here the film points with humorous self-reflexivity to its own incompatibility with the South Seas fantasies and aligns itself with the demystifying forces of civilization. The film's voyeuristic apparatus is made conspicuous through the use of sound and destroys the silent contemplative image along with its conventions of concealing the production technology of film.

Rogin notes how the use of sound in *The Jazz Singer* (1927) challenged the stylistic conventions of narrative silent films, reviving early cinema and its vaudeville atmosphere more closely linked with minstrelsy performances: "Classical movies, culminating in sound, may have replaced stock vaudeville caricatures with individuated, interior characters, but Jack develops his character—expresses his interior, finds his own voice—by employing blackface caricature. Blackface reinstated the exaggerated pantomime that restrained filmic gestures had supposedly displaced."[35] While the humorous self-reflexive use of sound in *White Shadows* serves a critical function in unveiling the South Seas cinematic illusion and voyeurism, it also highlights the film's affinity with vaudeville traditions and minstrelsy. Sound is treated as a vaudeville novelty act with which the first spoken utterance "hello" destroys the Edenic island paradise, comically revealing a voyeur hiding among the tropical foliage and spying on silent bathing island beauties. It is at this point, when the film introduces sound, that it radically shifts gears, abandons its realism, and reverts to racial caricatures. Although *White Shadows* refrains from using literal black-face performances, it does subscribe to minstrel stereotypes depicting the natives' happy subservience to the white settler. W. S. Van Dyke, a childhood actor on the vaudeville circuit, was familiar with its conventions and had also served as an assistant director under Griffith for his film *Intolerance* (1916) and was well acquainted with the racial ideologies that were embedded into classical Hollywood narration. *White Shadows'* South Seas fantasy proceeds with a changed emphasis on caricatures rather than realistic portrayals of natives, as seen in the film's critical opening sequence, once Lloyd makes contact with the native tribe.

After his first voyeuristic forays on the island, Lloyd eventually succumbs to exhaustion. The native women find and revive him with the local coconut oil massage *lomilomi*, fulfilling tacit sexual fantasies for audiences with quasi-erotic massages administered to Lloyd by South Seas beauties. As he befriends the locals and helps them with his medical knowledge in their distress, he is welcomed into their fold, treated to a festive luau and ceremonial dances, and permitted to date the chief's daughter upon saving the life of her younger brother. The island population, so to speak, embalms the white visitor and performs its rituals and ceremonies for him as if he were a white god. Gifts of women repay him for his efforts, as the virginal taboo on Fayaway, the chief's daughter, is quickly lifted. These sequences are shot with emphasis on visual spectacle and heightened melodrama, producing the South Seas as an intensely engaging screen and racial fantasy.

As Lloyd eventually goes native and takes the name Matta Loa, a subtle return to realism is signaled. The shot sequences now document in an observational manner the harvesting of oyster shells in the style of Flaherty. Similarly, Lloyd's original cultural heritage comes to the foreground, as he cannot resist a residual capitalist fascination for the economy of pearls. Having gathered a stockpile of pearls, he signals with fire at night in order to be rescued from the island. Confronted by his love interest Fayaway over this betrayal of their native bliss, he shows regret and throws the pearls into the ocean. His enlightenment, however, comes too late, as white shadows (sails of ships) approach on the horizon. Sebastian comes ashore and wins over the natives, and Lloyd is shot and killed by one of his men. After the villagers mourn his death, the film replicates the initial realistic tracking shots, focusing now almost exclusively on the trading post and emphasizing that white civilization is here to stay. As native dancers entertain white guests in the bar and a young native boy delivers coconuts in a commercial crate, the lonely widow leans against a tiki idol as black veils descend upon the screen, darkening it. The idyllic island image is destroyed and the interracial marriage is safely aborted before a mixed-race family is formed. *White Shadows* offers an ambivalent portrayal of the

South Seas with its remarkable cinematography and casting. However, it ultimately remains safely within the conventions of racial and gender depiction that characterize Hollywood films. While the film does suggest a strong critique of colonialist and imperialist practices, it also allows the audience to ignore them as the melodramatic narrative clearly outweighs the film's critical realism.

Victor Fleming's *Hula* (1927), starring Hollywood's "it girl" Clara Bow, bypasses the moral undertones found in *White Shadows* altogether. Instead of indulging in nostalgic mourning over the imminent loss of an indigenous Polynesian culture, the film's depiction of Hawaii is oddly realistic as it shows the islands already transformed and run by white landowners with the local population playing only a marginal role. As a progressive depiction of the modern woman, Bow's character also cuts against gender stereotypes that are often found in highly fetishized representations of submissive or exotic women. In *Hula*, woman's sexuality is owned by the female lead, provocatively and playfully flaunted, challenging gender conventions. This progressive aspect of the film appears at first to weaken or challenge the film's colonial discourse; however, at bottom it does not question it, since *Hula* has gone fully native and annexed Hawaiian culture altogether.

The film's opening intertitle evokes the setting of Hawaii as a sexualized backdrop for Bow's irreverent feminist flapper persona of the new woman: "A Hawaiian isle—a land of singing seas and swinging hips—where volcanoes are often active—and maidens always are." The film subsequently launches into a complex narrative of annexation with regard to Hawaii's native territory. Three island shots give a condensed chronology of Hawaii's settlement: first an uninhabited nature paradise, then a single person riding down a riverbed in the style of the lone Western hero, and finally local Hawaiians working and walking past the camera carrying supplies ashore. In a subtle reversal of chronology, the white settler associated with the Western genre precedes the shot of the original inhabitants, aligning the film with the mythology of the Western and America's westward expansion. After these initial shots of the island, a long shot reveals the character of Hula bathing nude in a pond, evoking images of the birth of Venus or Eve in paradise. This sequence is briefly interrupted by the intertitle introducing the star: "CLARA BOW as Hula Calhoun." The next shot offers a close-up of Hula's face, followed by several cuts between long shots and close-ups of the bathing nude. The scene is purposely transgressive and provocatively features the flesh of the heroine, particularly close-ups of her legs and her foot reaching for a tropical flower also shown in close-up. In these shots the tropical nature is directly transferred from the island setting onto Hula's sexualized body. To be sure, Hula becomes the islands. In the next scene, Hula is further legitimated in her native status. Stung by an insect, Hula returns home to be cared for by her guardian introduced as "Kahana, half-Hawaiian ranch foreman—Hula Calhoun's nursemaid and bodyguard since her baby days."

While Bow's screen personality certainly advances the image of a modern independent woman, such independence is not granted to her Hawaiian caretaker. In the tradition of American slavery and plantation culture, Kahana serves the heroine in the double function of mammy and servant. As with Fleming's *Gone with the Wind* (1939), racial minorities "are no more than conveniences, psychic extensions of the whites, intended to prop them up."[36] This subservience is all the more surprising since Kahana is also introduced as a ranch foreman of Hawaiian paniolo cowboys. Hawaii has a rich cultural tradition centering around the skilled paniolo cowboys, dating back to 1798 when King Kamehameha I was given a gift of cattle by Captain George Vancouver of the British Royal Navy. Mexican *vaqueros* were invited to Hawaii to train cowboys, with many remaining on the islands, forming Hawaiian ranching families still in business today. As a Hawaiian paniolo, Kahana has a respected social position; however, in the film his position and skills are transferred to Hula, who is an avid horseback rider and mingles with the paniolos in tomboy fashion, representing the new frontier spirit of women. Kahana presents Hula on her birthday with a prized paniolo horsewhip onto which he has carved her name, passing on his authority as a skilled paniolo to her. In the tradition of plantation culture, however, Kahana as a racial Other also becomes Hula's "mammy." It appears, then, that Kahana also transfers his masculinity to Hula. The intertitles state that Hula has celebrated all her birthdays since the death of her mother at Kahana's house, turning him into her substitute mother. In addition, in a disturbing scene Kahana is shown dressing the adult Hula, pulling her pants over her legs as if she were still an infant (see Figure 3). This scene clearly desexualizes and emasculates Kahana as he dresses a grown woman in intimate fashion more reminiscent of a maidservant. This scene also anticipates the famous dressing scenes in which Mammy (Hattie McDaniel) dresses Scarlett (Vivian Leigh) in Fleming's later film, *Gone with the Wind*.

Throughout the film, Kahana simply affirms Hula's romantic choices and serves as her emotional echo, while granting her native and paniolo status as a white settler (see Figure 4). Kahana, as the emasculated father figure, becomes the foundational mother figure for Hula, as only he can grant her legitimate island status, unlike her biological father or deceased mother. Rogin's comments on the role of the mammy in connection with blackface are very much to the point in *Hula*: "Blackface operates as vehicle for sexual as for ethnic mobility by offering freedom for whites at the price of fixedness for blacks. The white man plays with a nurturing, emotional identity that fixes black man, like white woman, as mother and child."[37] While *Hula* shies away from blackface performance, it nevertheless uses its dynamics in casting the local Kahana as a quasi-mammy, a nourishing racial mother figure for the white upward mobility of Clara Bow's character. Producers Adolph Zukor and Jesse L. Lasky at Paramount Pictures, with whom Bow had signed a highly lucrative five-year contract, making her the highest paid silent star in the late 1920s, launched *Hula* along with other hit vehicles such as *Mantrap* (1926), *Wings* (1927), and *It* (1927). Economic mobility constituted a significant part of the studio's publicity campaign that construed Bow into the mythic "it girl," an unknown aspiring model discovered by the studio and transformed into an overnight star. As Marsha Orgeron remarks, "'Making it' is a colloquial term of achievement, in this case by Clara Bow, whose fleeting but magnificent Hollywood success was facilitated by the popular medium of the fan magazine."[38] Bow's career began with the Fame and Fortune Contest of 1921 that solicited photographs of aspiring starlets.[39] Via this type of public recruitment of its stars, Hollywood stressed its democratic openness and saw itself as the facilitator of the American Dream.[40] As part of its mythical dream factory, Hollywood was keen on reproducing this fantasy of economic mobility through star vehicles such as *Hula*.

It is interesting to note that Jewish producers such as Zukor and Lasky were influential in toning down the anti-Semitism of early immigrant ghetto films produced under Edison but exerted little influence on the deeper racial divide that ruled Hollywood cinema. As Hansen explains, "Because Jews were involved in film production early on, they had a certain input in the shaping of their public image from which other minorities, especially blacks, were barred."[41] The use of melodramatic "plot strategies that rewarded the character's striving for assimilation"[42] allowed white immigrant minorities such as Jews, Italians, and Irish to join an enlarged mainstream from which minorities of color were systematically excluded. The depiction of the white landowners in *Hula* offers a good example of this wider inclusiveness. The Calhouns are shown to be an eccentric Irish family of seasoned gamblers and alcoholics who have drinks for breakfast or enter the house's living room, as Hula does, on horseback. While treated comically, the Calhouns are nevertheless granted access to white entitlement. Whereas their lifestyle offers a refreshing fantasy of a remote island life unrestrained by tedious mainland conventions, such liberty is never granted to the locals who either work or perform for the white settlers. A romantic melodrama that ensues as Hula falls in love with the British engineer Anthony Haldane (Clive Brook), who happens to be already married, is designed merely to overcome such obstacles on the path to greater wealth and financial rewards as part of a typical Hollywood happy ending. In his dilemma, Anthony briefly envies the imagined freedom of the natives—"A native isn't tied by conventions. Gad, I wish we were natives"—but never seriously considers their socioeconomic situation. Their enviously presumed and imagined freedom is never shown on-screen. Instead, the audience is treated to images of a white settlement culture totally absorbed in its pursuit of pleasure or romantic adventure. The Calhouns' estate appears to run magically on its own, as family members are seen only drinking or partying and never working. Only toward the film's end will Hula use a single calculated ruse, faking an explosion of Haldane's dam, to trick Anthony's wife into signing the divorce papers as she presumes Haldane is now

FIGURE 3. Clara Bow in Victor Fleming's *Hula* (1927) being dressed by her native care-taker Kahana.

financially bankrupt. The modern heroine will top her financially pragmatic competitor and win both love and fortune.

Much of the film's narrative, focusing on Hula's marriage obstacles, serves simply as a pretext to highlight the flamboyant Clara Bow and her proactive spirit in securing the man of her choice. Haldane, observing British propriety, initially refuses to date Hula seriously until he is divorced. Her frustration with this impossible situation erupts during a luau as she purposely gets drunk, causing a public scene by performing an impromptu hula dance. On screen, this spectacle is portrayed in an overtly exhibitionist fashion. The scene opens with an expansive back-tracking shot, depicting the assembled guests decorated with leis at the luau festivities. Close-ups show Hula drinking avidly out of a coconut shell, playfully engaging Mr. Bane, and provoking Anthony's jealousy in an exchange of hostile looks. As the native dancers start their performance, Hula exclaims, "If that's what amuses our guests—I'll show them what my name means!" Tossing pieces of clothes from behind a bush, she spontaneously joins the group after a quick wardrobe change into a grass skirt. As she replaces the lead dancer, she launches into an indulgent dance imitating hula moves in highly amateurish and improvised fashion. The camera lavishes

FIGURE 4. Clara Bow as Hula with whip made by Kahana, assuming the masculine authority of the Hawaiian cowboy, the paniolo.

Hula with close attention, featuring her face, chest, and swaying hips and legs. Reverse shots show the merry excitement of Hula's father, the disapproving look of Anthony, and the drunken and leering fascination of Mr. Bane. He eventually seeks to join Hula in the dance, but a fight with Anthony erupts, further escalating the spectacle.

Hula is initially pleased with the fight's outcome; however, Anthony prevails and carries her off against her will to Kahana's house. She protests against this treatment and scolds Anthony: "You big bully! How dare you treat me like a baby—in front of everybody?" This remark, if seen critically, should strike the viewer as ironic as it is uttered in the presence of Kahana, who is belittled and infantilized throughout the entire film by the white settlers. Unfortunately, Bow's feminism does not show the same progressive spirit toward colonial subjects. Also, the film in many ways resurrects a plantation setting that stands in stark contradiction to its advocated liberal values of the new woman. What Rogin observes in Fleming's *Gone with the Wind* (1939) as well as *The Birth of a Nation* (1915) and *The Jazz Singer* (1927) is also applicable in this film: "From one thematic perspective these motion pictures describe a circle: an abolitionist plantation story is answered by the southern view of Reconstruction, which in turn is answered in the shift from southern racial hierarchy to northern immigrant opportunity."[43] In representing mass con-sumer culture and immigrant opportunity through the second-generation Scottish and Irish immigrant character, Clara Bow foreshadows her famous role as a sales-girl in *It* (1927). The promise of upward mobility does not extend beyond the white mainstream. Moreover, since cinema's mass appeal is intimately tied to the female spectator, a performance such as Bow's in *Hula* has wide ramifications for cultural norms, embedding the discourse of colonialism and imperialism deep in America's domestic fabric. As a result, the film indirectly conveys America's prevailing racial hierarchy to its viewers via economic opportunities held up to its white immigrant audiences relying heavily on the exotic location of Hawaii as an American colony producing easy wealth for its white landowners.

The discourse of colonial appropriation is amply displayed in *Hula* with its strong emphasis on exhibition and entertainment. In his essay "The Work of Art in the Age of Mechanical Reproduction," Walter Benjamin notes how pho-tography and film increasingly shift the traditional cultic value of art toward its more modern shallow and commercialized exhibition value: "Today, by the absolute emphasis on its exhibition value the work of art becomes a creation with entirely new functions, among which the one we are conscious of, the artistic function, later may be recognized as incidental. This much is certain: today photography and the film are the most serviceable exemplifications of this new function."[44] The ritual and cultic practice of Hawaiian hula dance ini-tially accompanied only the chanting of Hawaiian legends and sacred prayers. The film puts the dance performance center stage as a vulgar tourist display of spectacle, following the lead of popular culture that had converted hula into a tourist attraction. In traditional hula, as Adrienne Kaeppler notes, "dance was choreographed to illustrate selected words of the text" and "used to honor the gods."[45] Conversely, in modern acculturated hula we see an increasing secular-ization of its practices: "Ever since 1893 when Kalakaua's court dancers per-formed at the World's Columbian Exhibition in Chicago, Hawaiian dance has been exported as a feature of entertainment for visitors, until today one type of Hawaiian dance has become a kind of 'airport art' aimed primarily at tourists."[46] Jane C. Desmond links the exhibition culture of hula to its tourist appeal patterned on primitivism: "This specific formulation of reinvigoration through contact with 'authentic primitives' emerges in tourist advertisements of the 1920s."[47] Desmond speaks of an "ideology of restoration" that "depended upon specific representational strategies."[48] In Bow's version, the film not only hollows out any residual cultic element of the native dance but also further wrests it away from its original Hawaiian performers and transposes it into the space of pure cinematic spectacle. Bow's dance must in this sense be more properly seen as a performance in the American tradition of minstrelsy, which is now commercially combined with Hollywood's musical tradition.

Hula can be said to perform the nation in a new way, in contrast to Griffith's *The Birth of a Nation*, inspired by racial hatred and defensive attitudes toward modernization. *Hula*'s initial stress on images of birth (Hula bathing in the pond; Hula's birthday; Hula receiving the Hawaiian paniolo talisman with her name engraved) and the film's native Hawaiian dance performed by Hula suggest the inauguration of a new identity. As Hula goes native, so too does Clara Bow's audience. Bow's star qualities, underlined by the capital letters in the intertitles that stress her name over that of her character, produce an entirely new form of cultural annexation based on mass consumerism. As Richard Dyer notes, "The star phenomenon emphasizes the kind of the person the star is rather than the specific circumstances of specific roles."[49] On the American continent Bow represents a new imaginary of the uninhibited white modern woman who freely determines her choices in love and life. This freedom is well illustrated in *It* when Bow's character escapes her modest economic lot as a shopgirl and transforms into an upwardly mobile consumer. This capitalist fairy tale is more romantically depicted in *Hula* when Bow reaches for the outer edges of the American empire and goes native. Bow and her modern lifestyle represent the new exoticism of American mass consumer culture, promising the American Dream through direct participation in the market. As Miriam Hansen states, "The new culture of consumption blurred class and ethnic divisions in an elusive community of abundance; it also undermined bourgeois divisions of public and private, above all the hierarchy of male and female spheres. Crucial to the shift from a production-centered economy to one of mass consumption was the female shopper whose numbers had increased ever since the Civil War."[50] The Hawaiian Islands are accordingly commercially exploited for the symbolic representation of Bow as the new market force of woman. In this modern perspective, unfortunately, Hawaii has to remain premodern, locked into a plantation culture and mythologies of the Wild West as represented by the paniolos. Unlike Clara Bow, for whom Hawaii is just one of her many costumes, Hawaiian culture is ultimately not allowed to exist outside the parameters of its confining cinematic depiction.

A majority of South Seas films in the 1920s, as so far discussed, confront via first-contact narratives troubling questions of racial and interracial relationships, working to preserve existing American racial hierarchies on the mainland. In an imaginary leap into the past, these fantasies revisit the first encounters of Western Eurocentric culture with nonwhites and non-Europeans in the Pacific and seek to portray European or American imperialism as a benevolent form of uplifting so-called lower civilizations. Films such as *White Shadows* may cast a more critical light on colonialism but for the most part remain within the Eurocentric mold of thought. The blatant racism of these films should not be misconstrued as an exclusive Hollywood product, however, since its disseminated views were widely held in American society at the time. Harvard-educated Lothrop Stoddard published his xenophobic *The Rising Tide of Color Against White World-Supremacy* in 1920, attempting to prove the cultural superiority of white cultures from the northern temperate zones over nonwhite cultures from tropical and subtropical regions.[51] The Yale geographer and president of the board of the American Eugenics Society also endorsed similar views. In *Civilization and Climate* (1915), Ellsworth Huntington asserts, "a certain type of climate prevails wherever civilization is high."[52] Widely known pseudo-scientific studies such as these, which expressed New England core values for the nation, tried to cement the basis for racism and white racial superiority on the merits of objective science, moving beyond Christian religious prejudices held toward so-called heathen cultures of the South Pacific.

W. S. Van Dyke's *The Pagan* (1929) ironizes Christian expansion in the Pacific and offers for the first time a more explicit attempt to understand the economic exploitation perpetrated by Christian capitalism. While this film still includes many racially problematic fantasy elements, it also takes a more realistic approach toward Western expansion in the Pacific. Clyde de Vinna's cinematography again offers remarkable tracking shots, as seen in *White Shadows*, but in this later film shows a more commercialized infrastructure that resembles the setting of American small towns. The camera comes to a stop at a bank building, emphasizing a more modern economic and systematic takeover of the Pacific than suggested in *White Shadows*, with its individual pirate-like pearl traders. The major transaction that leads to the financial ruin of the mixed-race hero Henry Shoesmith Jr. is a contract he willingly signs with Mr. Roger Slater (Donald Crisp), allowing him to use his coconut harvest for the production of copra at no charge. The white trader marked with a pirate earring is presented as a type of loan shark disguised as a fair businessman in a suit and tie who purposely lures the naïve native into signing the contract in order to further indebt him. Forced to default, Henry is evicted from his land, which passes into white ownership. A romantic love story between Henry and Slater's ward of mixed race eventually culminates in a jealous triangle of possession with Slater attempting to murder Henry and his final demise as he is torn apart by sharks. Even though the happy ending restores the islands to their rightful native owners, viewers understand the pure retrospective fantasy. Scenes that focus specifically on financial transactions as well as the missionary church with its Christianized natives subtly suggest an intimate connection between Christian missionary efforts and capitalist expansion. Donald Crisp, who starred as Slater, was well known to audiences from Griffith's *Broken Blossoms* (1919) and in one of the most famous scenes in film history brutally beats his own daughter (Lilian Gish) to death for having fallen in love with a Chinese man. His appearance in *The Pagan*, in which he is marked as a pirate, hypocritically attends church, gushes insincere religious rhetoric, takes part in a quasi-incestuous marriage with his ward, and has repeated violent outbursts, strongly links Christianity and colonial violence.

This systematic capitalist violence is historically accurate when considering the expansion of New England missionary work in Hawaii. As Gary Okihiro points out, "New England missionaries, too, were empire builders, commissioned to recreate Hawaiian society in their own image of Christianity and capitalism."[53] What began as a "mission of mercy" and "uplift" quickly took on more shades of capitalist and colonialist self-interest: "Missionaries hastened the advent and kingdom of capitalism by inducing changes in the pattern of land tenure and system of labor."[54] Paralleling the film narrative in *The Pagan*, debts to the foreign settlers spelled the beginning of Hawaii's demise of sovereignty: "Caught in the web of foreign trade and mounting deficits, along with occasional visits and threats by armed ships and marines to force concessions, the king and chiefs relied increasingly upon the settlers, including missionaries, who advised the kingdom and served its offices."[55] By 1842, foreign settlers already "occupied twenty-eight of the thirty-four cabinet seats and 28 percent of the legislature, though they totaled only 7 percent of the population."[56] Subsequent years were marked by the 1850 act "that granted foreign settlers the right to buy, own and sell land in Hawai'i" as well as ensuing land grabs, dubious land purchases sanctioned by the settler-dominated legislature, and expanding business opportunities for white settlers: "A stranded sailor from Massachusetts, Benjamin F. Dillingham, wed a daughter of missionaries and sired a financial dynasty of extensive land holdings, a railroad, and a ship terminal with wharves and warehouses."[57] Further New England profiteers who would eventually assume the role of the Big Five, the white families who controlled the entire economy of Hawaii, included C. Brewer & Co. (sugar cane, macadamia nuts), Alexander & Baldwin (real estate, sugar cane, agriculture), and Castle & Cooke later merging with Dole (pineapple, fruits).

As the plantation culture collapsed in the South during and after the Civil War, Hawaii's white settlers quickly compensated for this deficit with their own new plantation culture exploiting indentured servitude and low-wage labor. Lorrin A. Thurston, grandson of Massachusetts's first Hawaiian missionaries of the 1820s, who also translated the Bible into Hawaiian, stands out as a key political player in the overthrow of Queen Liliuokalani and the annexation of the kingdom. He was also the owner of the *Pacific Commercial Advertiser*, the forerunner to Hawaii's daily *Honolulu Advertiser*. Sanford B. Dole, son of Daniel Dole, a missionary from Maine, assumed the role of the presidency of Hawaii's new provisional government in 1893 and eventually became the first governor of the US territory of Hawaii in 1900. Dole's cousin, James Dole, from Boston, arrived in Hawaii in 1899 and founded the Hawaiian Pineapple Company, later the Dole Food Company. As Gary Okihiro points out, Hawaii's Big Five were organized with utmost feudal efficiency: "That concentration of economic power was kept within a circle called 'the family compact,' in which missionary families and their relations through marriage predominated. At least one missionary descendant served on every Big Five board during the early twentieth century, and through a system of interlocking directorates the family compact was observed. An oligarchy, the Big Five wielded both economic and political power, installing governments at will and serving in their offices."[58] These entrenched power structures would prevail until World War II when the US military placed Hawaii under its own martial law and broke the monopoly of the *haole* elite.

While some South Seas films hint at the destruction of an imagined Pacific paradise culture through its contact with Western civilization, these narratives with their biblical undertones contribute mostly to the concealment of the colonial and economic exploitation that guided Western expansion. W. S. Van Dyke's *The Pagan* does offer a much needed more concrete economic perspective, but at a time when its history had long been written and become irreversible. As Glenn Man summarizes the evolution of the genre, "By the 1930s, the cultural politics of the South Seas genre film would include not only a critique of the white presence and its 'civilizing' influence, but also the tension between that critique and the dominant pro-Western ideology inherent in most, if not all, classical Hollywood films made during the heyday of the studio years. The genre's flirtation with miscegenation is one significant illustration of this underlying tension between a radical tendency and the prevalent ideology, between the appeal of taboo and its ultimate cancellation."[59] According to Man, the South Seas genre offers a curious blend of a routinized critique of self-weary Western civilization paired with a more ambitious Hollywood imperialist and expansionist rhetoric. In analogy, an equally ambivalent position on race emerges, one characterized by transgressive flirtation with miscegenation soon to be brought more fully under the control of Hollywood's solidifying codes of censorship.

MODERNISM, VISUAL ASSIMILATION, AND THE ABORTED INTERRACIAL ROMANCE

Cinema in the 1920s, as Miriam Hansen has pointed out, attempts to gain wider cultural currency by creating complex narratives that position a mainstream mass audience as its ideal spectator in the identity of the mass consumer. Creating a phantom public sphere for the masses, cinema moves segregated social and cultural groups such as the working classes, immigrants of white ethnicities, and white women into closer proximity to one another. In order to do so, the heterogeneous practices of early cinema and vaudeville had to be left behind, with newer, more gentrified narratives taking their place. Classical Hollywood editing was an important strategy to raise cinema from its humble lowbrow beginnings toward its socially respectable acceptance as a legitimate form of cultural and artistic expression. It is important, however, to acknowledge the many significant technological breakthroughs in the film industry such as the advent of sound, mobility of cameras, higher speeds of film stock, improved lens, and lighting and editing technology, which offered cinema further currency as a cutting-edge technology deeply connected with America's modern industrial lifestyle. If audiences discovered themselves in cinema as empowered consumers in a modern mass culture, they also absorbed a significant amount of national pride as citizens of a country boasting leading technological output. In fact, films in the 1930s would consciously advertise the new technological breakthroughs as part of the industry's pride in having become during the 1920s the world's leading and unchallenged power in film production.

King Vidor's *Bird of Paradise* (1932) can be seen as an example of this pride in modernization that is accomplished at the expense of Pacific Islanders. Vidor had already made the culturally significant film *Hallelujah!* in 1929, his first sound picture in which a major studio (MGM) used an all-black cast in a story depicting the fate of sharecroppers. This film was considered a venture risk and required Vidor's own investment in the production. While Vidor attempted to present a portrayal of African American life with relative fidelity to reality, the focus of the film does not exceed that of a premodern agricultural world and thereby remains trapped in plantation culture. Known for his portrayal of urban New York City life as seen in the highly acclaimed silent film *The Crowd* (1928), Vidor did not consider urban life part of the African American experience, contrary to the historical Great Migration, during which 1.6 million African Americans migrated to northern cities such as Chicago and New York between 1910 and 1930. Similarly, Pacific Islanders are depicted outside of modern culture in *Bird of Paradise* and cast into a precivilized existence. Though the film was shot in Hawaii, the fictive location is a remote Pacific island to which a contemporary American yacht mistakenly navigates. In this first encounter natives are shown diving for modern consumer items, which the visitors throw overboard, including a sun hat, a pipe, a soda bottle, dinner plates and silverware, and a knife that proves crucial in the rescue of one of the ship's crew members during a subsequent shark attack. The film recasts Edison's *Kanakas Diving* (1898) in a new light, replacing its coins with the products of modern consumer culture. At the same time, however, the film refuses to note the modernization to which the Pacific Islands had been subjected after more than a hundred years of contact with Western civilization. An encounter that may still have been possible in the 1820s is now staged as occurring in 1932, as the film specifically dates itself in one scene. This temporal distortion artificially widens the distance between modern American life and that of Pacific Islanders who are cast in blatant racist terms as savages enslaved to superstition, worshipping the Hawaiian volcano goddess Pele and atoning her anger with rituals of human sacrifice.

Clyde de Vinna, Oscar-winning cinematographer from *White Shadows*, once again produces stunning underwater photography in the opening action scene of a shark attack and idyllic tropical images very much reminiscent of *White*

Shadows. An initial overhead POV shot of the heroine Luana (Dolores del Rio) floating belly-up in the water adds to the fetishistic appropriation of the island cast as woman to be conquered. A highly risqué underwater scene showing her in full nudity at considerable length while swimming with Johnny still fell into pre-code Hollywood but created a public scandal. Similarly, a topless performance by del Rio in a frenzied Polynesian dance with leis barely covering her breasts further adds to the amalgamation of sexuality and primitivism (see Figure 5). Such provocative sexuality, the film suggests, asks to be taken up on its generous invitation. In a later scene, the heroine's first kiss is nonconsensual, as she is held down with force by Johnny (Joel McCrea) in what looks more like an assault or rape. Apart from visually stunning photography and smooth use of modern sound technology with a soundtrack often relying on Hawaiian slack guitar, the film indulges in colonial fantasies of domination and offers no realism whatsoever. While the Depression era may have encouraged such escape fantasies, the film makes sure to represent mainstream American lifestyle in its most up-to-date state. In one scene, the hero recruits the help of a native woman by giving her a gramophone that plays contemporary jazz music, a scene clearly meant to highlight the new technology of sound in cinema. Unlike earlier South Seas fantasies with their slow buildup to spectacle scenes such as ceremonial dances and festivities, the projected paradise in this film is voraciously consumed from the start of the film's action-packed beginning in which the heroine saves the hero from a shark attack. Their early love encounter immediately leads to screen kisses and the eventual theft of the beloved during a ceremony in which she is promised as a bride to one of the natives. The interracial romance is cast predictably with familiar faces. The Italian Agostino Borgato, who played Kahana in *Hula*, returns as a native medicine man. The native girl Luana is played by the Mexican Dolores del Rio, resembling the casting of *White Shadows*, where another light-skinned Mexican, Raquel Torres, played the female lead. This casting of Latin and European-descent actors would continue with Anthony Quinn in *Waikiki Wedding* (1937), giving Latino actors more visibility on American screens while, however, confining them to roles of exotic characters. Napoleon Pukui is cast as the only significant Hawaiian in the thankless role of the backward king who will eventually offer his daughter as a human sacrifice to the volcano goddess Pele. The casting overall reflects the wider participation of white ethnic minorities in films during the 1930s that would produce such stars as the Irish Americans James Cagney and Pat O'Brian, the Jewish Americans Edward G. Robinson and Paul Muni, and the Latinos Anthony Quinn, Dolores del Rio, and Rita Cansino (later Hayworth).

The ending of *Bird of Paradise* also reflects America's new isolationism during the Depression era, as the American sailors rescue their stranded companion, return him to mainland, and pronounce the ultimate verdict on the doomed interracial romance referring to Rudyard Kipling's famous verse from the poem "The

White Man's Burden": "East is East and West is West, and never the twain shall meet."[60] In the face of this verse and the film's emphasis on initial assault, it appears that the United States had forced its way into a culture that in the end cannot be converted to modern Western standards. While Luana in her temporary elopement with her American lover is subjected to a fast-paced English language education and emerges from initial gibberish to speaking fluent English, she does not ultimately benefit from this fast-track acculturation. The ending shows her lost in a modern kitchen in the ship's cabin before she eventually turns her back on modern culture and chooses instead the path of self-sacrifice (thrown to the volcano goddess) in a melodramatic final scene. Although *Bird of Paradise* by no means offers a critique of colonialism as given in *White Shadows*, it does acknowledge in its own culturally biased terms the failure of the nation's expansionist enterprise. However, it no longer does so with regard to the original historical conquest of the Pacific Islands but reflects upon it from the late stage of the 1930s, a time period when Hawaii had already been thoroughly incorporated as a US territory and possessed a modern urban American lifestyle in its capital of Honolulu. As one of the last precode South Seas fantasies that were still permitted to depict an interracial romance, *Bird of Paradise* nevertheless concludes on a racist note, reflecting the nation's deep misgivings about Hawaii's native population framed as stubbornly premodern and inassimilable.

W. S. Van Dyke's *Never the Twain Shall Meet* (1931) fully implements the new code by ridiculing in overt racist fashion the impossibility of an interracial relationship between Dan Pritchard, the white heir to a shipping business, and his Polynesian lover Tamea. What initially starts out as romantic comedy with Tamea dancing hula and playing the accordion in the uptight American environment of San Francisco turns into soured disenchantment with South Seas fantasies once Dan has made the bold move to follow Tamea to the South Seas. In close-ups of a rum bottle, Dan confides in a beachcomber that he must get rid both of his drinking habit and Tamea, linking the two via a form of intoxication, or, as the film puts it, tropical fever. Although Van Dyke had shown some critical insights into US colonialism in the South Seas in *White Shadows* and *Pagan*, he makes a radical about-face in *Never the Twain Shall Meet*. In this latter film, racial mixing is ridiculed and the narrative withdraws into the position of white insularity and American isolationism. Tamea's Polynesian tribe is depicted in primitive and Paleolithic terms during a luau, and Tamea herself debauched and promiscuous, taking on additional lovers in the stereotypical manner of the uncivilized savage. With the severe economic downturn of the Depression, Van Dyke's film retreats into protective racism that secures white entitlement and privilege and advances isolationism.

Due to its controversial subject matter concerning the hypocrisy of New England's missionary values, Raoul Walsh's silent film *Sadie Thompson* (1928) had to be produced as an independent film but nevertheless performed well at the box

FIGURE 5. Dolores Del Rio as Luana dancing the hula in scandalous topless fashion in King Vidor's *Bird of Paradise* (1932). The leis were kept in place with tape.

office. Walsh is known today for his highly acclaimed crime and noir films, including *The Roaring Twenties* (1939), *High Sierra* (1941), and *White Heat* (1949), as well as war films such as *Objective Burma* (1945) and *Battle Cry* (1955). In *Sadie Thompson*, Walsh stars across Gloria Swanson (Sadie Thompson) as Sergeant Timothy O'Hara vying with Lionel Barrymore in the role of the missionary Alfred Davidson for Sadie's attention. The film is set in the remote Pacific outpost of Pago Pago, where US Marines are stationed. All major characters have a temporary stopover at the hotel of the white trader Joe Horn who is married to the native woman Ameena, played by Sofia Ortega.[61] While interracial romance is a convention in pre-code South Seas films and usually safely aborted before its full fruition as a family, an actual interracial marriage is rarely shown. As an overweight native woman, Ameena is ridiculed throughout the film for being lazy and is the literal butt of jokes when her husband lights a match on her behind and kicks her in this same area. Interracial marriage is thus belittled via routines of minstrelsy and slapstick comedy. In contrast to *Bird of Paradise*, in *Sadie Thompson* natives are shown as part of the modern world and are not involved in any pagan or superstitious religious practices, but pursue the lifestyle of traditional fishermen.

The film's plot revolves around the white prostitute Sadie Thompson, who wishes to leave her disreputable life behind and marry Sergeant O'Hara. However, the fanatical missionary Davidson recruits the help of the governor and prevents her from leaving the island, forcing her to face up to her former life and return to San Francisco, where she faces a prison term. In melodramatic fashion, Sadie undergoes a religious conversion, only to be sexually assaulted by Davidson on the night before her departure to San Francisco. Davidson subsequently commits suicide, and all obstacles for the happy ending with O'Hara are removed. The film features extensive close-ups of Swanson as she engages in "unladylike behavior" such as an obscene verbal shouting match with Davidson, dancing, listening to jazz music, and drinking and hanging out with soldiers. With Swanson at the center of the drama, the film defends and indulges in the loose morality of the Jazz Age. It also shows a significant shift in the administration of the Pacific, which in the twentieth century had been taken over from the missionaries by the US military.

In Lewis Milestone's remake of *Sadie Thompson*, titled *Rain* (1932), an even stronger realism comes to the fore. The Russian-born director (formerly Leb Milstein) had won best director Oscars for *Two Arabian Nights* (1927) and his famous antiwar film *All Quiet on the Western Front* (1930). In *Rain* he collaborated with accomplished cinematographer Oliver T. Marsh, who had worked on several films with Robert Z. Leonard, Ernst Lubitsch, and Erich von Stroheim as well as with Raoul Walsh on *Sadie Thompson*. As a Russian Jewish immigrant to the United States, Milestone appears not familiar or comfortable with the American tradition of minstrelsy displayed in Walsh. While the interracial couple of the hotel keepers are still presented as sloppy and unattractive in appearance, Joe Horn is instead cast as the lazy character. His native wife Ameena, played by the Samoan Mary Shaw, is initially shown with several of her children, which makes this interracial marriage bolder than Walsh's parody of a childless couple. Family and children entertain friendly relations with the military and Marines hug and play with the children, giving the relationship a type of administrative approval. Throughout the film, Milestone refrains from any parody or minstrelsy regarding the couple and instead relies frequently on documentary photography in the style of Flaherty, showing natives in close-up performing their work as fishermen. While the native lifestyle serves mostly as a background to the drama, it is treated with respect and hence places the burden of conflict on the white civilization.

The realism in *Rain* is built on stunning cinematography that showcases the latest film technology. Opening shots in the mode of poetic realism depict extreme close-ups of rain drops causing ripples in puddles, falling on sand next to sea shells, and gathering on tropical palm leaves. These shots not only symbolically represent the island's fecund climate but also showcase a much improved lens technology with microscopic close-ups of nature. The film's main drama focuses on the conflict between the life-affirming outlook of Joe Horn and Sergeant O'Hara versus the life-negating Puritanism of the missionary Alfred Davidson. However, a secondary drama of equal importance contrasts a traditional native lifestyle with the intrusion of modern life as given in the military station, loose morals, and the decline of nineteenth-century missionary expansionism. Supporting the outcome of the film in which Davidson's sexual assault upon Sadie and his suicide expose his ideology as hypocritical and life-negating, the film aligns itself with the forces of modernism in multiple displays of iconic images. Fetish close-ups of Sadie's jewelry-decked arm reaching from behind a beaded curtain, her legs exposed provocatively, and her shoes protruding into the frame make for a dramatic entrance when the sultry heroine (played by Joan Crawford) finally enters into full view from off-screen space (see Figure 6). This shot also evokes the part-for-whole shots of the island's climate and associates Sadie with nature. Sadie's part-for-whole entrance shot is repeated at the end of the film as her stage exit, declaring the victory of the Jazz Age over New England Puritanism. In another scene, as the heroine enters the hotel lobby, a remarkable 360-degree continuous pan shot revolving around the assembled guests evokes the dizziness and fascination they experience in the presence of Sadie's flaunted sexuality. This circular pan foregrounds the new camera mobility of the modern era with its cinematically enhanced realism. Improved lenses also contribute to many shots with deep focus and skillful theatrical blocking, which André Bazin was to praise in pathbreaking films such as *Citizen Kane* as the mark of modern realism in cinema. Further cinematic highlights include an exquisitely framed low-angle shot of Sadie from behind the gramophone as well as an unexpected wipe with a close-up insert of Sadie after her confrontation with Davidson, thus giving her the last word.

Sadie's character of the fallen woman and her melodramatic resurrection in marriage to a US Marine encompass both natural island and modern life and resembles the skeptical vitalism of Nietzsche's Zarathustra, whom Horn quotes at one point in defiance of church morality. Whereas the film subjects religion to critical scrutiny and appears to have moved away from religiously inspired racism—something Milestone knew well from anti-Semitic Russian pogroms—it leaves the authority of the military entirely unquestioned.[62] What is the military's interest in the South Seas? What justifies its presence? None of these questions are raised as the film updates the nineteenth-century colonial discourse of religion and missionary work to that of a modern and abstract discourse of technocratic administration. Immediately after the opening nature shots, the Marines are shown alongside a native carrying a canoe, singing and marching. The camera tracks their movements horizontally multiple times in both screen directions and switches to occasional close-ups of the soldiers' feet stepping into water-drenched mud, thereby linking them closely to the soil. In their back-and-forth horizontal marching movement caught via tracking shots, the Marines also constitute the boundary of the island. Other images of wooden blinds and of Marines carrying wood underneath a seafront pier link them to the forces of modern building construction and gentrification. Sadie's rescue through marriage by Sergeant O'Hara is foreshadowed early on, as she naturally enjoys the company of the modern military associated with global commerce over the outdated missionary, installing thereby military rather than missionary presence in the Pacific as the new status quo (see Figure 7).

These combined images clearly endorse the military as a natural and modern presence, reinforced also by their friendly and progressive relations with the interracial family and their children. While *Rain* abandons the embarrassing images of blackface and racial minstrelsy seen in so many South Seas fantasies of the 1920s, the film upon close analysis has in fact sanitized them into the cleaner discourse of a modern American administrative apparatus that rules ultimately via military and technology. This shift eventually eclipses the more radical initial depiction of the happy interracial couple that is used as a catalyst for the central melodrama's happy ending, a rehabilitation of the unfettered island's spirit embodied by Sadie through her marriage to Sergeant O'Hara. As will be shown, the discourse of military administration will intensify during the 1930s when the Pacific Islands, and particularly Hawaii, attain high geopolitical and military importance for the United States facing down Japan's imperialist expansion in the Pacific. The film's progressive and provocative depiction of an interracial marriage and family would not be seen for a long time in American cinema, as the Hollywood production code would align itself firmly with national racist and misogynist ideology in 1934 and prohibit on-screen miscegenation, alongside depictions of nudity, sexual perversions, rape, sexual hygiene and venereal diseases, and childbirth.

The perception and representation of Pacific cultures is complicated once Hawaii's modern population consisting of Hawaiians and Asians is taken into full account. In contrast to a film like Milestone's *Rain* limited to a presentation of contact between native Pacific Islanders and Westerners, Josef von Sternberg's highly acclaimed *Shanghai Express* (1932) conventionally depicts the offspring of an interracial relationship in the mixed-race Eurasian character Henry Chang (Warner Oland) in highly negative fashion and in the terms of Hollywood code. This film released in the same year as *Rain* shows that Milestone's film emerged in a cultural climate still strongly dominated by racist and Orientalist perceptions of Asians as well as strong objections to racial mixing, outlawed as miscegenation. Yellowface performances like blackface performances were used to point to the inassimilable Asian Other, highlighting grotesqueness. In the case of Warner Oland, who would eventually morph from Asian villain into the beloved Honolulu detective Charlie Chan, it is helpful to recall some of his earlier yellowface performances. Hawaii with its Asian majority population serving as a cultural middle ground and gateway between East and West provides Hollywood with the opportunity to present a more modern perspective on Asian and Asian American culture that overlaps with Polynesian culture. The cost of this more "positive" presentation, as one sees with the Chan series, is that of assimilation and denial of a distinct Asian Hawaiian culture.

FIGURE 6. Joan Crawford as Sadie Thompson, the prostitute on the mend in Lewis Milestone's *Rain* (1932).

In the harsher Orientalist driven *Shanghai Express,* Chang (Oland), a disguised Communist revolutionary agent during the Chinese civil war, hijacks the Shanghai bound express train trying to secure a prisoner swap. During this mission, however, he also rapes Hui Fei (Anna May Wong), brands a German passenger with a hot iron, and coerces Shanghai Lily (Marlene Dietrich) to provide sexual favors under threat of blinding the captured British officer Captain Harvey (Clive Brook).

FIGURE 7. Sadie Thompson (Joan Crawford) morally rehabilitated by U.S. Marines stationed in the South Seas port of Pago Pago in *Rain* (1932).

While the depiction of Asian culture is often praised as evenhanded in this film, supported by Anna May Wong's captivating performance, one cannot overlook the yellowface performance of Warner Oland, which clearly subscribes to Hollywood's code against miscegenation by depicting the hybrid Eurasian as a morally depraved, vengeful, and evil character. Warner Oland's yellowface performance in *The Mysterious Dr. Fu Manchu* (Paramount, 1929) similarly provides a highly negative depiction of the wily and demonic Asian who is set to avenge losses suffered during the Boxer Rebellion with elaborate schemes to poison its British perpetrators in London. A young white British girl Lia left in his care and reared by Dr. Fu is mercilessly used as a weapon through powers of hypnosis. Lia is initially shown in Chinese dress living in the Chinese Limehouse district of London; yet the plot demonstrates that this cross-cultural appearance is a perverse anomaly and consequently restores her Western white identity by film's end.

Oland's yellowface performances in *Shanghai Express* and *The Mysterious Dr. Fu Manchu* reflect an Orientalism that subscribes to strong cultural and racial prejudices. While working on these films, however, Oland also produced another yellowface performance on film that would secure him huge success and cult status in American cinema as the beloved Honolulu detective Charlie Chan. It is remarkable that this character also played in the reactionary tradition of minstrelsy and yellowface is at the same time connoted in more progressive terms. Detective Chan emerges as a leading international authority on crime and is fully versed with the latest developments in criminal forensics. His procedures of inquiry frequently dispel myth and supernatural speculation and side strongly with modern science. His Asian American children speak the American lingo of the day in contrast to Chan's Hawaiian Chinese pidgin English, implying cultural assimilation and integration. With the exception of Chan the entire Chan family is cast with Asian Americans, permitting for a greater screen presence. By placing Chan's yellowface performance into the midst of a large Asian family, he is to some extent assimilated, ironically becoming Asian and blurring the binary that yellowface traditionally seeks to maintain. The older children, both male and female, also pursue college education in later films and his son Lee will even represent the American swimming team and win gold at the Olympics in 1936. It appears that the series develops a new type of Orientalism that would later become known as that of the exemplary Asian American model minority. At dinner, for example, Chan carefully checks up on his son's academic progress looking at his report card (see Figure 8). While Oland's yellowface performance is clearly meant to contain the character's Asian heritage, it provides in its use of an imaginary Hawaiian Chinese pidgin a transition toward an assimilation to normative Anglo American culture as seen in the children's diction. By contemporary standards, this progressive cultural opening would appear still firmly rooted in Eurocentric ideology and racism. However, when compared to the primitive and premodern depiction of the Pacific Islands and Hawaii in the South Seas fantasies, its significance as a radical change in representational strategies cannot be dismissed.

The potential modernism of Chan's screen persona eroding Hollywood's racial binary is underscored in the first Chan film set in Honolulu, *The Black Camel* (Twentieth Century Fox, 1931). The film's evocative Orientalist title promises an atmosphere of Asian corruption but locates this moral decline exclusively within the white community of Hollywood stars during a film production in Hawaii where the murder of one film star by his starlet wife is avenged with her own murder by a jealous second spouse. In stark contrast to South Seas fantasies with their obsession with premodern Polynesian culture, this film depicts Honolulu as a modern urban setting. The film with its self-reflexivity and its focus on Hollywood publicity and technology further endorses a modern atmosphere. It opens on tourist footage with the camera tracking alongside Hawaiian surfers approaching Waikiki Beach and Diamond Head and dissolves into a newspaper headline from the *Honolulu Star* announcing the arrival of a Hollywood production: "Honolulu Welcomes Hollywood Motion Picture Company." In tiny print the featured article further states: "Planning to spend a month with Hawaii's beaches and mountains as the background for their scenes, a group of 50 players and technicians from Hollywood studios will reach Honolulu this afternoon." A further dissolve highlights a page from the paper's gossip column about the star's prospective marriage: "Trip to Islands Brings Noted Pair Together; Secretly Engaged." The film's opening scene thus introduces tourism, Hollywood technology, and modern media publicity strategies as the first images of Hawaii rather than any remote island fantasy. In a final dissolve we see a white contemporary woman in modern swimwear approached by a native also in modern swimwear as the camera cuts in on their conversation on the beach. The conversation is suddenly interrupted by an off-screen call "cut!" as both characters begin to walk off screen. In a match action cut, the film star Shelah Fane reemerges in the next frame in front of a full film and lighting crew with the director expressing concern about her distracted performance. A further cut-in clearly highlights the camera equipment and thus brings the production apparatus more fully into view. The seemingly idyllic beach scene of Waikiki is relativized as a film production in progress. Further shots show the arrival of her assistant Julie in a car at her dressing room. Numerous other cars are parked nearby and the background reveals a network of modern housing and telephone wires. A curious crowd of spectators of ethnically diverse background dressed in contemporary fashion is also shown on the set. Chan's first appearance occurs at the famous Royal Hawaiian Hotel lavishly filmed on location as a tourist haven for the wealthy elite. It also designates the legacy of the Hawaiian monarchy in the commercial and modern terms of tourism. The smooth on location sound recording along with the superb cinematography consequently delivers a modern and thoroughly Americanized Hawaii as a realistic image fashioned with the most modern production standards of Hollywood.

The question remains to what extent this technological modernism and realism can also be transferred onto the film's ethnic population and protagonists. As stated, Warner Oland's appearance may have to be seen as performing a mediating function between traditional Orientalism and a modern perspective on Asian American life. This modern perspective is still mixed with considerable reservation as his Japanese sidekick Kashimo (Otto Yamaoka) is frequently ridiculed by Chan and may be perceived as a minstrel parody of his attempts to assimilate. Likewise, Hawaii's multicultural setting is not allowed to emerge on-screen and is instead managed with a single group strategy in which Chan's Chinese family stands in for the ethnic Other of Hawaii. Given the ethnic diversity of Hawaii, this portrayal appears severely limiting but is part of Hollywood's hierarchical integration of certain ethnic groups into the American mainstream within certain genre functions such as the gangster film (Irish and Italian Americans) or the musical (Latinos), and the romance genre mostly reserved for the white majority. In the Chan series, the later addition of Stepin Fetchit (*Charlie Chan in Egypt*, 1935) and Mantan Moreland's racial minstrelsy routine in multiple Chan films alerts one to Hollywood's continued adherence to racial binaries in which minorities of darker

FIGURE 8. Detective Charlie Chan (Warner Oland in yellowface) reading the report card of his model Asian son at the dinner table in *The Black Camel* (1931).

color are persistently shown as undeserving of the American Dream. Hollywood also persistently refused to cast a minority of color in a lead role, opting for yellowface in Chan's case. Similarly, Chinese American actress Anny Mae Wong failed to secure the lead role of the Chinese O-Lan in *The Good Earth* (1937), which was given instead to the German Jewish actress Luise Rainer, who starred across the Austrian Jewish actor Paul Muni, playing the farmer Wang. The Chinese on-screen romance in *The Good Earth*, in compliance with Hollywood code, could be done only in yellowface, and therefore Wong, who had already carried many lead roles in European films directed by the German Richard Eichberg, could not be cast.[63] Since a majority of Hollywood film uses the dual plot of romance alongside each given genre (comedy, thriller, Western), all lead roles ultimately go to actors drawn from the white majority. Representational breakthroughs occur instead in more limited fashion, as with the depiction of modern Hawaii, Chan's highly intelligent character, and his thoroughly Americanized and successful children.

In spite of the many claims that the Chan series provided a cultural opening for the higher visibility of Asian Americans, one should also not overlook its accompanying construction of normative whiteness. As Daniel Bernardi observes, "Sometimes whiteness lurks outside the shadows of mise-en-scène, engulfing color, as if to represent what it is not. In these instances, whiteness aspires to be what Richard

Dyer recognizes as 'invisible,' showing that it is there, in force, a natural divine norm to be pursued but not to be questioned. This form of whiteness is nonetheless visible as white, replete with its own body of visual and narratological evidence. Ranging from white characters to white lighting techniques to stories of white superiority, this evidence is the stuff of texts and tales."[64] In *The Black Camel*, every attempt is made to surround Chan with whiteness. Initial shots of Shelah Fane in white swimwear and a radiant white robe show her on a sun-bleached white beach; she is filmed with high key lighting that stands in stark binary contrast to the native Hawaiian who approaches her and the native surfers. As Shelah Fane withdraws to a tent for a wardrobe change, the color of white is again predominantly featured in her dress. Chan's first entrance is also carefully staged at the Royal Hawaiian Hotel, which opened in 1927 as an exclusive resort to white elites from the mainland. As Yunte Huang comments, during its opening ceremony all twelve hundred invited guests were white: "On an island where four out of five people were nonwhite at the time, the Royal Hawaiian Hotel was as much a symbol of racial hierarchy as an icon of Hawaiian tourism."[65] The hotel appears as an appropriate set since it very much resembles movie palaces from the 1920s and 1930s in its architectural structure: "With a bright-pink Moorish-style stucco façade, The Royal Hawaiian owed its architectural influence to Hollywood, especially Rudolph Valentino and his Arabian movies. . . . Adding to its exotic charm, the hotel bellhops all wore pseudo-Chinese costumes."[66] In the black-and-white film, the Royal Hawaiian Hotel appears as a white rather than pink palace, shown in an extreme long shot from an offshore perspective resembling a luxury tourism ad or postcard of Hawaii. Once inside the hotel the camera follows an Asian bellhop in a modern Western uniform as he makes his rounds through the hotel to deliver a message. All the assembled guests in the hotel are white, until we finally see Chan in modern suit and white Panama hat and his overeager Japanese assistant Kashimo, who, after being ridiculed by Chan, quickly leaves the premises. The initial shot of the bellhop stressing his role as a servant is by association now also conferred onto Chan, the only other nonwhite character still present in the hotel.

During the entire film it will be Chan's task to solve a crime in an all-white community living aloof in a separate space of whiteness and having little contact with the island's ethnically diverse population. In two brief scenes, this diversity is shown with onlookers on the film set and children playing on the beach. Both scenes, shot in deep focus, relegate the nonwhite ethnic population to the background and highlight the white actors who occupy the foreground. Further scenes feature a Chinese cook (James Wang), stressing subservience and a stereotypical romance between the native girl Luana, played by the Mexican actress Rita Rozelle, and the white alcoholic painter Archie Smith, who is fatally shot, thereby negating the film's subplot of an interracial South Seas fantasy. The Hungarian actor Bela Lugosi, well known for his performance of Count Dracula and usually typecast as a horror film villain, stars as a mystic adviser in disguise, making Chan by contrast appear more transparent and trustworthy. In a separate scene, perhaps typical of America's apartheid society, the entire Chan family is featured in animated conversation during a family dinner. Though Chan and his family provide a higher visibility of Asian Americans on-screen, the native population of Hawaii featured initially in the film disappears altogether and is given virtually no narrative voice. Chan also bears little resemblance to the original Honolulu detective Chang Apana, upon whom his persona was modeled by the New England novelist Earl Derr Biggers. In contrast to Apana, who along with other minority detectives was excluded from working on high-profile cases, which was the official racial policy at the Hawaii Police Department at the time, Chan functions almost exclusively in the circles of the white upper classes.[67] A paniolo cowboy who worked at Parker Ranch, Apana started originally with animal abuse cases.[68] His later cases involving gambling and racketeering required a hands-on approach, as evidenced by the many injuries suffered by the famous and tenacious detective. Unlike Apana, Chan instead appears to be more a version of a Hawaiian Sherlock Holmes who solves most cases with a cerebral approach employing the latest innovations in criminal forensics.

The Black Camel provides a first example of films about Hawaii that begin to modify South Seas fantasies from the mid-1930s onward. Abandoning the traditional narrative of first encounters between white colonizers and natives, these films instead show America's colonizers fully acculturated in the Pacific and at home on Hawaii's islands. In ironic reversal, the natives appear as intruders. This annexation of Hawaii as a native turf is demonstrated in its most extreme form in Irving Cummings's *Curly Top* (1935), starring Shirley Temple in an adoption fantasy plot involving a rich bachelor who falls in love with her orphan sister. Shot in Hawaii, the film was promoted through a newsreel with the opening captions, "Whether in Hollywood or Honolulu, or New York City, 'Our Little Girl' managed to make the whole country her backyard." In the footage Temple is honorably inducted into Waikiki's beach patrol as the voice-over narrator states, "Right now the little colonel wants to be a little captain." In the short publicity film, Temple inspects a lineup of lifeguards with surfboards standing at attention and expresses her wish to return to Honolulu again. The actual film *Curly Top*, strangely enough, is set not in Hawaii at all but at a beach mansion in Southampton, New York. As an exclusively white social mobility fantasy during America's dire years of the Depression, the film enjoyed great success at the box office. The only residual appearance of Hawaii occurs during one scene when Elizabeth Blair (Shirley Temple) is looking through the funny pages and chances upon a comical drawing of dark islanders running around in grass skirts. A brief prior scene of Temple dancing the hula topless and in a grass skirt was eventually cut, as it violated the Motion Picture Production Code, which was strictly enforced starting in 1934. However, before the film tracks in on Temple reading the funny pages and presents the comics in close-up as a full frame, it obscenely creeps up the child's rear end in a surprising fetish shot usually reserved for sexualized adult women, perhaps trying to circumvent the code. Temple would eventually return to Honolulu and meet her second husband, Charles Alden Black, a former Navy intelligence officer who worked as the assistant to the president of the Hawaiian Pineapple Company. In both *The Black Camel* and *Curly Top*, Hollywood addresses in a more realistic fashion the subjects of crime, poverty, and orphanages. Hawaii's beaches as the playground of the wealthy, whether real or displaced onto Southampton, nevertheless retain a fantasy function in motivating plots of social mobility and serve as a catalyst for the restoration of white wealth. The fate of the colonized subjects is in fact even more repressed than in earlier South Seas fantasies and disappears into quasi-invisibility.

MASS ORNAMENT, PLANTATION CULTURE, AND THE SPECTACLE OF NATIONHOOD

In response to growing and aggressive expansion of the Empire of Japan in the 1930s, new US geopolitical realignments ensured that the borders of the American empire in the Pacific remained stable and unchallenged. Denigrating images of Asians as seen in *Fu Manchu* and other films depicting demonic Orientals did not find favor with the Chinese government and were eventually phased out in Hollywood to secure wider international box office appeal and align with new US foreign policy courting China as an ally. As Huang notes in the case of *Fu Manchu*, "In 1932, when MGM tried to make a new Fu Manchu number after four popular earlier films, the Chinese Embassy vehemently protested. The United States, at that point alarmed by the rapid and ambitious expansion by Japan in the Far East, wanted to recruit China as an ally against the Japanese threat. As a result, the American government pressured MGM to pull the plug on the production."[69] One can easily see that the global popularity of the Chan series with its amiable Hawaiian Chinese detective suited the State Department quite well in recruiting international allies and dispelling fears of racial or national hatred abroad. Huang suggests that Chinese censorship may have had a significant impact upon this new direction in Hollywood:

After Chiang Kai-shek gained control of China in 1927, his Nationalist government established a review board that maintained an iron grip on the importation of foreign films. The board regularly banned foreign imports that, in its view, either portrayed Chinese in a negative manner or demonstrated any hostility toward Chinese. Famous English titles in the banned list included *The Thief of Bagdad*, *Shanghai Express*, and *The Bitter Tea of General Yen.* . . . The Charlie Chan series, however, easily passed muster with the board because these movies were regarded as the first American films with a positive, let alone brilliant and funny,

Chinese character. Not only was Chan, in the eyes of the Chinese, a sea change from the sinister Fu Manchu stereotypes in earlier movies, but also, as a Chinese hero he appeared at a time when China was looked down upon by the Western powers.[70]

A growing need to address America's own national and military strength became increasingly imperative in a geopolitical climate troubled by Japan's militarism, Russia's Stalinism, and Germany's fascism. Diplomatic engagement of allies such as China via cultural exports would support this mission abroad.

At home, the Hollywood musical, with its assembly-line choreographies of human bodies, appears as a highly suitable vehicle to address these new national concerns for unity in film. As a mass ornament perfected in the elaborate musicals of Busby Berkeley, the musical not only brought escapist fantasies to the screen via the new technology of sound but also demonstrated a national body moving, dancing, and singing to the same beat. In this respect, the musical resembled military marching drills and elaborate military parades with their intent to form and represent a unified and homogeneous fighting body of the army. In his analysis of mass ornament, German sociologist, cultural critic, and film theorist Siegfried Kracauer first discovered its novel form of expression in the vaudeville performances of the Tiller Girls on tour in Berlin. Describing their chorus and assembly-line appearances on-stage, Kracauer notes, "These products of American distraction factories are no longer individual girls, but indissoluble girl clusters whose movements are demonstrations in mathematics."[71] Their wider dissemination via newsreels at the movies lends an even further element of abstraction to their already dehumanized bodies: "One need only glance at the screen to learn that the ornaments are composed of thousands of bodies, sexless bodies in bathing suits. The regularity of their patterns is cheered by the masses, themselves arranged by the stands in tier upon tier."[72]

In this reciprocity of mass audience and mass-orchestrated performance, a new totalitarian logic comes to the fore: "Only as parts of a mass, not as individuals who believe themselves to be formed from within, do people become fractions of a figure."[73] This new mass aesthetics initially brings about a break with nineteenth-century bourgeois traditions of subjectivity and interiority and gives voice instead to the modern anonymous urban masses. As such, these masses can be subjected to variables of the mass ornament within a given ideological system, such as Hitler's racist and eugenicist blood and soil populism, Stalin's communist revolt of class war, and America's capitalist mass consumer culture. In cinema these ideologies found their expression in Leni Riefenstahl's *Triumph of the Will* (1935), depicting a Nazi mass rally at Nuremberg with Hitler figuring as the part-for-whole stand-in of the will of the masses and its postulated white Aryan body; in Sergei Eisenstein's Odessa staircase scene from *Battleship Potemkin* (1925), with its oppressed revolutionary masses engaging in spontaneous uprising and conflict with the repressive and regimented body of czarist government soldiers and Cossack cavalry; and in Busby Berkeley's *Gold Diggers of 1933* (1933) with its coin-bedecked chorus line of girls celebrating the recovery of the dollar with the song "We're in the Money" as the anthem of an invincible American capitalism.

While these three cultural and political ideologies are highly divergent in their visions of society, they do share the deterministic sense of a system to which the individual is subordinated. The musical performs in this sense what Walter Benjamin calls the function of the aestheticization of politics. Forever cheerful and arranged with military precision, the hyperbolic chorus sequences display the wholesale eroticization of consumerism, as each of the chorus girls turns into a mass-manufactured commodity, representing the capitalist system in the fetishized body of the woman. As Patricia Mellencamp notes in the case of Berkeley's *Gold Diggers*, "Factory principles of standardization . . . operate in Berkeley's female formations of assembly-line symmetry, harmony, anonymity, perfection. The chorus lines are a combination of Freud's sexual fetish and Marx's commodity fetish, lining up with the mechanical studies of human labor taken into pleasure and leisure, like the history of cinema itself—popular culture as the flip side of industrial culture."[74] Apart from its erotized commodity focus, Berkeley's *Gold Diggers* also features some historical tableaux focusing on war in the number "Remember My Forgotten Man": "Scenes of soldiers marching off to war transform into war's aftermath of wounded, bleeding, bandaged veterans of World War I."[75] While these scenes may stress the economic fallout of war, they also highlight a different form of labor, namely nation building. It appears that the sacrifices of soldiers and veterans have been bypassed in a brutal economic system run by big finance. Beneath the surface of the musical's intent to jump-start the economy by savvy investment and marriage schemes that allow for the show to go on and provide the film's happy ending, one also detects a rallying call for renewed patriotism expressed via the war sequences. In Berkeley's musicals there is no attempt to hide the apparatus that fuels the nation, whether it refers to the economy, as shown in the backstage and production narrative, or war as the labor of nation building. Later musicals, particularly Mark Sandrich's Astaire and Rogers series, will shy away from an explicit backstage plot, which includes economic activities such as fund-raising, to put on a stage production and instead focus on a more concealed setting to foreground ease, effortlessness, and simplicity in their dance numbers. As Martin Rubin points out, "Performance space in the R-K-O/Astaire musicals is not confined to a separate compartmentalized domain such as a theatrical stage. Instead, any place becomes a potential performance space."[76] Thus, labor, which was dealt with explicitly in Berkeley, is now concealed in the performances of Astaire and Rogers that showcase a dance as the expression of everyday activities rather than stage performances operating under the pressure of a profit-oriented market economy.

It is precisely in moments of national crisis such as the onset of the Great Depression or impending war that film will reveal its own apparatus of labor that is usually concealed to ensure undisturbed entertainment. As a national imaginary, film not only constitutes an economic enterprise but also is linked to the work of building a nation's symbolic rituals of expression, creating Benedict Anderson's imagined community. It is therefore not surprising that an unlikely element such as war or the military can be perfectly integrated into a musical, particularly in the face of national and pressing historical circumstances. In the 1930s, the United States faced an increasingly hostile global environment with the Nazi rise to power in Europe and Japan's expansion on the Asian continent. While the country's severe economic woes may have first favored isolationism, the looming crisis did not entirely disappear from the nation's awareness. The musical *Flirtation Walk* (1934), starring Dick Powell, well known from his performance in *Gold Diggers of 1933*, combines what would appear as the rather remote narrative of a Hawaiian romance and marriage plot with a social mobility narrative in which its hero pursues an officer's career at West Point. After having been featured repeatedly in nostalgic and utopian South Seas romances during the 1920s, Hawaii's Pacific islands are now abruptly recontextualized in terms of war mobilization and military. Rather than performed in female chorus lines, the mass ornament in *Flirtation Walk* is accordingly linked to military drills and exercises. In this sense, the film also brings full circle the history of film documenting Hawaii that took its origins in the Spanish-American War in 1898, the year of Hawaii's annexation. Edison's film crew on their way to the Philippines made sure to document the new acquisition of Hawaii during a stopover in Honolulu. Since this time Hawaii had become heavily Anglicized in its power structure, representing the outer boundary of the United States as gateway to the Pacific. While the Pacific Fleet still had its permanent base in San Diego, the Navy was already in the process of relocating to Pearl Harbor. And though Hawaii in *Flirtation Walk* mostly occupies the background as a South Sea fantasy facilitating a marriage plot, it is nevertheless given strategic importance with the nation stretching from West Point to Honolulu.

Released in 1934 and directed by Frank Borzage, *Flirtation Walk* ushers in a new era of the strict self-imposed Motion Picture Production Code through which Hollywood aligned itself with national norms concerning the perception of race, sexuality, and violence.[77] This censorship code no longer accommodated traditional South Seas interracial romance. Instead, Hawaii now serves as the catalyst for a white romance starring Dick Powell, cast as a young private who becomes involved with the general's daughter, played by Ruby Keeler, well known for starring opposite Powell in seven musicals, including *42nd Street* (1933), *Gold Diggers of 1933* (1933), and *Footlight Parade* (1933).[78] However, before the romance in *Flirtation*

Walk is fully under way, the film opens in an unusual and alarming fashion with combined Navy and Air Force war maneuvers. The opening shot features a military document that spells out the mission:

WAR DEPARTMENT

THE ADJUTANT GENERAL'S OFFICE

WASHINGTON

SUBJECT: WAR MANEUVERS—LAND DEFENSE OF THE
HAWAIIAN ISLANDS.

TO: COMMANDING OFFICER, SCHOFIELD BARRACKS,
HONOLULU T. H.

1. ON OCTOBER 15, THE COMBINED NAVAL AND AIR FORCES WILL
ATTACK THE HAWAIIAN ISLANDS.

2. USING ALL ELEMENTS IN YOUR COMMAND, YOU WILL REPEL THIS
ATTACK

The film then launches into documentary footage of military maneuvers, featuring the latest military equipment in carriers and naval destroyers as well as slightly old-fashioned twin propeller airplanes flying in attack formation. Further shots feature target practice with heavy artillery and an artillery gun directly aimed at the viewer. This in-your-face presentation of the military can be construed as a call to arms or as a call for military alertness in an era of geopolitical developments threatening the United States. In a final dissolve the film's opening sequence shows the entrance gate to Schofield Barracks, the military base that would eventually become known to the world in the aftermath of the attack on Pearl Harbor. While such a military opening may seem rather unusual for a romantic musical, it stresses the genre's strong connection to the mass ornament, which highlights nation building in its complex choreography of masses.

The military narrative blends seamlessly with that of romance, stressing marriage prospects along with economic mobility. On duty as the general's driver, Dick Dorcy (Dick Powell) becomes involved with his daughter in a spontaneous romantic adventure when they tour the island and chance upon Hawaiian torch fishermen and an ensuing luau festivity. The film repeatedly highlights the POV and eye line of hero and heroine as their looks authorize the local spectacle, cutting to overhead and long shots that show us the circular choreography of the Hawaiian dancers and drummers aligned in elaborate patterns similar to a Busby Berkeley number. The Hawaiian mass ornament underlined by war chants will return later in the film again as the military mass ornament of drill exercises at West Point, connecting the tropical islands to the strategic interest of the country. As the couple nears the performance, the music shifts to the more romantic hula and features a female Hawaiian dancer. Love and nation are strongly foregrounded in a circular petal flower dance arrangement accompanied by Hawaii's unofficial anthem "Aloha Oe," written by the deposed Queen Liliuokalani. Hawaii is further shown as an extension of the United States as Dick Powell's character speaks fluent Hawaiian and converses with the locals before launching into a Hawaiian song. Reaction shots feature well-known Hawaiian musicians Sol Hoopi and Sol Kekipi Bright, embedding Powell as a quasi-native Hawaiian. Powell delivers the song in Hawaiian and in the authentic falsetto voice typical of popular Hawaiian music. His performance by far surpasses the usual facile impersonations of screen Hawaiians as seen, for example, in Clara Bow's Hula but conveys a genuine transcultural musical sensitivity. For the film's purpose, however, Hawaiian culture is now fully owned by its white colonizers and internalized into the national imaginary. In this sense, Dick Powell's character, Dick Canary Dorcy, becomes the enunciator of Hawaiian culture as the natives and his date look at him in admiration.

Kracauer views the system of the mass ornament as indigenous to America where capitalism reigns as its national ideology: "In America surplus profits are directed to spiritual shelters such as libraries and universities, which cultivate intellectuals whose later endeavors repay with interest the previously advanced capital."[79] In this light, the mass ornament does express the spirit of a national community, albeit with the shallow value set of monetary capitalism. *Flirtation Walk* demonstrates this connection of capitalism and national community. As Dorcy attends military academy at West Point, he also improves his social and economic standing and is finally deemed worthy to marry the general's daughter. The military career path is presented as a sound investment strategy that will repay one's labor with increased social standing and an upwardly mobile family. The formerly erotic flirtations in Hawaii reemerge with the young couple as they date on West Point's flirtation walk, a preset path for love and marriage. The military is shown to be the big family, the total community, to which its participants aspire to belong. The spiritual expression of the American nation reflects Max Weber's thesis on the unification of monetary and spiritual concerns in the Protestant work ethic. Spanning from Honolulu to West Point, the film ends on elaborate displays of mass ornaments now presented in the form of military choreography, paralleling the ornamental displays shown earlier in Hawaii. *New York Times* film critic Andre Sennwald captures this excess of national and patriotic emotion in his review of the film's premiere: "A rousing recruiting poster, the new photoplay tells of the raptures, the sentimental joys, the minor difficulties and the collegiate fun of life among the institutional lads at the Military Academy. Mr. Borzage, for the benefit of those who came in late, gives the last scene everything he has. On a widened screen the Cadets march sternly and proudly to receive their commissions and take up their glorious destinies as defenders of the Constitution. In the grandstand, Ruby Keeler and Sergeant Pat O'Brien lift their tear-filled eyes as Dick Powell marches past at the head of the parade, while a stiff breeze whips the flag gallantly across the screen."[80] *Flirtation Walk* anticipates a military crisis for the United States at its outer borders in the Pacific in its opening sequence and eventually settles for a rallying call for patriotism and capitalism. Walter Benjamin's dire prediction, however, that "all efforts to render politics aesthetic culminate in one thing: war" cannot be entirely dismissed.[81] The film's romantic setting in Hawaii cannot conceal the geopolitical and strategic value of this territory as a major military hub for the Pacific Fleet.

Films about Hawaii during the late 1930s continue in a less war-like atmosphere, stressing instead its deep national ties to the mainland via the industry of tourism and the export of Hawaiian culture to the mainland via film and musical and dance performance circuits. As Adria Imada sums up the development of the 1930s,

> Americans on the continent did not, however, come into close contact with Hawaiians on a wide scale until the 1930s. In the years prior to World War II, as the Pacific colony grew more important to national security, Americans needed to define Hawai'i and Hawaiians for their own interest. Concomitant with tourism, American military operations were mounted in Hawai'i, where the United States required a foothold to assert itself against Japan. In an era before jet planes delivered Americans to the islands, Americans came to experience Hawai'i through live performances on the U.S. continent. The imperial hula circuits of the 1930s and 1940s produced what I call an "imagined intimacy" between Hawai'i and the United States. A fantasy of reciprocal attachment, this "imagined intimacy" made it impossible, indeed unimaginable, for Americans to part from their colony.[82]

Imada further discusses the "greatest hula contest ever staged in the Islands,"[83] sponsored by MGM studios in 1938 as part of a Hollywood promotion campaign. This marketing ploy can be seen as indicative of the increasing incorporation of Hawaiian music and dance performances in the sound pictures of the 1930s. While Imada focuses on Hawaiian performance circuits on the mainland, it is equally important to consider the role of film during the 1930s as the most widely disseminated mass medium, reaching sixty to eighty million viewers, half of America's population, on a weekly basis. Audiences who did not have a chance to witness hula performances or Hawaiian music events could do so through movies that featured music and guest appearances by Andy Iona and His Islanders, Sol Hoopi, Sol Bright, Harry Owens and the Royal Hawaiian Orchestra, as well as dancers such as Kealohu Holt and Hilo Hattie. Through the medium of film, along with radio, Hawaiian showrooms in various hotels around the country, and tourist magazines, Hawaii assumed a more concrete position in the national imaginary than it had in prior decades. The "imagined intimacy," to which Imada refers, had also evolved from exotic island and sexual conquest fantasies, as seen in the more vaudeville-oriented hula shows resembling the Harlem clubs of the 1920s, into more realistic and contemporary fantasies of commercial and romantic interaction for the masses, as featured in cinema's imaginary.

If hula performances at the various Hawaiian showrooms belonged more in the realm of adult and night entertainment, film managed to deliver a more day-time atmosphere along with the cleaned-up vaudeville elements that had to meet Hollywood's own censorhip code, the Motion Picture Production Code, enforced in 1934, with its goal to ensure wholesome and respectable mainstream entertainment. Along with the tourist illusions offered by cinema in an era where mass tourism had not yet been developed, Pacific musicals further contributed to the national mass ornament in their invocation of the plantation system. During the 1930s, an era that marks the final stages of an irreversible transition in the United States from an agricultural toward a modern industrial and urban society, numerous Hollywood films (*The Little Colonel*, 1935; *The Littlest Rebel*, 1935, starring Shirley Temple and Bill "Bojangles" Robinson; *Jezebel*, 1938, starring Bette Davis; *Gone with Wind*, 1939) and film musicals (*Mississippi*, 1935; *Show Boat*, 1936; *Way Down South*, 1939) evoked an antebellum nostalgia for southern plantation culture. This nostalgia extended to both rural preindustrial culture and America's pre–Civil War racial hierarchy, reinforcing the apartheid logic of Jim Crow as a quasi-natural, eco-friendly, and racially eugenic mythology. Because such films were always traumatically tainted with the legacy of slavery, similar plantation dramas set in the South Seas and the South Pacific appeared all the more appealing as they resurrected plantation culture in a post–Civil War America and hence had seemingly moved beyond slavery.

As Gary Okihiro points out, sugar cane and pineapple plantations in Hawaii accelerated their production in the wake of the Civil War and rose to national prominence due to postwar shortages on the American continent. By 1910, more than 90 percent of the production of sugar cane and pineapple in Hawaii was run by five big former missionary families (the Big Five) who had originally hailed from New England.[84] This expansion also embraced many of the cultural values of the plantation system and modified them only slightly to dismiss the crude practices of slavery while retaining white supremacy. The updated and modern Hawaiian plantation system provided in this case the template for America's twentieth-century imperialist ambitions with which it sought economic and administrative control in the Pacific. In films depicting Hawaiian plantation culture such as Victor Fleming's *Hula* (1927) or the musicals *Honolulu* (1939) and *Song of the Islands* (1942), the generic conventions of southern plantation dramas could be easily reactivated, exoticized, and served up to a contemporary audience. *Flirtation Walk* (1934), *Waikiki Wedding* (1937), and *Honolulu* (1939) perhaps stand out among the South Seas fantasies, as these romantic musicals also highlight changing economic structures built on the increased role of the US military in the Pacific as well as modern advertisement and tourism, questioning the naïve soil and agricultural mythology of plantation culture. However, even these more modern films still utilize rural Hawaii as the romantic and idyllic backdrop serving as the catalyst for the production of the white heterosexual romance at the center of these films. In addition, the Hollywood formula of the happy ending for the white and prosperous couple continues to borrow heavily from the racial hierarchy of plantation melodramas. To be sure, the southern plantation system had simply been modernized and updated in South Seas fantasies and was repackaged for mass consumption in the lighter genre of South Seas musicals. For instance, for many American GIs stationed in the Pacific theater during World War II, Hawaii often provided the first direct contact with non-European races. Hollywood films offered the necessary social and cultural contexts for such encounters. South Seas musicals also provided a more upbeat outlook, abandoning the melodramatic and tragic dimensions of the filmic antebellum South. Musicals, in particular, promoted a new mass choreography of nationhood and race in which old racial hierarchies were cheerfully updated and celebrated, maintaining the status quo.

In her discussion of European imperialism, Hannah Arendt points to the many tensions and contradictions between global economic expansion and the homogeneous nation-state: "In contrast to the economic structure, the political structure cannot be extended indefinitely."[85] The encounter with non-European civilizations for the purposes of economic expansion posed considerable problems of political and cultural integration of these new territories with its nonwhite populations.[86] This dynamic of Eurocentric imperialism also applies to the American expansion in the Pacific, requiring repeated explanation of the country's mission in these non-European and often non-Christian territories. The plantation system, which in itself was built on a colonizing effort on the US continent, assists here with convenient answers for America's new expansionary efforts. The medium of film, which disseminated these ideologies in mass culture, simply repurposed the old southern plantation logic for its new territories in the Pacific.

Waikiki Wedding (Frank Tuttle, 1937) offers a sophisticated example of enlightened consumerism in which film can critique its own interest in financial profit, while exploiting the message of critique as yet another marketable product. Similar to MGM's promotion campaign of a hula contest with winners having a chance to visit Hollywood, the film features the contest winner of a mainland promotion for the Hawaiian pineapple industry. As part of the contract, the beauty pageant winner is crowned "Miss Pineapple Princess" and is sent on a romantic vacation to Hawaii. As part of the publicity campaign, she will report her experiences in several newspaper installments. However, the beauty queen Georgia Smith (Shirley Ross) does not find the expected romance on the islands and quickly tires of her vacation, threatening to leave abruptly and write about her unhappiness in the newspaper. Tony Marvin (Bing Crosby), the ad agent who devised the original promotional scheme, is called upon to remedy the crisis. What follows is an elaborately staged and prescripted Hawaiian romantic adventure to make the heroine fall in love and avert the publicity disaster of a disenchanted tourist and contest winner. With the help of his Hawaiian friend Kimo (Anthony Quinn), Marvin stages an elaborate Polynesian theme show, involving the clichéd luau, ceremonial and sacrificial festivities, as well as a faked volcano explosion. As expected, feigned love turns real, but the happy ending is temporarily suspended when Georgia discovers that she has been duped by Marvin's Hawaiian show. In a final ruse, Marvin hires an older woman to play the part of his mother and convince Georgia not to leave the island. Georgia accepts Marvin's proposal, realizes that she has been duped again, but now values the ingenuity of Marvin's stagecraft. In similar fashion, the film blurs the boundaries between fact and fiction and elevates the entertainment industry with its commercial interests into a position of sincerity in spite of its staged and invented screen realities.

The film opens with a cheerful Hawaiian wedding spectacle as the establishing scene of Marvin's legitimate claim to the island. A long tracking shot reminiscent of those in *White Shadows* follows the hula dance of a teenage native female as she passes rows of women covered in flower leis holding a chain lei. The chain brings together all the people present, creating a communal mass ornament. The camera eventually rests on a close-up of the soon-to-be-wed young Hawaiian couple. As the *kahuna* or Hawaiian priest performs the ceremony in Hawaiian, the camera swerves to the left and Tony Marvin (Bing Crosby) and his friend come into full view. Marvin translates the Hawaiian prayers effortlessly to his white friend and is shortly thereafter called upon by the groom to perform a good luck ritual as the best man: "For the ceremony of the bowl I choose my friend, the friend of all my friends, I choose the *haole*." All the natives cheer on the *haole* as he performs the ceremony and soon after launches into a Hawaiian song rendered in the native language. The white insider to Hawaiian culture is once again established similar to Dick Powell's Hawaiian song performance in *Flirtation Walk*. Close-ups of Crosby, now wearing a thick, glowing white lei, make this scene a sumptuous spectacle. The scene ends with him carrying off a young female native dancer on his shoulder in paternalistic fashion, presenting him as a father figure to the natives (see Figure 9). The imagery of the leis as a motif that represents a natural or organic community not only foregrounds Tony Marvin as a member but also shows his elevated status in the social hierarchy as his lei is thicker, whiter, and more luxurious than those of the natives. His status is further affirmed via POV shots and close-ups. At this point, however, the illusion of Hawaiian nativism is suddenly disturbed and dismantled. The camera settles on medium shots of elderly male native drummers, the real fathers of the islands, then dissolves into an island shot, followed by another dissolve inside a pineapple plant with exhausted Asian and Hawaiian women wearing Imperial Pineapple uniforms, manning an assembly line. The sound bridge of the drumming from the wedding scene carries over into the monotonous mechanical sound rhythm of the assembly line. The entire dissolve shot sequence deconstructs the mass ornament as it reveals the monotonous labor that is required to sustain its illusion. A final dissolve rests on an office door highlighting the huge and pompously lettered name of J. P. Todhunter, president of the pineapple company. In this swift transition, the film condenses the entire history of Hawaii's economic exploitation by the powerful white mainland families, the Big Five, and invites viewers to reexamine critically their exotic island fantasies in a more realistic light.

What follows, however, is not a disavowal of white rule but rather a generational struggle between two competing white father figures who determine the economic fate of Hawaii. Representing Hawaii's older, established, and profitable pineapple industry, Todhunter is challenged by Marvin, who represents a younger and modern generation, placing its bet on tourism as the new market expansion for Hawaii's future. Todhunter's son and assistant speaks with a southern accent, evoking traditional feudal plantation culture associated with slavery, whereas Marvin's assistant is a young female Hawaiian Asian professional who edits his prescripted installments to the mainland newspapers and provides a modern liberal perspective on Hawaii. While the film conventionally casts the Mexican American Anthony Quinn as Marvin's Hawaiian friend Kimo, reminiscent of the many Hawaiian brownface performances in cinema, the film also relies on contemporary casting of Asian Americans in the modern workforce. In addition, the audience sees Kimo performing scripted Hawaiian clichés for the tourist visitor and understands that his role of the exotic Hawaiian is nothing more than an act or a cinematic myth. In another transgressive scene, Marvin and Georgia cradle a native child in a hammock, providing an unusual family shot with a nonwhite child and allowing the film to bypass Hollywood's restrictive censorship codes on miscegenation and mixed-race offspring. The lullaby song "Sweet Leilani," which was awarded an Oscar for best song in 1937, underlines this provocative and utopian scene. In its progressive outlook, the film also stresses a middle-class perspective catering to American mass audiences who identify with Marvin and his easygoing friends in contrast to Todhunter, who represents the staunch and crusty white business elite. However, as the film goes on to show, the world of advertising is deceptive and, like a mass ornament, an empty surface expression that can be manipulated to accommodate multiple ideologies. In typical Hollywood fashion, the film serves up a mixed dish of progressive and conservative outlooks, ultimately maintaining the status quo of American culture and politics.

The final part of the film is devoted to the restoration of the white middle-class couple to its top position in America's social and racial hierarchy. The couple's position is buttressed by a comedic couple, representing uneducated lower-class whites (Myrtle and Shad played by comedians Martha Raye and Bob Burns) and serving as a stark contrast. It is interesting to note here that traditional blackface minstrelsy as seen in Griffith or Walsh's South Seas films is now displaced onto the lower-class white couple. Myrtle and Shad are paired up in comedic scenes with a monkey and pig, respectively, becoming the laughingstock of even native Hawaiians. Myrtle in particular is subjected to considerable misogynist slapstick violence such as falling face down into a bowl of the Hawaiian moonshine *okolehao* and later falling drunkenly from a thatched roof. This strategy allows Hollywood to retain its tradition of minstrelsy while also elevating the Hawaiians who are no longer the butt of its jokes. At the same time, the social and racial hierarchy is reestablished in deceptively liberal terms. The Hawaiians gladly spend entire days to help out their best friend Marvin and eventually disappear discretely when the film's happy ending celebrates the restoration of the white middle-class couple. Throughout the film, the same rhetorical device of revealing and concealing the apparatus of production is repeatedly used, trapping the viewer in the inevitability of white capitalism as the only true guardian for Hawaii. Everything, as cinema has its audience believe, is show business.

Waikiki Wedding suggests in its plot a generational change and transition from the agricultural to the tourist industry; yet, this imagined reality was more visionary in nature since mass tourism did not come to Hawaii until the 1960s. Prior to this period, only wealthy elites could afford to vacation there. However, what the film credibly promotes is Hawaii as a commodity and brand with products such as pineapple canned in assembly-line fashion and sold on the US continent as an exotic staple. Marvin, the millionaire version of a beachcomber, manipulates and guides Hawaii's modern advertising in seemingly effortless manner, as he relaxes on his sailboat, dreaming up original ad ideas that control the representation of Hawaii. Meanwhile, the local labor pool of women is put to good use in the factory and contributes to American affluence, suggesting a top-down hierarchy of American business ingenuity administering local labor and its emerging service industries. This sanitized version of the southern plantation system is sold to mainland audiences as the latest modernization on the labor market, combining white know-how with brown labor. The pineapple plays a crucial role as a major signifier for Hawaiian aloha and accordingly becomes the metaphor for the modern plantation. While the pineapple industry had suffered some setbacks during the Depression, it had fully recovered by 1937 and excelled in the combination of modern production techniques and advertising, or what Gary Okihiro aptly calls "Pineapple Modern":

The genius of Hawai'i's pineapple producers illustrated in the spectacular rise of the industry and its influence in the U.S. marketplace of consumption and image making derived at core from its partnership with modernity. . . . It created for itself machines to reduce the need for stoop labor; the sanitary, efficient canneries, and their lines of uniformed and gloved women who nursed the naturally

FIGURE 9. Bing Crosby portraying Tony Marvin, the paternalistic guardian of Hawaiian culture and Hawaiians, in *Waikiki Wedding* (1937).

wild, prickly fruit made tame by peeling and slicing it for civilized tongues; and the advertising campaign aimed at white middle-class women and orchestrated by modern artists, graphic designers, and writers whose productions tapped inchoate desires for fashion and style, sensual abandon, and convenience.[87]

As a product of improved nature, the canned pineapple could also cross climate zones and find itself on store shelves in colder climates.[88] This abstraction of the fruit from its natural environment, needed to become a proper consumer product, was best suggested in modernist design techniques that highlighted in their labeling of products surface silhouettes and converted Hawaiian images into surface ornaments. Design arts that control the modern representation of marketable commodities thereby assume equal importance alongside the product in advertising a tropical modernism. Among the many designers for Hawaiian products and tourism, Frank Mcintosh stands out for his techniques indebted to Japanese print and Asian art. Most notably, Mcintosh designed the luggage sticker for the Matson shipping company, which brought American visitors to the islands. As DeSoto Brown notes, "The greatest triumph, however, was his series of six menu covers in gorgeous colors and streamlined airbrush lines; beautifully abstracted, yet clearly Hawaiian."[89] Dole's Hawaiian Pineapple

Company enlisted none other than the modernist artist Georgia O'Keeffe, whose work similarly uses surface texture and fabric-like print patterns with abstractions of organic nature, for its advertising campaign.[90] This abstraction from nature to design allows for Hawaii to become an enlarged franchise of a variety of consumer items such as ukuleles, hula skirts, hula girl dolls, leis, shells, wooden carved pineapple ornaments, tiki statues, Hawaiian music, Hawaiian liquor, Hawaiian muumuus, Hawaiian fabrics, aloha shirts, and all other things Hawaiian. These consumer items enabled those who did not have the means to travel to Hawaii to nevertheless own a piece of the islands.

A similar modernist style of abstract advertising appears prominently in the opening credits of the MGM film musical *Honolulu* (Edward Buzzell, 1939), with silhouette and streamlined art deco designs. As the culmination of Hollywood's increasingly self-revelatory style as an entertainment product, this musical packages itself in the stylized form of modern consumer items from Hawaii. The radical emphasis on surface ornament is reciprocated in the musical's many mass ornamental choreographies and its plot of the interchangeable lives of a film celebrity and a commoner. Tired of his celebrity movie star status, the hero Brooks Mason (Robert Young) switches roles with his look-alike George Smith, who happens to be from Honolulu and a plantation owner. In an irony that escapes the filmmakers, this switch links Hollywood to the southern institution of plantation culture and slavery. In the ensuing comedy of errors, the film demonstrates that the white consumer is king and can impersonate anyone. Commodity is thus linked not only to consumer items but also to identity. In stark contrast to the film's seemingly open market on identities for white consumers, the featured minorities cannot take part in this freedom but must remain exactly who they are, namely part of the ethnic or racial servant class. Race offers no obstacle for whites as one musical number clearly shows with its return to minstrelsy performance. In the case of white female dancer Dorothy March (Eleanor Powell), race and gender boundaries are crossed when she impersonates the racial Other in a so-called tribute to the "King of Harlem," Bill Bojangles Robinson, done in blackface. The Hawaiian servant Fong (Willie Fung) and the black butler Washington (Eddie Rochester Anderson) by contrast not only are locked into their socioeconomic role as servants but also are obliged by Hollywood to perform their roles in the manner of self-degrading minstrelsy.

In the socioeconomic system depicted in *Honolulu*, subaltern and marginalized identities are the cheapest commodities and can be purchased by any white consumer. In this context, Kealoha Holt's Hawaiian dance performance is not so much an expression of Hawaiian identity but simply provides the garment for Dorothy March's Hawaiian makeover. The ownership of cultural identity, as the film suggests, belongs foremost to its entitled white characters who can adumbrate themselves with the creativity of racial and ethnic minorities, black, Hawaiian, Asian,

or Jewish. As Carol J. Clover points out in relation to *The Jazz Singer* and *Singin'*
in the Rain, with their uneasy relation to race and use of black music and dance
styles, "These moments point to the immensely popular tradition, on stage and
film, of the performance, by whites in blackface and often in venues that did not
admit African American performers, of music and dance deeply indebted to those
performers. The film musical in particular drew heavily and variously on black art
and talent. Only in the 'Negro musical' was that talent front and center."[91] Likewise,
Hawaiian music and dance, as seen in the many South Seas films, are in the end
the property of the white American elite and not to be confused with the expression of genuine Hawaiian culture. While overt racism as seen in *The Idol Dancer*
and *The Jazz Singer* slowly disappeared in Hollywood, it was simply replaced by
a more insidious economic system of market colonization and annexation of cultural identities via commodity fetish. This socioeconomic disenfranchisement
is comparable to the contemporary notion of theft of intellectual property, since
Hollywood rewarded its white performers handsomely for impersonating and performing the cultural Other and paid only the standard lower wages to the origina-
tors of Hawaiian or black music and dance idioms.

The system of exploitation is perhaps best demonstrated in the film's two other
interchangeable characters, namely the black servant Washington in New York
and the Chinese Hawaiian servant Fong in Honolulu. Both are curiously linked
via the plantation system and their minstrelsy performances, which are meant to
adumbrate the lifestyles of their masters. Washington gives the routine minstrelsy
performance of the dumbfounded and intellectually inferior black butler who is
totally mystified when dealing with the coming and going appearances of Mason
and his lookalike Smith and their simultaneous preference and dislike for a cup
of coffee. The Chinese Hawaiian servant Fong illustrates the updated code as his
duties betray a more strategic subversive nature of deliberate forgetfulness of the
master's orders, landing the master temporarily in jail as a suspected impostor. Like
Washington, Fong is cast intellectually inferior but is beginning to emerge tacitly
as smarter than he would lead one to believe, negating the master's dominance in a
type of subversive minstrelsy.

In the costume ball "Come as Your Favorite Star Tonight," the audience sees
Eleanor Powell blacking up in a scene reminiscent of *The Jazz Singer* but now in
a frontal shot facing directly the viewer who takes the position of the mirror. This
conspicuous display of corking up is needed to inscribe the system of white racial
superiority. Her musical tribute to the legendary Bill Bojangles Robinson—based
on his tap dance performance on a set of ascending and descending stairs in *Har-*
lem Is Heaven (1932) and its repeat version in *The Little Colonel* (1935) together with
Shirley Temple on a staircase inside a southern colonial mansion—is underlined
at one point with a single violin plucking the melody of Dixie, linking the performance with southern plantation culture rather than Harlem. As the performance

ends, the film cuts to a clichéd image of the South Seas and underscores it musically with "Aloha Oe." This sound bridge from "Dixie" to "Aloha Oe," from plucked fiddle to Hawaiian slack key guitar, presents Hawaii as the new sanitized plantation culture in which slavery no longer exists but the ideology of Jim Crow endures. In symmetry with her Bojangles tribute, Dorothy March (Eleanor Powell) eventually performs a tribute to hula and a native war dance. Backed by Andy Iona's orchestra, the film merges the traditions of black minstrelsy and tap dancing with the Hawaiian traditions of hula. At the center of an elaborate ornament, the white female dancer emerges surrounded by Hawaiian dancers who bow to her in prayer-like manner and encircle her as the ultimate national signifier (see Figure 10). The final double wedding starring Robert Young as both Mason and Smith multiplies the power of the white wealthy male and enthrones him ultimately at the top of the nation's hierarchy.

IMMINENT WAR AND THE END OF SOUTH SEAS FANTASIES

The increasing militarization of Hawaii and American culture can be seen in the musical *Flirtation Walk* (1934) as well as in the regimented mass ornament of less belligerent musicals such as *Waikiki Wedding* (1937) and *Honolulu* (1939). In 1931 Japan invaded Manchuria and established the puppet state Manchukuo, first hinting at their expansionist ambition. In 1937 the Japanese military attacked the USS *Panay*, an American gunboat, on the Yangtze River, claiming that officials had not seen the ship's flag. The subsequent Allison incident (January 1938), in which a Japanese soldier struck an American consul in Nanking, further added to the already strained political climate between the United States and Japan, not to mention the Nanking Massacre of 1937, which had given America a drastic impression of Japan's brutal expansionist agenda. It is not surprising that John Ford's only South Seas film, *The Hurricane* (1937), took on a much darker tone in its representation of French colonial power and institutional racism in the Pacific, culminating in a hurricane to end the Western fantasy of the Pacific, the quiet or peaceful ocean as it had been dubbed upon its discovery. In early 1941 President Roosevelt moved the Pacific Fleet from its base in San Diego (as seen in *Flirtation Walk*) to the outer boundary of the American empire, namely Hawaii's Pearl Harbor, and ordered a military buildup of the Philippines. In the wake of these developments, American film audiences witness one more final change in the South Seas musical, anticipating the multiracial combat films that were to follow in the 1940s. In contrast to the exclusionary logic of the earlier musicals, these late musicals such as *Hawaii Calls*, *Honolulu Lu*, and *Song of the Islands* are overshadowed by imminent war. As such, their role changes to an even more comprehensive rallying call for the nation and they include minorities more extensively. *Hawaii Calls* (1938) features the story of two stowaway children who board a ship to Honolulu. In the assimilative gesture of Jewish ghetto films from the 1920s that often brought together Irish and Jewish American families, allowing Jewish characters to enter the social hierarchy at the lower level of ethnic white American immigrants, this film similarly pairs up an Irish American orphan, Billy, with his buddy, the Hawaiian native Pua.[92] In Hawaii, Billy is welcomed by Pua's family, which includes Hawaiian actress Mamo Clark, known for her roles in *Mutiny on the Bounty* (1935) and *The Hurricane* (1937), and is given a full tour of native Hawaiian pastimes. Throughout much of this musical, Billy sings lead in numerous Hawaiian songs frequently surrounded by a cast of native dancers and musicians. Accidentally, the two children also uncover a major plot of sabotage and help retrieve the strategic defense plans stolen from Commander Milburn. Korean American actor Philip Ahn plays the role of the Japanese traitor and house servant Julius, expressing suspicion toward Japanese expansionism in the Pacific and possible collaboration by Japanese Hawaiians. The film offers a more friendly inclusion of Hawaiians in national affairs, though not without marginalizing the largest ethnic group of Hawaii, namely Japanese Hawaiians.[93]

Honolulu Lu (1941), shot before the attack on Pearl Harbor and released shortly after, features Mexican dancer Consuelo Cordoba (Lupe Velez) as the film's main character. On the lam in Hawaii with her con-artist uncle Don Esteban Cordoba, Consuelo is helped by a local Hawaiian woman in her pursuit of an honest career as a cabaret dancer entertaining young sailors. Eventually, Consuelo also succeeds in reforming her uncle, presenting viewers with newly reliable and patriotic Latino and Hawaiian characters. The light musical comedy also features American sailors as a significant part of Honolulu's population, thereby changing the island's image from a wealthy tourist or leisure site into a military base. *Song of the Islands*, released in March 1942, would appear to take on a more fantasy-like tone in its glorious use of color film but again shows a wider inclusiveness of heretofore excluded minorities and clearly plays to a different audience in its emphasis on lowbrow comedy. At the center of this musical comedy is a dispute between two landowners pursuing different cultural and commercial agendas in their use of the South Seas islands. The Irish American Dennis O'Brien (Thomas Mitchell) believes in preserving his plantation as a natural sanctuary and resists any modernization.[94] Conversely, the Anglo American Jefferson Harper Sr. wishes to buy land from O'Brien so that he can build a loading ramp for his profitable cattle farm. The Italian American actor Victor Mature plays Harper's son and soon develops a romantic interest in O'Brien's daughter Eileen (Betty Grable).[95] Eventually, cultural and business differences are set aside and culminate in a hula festival on Saint Patrick's Day, incorporating Irish dance steps and green costumes into hula dances. The film thus renegotiates white ethnic diversity (Anglo, Irish, and indirectly Italian American) into a family merger of mutual interest staged in the terms

FIGURE 10. Eleanor Powell as Dorothy March in the film musical *Honolulu* (1939), at the center of a petal mass ornament, highlighting the controlling dominance of the white signifier.

of plantation culture. Musically, the film links Western and country music with the music culture of Hawaiian slack key guitar and Hawaiian cowboy or paniolo culture. In addition, it features lengthy cameo scenes of Hawaii's comedic hula dancer Hilo Hattie, providing a burlesque element for the sake of mass entertainment, since Hattie proved to be tremendously popular with the American military.

Hattie is featured as Palola, Grable's childhood nurse, and sings two major songs, "Hawaiian War Chant" and "Cockeyed Mayor of Kaunakakai." She is frequently degraded as she chases Harper's friend Rusty Smith, trying to coerce him into marriage. Humor concerning her family's cannibalism adds further to the depiction of Hawaii in the manner of minstrelsy but is also motivated by the style of lowbrow burlesque comedy. It is interesting to note that as a propaganda musical for American unity, the film resorts to the premodern concept of plantation culture, linking all its participants into feudal family bonds. On December 7, 1941, these imagined communities met with the startling intervention of reality, escalating the ongoing global contestation of territories and geopolitical dominance in the Pacific into America's entrance into World War II. As will be discussed in the next chapter, the South Seas fantasy had to surrender to the more realistic genres of war and combat film in which Hawaii and the Pacific would once again be restaged as crucial to US interests.

One such last South Seas fantasy is the adventure drama *South of Pago Pago* (Alfred E. Green, 1940), shot mainly on Hawaii's Kona Coast and American Samoa and involving numerous Hawaiian extras. Set in the 1880s, the film features pirate-like Western intruders on the island of Manoa, attempting to secure precious pearls. While the film follows clichéd plotlines of naïve natives quickly subjugated by white intruders along with the usual interracial romance, it does so with a new twist that points to the genre's end and imminent war in the Pacific. The romantic plot deviates from the standard aborted interracial marriage trope in that a marriage ceremony between the white heroine (rather than the usual Polynesian female love interest) and her Polynesian lover Kehane does indeed take place. Jon Hall, alias Felix Locher, of Swiss and Tahitian descent, is boldly cast as a native hero who wins the heart of the white woman with on-screen interracial kissing scenes, something usually prevented by Hollywood codes. Though the heroine Ruby Taylor is of dubious reputation, much like Dallas as the prostitute with a heart of gold in John Ford's *Stagecoach* (1939), she is ennobled by Kehane's genuine love and eventually sacrifices herself by taking a bullet for him. In the film's culminating scene, the natives rebel against the white intruders and die in great numbers, while fighting their explosives and superior guns. With persistence, however, they capture the ship, kill the villainous captain, and tie the remaining survivors onto masts with a sign "So That Other White Men Will Remember Manoa," setting the ship adrift as a warning. Final shots show natives in full possession of the sovereignty of their island and the hero's second marriage to the native Malia. With its relaxation of casting codes and unusually violent and warlike ending, *South of Pago Pago* indicates that the Pacific may soon see conflict and that Americans need allies rather than colonial subjects.

As has been discussed in this chapter, the representation of Hawaii in Hollywood cinema articulates the national imaginary of the United States. As Amy

Kaplan points out, with the end of America's expansionist era at the turn of the previous century, overseas possessions took on a symbolic function for American desire as represented by its goal of overseas markets and cultural expansion with its forms of free-market capitalism and democracy as a world model: "With the end of continental expansion, national power was no longer measured by the settlement and incorporation of new territory consolidated into a united state, but rather by the expansion of vaster yet less tangible networks of international markets and political influence. Even the annexation of Hawaii and the Philippines was valued primarily as providing way stations to the fabled China markets, just as Cuba became the gateway to the Caribbean. . . . These islands, despite their bounded nature, became projections of the desire for an ever-growing expansion that seemed directed at non-corporeal goals."[96] What Wheeler Winston Dixon identifies as the Edenic utopian dimension in South Seas fantasies pairs well with America's political agenda,[97] described by Emily S. Rosenberg as the unique blend of the interests of "Capitalists, Christians, [and] Cowboys."[98] As Rosenberg points out, McKinley's Open Door Note in 1899, "asking all nations to respect the principle of equal commercial opportunity in China,"[99] became the cornerstone for America's expansionist ideology. It would appear that in this grander scheme of things, the territorial sovereignty of Hawaii had to be sacrificed, framing the islands as cultural fantasies for a Christian capitalist world conversion. Hollywood, itself an economic enterprise, was only too glad to support these national fantasies as part of the productions emerging from its dream factory.

2 ❀ WORLD WAR II HAWAII
Orientalism and the American Century

On the eve of America's entry into World War II, Henry Luce, founder of magazines such as *Time, Fortune,* and *Life,* predicted in a now famous *Life* editorial the coming of the American Century. "So far," writes Luce in February 1941, "this century of ours has been a profound and tragic disappointment."[1] The time has come, Luce writes, for the United States to cast aside its isolationism and provincial perspective and assume its rightful position as an international leader. The "20th Century," he argues, "must be to a significant degree an American Century":

> Under [Roosevelt] and with his leadership we can make isolationism as dead an issue as slavery, and we can make a truly *American* internationalism as natural to us in our time as the airplane or the radio.... [We need] to accept wholeheartedly our duty and our opportunity as the most powerful and vital nation of the world and in consequence to assert upon the world the full impact of our influence, for such means as we see fit.... Once we cease to distract ourselves with lifeless arguments about isolationism, we shall be amazed to discover that there is already an immense American internationalism. American Jazz, Hollywood movies, American slang, American machines and patented products, are in fact the only things that every community in the world, from Zanzibar to Hamburg, recognizes in common.... America is already the intellectual, scientific and artistic capital of the world. Americans—*midwestern* Americans—are today the least provincial people in the world.[2]

Luce's confident, if arrogant, vision of America's global expansion inaugurates a liberal capitalist internationalism born in the crisis of World War II. Luce's "American internationalism," however, is a contradiction in terms since it transforms "*midwestern* Americans" into cosmopolitans merely by dint of its escalating global economy. It unabashedly celebrates a global environment of

Anglo-American culture and values conducive to the economic expansion of American markets and capitalism. In his interesting pronouncement that isolationism can become as dead an issue as slavery, Luce also implies that American internationalism and market expansion are essentially democratic, liberating, and, above all, morally just. Slavery, like isolationism, is simply treated as an unfortunate aspect of US history, obscuring its legacy of Jim Crow race relations.

Indeed, Luce's project of global domination is presented not simply in the vocabulary of finance and economy but in terms of a quasi-religious morality, "an international moral order," defined as a providential American capitalism.[3] And most significantly, it calls for an active interference in East Asian affairs. Luce's manifesto is much more than a rallying cry for the impending world war, articulating instead an updated version of Manifest Destiny or what Luce calls in his essay "manifest duty." In addition to supplying the world with its free economic system as well as "engineers, scientists, doctors, movie men, . . . teachers, and educators," it is the "manifest duty of this country," argues Luce, "to undertake to be the Good Samaritan of the entire world."[4] Luce's "American Century," then, lays the foundation for a form of nationalism masked as internationalism, envisioning a new world order based on all things American.

As historians have argued, Manifest Destiny is a peculiar "expression of American romanticism, a blending of divinely ordained mission and expansion," one in which race plays an important function.[5] This obscured but seminal role of race is seen both in Luce's pronouncement that slavery is dead and in his representation of the Orient. As Michael Hunt points out, Luce's international perspective is informed by his place of birth and childhood, China, and his belief that it was in great need of American uplift and culture. His parents were prominent missionaries whose fund-raising helped sustain American schools such as Yenching University in Beijing. According to Hunt, Luce, like his parents, held an "ethnocentric, self-righteous, almost cartoonish conception of China. . . . He appears to have known little about the very people with whom he would come to closely identify, and he would never learn the language of the country for which he claimed to speak. Unfortunately, for Americans and Asians alike, the resulting simple, superficial conception of China . . . would . . . shape Luce's general approach to Cold War Asia."[6] Indeed, Luce's Orientalism manufactures China (and later Japan, Korea, and Vietnam) as an imaginary ideal, legitimating the global expansion of American influence and providing a national myth. The national issue of isolationism, and by association the "dead" institution of slavery (and race), is overcome by being displaced onto the international plane of global domination, involving yet again the containment of the racial Other. Luce's Orientalism ultimately transforms the premodern narrative of the master/slave relationship into a master narrative of global domination and administration that rearticulates the American credo of Manifest Destiny in modern terms, fusing economic expansion into the East with faith and divine provenance.[7]

The critique of Orientalism has been widely discussed in the context of European imperialism. In particular, Edward Said's influential work has claimed that Orientalism is not merely the academic study of the Orient as practiced by Orientalists but a cultural tool used in Europe's acquisition of empires.[8] As a Western system of representation that frames, manages, and produces the Orient, Orientalism is now commonly viewed as a discourse, an imaginary geography that articulates a specific global order and the fundamental distinction between East and West. In recent refinements to Said's theory, Orientalism is also seen as defining Western culture in reverse, showing that it is itself a product of its Orientalist imaginary.[9] Indeed, Orientalism paradoxically regulates and codifies not only the East but the West as well, organizing and ranking the various domains and institutions of Western culture. As Deborah Gewertz and Frederick Errington argue, Orientalisms can be discussed only in terms of Occidentalisms and vice versa, since both are necessarily defined by their differences to one another.[10] American Orientalism has been shaped by its European inheritance, especially the extensive tradition of Orientalism,[11] and since the eighteenth century has figured prominently in the American imaginary.[12] However, it is during the crisis of World War II that a new preeminent American Orientalism, superseding South Seas fantasy, was born, facilitating the nation's rise to the world's strongest superpower. The Orientalism embedded in South Seas fantasies, as we have seen, is a mixture of racial, ethnographic, and colonial rhetoric built on a Western teleological understanding of the history of mankind and civilization, placing Europe and even more so the United States at the top of its hierarchy. South Seas Orientalism is frequently conflated with Africanism, pointing to presumed lower Pacific tribal cultures, as is commonly also done in Hollywood's stereotyping of Africa. For example, the 1933 version of *King Kong* arbitrarily depicts Skull Island as a mixture of Malayo-Polynesian culture and African tribalism.[13] Beginning with World War II Orientalism, these fundamental racial discourses are pushed into the back and concealed by a new pragmatic, geopolitical, and administrative perspective. Liberal developmentalism, to borrow Emily Rosenberg's term, views itself as enabling foreign territories and markets to share in the capitalist vision advanced by American Christian democracy. The United States sees itself no longer as a colonial oppressor or imperialist power but rather as a global protector of its democratic freedoms and capitalist practices. Of course, in order to implement this role of world leadership considerable military power is required.

This chapter explores forms of this new wartime American imaginary and its production and management of the East as articulated in the vernacular Orientalisms of Henry Luce and particularly John Ford, before turning to cruder forms of Orientalism in B films that expose the persistent racist underbelly of American society. Examining Ford's war documentaries, *December 7th* (1943) and *The Battle of Midway* (1942), I discuss the significance of American Orientalism as a pragmatic and more efficient version of European Orientalism. I also explore the differences between the Orientalisms of Luce and Ford, arguing that the latter stresses an entirely new ingredient, namely that of multiculturalism, absent in most other forms of Orientalism. In this context, Ford's Orientalism paradoxically not only provides a new national narrative that articulates a wartime imperialist agenda justifying expansion into the East but also puts forward a constructive critique of this ideology. This latter subversive aspect is most clearly seen in *December 7th* and its depiction of Hawaii's multiracial society, which assumes in Ford's work the crucial role of a cultural and geographic avant-garde, an offshore site of experimentation for multiculturalism yet to be implemented on the mainland. To be sure, Hawaii's own population experienced the military not in the progressive terms outlined by Ford for the mainland. As Haunani-Kay Trask notes, "Throughout the Second World War and its aftermath, Hawai'i was under martial law for seven years, during which time over 600,000 acres of land was confiscated, civil rights were held in abeyance, and a general atmosphere of military intimidation reigned."[14] While Ford's Orientalism is without doubt an example of American imperialism, it nevertheless motivates significant progressive tendencies on the mainland that cannot be found in Luce's exuberant and uncritical version of expansionism.

JOHN FORD'S ORIENTALISM

Like Luce's liberal capitalism in which American products, culture, and technology populate the globe, Ford's Orientalism extends the national frontier of the West into the East.[15] It is commonly noted that Ford's celebrated Western films capture the quintessential spirit of American identity. Conquest of the land, securing of national borders, a diverse people forming a unified and meaningful community are key themes in Ford's mythic depictions of the nation's westward expansion. In classic Westerns such as *Stagecoach* (1939), *The Searchers* (1956), and *The Man Who Shot Liberty Valance* (1962), Ford recounts again and again the tale of America's birth and its ethos of democracy as that which legitimates its nationhood. Ford's World War II films similarly tell another tale of the nation's birth, that of Luce's American Century. Certainly, Luce and Ford share a similar pragmatic approach to Orientalism, viewing it not as the colonization of another culture as given in nineteenth-century European imperialism but as the benign modern management of another cultural space with the superior tools of self-government and free-market strategies that empower other nations to assume the shape of American democracy.

However, unlike Luce's Orientalism that obscures the role of race and uses it as a tool to legitimate market expansion, Ford's Orientalism actively incorporates race as foundational to the narration of nation. His war documentaries help establish conventions of the World War II combat film with its imaginary depictions of multicultural combat units consisting of every type of American ethnic and race group (Black, Mexican, Jewish, Polish, Irish, Filipino) fighting side by side. Recasting Luce's international vision in narrative and melodramatic terms, Ford makes it available not merely as a commodity and tool but as a legacy that documents America's struggle to achieve its vision of democracy in its westward/eastward expansion. Hence Ford's complex form of American Orientalism destabilizes the restrictive binary perspective of black versus white that regulated national discourse in the prewar era. Indeed, Ford's American Century takes on a peculiar mix of sophisticated international and plain homespun ideals, expressing a nascent multiculturalism. In his films, these deceptively naïve democratic values are strategically deployed to promote complex and often conflicting national interests that identify its Oriental enemy as hostile to Occidental democracy (Japan) and to broadcast democratic values among America's World War II Oriental allies (China, Korea, the US territories of the Philippines and Hawaii). In spite of its conservative attempt to manage the Orient and America's racial hierarchy (via assimilation and Americanization), Ford's Orientalism contributes paradoxically to a more complex and diverse understanding of race and ethnicity, acting as a catalyst for a new multiethnic configuration of American nationhood. It transforms the binary logic of majority and minority discourses into a more complex field of cross-ethnic elective affinities, thereby breaking open the hegemony of Anglo-American cultural standards too readily presumed as the foundation of American identity. To be sure, while Ford's vision of a new international America similarly transforms midwestern Americans into cosmopolitans and attempts to manage America's racial hierarchy, it also documents America's struggle to overcome its midwestern provincialism, xenophobia, and racism.

Before discussing Ford's new version of World War II Orientalism, it will be necessary to review some of the films John Ford shot in the 1930s, leading up to his new paradigm. *Judge Priest* (1934) offers the failed attempt of a southern postbellum comedy, promoting racial harmony and reconciliation. Not unlike Luce, Ford wishes to put slavery to rest and fails to recognize the virulent systemic racism of Jim Crow in full force at the time of the film's release, one still occurring today in forms of white entitlements and systemic exclusions based on race. Since the history of the American South, in contrast to the western frontiers or the South Seas, does not provide a utopian margin due to the brutal social reality of racism, Ford's eccentric Judge Priest (Will Rogers), who is best friends with the happy and carefree Negro Jeff Poindexter (Stepin Fetchit), amounts simply to nonrealistic and fantastic nonsense, belittling the violent history of slavery and whitewashing it with paternalism and nostalgia. The opening credits introduce Judge Priest in 1890 Kentucky in an apologetic and nostalgically obscured description as "typical

of the tolerance of that day and the wisdom of that almost vanished generation."
As an eccentric judge, Priest resembles later Ford figures such as the drunken
doctor Kersaint or Boone (both played by Thomas Mitchell) who operate outside the conventions of society. The latter do so, however, in locations associated
with openness and mythopoeic qualities (South Seas, Wild West) and not with
three hundred years of slavery and strictly enforced postbellum Jim Crow rule.
Due to this imperative of realism on American soil, Ford's utopian vision cannot
credibly take off and instead reinforces an amnesiac denial of history, upholding a
pet Negro stereotype in the minstrel character performed by Stepin Fetchit. The
only progressive element in the film is that of white class mobility, which allows
the northern-educated nephew of Judge Priest to marry the orphan girl Ellie May
Gillespie, who naturally turns out to have a secret father and who despite being a
chain-gang prisoner conducted himself nobly as a soldier in the Civil War and has
provided secretly for his daughter's education. Conversely, black characters such
as Poindexter and Aunt Dilsey (Hattie McDaniel) are locked in plantation stereotypes of happy subservience, denying the reality of the violent institution of slavery, the failure of Reconstruction, and the postbellum Jim Crow rule of apartheid
segregation.

Released in the same year as *Judge Priest*, *The Lost Patrol* (1934) shows Ford in a
much more credible position where he is allowed to engage uncharted and utopian
locations such as the North African desert, away from America's racist landscape.
In 1928 the popular British suspense writer Philip MacDonald published *The Patrol*,
the story of a World War I British detachment lost in the Mesopotamian desert. A
young John Ford immediately bought the screen rights and, working with several
writers, adapted it into a convincing film script. In 1933 a hesitant RKO Pictures
granted him a small budget to direct the film. Using a largely British cast of actors,
The Lost Patrol was moderately successful and, more importantly, launched Ford's
historic career. Ford is especially celebrated for his war films and Westerns, two
genres profoundly concerned with representation of nation. *The Lost Patrol* itself
went on to have a major impact on World War II combat film, establishing conventions of framing friendly and enemy Asians (as well as model and nonmodel
minorities) and their relation to the West. Ford's remodeling of its narrative allows
us to compare and discuss various forms of Orientalisms, exploring where the film
draws and departs from its European predecessor and how it forms the basis for
the American World War II model.

As an Orientalist thriller, MacDonald's novel *The Patrol* follows in the tradition
of the popular detective genre that became fashionable in the latter half of the nineteenth century. Exemplified by works such as Wilkie Collins's novel *The Moon-
stone* (considered the first British detective work), the genre effectively conflated
mystery and Orientalism. As a late stage in Europe's Orientalism, these Oriental
mysteries appeal to mass culture and are less concerned with esoteric or erudite

knowledge of the Orient. Instead, images of the Orient are starkly reduced and simplified, thereby achieving mass currency. Said notes that twentieth-century Orientalism likewise shows a simplification of approach, steering away from the old scholarly and philological immersions of the nineteenth century toward a more modern, pragmatic, and administrative management of Oriental affairs. Knowledge of Oriental languages and cultures become secondary, if not altogether useless in some cases, to the geopolitical bureaucratic management of colonies and territories.

It is precisely at this stage that the United States, with its ascending geopolitical and economic imperialism during the World War II era, would replace the former colonial powers of France and Britain. Cinema with its mass cultural appeal early on took a strong interest in Orientalism and seemed perfectly suited for its modern-day shorthand rendition of Oriental stereotypes. Philip MacDonald, the author of *The Patrol*, subsequently moved to the United States after his collaboration with Ford and had a successful career as a Hollywood scriptwriter. He authored several scripts of interest to us here, including *Charlie Chan in London* and *Charlie Chan in Paris* (Chan's creator Earl Derr Biggers died in 1933 and MacDonald effectively followed in his footsteps) as well as *Mysterious Mr. Moto* and *Mr. Moto's Last Warning*, which feature a similar wily Asian detective played in yellowface by Peter Lorre, a Jewish exile from Vienna especially known for his appearances in other Orientalist mysteries such as *The Maltese Falcon* and *Casablanca* that incorporated Orientalist themes into that of resistance.

Filmed on location in the desert of Yuma, Arizona, Ford's adaptation of MacDonald's Orientalist thriller retains much of the novel's heavy-handed stereotypes. As will be seen, however, Ford's 1934 film has two significant Orientalist agendas: the required representation of the Orient and, more important, the American agenda of challenging and replacing the British claim to global leadership complicated by America's post–World War I pacifist stance and isolationism. The film, with its story of a lost British patrol that is slowly picked off by unseen Arab enemies, represents the Orient in typical occidental manner as described by Said: "In the Orient one suddenly [confronts] unimaginable antiquity, inhuman beauty, boundless distance."[16] This idea of a primitive and brutal vastness is communicated instantly in the film's stark images and opening dedication. The dedication places us directly in the Mesopotamian desert in the year 1917: "While the World War raged in Europe, British troops were fighting in a far corner of the world. Small solitary patrols moved over the vast Mesopotamian desert that seemed on fire with the sun. The molten sky gloated over them. The endless desert wore the blank look of death. Yet these men marched on without a murmur, fighting an unseen Arab enemy who always struck in the dark—like a relentless ghost!" In the backdrop accompanied by recognizable Middle Eastern music, the audience sees the immense undulating desert at high noon with a procession of men on horseback.

The dominance of the desert is depicted in the distance of the framing (extreme long shot), the composition within the frame (the men are pushed to one side of the screen, with the desert taking up the mass of the space), and the repetition of the desert's swelling mounds in the hypnotic, rhythmic music as well as in the rolling line of soldiers proceeding in single file. The dedication is followed by an extreme long shot of a lone soldier on horseback centrally framed, appearing insignificant if not lost in the enveloping desert. We hear the swishing sound of a bullet and in the second shot see him hit the ground dead.

Said has discussed the tension between vision and narration in Orientalist narratives. The vision of the Orientalist is panoptic, says Said, that is, it can see the entirety of the Orient in a single view.[17] This static panoptical vision, he notes, is pressured by the temporality of narrative, which introduces change and development. With its simple and economical narrative, The Lost Patrol deftly maintains the panoptical vision of primitive vastness represented in the central image of the desert. For the remainder of the film, members of the patrol (now lost without their commanding officer) are eliminated one at a time by invisible Arabs who attack either from a distance (sniping) or stealthily under the cover of darkness. The Arabs remain literally unseen for the entire film, relegated to off-screen space, except for a brief moment at the film's end when they enter screen space to kill the remaining survivor, the sergeant. When we do finally see them, the Arabs are framed in extreme long shots (like the desert landscape of which they are a part) as a group and are completely covered by their dress. Having no individual features, they are represented not as distinct, complex subjects but simply as a nameless, primitive drive compelled to destroy civilization. Like the desert, the invisible Arabs are an incomprehensible force, transcending time and humanity.

In contrast to the relentless monotony of the desert and its inhabitants, the patrol members are a motley and complicated crew representing the various cosmopolitan members of the British Empire with their competing dialects, values, social systems, and religions. Everything we perceive and learn about Arabic characters in The Lost Patrol is mediated through the various members of the patrol who speak and act in their stead. In keeping with Orientalism, history, narrative, speech, complexity, and development are associated with the West whereas image, stasis, and myth characterize the East. At the same time, the film undermines this traditional Orientalist binary by questioning the act of war and British imperialism. Framed in the convention of the World War I film genre and reflecting America's own stance toward impending war, The Lost Patrol represents war strictly in pacifist terms. The British patrol is absolutely out of sync with its surroundings and war is reduced to absurdity. Throughout the course of the narrative, the film highlights the patrol's poor training, its inability to focus on the task at hand, and the arrogance of its officers. The patrol is lost due to the blundering incompetence of its young commanding officer, who is killed before articulating the mission. The men seem unable to comprehend the concept of sniping and are easy targets, as they constantly fight and bicker among themselves. They station as night sentry a young, idealistic recruit who foolishly thinks of Kipling when looking at the moon and are surprised when the next morning he's dead and the horses are gone. Another soldier is a religious fanatic who attempts to redeem and later kill his fellow soldiers—he's shot by Arabs as he wanders into the desert carrying a crudely made cross and has a fellow comrade killed. A pilot is shot dead as he struts toward the lost troops unaware of the dangers of war, and the lone surviving sergeant, who is finally rescued by another patrol, goes mad and continues to talk to his dead comrades. From the opening scene to the last, the British are represented as inept, decadent, and patronizing bunglers who have only themselves to blame for their fate in the Orient. The patrol is not simply lost in a desert but lost morally and culturally as well. With this critique of the outdated nature of British Orientalism and global leadership, Ford paves the way for his own emerging utopian vision of the American Century based on a new and progressive model of Orientalism.

Wee Willie Winkie (1937), released in July, shows a first attempt of Ford to inject his Orientalism with a utopian dimension rather than the purely critical stance taken toward British colonialism in *The Lost Patrol*. He does so through the character of Priscilla Winkie Williams (Shirley Temple), who witnesses the British colonial apparatus with the untainted lenses of a child who finds herself along with her widowed American mother in colonized India as guest at the regiment of her Scottish grandfather. In contrast to Temple's reactionary and racist roles in *The Little Colonel* (1935) and *The Littlest Rebel* (1935), where she seamlessly blends into the southern plantation drama, Ford's film casts her as naïve and innocent observer to colonial violence with spontaneous affection for both sides of the conflict. Witnessing the arrest of rebel leader Khoda Khan, she immediately takes his side, visits him in prison, and delivers without her direct knowledge a secret message that allows Khan to be freed by the rebels. In more humorous pursuits, Winkie is seen marching and acquiring basic military skills as she establishes a strong emotional bond with Sergeant Donald McDuff. Through the use of comedy that levels the seriousness of the colonial conflict into a family melodrama, Ford steps outside of the deadlocked positions in the conflict and envisions a utopian, peaceful coexistence of both parties (see Figure 11). When Winkie is abducted and held at Khan's camp, the brewing military conflict is averted with the grandfather boldly meeting Khan on his own and establishing a diplomatic rather than a military position toward the rebels. Even though Ford's lighthearted drama can hardly be taken seriously as an adequate representation of British colonialism, the film offers a new American Orientalism based on a utopian model of cooperation and peaceful coexistence rather than an oppressive military apparatus. The tragic death of the beloved McDuff during Khan's jailbreak also inserts a dose of realism into Winkie's infant world, an existential limit that is typical of Ford's films. These limits seek

FIGURE 11. John Ford's benign Orientalist fantasy *Wee Willie Winkie* (1937), depicting peaceful coexistence of East and West in the encounter of Priscilla (Shirley Temple) and the leader of the resistance Khoda Khan (Cesar Romero).

to curb the seemingly boundless expansion of Western civilization and establish instead a common denominator of death, birth, marriage, and other existential rituals that tie mankind together as a shared humanity. In more critical terms, as Ella Shohat and Robert Stam note, the film and its go-between figure of Shirley Temple reflect "the historical in-betweenness of the U.S. itself, as at once an anticolonial revolutionary power in relation to Europe, and a colonizing, hegemonic power in relation to Native Americans and African peoples."[18] Shohat and Stam fail to mention the US colonial expansion into Pacific territories that completes the picture of its reach for total global hegemony.

John Ford's *The Hurricane* (1937), released in November, filmed on location in Pago Pago and American Samoa, would superficially appear to offer yet another South Seas fantasy, but on closer analysis the film critically confronts the genre's imperialist rhetoric, seeking to expose and dismantle it. *The Hurricane* received a promotional photo spread in Henry Luce's *Life* magazine (November 22, 1937), which also featured stories about the Japanese takeover of Shanghai and the call of Joseph Kennedy, chairman of the Maritime Commission, for war buildup and battle-fit merchant ships. The film opens with a teary-eyed Dr. Kersaint (Thomas Mitchell) and a female tourist companion passing the deserted and destroyed

FIGURE 12. John Ford's *The Hurricane* (1937), starring Polynesian actor Jon Hall and Dorothy Lamour, in which the Polynesian couple takes center stage in the film.

island Manukura in the vicinity of Tahiti on a cruise ship, triggering his melancholic retrospective narration leading up to the island's destruction. Dr. Kersaint states that the island, once mentioned in the travel folders along with other South Seas isles, "made the mistake from being born in the heart of the hurricane belt." However, as Ford's film will clearly show, these hurricanes metaphorically extend to the devastation brought about by European colonialism, anticipating escalating war in the Pacific. The unfolding tale is signaled with the eager tourist taking film footage of the destroyed island before dissolving into the narration of the film. The film slowly tracks left, beginning with idyllic nature images of palms and ocean, then revealing a small missionary church, natives fishing at the beach, and the governor's mansion, finally resting on a close-up of the French flag. Mitchell, in the role of a drunken doctor, which he would famously reprise in *Stagecoach* (1939), assumes the position of a socially unhinged and intoxicated detached observer who cannot be brought entirely under the rational control of the French colonial administration that oversees Manukura's affairs. His worldview differs strongly from that of the fanatic French colonial governor DeLaage, who deals out harsh sentences to natives for minor offenses, establishing a brutal penal system under the guise of Western civilization. Dr. Kersaint defends one islander for having stolen a canoe in equally patronizing terms, pointing to the childlike and innocent behavior of natives best left alone. The film, though dealing with French colonialism in Tahiti, establishes an unmistakable connection to the US involvement in the Pacific via the Hawaiian musical theme of "Aloha Oe" played at the harbor upon the arrival of the governor's wife.[19]

At this point, the focus shifts to the native sailor Teranga, played by Tahitian Swiss actor Jon Hall, who dives from the top of the ship's mast into the ocean, instilling envy in the governor, as if having committed hubris with his high-wire acrobatic act. Teranga subsequently marries his native sweetheart Marama (Dorothy Lamour) and does so twice at the Christian church and with the blessings of the island's chief, his father Mehevi, played by Hawaiian actor Al Kikume. Ford substitutes here the traditional temporary interracial romance with a lasting marriage of a native couple presented alongside the French European couple (see Figure 12). During the wedding festivities, Ford also chooses a presentation that is different from *Waikiki Wedding* (1937), where Bing Crosby's character commands the center of attention during a similar ceremony. As Dr. Kersaint wishes to offer a toast at the festivities, the couple simply ignores him and runs off, leaving the doctor standing there staring at the empty spot, subjected to the laughter of the natives. White officiating is ridiculed here as a pompous colonial European practice and negated by the native couple that does not abandon its native customs and shows self-sufficiency. The couple is subsequently shown in a typical South Seas fantasy silhouette shot against sea and sky, one usually reserved for white couples or interracial romance. By establishing a "native" couple within these conventions, Ford lends significantly more screen agency to natives than is traditionally seen in South Seas scenarios. As DeLaage's earlier envious look at Teranga shows, it is this self-sufficiency and functioning family structure that his parasitic colonialism seeks to destroy.

Colonialism as a harshly administered penal system is questioned throughout the film so as to make way for an American Orientalist version of benevolent colonialism, based on the peaceful coexistence of cultures. Recruited as a sailor of higher rank, Teranga takes temporary leave of his wife and sails to Tahiti. Upon visiting a bar during his stopover, he is met with both racism and the relentless power of the law. The bar features a native singer, singing in French "I Can't Give You Anything but Love," pointing to the spreading American influence in the Pacific. In the bar, Teranga unpacks and inspects a gift for his wife, a wind-up hula doll shown dancing in close-up. This seemingly harmless consumer item representing Western capitalism visually turns into an omen foreboding Teranga's downfall and that of the entire island. Immediately after the close-up of the mechanical doll, a white man tells him to vacate his seat and a fight erupts triggered by the racist remark. Teranga is subsequently arrested and must spend six months in prison. Shown in medium close-up behind bars and facing barbed wire overlooking the open sea, the film conveys the image of a colony turned penal society. Needless criminalization of minor offenses and biased judgment—Teranga is sentenced to sixteen years after his first escape—expose the colonial apparatus as a brutal regime bent on breaking the will of natives. John Carradine, in the role of a sadistic jailor, states explicitly that he will eventually break his native prisoner. Teranga attempts

FIGURE 13. John Ford's *The Hurricane* (1937), depicting in unusual fashion the rescue of a Polynesian family as the culminating happy ending of the film.

multiple jailbreaks and is repeatedly incarcerated, sentenced to longer terms, and chained to a wheel under the supervision of his jailor. After eight years, he succeeds in another daring escape but accidentally kills a man. When Father Paul comes across the marooned Teranga, he believes his story and carries him to safety, allowing for a reunification with his wife Marama and daughter Tita.

The representation of the church's role in the colonial enterprise appears at first idealized, as Father Paul resists DeLaage's pleas to deliver the criminal. As a hurricane approaches, DeLaage commissions Captain Nagle's ship in his fanatic search for Teranga, who he believes is still at sea, leaving his own wife behind to deal with the storm on her own. During this storm, Dr. Kersaint's prediction that DeLaage will meet with a force higher than the legal code will come true, though not necessarily with the implied religious overtones. Ford's ambivalence toward institutionalized religion is shown as the natives follow Father Paul to the church as a sanctuary but will perish with him. Ironically, Teranga, returning from his hideout, rescues DeLaage's wife from the church and her certain fate of drowning. Teranga, his family (see Figure 13), and DeLaage's wife make it safely to a small island, where the governor is eventually reunited with his wife, allowing Teranga's family to move on, forgoing any further prosecution. In another scopic episode that recalls the tourist filming the island at the beginning of the film, DeLaage looks through the binoculars and goes along with the protective lie of his wife, by stating he can see only a log drifting in the water, rather than Teranga and his family making a final escape. Thus, the visual recognition of the native is still out of focus for the softened French governor. However, the film will bring this recognition into focus for its viewers.

On another boat, Chief Mehevi and Marama's sister also survive the storm with Dr. Kersaint, who delivers her child. The film ends on the chastened insight of DeLaage and reunites Teranga's immediate family and also saves his extended family (his father Chief Mehevi and his sister-in-law and her baby), pointing to the possible coexistence of Western and non-Western family structures. The structure of the family melodrama, usually not granted in Hollywood to minorities with their truncated, dysfunctional, or nonexistent families, is of major importance in Ford's film, where it takes center stage as a Tahitian family melodrama with a full genealogy ranging from grandfather to grandchild.[20] In its representation of the institutions of law, religion, and medicine impacting on this family structure, the latter with its protection of life is clearly favored in Ford's film as the most productive engagement with South Pacific cultures. This utopian perspective for a new type of American Orientalism, which contrasts starkly with its European forebear as well as with South Seas fantasy films, will become the guiding vision for Ford's World War II films. In anticipation of the World War II Office of War Information censorship codes and its recommendations for the representation of minorities, the film also desists from using mocking stereotypes and minstrelsy clichés regularly seen in South Seas films of the 1930s. More critically, the film ushers in the vision of a new engagement with overseas territories through a neutral administrative apparatus of co-opted care and technology systems rather than traditional colonial and penal rule with its heavy-handed subjugation of local populations based on overt practices of racism.

HAWAII AND WORLD WAR II ORIENTALISM

Like Luce, the forty-seven-year-old John Ford was eager to be a part of the impending war and in late 1939 began, while continuing to direct films, to create a naval reserve unit made of professional filmmakers that could be of use to the government. Calling his outfit the Naval Field Photographic Reserve (also referred to as John Ford's navy), he managed to enlist the biggest names in Hollywood, including cinematographer Gregg Toland and editor Robert Parrish. The combat photo and film unit trained and lobbied for naval recognition for eight months before authorization was finally given later that year. It became part of the Navy's clandestine intelligence service, which transformed early in the war into the OSS (Office of Strategic Services), the predecessor to the postwar Central Intelligence Agency. The unit worked mainly on secret missions, photographing the work of guerrillas and saboteurs as well as filming battle footage for newsreels and the government; however, several field photo documentaries were released to the public, with Ford's *December 7th* and *The Battle of Midway* garnering Academy Awards.

It is in these two war docudramas along with the feature film *They Were Expendable* (1945) that we see a developed articulation of Ford's American brand of Orientalism. An analysis of *December 7th* and *The Battle of Midway* demonstrates how Ford's Orientalism created a sustaining popular vision of nationhood, one that enabled American citizens to come to grips with World War II and spell out exactly what they were fighting for in compelling cinematic terms. Rather than arguing for the annexation of territories framed in a premodern Eurocentric view, American Orientalism embraces a pragmatic view, legitimating its expansion into the Far East on the basis of its economic and democratic benefits that it will bring to these areas as the representative of administrative and technological modernization. In Ford's films, particularly *December 7th*, the audience also sees the significance of wartime Hawaii that is not only attacked by the Japanese but annexed as well as an extension of the American mainland. The attack on Pearl Harbor, as is generally agreed, transformed an isolationist America into the world power that it is today. Such a complete reorientation also required a new vision of America, entitling it fully to territories beyond its continent. Hawaii, a Pacific outpost of the United States, transforms from a trading gateway to the East to a fully militarized hub of American naval forces, playing a crucial role in the readjustment of America's vision from an isolationist into an Orientalist one, from a continental to a world power. Whereas South Seas dramas mostly represented US commercial and cultural expansion, World War II Hawaii now takes on global military importance in the US effort of pushing back Japanese expansion in the Pacific and later to assert geopolitical dominance in a Cold War world.

December 7th was originally shot and directed by cinematographer Gregg Toland; however, the Navy refused to release the film as he had originally conceived it. As the producer of the film, Ford shot new footage and hired Robert Parrish to reedit the film, cutting out offensive elements and considerably shortening it from eighty-two to thirty-four minutes.[21] This newly censored version was released in 1943 by the Navy and War Department but was restricted to servicemen/women, military personnel, government employees, and war workers as part of the government's extensive mobilization efforts, especially the "Industrial Incentives Program," sponsored by the newly created Office of War Mobilization.[22] While bypassing the regular theater circuit, the film nevertheless reached an audience of several million viewers. The uncensored version would be released to the public only in 1991, almost fifty years later.[23] In spite of its limited release, *December 7th* would have a profound impact on both the nation's historical reception of the event itself and the developing genres of war documentary and combat film. In the postwar era, the censured version has been featured repeatedly on national, public, and cable television, arguably becoming the nation's popular account of the event. And regardless of the controversy surrounding it and the criticism by film critics, feature films and documentaries continue to quote from it, showing "real-life excerpts" of the Pearl Harbor attack.

A controversial film on several levels, *December 7th* aroused anger particularly on the two subjects of military preparedness and race.[24] Responding to a naval request, Field Photo initially conceived of it as "a complete motion picture factual presentation of the attack."[25] However, under Toland's directorship it transformed into a critical investigation foregrounding naval intelligence failure. Not only did the film stress military inadequacy, it moreover was blatantly racist, charging that the Japanese of Hawaii were a security threat. In line with Roosevelt's Executive Order 9066, which led to the internment of over 120,000 Japanese Americans on the mainland, the film suggested similar treatment of Japanese Hawaiians. At the Honouliuli Internment Camp in Oahu, eventually 1,400 Japanese Hawaiians were interned.[26] In addition to these controversies, the Navy was ashamed of the film's poor re-creation of the historic attack and its utilization of studio actors and rear projection screening. To the trained eyes of Navy officials, it was clearly not news footage but a mock-up studio reproduction of the bombing that made poor use of ship and plane models. The attacking planes were perceptibly not Mitsubishi Zeros but American Dauntless bombers flying maneuvers. The film moreover was filled with gross inaccuracies and misinformation.

Not surprisingly, the War Department confiscated and banned Toland's film. And finally, in an attempt to reign in John Ford and his nonconformist unit, the Joint Chiefs of Staff and Roosevelt himself "issued a directive that all Field Photo material henceforth would be subjected to censorship."[27] Ford's reedited version would address all these issues, turning Toland's military critique into a patriotic paean celebrating the Navy's ability to face defeat and make a triumphal comeback. Similarly, the suspicion toward Japanese Hawaiians is converted into an acknowledgment of their patriotism, framing only the Japanese enemy in racist terms. The film's popular success lies in its ability to depict the turnaround from initial humiliating defeat to a powerful comeback as a national melodrama, one that anticipates, like Luce's essay, the coming of the American Century. Key to Ford's visual narration of a nation at war is the site of Hawaii as the gateway to the East, signaling a new era in American expansionism and an equally new sense of multiculturalism.

Prior to the events of December 7, few Americans had any intimate knowledge of Hawaii, viewing it as a faraway tropical paradise, the vacation choice of wealthy celebrities. Popular films such as Victor Fleming's *Hula* (1927), *Waikiki Wedding* (1937) starring Bing Crosby, and MGM's *Honolulu* (1939), featuring swivel-hipped hula girls, beautiful beaches, palm trees, and an easygoing, decadent lifestyle, expressed this stereotypical view. Most Americans had never heard of Pearl Harbor or knew that it was the main base of operation for the Pacific Fleet. "Who's Pearl Harbor?" asks Woody Allen's comical heroine Sally White (Mia Farrow) in a thick Bronx accent upon hearing the breaking news of the Japanese attack in *Radio Days* (1987). The attack would indeed change all of this, transforming Hawaii overnight from a tiny island territory located in the distant reaches of the Pacific into a central site of national importance. President Roosevelt's celebrated infamy speech is significant in that it not only marks the entrance of the United States into World War II but also makes the exceptional statement in which a colonial territory is *equated* with mainland America: "The United States of America was suddenly and deliberately attacked by naval and air forces of the Empire of Japan."[28] Roosevelt's official speech linguistically converts Hawaii into the United States, allowing thereby for a declaration of war. Ford's shortened version of *December 7th* would stress this representation of Hawaii as America, a difficult task since most Americans viewed it as an exotic, faraway land. Indeed, in spite of Roosevelt's declaration, Hawaii was not by any stretch of the imagination "American," having a radically different culture and history and a large population consisting of various nationalities and nonwhite races. Ford's film, like Roosevelt's speech, forcefully annexes the islands for national purposes, violently transforming Hawaii into an extension of America. This transformation of Hawaii into America would be complete in 1959 when it became the nation's fiftieth state.[29]

A multiracial and multinational society, Hawaii was often touted by its white elite as "a paradigm of racial harmony."[30] While this perspective obscures the actual exclusionary race and social practices of the white elite that kept political and economic power firmly in its grip, it points to Hawaii's unique configuration of race and cultural relations. As Beth Bailey and David Farber write in their study on wartime Hawaii, this island territory was "the first strange place"[31] in America's passage to a new postwar era in which cultural and ethnic minorities (as well as women) would actively participate: "Hawai'i, where Americans came together in the common cause of waging war was a liminal place. That liminality, combined with Hawai'i's specific society and culture and the ever-present fact of war, created a highly charged arena in which the individual dramas of cultural contact were played out. In Hawai'i during WWII, people of different backgrounds were brought together in a common cause. This contact—collision, even—of cultures led to struggle and contestation, and sometimes to negotiation, improved understanding, or change."[32] As the "first strange place" in which Americans would come into contact with cultural and ethnic Others, Hawaii and its multicultural society presented new possibilities for a nation plagued with racism and ironically fighting a war in the name of democracy. The island's model of racial coexistence, one facilitated by its multiracial and multinational shadings of identity, challenges the reductive black-and-white binary that dominated race discourse on the American mainland. Unlike Luce, Ford grasped the significance of race relations, perceiving race and nationality as intimately linked. His edited version foregrounds the role of race in his new vision of an international America, incorporating Hawaii's multi-ethnic population into the nation rather than vilifying it.

In many ways, *December 7th* can also be seen as depicting Ford's personal struggle with race. According to Geoffrey White and Jane Yi, the original version accurately reflects Ford and Toland's racist suspicions toward Hawaii's Japanese population, which motivated them "to devote the first half of their film to a fictionalized portrayal of Hawaii's Japanese residents as extensively involved in subversive activities."[33] Quoting from a letter to his naval superior, in which Ford writes about "how very Oriental Honolulu appears—thousands upon thousands of Jap faces," White and Yi argue that the opening scenes "closely reflect the paranoid vision of Ford."[34] While White and Yi are certainly justified in pointing out Ford's racist views, more differentiation and context are needed for this discussion. The contradictions expressed in Ford and Toland's original version, particularly its racist views of Hawaii's Japanese, making up 40 percent of Hawaii's population, and its simultaneous celebration of Hawaii's multiculturalism, become much clearer when considering the film in its proper historical context of pre–civil rights America and its ubiquitous standard of whiteness. As Bailey and Farber point out, "whiteness was the 'natural' condition" in 1940s America: "Beyond that unvoiced assumption about their own normality, many white Americans gave little thought to the issue of race as it had to with others. Many Americans of European ancestry had never even spoken to an African American, a Hispanic, or to someone of Asian ancestry. They rarely encountered nonwhites in their daily lives and almost never on the public stage of national events."[35] As Barley and Farber further argue, Hawaii would challenge this racialized, provincial outlook, shocking "white men [who] were suddenly made to feel that *they* were the ones who were different": "Hawaiʻi's population was a mixture of racial and ethnic groups unlike anywhere else in the United States. In Hawaiʻi, white Americans were not in the majority, and though racial and ethnic hierarchies undeniably existed, they differed from those on the mainland. In Hawaiʻi, 'whiteness' was not the natural condition. . . . Such a reversal of 'normality' was all the more disconcerting because it took place in what was, after all, America. Few of the white mainlanders really understood the complexities of Hawaiʻi's racial system."[36] Ford's shock at seeing "thousands upon thousands of Jap faces" in a "very Oriental Honolulu" reflects this disconcerting reversal of normality with its unquestioned racial hierarchy based on the no-contact apartheid policy of Jim Crow. If, then, the first version of *December 7th* reflects Ford's own racist outlook, as White and Yi argue, we can also see how Ford attempts to work through it in the second version and articulate from within Hawaii's context a new understanding of democracy and equality more commensurate with America's increasing global perspective. The remaining contradictions within the film reflect the problematic nationalism of World War II America, namely the inability to articulate an authentic expression of democracy and multiculturalism in a Jim Crow society.

To be sure, the majority of mainstream white Americans saw ethnic Others only on the silver screen, where they were represented in typical Hollywood treatment as caricatures and grotesques. Hollywood's long tradition of racism is seen especially in its use of minstrelsy, blackface, yellowface, redface, and other demeaning stereotypes. As Daniel Bernardi argues, the classical Hollywood system, like early American cinema, used race in "distinct ways" to create "movie magic" with "the studios [systematizing] the popularization of American whiteness": "[Race] informed our classics, directed aesthetic choices, collaborated in the moral voice of popular narratives, enhanced the star system, promoted and sometimes bypassed censorship, and drew upon national and international events. . . . [W]hiteness remained the 'norm by which all "Others" fail by comparison.'"[37] As Hollywood studio insiders, Ford and Toland certainly helped to promote a vernacular myth of whiteness critical to cinema. Considering this popular ideology of "classic whiteness," images of minority Others portrayed in non-grotesque and more realistic and sober manner are therefore exceptional. In this context, the significant close-up shot in *December 7th* of the African American soldier (representing the real-life Dorie Miller, USN, mess attendant, third class) heroically manning an antiaircraft machine gun and dying for his country is quite radical for its time, especially in view of the fact that the segregated military systematically assigned blacks into noncombatant, subservient positions (see Figure 14).[38] Similarly, the images of actual minority soldiers who died at Pearl Harbor as well as those of Hawaii's various Asian/Pacific Islander populations function to humanize rather than demean ethnic Others. White and Yi skeptically view these images as a version of the multicultural melting pot myth that renders minorities, particularly Hawaii's Japanese, invisible. Given the context of Jim Crow and Hollywood, however, one can also view these images as more subversive, incorporating heretofore alien Others into the fabric of mainstream American life. While there is no doubt that the underlying melting pot ideology of Americanization maintains the nation's status quo, it also acknowledges ethnic Others for the first time as American citizens. Indeed, Hollywood's decision, following the Office of War Information race-neutral guidelines, to begin broadcasting positive images of ethnic Others would have a significant impact in forcing the armed forces to desegregate after the war.

Refining Étienne Balibar's discussion on the intimate relations between race and nationalism, Takashi Fujitani has discussed how the success of American national discourse in the World War II era necessarily depended upon the official disavowal of racism. Modern nation-states, writes Fujitani, routinely "deny that they condone racial discrimination even as they continually reproduce it in close alliance with nationalism."[39] This disavowal of racism is certainly evident in the nationalist rhetoric of both Luce's essay and Ford's war films, which is meant

FIGURE 14. John Ford's *December 7th* (1943), reenacting the heroics of African American sailor Dorie Miller manning a machine gun during the attack on Pearl Harbor.

primarily to rally war support and motivate patriotism. However, their disavowals of racism take startlingly different forms, influencing their respective Orientalisms. Luce's declaration that slavery is a dead issue works to create a tabula rasa by erasing a burdensome national history. It enables a fresh start that heralds the seemingly innocent beginnings of a new American Century. However, Ford's disavowal of America's history of racism does not so much deny the past as envision a national future based on ideals of democracy and racial equality. Ford's emphasis on a utopian vision of radical democracy seeks to reconfigure America's troubled history in its imagining and projection of a multicultural society. While Ford's depiction of race is certainly not unproblematic, it begins to question the formerly unchallenged authority of white Anglo-Saxon middle-class America. Extending democracy to disenfranchised groups is characteristic of many of Ford's films, including *The Grapes of Wrath* (1940), which tells John Steinbeck's historically accurate story of Depression-era "Okies," poor midwestern farmers forced to migrate to California; *Stagecoach* (1939), which questions middle-class mores of class and social status; and *The Searchers* (1956), which explores issues of race, miscegenation, and hybridity in the context of a burgeoning civil rights movement.

WARTIME HAWAII AS NATIONAL MASS ORNAMENT

In its visual performance of national rituals, Ford's film heavily employs what Siegfried Kracauer calls the mass ornament. For example, in the reedited version of *December 7th*, the laying to rest of the dead is depicted in a unique and somber configuration of the mass ornament, appearing as a significant aspect of the attack. According to Kracauer, the mass ornament is a visual construct or spectacle that consists of patterns of body formations or choreographic representations of mechanical objects. An aesthetic that delights in the ostentatious mass display of surface, ceremony, and contemporaneity, it articulates the desires of the mass as its visible surface expression: "Although the masses give rise to the [mass] ornament, they are not involved in thinking it through. As linear as it may be, there is no line that extends from the photographs of landscapes and cities in that it does not emerge out of the interior of the given conditions, but rather appears above them. Actors likewise never grasp the stage setting in its totality, yet they consciously take part in its construction; and even in the case of ballet dancers, the figure is still subject to the influence of its performers."[40] A purely performative act, mass ornament visually enacts the mechanical coordination of the social body and displays the coming together of mass reality and surface spectacle. Examples include parades, dancing girls, military formations, and the gaudy motion picture palaces of the 1920s that stress ornament and surface brightness.

In Ford's film, mass ornament enacts the rituals and spectacle of nationhood as an activity of communal solidarity expressed in the coordination of its various parts into an indivisible whole. This conflation of mass ornament and nationalism is depicted in the flight formation of the Japanese planes, in the arrangement of US planes queued in orderly linear formation on the ground and totally exposed in open airfields, in the aerial shots of the Pacific Fleet ships ablaze and trapped in the harbor as immobile targets, in the military funeral, and in the depiction of uniformed soldiers fighting side by side against a common enemy. As such, the mass ornament lifts the entire event above the level of the individual and instead stages it as a collective history unfolding in front of the viewer, visually performing the narration of nation. In this respect, the Navy's criticism of the film's use of props, ship and plane models, rear screen projection, actors staging histrionic deaths, and so on entirely misses the film's point as a national melodrama. *December 7th* is not an exercise in documentary realism or war reportage; rather, it deliberately shows itself to be a melodramatic reconstruction and staged performance of the attack, demonstrating that it, like the concept of nation itself, is a cultural and imagined construct open to interpretation.

Whereas Toland's uncensored version starts with a tediously protracted conversation between Uncle Sam and Mr. Conscience that provides an analysis of Hawaii and the merits and negative aspects of Japanese Hawaiians, Ford's edited account jumps almost immediately into the attack. The opening scene features Uncle Sam deep asleep in a tropical setting on the early Sunday morning of December 7, stressing the slyness of the surprise attack. Similarly, "the city of Honolulu," the narrator tells us, "like many other unsuspecting American communities, was fast asleep." Tranquil shots of Diamond Head, Oahu's picturesque harbors and beaches, the Koolau Mountain Range, and the Nuuanu Pali shrouded in hazy morning mist emphasize a soothing, sleepy atmosphere befitting the untroubled island paradise. Similarly, the island's military bases, Hickam and Wheeler Fields, Kaneohe, and Pearl Harbor, complacently conduct their weekend routines. Sailors play a lazy game of catch, while other soldiers attend Sunday mass. The leisurely paced editing and camera allows the viewer to participate in the mass as the audience hears the minister urging the young men, who are presented in affective close-ups, to send Christmas gifts to family and loved ones on the mainland.

However, a bell tolls ominously throughout the scene, generating a subtle but pervasive sense of danger. The viewer notes that the natural beauty of the beaches is marred by the presence of patrolling armed troops and barbed wire, bases are on high alert, weapons are being readied, and the narrator reports that Uncle Sam has spent a long difficult night wrangling with his conscience as the equally difficult year of 1941 comes to a close. The droning of planes is heard in the distance as Japanese squadrons appear on the horizon. Once again, the viewer is treated to the picturesque scenery of Oahu as the bombers fly "over the Koolau Range, past the Pali, past Diamond Head, over Waikiki Beach" with the film's narrator carefully enunciating each site's name. It is important to note that the flight plan of the Japanese bombers shown here is flagrantly false, depicting instead a filmic sightseeing tour that introduces mainland US citizens to the island's most prominent sites.[41] The repeated viewing of famous landmarks recalls the earlier depiction of the island as a tourist paradise that is now being forcefully converted into a military staging ground, suggesting that the former was merely a phantom with the reality of war lurking beneath its alluring specter. Blending the two incompatible images of the island, idyllic, peaceful nature and staging ground for modern warfare, Ford's film achieves a narrative tension that takes the war documentary beyond the mere factual account of military events. Fact and fiction become inseparable in *December 7th*, articulating an existential national melodrama. Warfare becomes a battle of competing visions, opening the realism of the war and documentary genres to the aesthetic and the imaginary. Similarly, the repeated enunciation of the various sites by the narrator functions as a dramatic documentary device, familiarizing an American audience with the alien geography and language of Hawaii and somehow naturalizing it.

Both Luce and Ford offer a similar vision of a larger global role for America, albeit in the different and complementary terms of the pragmatic and existential. Highlighting a somnolent United States in the form of a sleeping Uncle Sam not yet awoken to its new realities, Ford's expertly edited opening scene resembles Luce's message of the unhappy and unrealized American similarly unaware of his global importance. In his opening argument, Luce compares the troubled and unhappy American psyche to that of the British now at war with Germany:

> We Americans are unhappy. We are not happy about America. We are not happy about ourselves in relation to America. We are nervous—or—gloomy or apathetic. . . . This is a striking contrast between our state of mind and that of the British people. . . . The British people are profoundly calm. There seems to be a complete absence of nervousness. It seems as if all the neuroses of modern life had vanished from England. . . . The British are calm in their spirit not because they have nothing to worry about but because they are fighting for their lives.

> With us it is different. We do not have to face any attack tomorrow or the next day. Yet we are faced with something almost as difficult. We are faced with great decisions.[42]

In Ford's scenario, Uncle Sam, like Luce's American public, is faced with decisions, ultimately hesitating to take the final step and acknowledge that we indeed are already at war. When Japanese bombers "[swoop] down like tiny locusts in the sky" delivering "man-made hell, made in Japan," it is presented not as the start of war but as an outcome of an event already in motion. The nation simply needs to wake up to the reality of war. By film's end, the armed forces and Hawaii's local population (now an extension of the American public) have lost any sense of nervousness and are resolutely committed to the war. Like Luce's British "they are calm in their spirit . . . because they are fighting for their lives."[43] No longer seen as a sleepy tropical paradise, Hawaii is now portrayed as a strategic war site as represented in the island's famous tourist landmark, the Aloha Tower, painted in camouflage.

Repeatedly featured in the film, the Aloha Tower, a maritime communication center and observation deck that provides sweeping views of Honolulu and the Pacific, embodies a triple function: a watchtower or strategic observation point, a clock tower, and a welcome beacon for those entering Honolulu Harbor, with aloha chiseled in large letters on its face. In Ford's film, the tower takes on an additional iconic function, with the frozen clock capturing the moment immediately before the attack, seven fifty in the morning, a significant caesura frozen in the nation's history. The Aloha Tower no longer measures simply the local time of Hawaii but a national time, performing what Homi Bhabha calls the lived time of the nation.[44] This transformation, in which a tourist landmark and welcome beacon becomes a national symbol of war and dons camouflage paint, signals at once the birth of a new national era and that of Hawaii as a de facto American state, eliding the fact of Hawaii's own colonial status. Indeed, Ford's film visually recapitulates the act of American imperialism and Hawaii's illegal annexation in 1898 by reappropriating its cultural landmarks for America's war machine. In short, Luce's American Century, one marked by the nation's economic and military expansion into the Far East with Hawaii as its gateway, officially begins.

Unlike Luce's optimistic pragmatic vision of an era of global American economic domination, however, Ford's darker existential perspective in *December 7th* stresses the limits of human endeavor found in expansionism, warfare, struggle, death, and sacrifice. The project of global expansion is presented more soberly as a residual utopian hope projected from the partial failure in the present onto a future of remaining possibilities. While Luce does acknowledge past and present failures—namely the failed internationalism of the Wilson administration and the present isolationism and aversion to war—a firm belief in the teleology of progress dominates his argument. The past and present for Luce are incomplete realizations of a better future. Similarly, death, poverty, and limitation give way to the great possibilities of America's future as world leader. In the Fordian existential economy, however, the future and its possibilities are built on a history of human loss and sacrifice. The realization of national identity is not simply the overcoming of failure and limitations but learning to accept and coexist with them. In this respect, Ford's concept of nation closely resembles that of Benedict Anderson, one founded on a profound sense of irrecoverable loss, fulfilling a vital need for communal and collective affiliation.

As Anderson tells us, nationalism is not an ideology.[45] The love people feel for their nation cannot be succinctly expressed in an ideological principle, since it cannot begin to explain why people are willing to die in its name. Suffering from "philosophical poverty" and incoherence, the concept of nationalism instead points to a form of modern kinship, a community passionately imagined into existence and invested with sacred and sentimental musings that symbolically, even mythically, represent its people, culture, language, history, and values.[46] By linking national affinities to those of family and religion, Anderson foregrounds the existential and profound sense of passion that surrounds and legitimates the discourse of nationalism. Like religion, it attempts to answer large, unanswerable questions, defining who and what a nation is as a collective being—how, out of many, it becomes one. And like family, the nation perceives these sacred bonds as somehow natural and pure in origin. Similarly, Ford's *December 7th* strategically makes use of the conventions of melodrama to explain to its citizens why the United States is at war. Like Anderson's nationalism that is defined in the emotional and intimate terms of kinship and religion, Ford's national melodrama transforms public concerns of war and imperialism into a personal and domestic narrative. This vision of the nation is not merely a naïve aesthetic adumbration of nationalism but places it into the abyss of crisis, indicating a simultaneous aspiration and loss. Accordingly, Ford's films contain numerous scenes of death and sacrifice, particularly funerals as the ritual bond between self, territory, and nationhood that mark at once a horizon of expansion and limit.

According to Kracauer, the seemingly empty surface expression of the mass ornament is more indicative of contemporary culture than narratives appealing to substance and psychological interiority.[47] This paradoxically empty but emotionally laden aspect of the mass ornament is also seen in Benedict Anderson's well-known example of cenotaphs and tombs of unknown soldiers: "No more arresting emblems of the modern culture of nationalism exist than cenotaphs and tombs of Unknown Soldiers. The public ceremonial reverence accorded these monuments precisely because they are either deliberately empty or no one knows who lies inside them, has no precedents in earlier times. . . . Yet void as these tombs are of identifiable mortal remains or immortal souls, they are nonetheless saturated with ghostly national imaginings."[48] Similarly, Ford and Toland's film strips soldiers of any individual personality, while according them the highest official honor. The film's strong use of mass ornament goes so far as to conflate the destruction of the US ships and equipment with the death of the soldiers, further blurring the line between technology and man, between the inorganic and the organic, between nation and individual. Reading Ford's film in the combined contexts of Kracauer's mass ornament and Anderson's sacrificial nationalism, one begins to appreciate more fully its depiction of the performativity of national identity, race, and diversity.

The funeral service of the soldiers appropriately follows the shots of wreckage without break, creating a unified ceremonial tribute. And although the viewer is introduced to a few of the deceased soldiers (via photographs) as well as their families, the serialized nature of the mass ornament is retained. Not only do the introductions evoke the military protocol of the roll call, a convention of combat films, but also the same voice speaks for all of them, introducing selected soldiers and their towns and families. Befitting a democracy, the soldiers represent the nation's various ethnicities and races, hailing from different regions. The departed soldiers and their respective families function as a demographic sampling, mapping out and representing a democratic society, the many as one, configured via mass ornament. When questioned by the narrator why all of the soldiers "sound and talk alike," the voice from beyond responds, "We are all alike. We are all Americans." And though this voice represents white middle-class America in its use of Standard English, the film also incorporates voices of cultural Others as given in the accompanying music, "My Country, 'Tis of Thee," sung as an African American spiritual. Similarly,

FIGURE 15. John Ford's *December 7th* (1943), depicting the funeral of fallen sailors with Hawaiian leis marking their graves.

the Christian funeral service incorporates aspects of Hawaiian culture, depicting soldiers placing leis (flower wreaths) on graves of the dead (see Figure 15). While the mass ornament stresses the many as one, implying a narrative of assimilation and Americanization with whiteness as its norm, it also has the potential to project diverse voices.

The film's final scenes depict images, configured again in the mass ornament, of a nation coming together and rallying against its Japanese enemy. Using crane, aerial, and tracking shots for maximum effect, the film shows supplies, troops, and ships arriving in Hawaii. The subsequent introduction to Hawaii's multiethnic and multiracial inhabitants, who have always aroused the anxiety of white mainstream America, is likewise presented in terms of the mass ornament, with Hawaii now referred to as "America's tropical suburb." The viewer is first introduced to the island's "civilian army," "Oahu's civil defense committee, 4,000 men and women," framed in an aerial shot and grouped in rank and file wearing uniforms and helmets. Ensuing shots reveal individuals of various races and ethnicities, Korean, Filipino, Japanese, Chinese, Pacific Islanders, and so on; however, like the departed soldiers they function as a representative sampling. The film's strategic use of mass ornament transforms them into an extension of the United States, and they become legitimate American citizens, fighting a war on American soil. Similarly, images of innocent Hawaiian children at school practicing drills in trenches and learning how to dodge bullets and shrapnel by moving in zigzag patterns heighten the film's melodramatic content. "For the first time in history," the narrator reports, "American schoolchildren were brought face to face with the grim reality of war." Hawaii's Japanese are given a special tribute, showing them in a series of prominent close-ups donating blood and ordering war bonds in Japanese via a translator. Though a few suspected enemy agents were interned, the narrator is pleased to report that "not one, single solitary act of sabotage was committed on the 7th." Unlike Toland's version, which cast doubt and suspicion on Japanese residents of Hawaii, Ford's account reserves its enmity and racist rhetoric mainly for the Empire of Japan and envisions instead a multicultural narration of nation via the mass ornament.

This democratic utopia, while standing at radical odds with a sexist, hierarchical, and pre–civil rights America, would not only establish significant genre conventions in war and combat films, but also create a visual national myth to sustain a country at war both abroad and at home, a nation struggling to come to terms with its new role as democratic leader of the free world and its most powerful economic force. At the same time, *December 7th*'s repeated depiction of various races of Americans destabilizes the notion of a homogeneous Anglo-dominated America, anticipating a more multicultural America that begins to express itself in the postwar civil rights movement. Also significant is the film's representation of various Asians, breaking down the stereotypical image of an undifferentiated and vast Orient. Prior to the war, American society did not distinguish between its various Asian inhabitants, categorizing them under the catchall rubric of "Oriental." However, World War II forces the United States to discriminate between its various Asian allies and enemies as well as its Asian citizens. This new perspective is clearly seen in Hollywood World War II combat films, which by convention feature American soldiers fighting side by side with their Filipino, Chinese, and Korean allies (*Bataan*, 1943; *Thirty Seconds over Tokyo*, 1944; *Back to Bataan*, 1945; *First Yank into Tokyo*, 1945). Taking this perspective of multiculturalism ever further, postwar combat films such as MGM's *Go for Broke!* (1951) draw attention to the ambivalent position of Japanese American soldiers, mostly from Hawaii, fighting in Europe while their families are interned. Ford's edited version of *December 7th* is one of the first clear articulations of a multicultural nation foregrounding the multicultural society of Hawaii as a utopian model of a new America.

As bold as Ford's "democratic Orientalism" may be, however, it is not without significant problems and contradictions, especially in its use of two diametrically opposed paradigms. On the one hand, the film promotes a multiculturalism based on the Hawaii model; and on the other, it appears to have no problem with America's various strategic expansionist agendas in the Pacific that had heavily interfered in Hawaii's internal affairs, dissolving its incumbent monarchy in 1895 and annexing it as a US colony in 1898. Nor does Ford have any problem using racist rhetoric, as seen in his use of yellowface as a sonic device to construe a clichéd Asian voice in his representation of the Japanese enemy. Moreover, the film's use of the mass ornament as a collective and national aesthetic obscures the underlying practices of coercive assimilation and standardization. If all soldiers in *December 7th*, regardless of race, creed, or color, sound alike, it begs the question as to whose voice is doing the actual speaking. Is this voice democratic or a standardized and invisible Anglo-American norm? Does this process of standardization transform ethnic minorities into model minorities? Similarly, how does one even begin to justify the transformation of Hawaii into a military zone and that of its inhabitants into a "civilian army" simply for the protection of the United States?[49] To be sure, Ford's Orientalism is part and parcel of America's benevolent imperialism, combining a call for democratic freedom with territorial hegemony. Ford's narration of nation produces what Bhabha calls the double time of the nation in both progressive multiculturalist and regressive nationalist terms. These contradictory agendas create ultimately the tension in Ford's war films (and Westerns), reflecting an internally divided nation striving to articulate the many as one.

AMERICAN MIDWESTERNERS IN THE PACIFIC: *THE BATTLE OF MIDWAY*

The westernmost part of the Hawaiian Islands Archipelago, Midway Atoll, is situated in the center of the Pacific approximately thirteen hundred miles northwest of Honolulu. Consisting of two main small coral islands inhabited mainly by a type of albatross known as the gooney bird, Midway functioned during the war as a strategic and refueling base for the US Navy. It was often called the "sentry to Hawaii," becoming after the fall of Wake Island the most remote US Pacific outpost. The small coral atoll occupies an important place in history as the site of the world's largest sea battle, the Battle of Midway, occurring over three days in early June 1942 between the Japanese Imperial and the US Pacific Fleets. The battle was a turning point in World War II, signaling the end of Japan's domination of the Pacific.

Due to decoded intelligence, the US military had advance detailed information of Japan's plans to capture Midway and was able to trap and destroy a significant part of the Imperial Fleet, including irreplaceable carriers and aircraft. Shortly before the battle, at the end of May, Admiral Chester W. Nimitz, commander-in-chief of the Pacific Fleet, requested that Ford send a Field Photo representative to document "a dangerous mission."[50] Ford himself volunteered, taking with him a young assistant photographer, Jack MacKenzie, who like his well-known father had been an RKO cameraman. And thus, writes Joseph McBride, "as Japanese divebombers and fighter planes swooped over the Midway Atoll in the central Pacific on the morning of June 4, 1942, America's greatest filmmaker was there filming the attack for history" atop the roof of the base's power house with his handheld sixteen-millimeter Eyemo camera, eventually receiving the Purple Heart for injuries sustained during his filming.[51]

An extraordinary film, *The Battle of Midway* (1942), contains now famous authentic scenes of battle. However, what is even more remarkable and significant about Ford's film, above its appeal to authenticity, is its playful manipulation and use of the entire range of cinematic illusion to create the narration of nation as a docudrama. Unlike newsreels of the era, Ford's film uses real-life photography in new and inventive ways, juxtaposing unrelated, even incompatible, material. Formal aspects of camera framing, editing, sound, and color are creatively and jarringly used. In addition, Ford plots the film with a strange combination of linear and nonlinear narrative techniques. In doing so, his documentary lays bare its own codes of production, demonstrating that history is not objectively witnessed and recorded but created, constructed, and manipulated. In *The Battle of Midway*, then, history is documented as a consciously imagined narration of nation.

Accordingly, the film begins not with *Midway*'s famous "authentic" scenes of battle but with an introduction to Midway and the soldiers as they prepare for battle. The docudrama starts with intertitles asserting, "This is the actual photographic report of the Battle of Midway." A map shows Midway situated between Japan and the United States and northwest of Hawaii. Though both intertitles and map are used to demonstrate authenticity, they are also conventions of the combat genre used to enhance realism as seen in early classic combat films such as *Bataan* and *Guadalcanal Diary*, also released in 1943. Filmed in glorious Technicolor, *Midway*'s opening image is a reconnaissance plane flying against a preternatural blue sky. From the plane, the viewer is introduced to Midway via an aerial shot as the narrator comments in folksy fashion, "Midway Islands. Not much land right enough but it's our outpost, your front yard."[52] As in the previous shots, the unnatural bright blue of Technicolor predominates (the ocean), placing the viewer into the unreal space of the national imagination. As the men prepare for the big battle, the viewer, oddly enough, is indulged with a small parade, one befitting a celebration that should take place *after* the attack and not prior to it. The parade of Marines marching to the "Marines' Hymn" and proudly displaying the US and Marine Corps flags functions as a framing mass ornament, paying patriotic tribute.[53]

Perhaps the most fascinating aspect of *Midway* is Ford's bold pastiche of seemingly incompatible cinematic genres, including slapstick comedy, high melodrama, combat film, documentary, and patriotic propaganda. Following the upbeat and deliberately propagandistic treatment of the opening shots, Ford immediately moves into grotesque comedy as he introduces the "natives" of Midway, the loveable gooney bird. Known for its clumsy, ungainly walk (which contrasts its beauty in flight), the bird, a type of black-footed albatross, successfully provides comic relief and a chance to rail against the Japanese. Accompanied with onomatopoetic sound effects and music mimicking the bobbing, awkward gait of the gooney bird, the narrator's deadpan comedic delivery informs the viewer, "These are the natives of Midway. Tojo has sworn to liberate them." This comical reference to US national enemies is a far cry from the racist treatment of the Japanese enemy in *December 7th*, following instead the rules of the government's Office of War Information (OWI). Created officially in the summer of 1942 (too late to influence *December 7th*) as a form of tacit censorship imposed on Hollywood, the OWI called for a ban on the studios' typical racist treatment of blacks, Latinos, Asians, and women. The OWI manual also requested that national enemies be depicted not as racial groups but as misguided people who wrongly advocate fascist values. "The war," it stated, "was a people's struggle, not a national, class or race war."[54] *Midway* strongly adheres to this democratic ideal of fair struggle.

As quickly as the film moves into the comical, it abruptly becomes reflective and poetic. The amusing gooney birds sense something is wrong, suddenly taking flight as the narrator describes them as "nervous" and the skies turn a rich red and orange. The following shots of the men (mostly in silhouette) relaxing against a sublime sunset and a fading horizon poetically depict the calm before the storm. The US flag waves regally in the wind while the men smoke, play the accordion, and prepare for battle. Though optimism reigns, the darkening skies and somber faces of the men (shot in deep shadow) reveal that death is never far away. *Midway*'s opening scenes work not so much to place the viewer realistically into battle but to extend symbolically the American frontier, pushing ever westward into the East. This theme of expansion is depicted in the repeated panning shots of the bombers taking off from left to right; in the depiction of a soldier's father who is a railroad engineer tending to a locomotive; in the soldiers making themselves at home in Midway and playing the unlikely instrument of the accordion; and in the use of well-known *Grapes of Wrath* actors Jane Darwell and Henry Fonda as additional narrators. This deliberate citation from Ford's popular Oscar-winning film (best director, seven nominations, 1941), which depicted the migratory movement of midwesterners (Okies) to California, now functions as a symbolic extension of Ford's cinematic world to Midway. The midwesterner, given in the folksy and familiar voices of Darwell and Fonda (Ma Joad and her son Tom Joad), has become the cosmopolitan that Luce envisioned, confidently asserting America's global significance.

While celebrated as one of the finest examples of realism, *The Battle of Midway* unashamedly uses every type of cinematic technique to seduce the viewer. Sound, framing, narration, and editing play invaluable roles in creating the film's "authentic" battle scenes. Shots of planes swooping down, gunners returning fire, buildings ablaze and collapsing are edited and framed for maximum effect. Similarly, the US flag rises in the midst of battle, framed in a low angle and accompanied by "The Star-Spangled Banner" with the narrator exclaiming in hushed tones, "Yes, this really happened." The narrative voice asserts the conventional view that documentaries deliver the real, as if to remind the viewer that Ford is not toying with reality in his idiosyncratic and multiple uses of cinematic techniques. At the same time, the voice may also be said to express Ford's own view that reality becomes real only after it has been reconstructed and arranged.

The famous shot in which exploding shrapnel hurls toward Ford as the camera absorbs the resulting tremors depicts more than the mere reality of war, working paradoxically to destabilize the narrative of nation. It is here where the film's discourse of nation literally comes undone and reveals in disconcerting ways what Bhabha calls the double time of the nation, national discourse in conflict with its own aspirations. The film, while reassuring American viewers of the nation's project in the Pacific, shows quite clearly its cost and losses. Indeed, images of war, replete with exploding buildings, ships, and planes and above all death, create anxiety and cast strong doubt on national aspirations. The authentic battle scenes stressing death, chaos, and ruin are incompatible with the calm serenity of patriotism or the humor of the gooney birds evoked earlier as well as with film's triumphant ending and its bold brushstrokes of the victory sign. As in Spielberg's *Saving Private Ryan* (1998), in which the extreme violence of the prolonged D-Day scene challenges the film's overall conservative treatment of patriotism, *Midway*'s nationalism and patriotic fervor become contaminated by feelings of anxiety, doubt, and ambivalence.

In contrast to that in *December 7th*, Ford's Orientalism in *The Battle of Midway* is almost not palpable and appears to be absent. Rather, the film follows closely the race-neutral guidelines of the OWI, and America's growing sense of becoming a global power takes center stage. Its Orientalism is more evident in the depiction of America's sense of entitlement to the Far East with which it seeks to secure its expanding borders. For instance, this confidence is displayed in the film's coda in which bold brushstrokes, reminiscent of Japanese and Chinese ideogram painting techniques, paint a large V sign signaling victory in dripping red across a canvas. The Asian writing system is thus symbolically disowned and annexed by the American victor. This expansionist vision, akin to that of Luce, is based on an inherited legacy of Eurocentrism that now operates from within Anglo-American culture and once again, as with the former European imperialism, sees itself entitled to the world. Its unspoken rhetoric stems from a sense of civilizational superiority bolstered by the achievements of the military, technology, market economy, and governance. Similarly, in the film's adherence to OWI guidelines, nineteenth-century notions of racial superiority are checked but not entirely suspended; rather they are rescripted in seemingly more benign terms.

Ford's presentation of America's global significance is not depicted naïvely as with Luce but anchored in an existential narration of nationhood that involves death, sacrifice, loss, and particularly the perplexing question of race. No triumph in victory but rather the uneasy sense of having to face death and annihilation mark the skeptical and ambivalent discourse of Ford. Also, Ford's highly original use of multiple and contradictory genres gives his war documentaries a plurivocal quality, complementing the ideals of democracy. Unlike, for example, Leni Riefenstahl's propaganda films that aim for seamless fluidity and stress total cultural homogeneity and blind belief in national ideology, Ford's cinematic vision spells out in aesthetic and thematic terms the heterogeneity of America's democratic tradition and reveals a more skeptical outlook concerning the prospects of ultimate conquest. Regardless of its political blind spots and conservatism, Ford's radical reinvention of the documentary as an open and skeptical form allows for an entirely new approach to this genre as a democratic vehicle that can incorporate change and debate.

Ford's unorthodox approach to Orientalism, one in which the nation's narration is placed into conflict with itself and its desire for mythic totality, helped ultimately to destabilize the racial map of the United States, chipping away at the prewar binary perspective (white vs. black, East vs. West) and moving closer toward multiracial and multicultural models of national identity. Whatever personal conservative ideologies may have informed Ford's films, they are undermined by his own visual aesthetics of American Orientalism, depicting the narration of nation as open-ended and evading closure. Just as Ford's Westerns depict the historical end of America's westward expansion and its accompanying frontier myths, his war documentaries likewise represent America's new national discourse as that of a global power with similarly contradictory and ambivalent insights, creating a national mythology that simultaneously demystifies itself.

As part of the American apartheid culture of race, however, John Ford could not successfully translate his progressive Orientalism, developed during a time of national crisis, to the postwar era, with its pressing and long-overdue issues of racial injustice on the home continent. Two attempts to tackle these issues, *The Sun Shines Bright* (1953) and *Sergeant Rutledge* (1960), are seriously marred by the outdated perspective of Ford's generation. In fairness, one should note that filmmakers of his generation such as John Huston, Howard Hawks, Raoul Walsh, George Cukor, Orson Welles, Billy Wilder, and Alfred Hitchcock, had practically nothing to say about Jim Crow segregation. Otto Preminger's *Carmen Jones* (1954), with Dorothy Dandridge and Harry Belafonte in lead roles and an all African American cast, shows a bolder inclusive effort but could not speak to contemporary matters such as *Brown v. Board of Education* (1954). Joseph L. Mankiewicz's *No Way Out* (1950) offers an early example of contemporary racism when a black doctor (Sidney Poitier) is asked to treat two racist patients, escalating into racial tension. Other directors such as Douglas Sirk (*Imitation of Life*, 1958), John Cassavetes (*Shadows*, 1960), Daniel Petrie (*A Raisin in the Sun*, 1961), Robert Mulligan (*To Kill a Mockingbird*, 1962), Guy Green (*Diamond Head*, 1963; *Patch of Blue*, 1965), and the seasoned Stanley Kramer (*The Defiant Ones*, 1958; *Guess Who's Coming to Dinner*, 1968) would begin to address contemporary issues on race in America in an incomplete but more adequate manner.

Ford's *The Sun Shines Bright* (1953) is a remake of his paternalistic and problematic *Judge Priest* (1934) and barely fares better than its infamous forebear. The film includes a starker episode of racism omitted in the 1934 version as Judge Priest, staking his entire career on an act of personal intervention, saves a young African American from a lynch mob after false accusations of rape. However, the film seriously mars and obscures the message with its inclusion of Stepin Fetchit's minstrelsy performance of the lazy Negro, its frequent waving of the southern Confederate flag alongside the US flag, and its strong class bias in attributing racial violence solely to the neighboring poor district of Tornado, thereby exempting the entire southern elite, the original slave owners, from any complicity. The film also shows disturbing paternalistic tendencies with all black life centering around the Honorable Judge who is revered, with a black choir singing Negro spirituals in his honor as the white savior. Even the lynch mob, the Tornado boys, wave a banner reading "He saved us from ourselves" at the end of the film, as they join in the celebration of the Judge's reelection victory against a "carpet bagging Yankee" who loses by only one vote. Systemic racism is thereby belittled and sentimentalized as a temporary lapse from morality that can be quickly corrected without any larger intervention on the part of the legal, social, and economic systems. The Judge's sense of justice is parochially limited to notions of honor, which force him to make a stance against false criminalization, ensuring only a bare minimum of human rights for the African American community. At the same time, the Judge exonerates a dying white prostitute and gives her a grand funeral parade at the conclusion of the film, reuniting the town around the sentimental cause of a fallen white woman. *Sergeant Rutledge* (1960) more progressively features an African American buffalo soldier (Woody Strode) who likewise stands falsely accused of rape but is exonerated in a court of law and more properly seen as a valiant soldier and hero. This film is not tainted with plantation culture stereotypes but once again places the conflict of race in America in the manner of *Searchers* (1956) into a remote past, thereby saying nothing about the civil rights movement and systemic racism of the present.

IMAGINING A MULTIETHNIC AMERICA: ORIENTALISM AND WORLD WAR II PACIFIC COMBAT FILMS

When exploring the national imaginings represented in American World War II Pacific combat films, the confusion and ambiguity created in their visual narration of the nation stand out as a striking feature. Combat films of this era provide an especially fertile ground for such an exploration since they articulate a new sense of nation growing directly out of the unique experience of World War II. Born in this historical event, the combat genre vividly depicts the simultaneous emergence of a new kind of nationalist culture in a moment of acute historical crisis. The effectiveness of the genre's production of a novel representation of the nation lies in its exploitation of nationalist feelings aroused in the absolute embracing of warfare with its extreme existential border situations of loyalty and heroic death. The pathological aspect of love for one's nation, combat not only expresses the ultimate test of national membership, namely self-sacrifice, but also reveals underlying patterns of racial identification and demarcation against national enemies and foreign Others.

Examining the distinct but overlapping concerns of race and nationhood, this section discusses the phenomenon of American Orientalism as it manifests itself in World War II and its significance in nation building. Since the 1850s Orientalism of one kind or another has figured prominently in American's national imaginary. In the World War II era it takes on a particular importance where it is specifically deployed to promote America's ascendancy as a global military power. Oriental-ism is explored here as the underlying cultural semiotics of nation as depicted in the two significant World War II combat films *Bataan* (1943) and *Back to Bataan* (1945). The discussion of these films is especially interested in the double bind of American Orientalism that identifies its Oriental enemy as hostile to occidental democracy while having to propagate democratic values among its Asian allies and immigrants. As will be discussed, Orientalism contributes paradoxically to a differ-entiated understanding of Asian cultures and to an increasing democratic recogni-tion of Asian immigrants living within the United States. As an analysis of *Bataan* and *Back to Bataan* demonstrates, the complex discourse of Orientalism destabi-lizes the traditional racial map of the United States by advancing a multiethnic and multiracial configuration of nationhood and thereby also diffusing the adversarial binary perspective of traditional racial conflict.

When Japan attacked Pearl Harbor on December 7, 1941, a new historical stage was set that signaled not only the entry of the United States into the war and the overturning of its isolationist policy but its ascendancy as a world interventionist power. This watershed event worked in particular to invent American notions of nationhood against those of its Asian rival, the Empire of Japan. The new enemy-friend configuration not only changed America's foreign relations to Asia and the world but also internally redefined the status of Asian immigrants living in Amer-ica. Lisa Lowe has discussed how since the middle of the nineteenth century, the American citizen has been defined against the Asian immigrant (immigrant exclu-sion acts, antinaturalization laws, repeal acts, wars, etc.).[55] Lowe points out how in times of war with Asia (specifically the Philippine-American War, World War II, the Korean and Vietnam Wars), "American orientalism displaced U.S. expansionist interests in Asia onto racialized figurations of Asian workers within the national space."⁵⁶ Viewing Asian immigrants as a foreign threat to national concerns even while being American born and recruited into its armed services, the United States was unwilling to accept them as citizens and in times of war to distinguish them legally, racially, and culturally from its Asian enemies.⁵⁷

With the start of World War II, America was forced to reconsider its racial policy of barring citizenship to its Asian immigrants who heretofore were viewed mainly as members of an exploitable labor force. While anti-Asian sentiments certainly increased within the United States during times of conflict in Asia, World War II challenged America to enter into a more complex process of differentiation among its Asian allies and enemies and thereby to question its monocultural and racial perceptions of Asians and American Asians. Those once conveniently grouped under the single rubric of Asians or Orientals, now called for distinctions between America's Filipino and Chinese allies, between anti-Japanese Korean nationalists who were still considered by America subjects of its conqueror Japan, and between pro- and anti-American Japanese immigrants. Similarly, the impact of World War II created, writes Ronald Takaki, a "crucial dividing line in the history of Asian American communities," forcing them "to determine more sharply than ever before their identities as Asians and as Americans."⁵⁸ To promote their differences and distinguish themselves from the Japanese, many Asian Americans wore buttons identifying their ethnic groups.

Combat films in particular reflect this difference in America's perception of Asians. "You're our kind of people," says the American hero in *Thirty Seconds over Tokyo* (1944) to his Chinese ally. The many combat films about the Battle of Bataan and the "liberation" of the Philippines depict Filipino and American soldiers fighting shoulder to shoulder. *Go for Broke!* (1951) recounts the true story of the 442nd Regimental Combat Team, a Japanese American army unit that was the most decorated in World War II. Even treatment of the Japanese enemy had to be considered within the more recognizable context of European fascisms. Japan was a *fascist* enemy, the OWI declared, encouraging the avoidance of racial stereotypes. Of course, the internment of Japanese Americans reveals the limits of this conception of democracy, demonstrating yet again the nation's refusal to accept its Asian immigrants as legitimate citizens and view them as distinct from its enemies.⁵⁹ However, in spite of the prevailing xenophobia and Orientalism, a more differentiated view of Asians and Asian American immigrants nevertheless found its way into World War II combat films, reaching a larger public with its reconfigurative notions of American nationhood and ethnic identity.⁶⁰

Ten days after Pearl Harbor, FDR appointed a coordinator of government films to establish a liaison between Hollywood and the government, citing in his executive order that "motion pictures could be one of the most effective tools in 'informing' the public."⁶¹ This office would later become part of the newly created OWI in June 1942, upholding a liberal New Deal perspective as it worked with Hollywood on the delicate mix of propaganda and entertainment.[62] Responding to the studios' quick cranking out of films that used the war as a mere backdrop to entertainment, the OWI attempted to curb the blatant racism and shallow representations of America's enemies and the war in general.

In the summer of 1942 the OWI released the "Government Information Manual for the Motion Picture Industry," outlining to Hollywood in detail what it expected in an American war film. As Clayton Koppes and Gregory Black point out in their analysis of OWI materials, the manual is a key document in understanding the relationship between Hollywood and the government, between film and propaganda: "More than a 'how to' handbook, the manual was a comprehensive statement of OWI's vision of America, the war, and the world."[63] Of particular importance to the left-leaning war office was the representation of democracy as an ideal of the average person, one that apparently transcended race, class, religion, and gender. To this end, it called for a ban on Hollywood's typical treatment of minorities, especially blacks, Asians, and women, who should now be shown as loyal and concerned citizens and resident immigrants ready to support the national cause. Furthering an anti-imperialist stance, the manual emphasized that "the war was a people's struggle, not a national, class or race war."[64] Enemies should be depicted not as racial groups but as misguided people who wrongly advocate fascist values. Through a variety of strategic maneuvers, including the significant threat to halt film distribution to foreign markets, the OWI influenced and pressured the studios into a form of acceptance of its manual.[65] By the fall of 1942, as Koppes and Black note, the OWI had firm control over the industry "whether through script review or application of the manual."[66]

Released in June 1943 with the OWI's full approval, *Bataan*, as Jeanine Basinger has pointed out, is *the* seminal film of the combat genre, marking the birth of the genre at a distinct moment in American history.[67] Basinger goes so far as to use the film as a categorization device, dividing the seminal year of 1943 into "Before *Bataan*" and "After *Bataan*."[68] This temporal caesura can also be seen in the work of Tay Garnett, the film's director. Before establishing the multicultural template of the combat film, Garnett was known for films such as *China Seas* (1935), a modern adventure and pirate story in the Pacific with stereotypical Orientalism in its subplots and lower decks, and more notoriously for *Slave Ship* (1937), a swashbuckler comedy in which a lifelong slave trader repents upon marrying, helps to set his slaves free in the film's finale, and is pardoned whereas his subordinates, who insisted on continuing in the outlawed business, receive the death penalty. *Slave Ship*, though not capable of questioning the entitlements of its leading white couple and problematic on several levels, was one of the first films openly addressing the violence of slavery, a topic usually considered unfit for Hollywood's screens. *Bataan*'s significance to the genre lies in its being the first infantry film entirely situated in and committed to warfare, transforming war into a national masculine love story of military and multicultural cooperation that quickly establishes itself as the combat genre. According to Basinger, the introductory stage of the genre occurs immediately after Pearl Harbor and moves into the second stage, emergence of the definition, with the release of *Bataan*, and in 1944 is followed by a final stage, repeat of the definition.[69]

Prior to this development, one can indeed speak of nationalistic war films and the depiction of lengthy combat scenes. One thinks especially of the great World War I combat films, Milestone's *All Quiet on the Western Front* (1930), Vidor's *The Big Parade* (1925), or Griffith's *The Birth of a Nation* (1915). However, these films also portray war as a futile act of devastation, questioning, even subverting, traditional concepts of national loyalty and duty. "When it comes to dying for your country, it's better not to die at all," Paul Bauman, the hero of *All Quiet on the Western Front*, tells young students eager to fight for their country. Told from the German enemy's point of view in English, the film posits a universal understanding of humanity that transcends petty national concerns. In spite of its magnificent representation of trench warfare and wartime themes that would become established conventions in the combat genre, *All Quiet on the Western Front*, like most World War I combat films, is in the end a pacifist film that narrates the horrors of war and condemns national pride for demanding such sacrifices. That it was banned in countries preparing for war reveals its success as an antiwar film.

Bataan, the story of a patrol that has volunteered for a death mission, marks a turning point in the history of combat film with its persuasive twofold story of love and war, fusing individual familial passions and masculine national desires. Taking its cue from patriotic wartime newsreels and documents as well as national interest narratives like that of the OWI, the World War II combat film foregrounds the living legacy derived from heroic death. It monumentalizes soldiers before they die, turning them into cenotaphs for patriotic achievement. This trait is immediately presented in *Bataan* with its opening dedication superimposed on the map of the Philippines, setting the tone of the film: "When Japan struck, our desperate need was time—time to martial our new armies. Ninety-six priceless days were bought for us—with their lives—by the defenders of Bataan, the Philippine army which formed the bulk of MacArthur's infantry fighting shoulder to shoulder with Americans. To those immortal dead, who heroically stayed the wave of barbaric conquest, this picture is reverently dedicated."[70] This dedication, stressing heroic sacrifice at the expense of strategic and military inferiority, transforms the demoralizing defeat of Bataan into a belated national success. As a tactical battle of delay, it succinctly gives the mission its national character of ultimate commitment even when no immediate victory is in sight. Its metaleptic temporality undoes the earlier defeat at Pearl Harbor, sanctions the subsequent defeat at Bataan, and restores the possibility of victory in the future. By the time *Bataan* is released in 1943, the United States is already making significant advances in the Asian theater of war and can confidently defend its military humiliations as necessary national trials on the road toward ultimate victory. The map underscores the revisionist temporality of the dedication by envisioning the territory of the Philippines as a restored sovereign nation. Ironically, the map covers up the fact that the United States itself had brutally suppressed national sovereignty in the Philippine-American War (1899–1902), turning the Philippines into a colonized US protectorate.

Like Pearl Harbor, the Battle of Bataan was not simply a loss but a national humiliation. After the Japanese invasion of the Philippines, which occurred on the same day as Pearl Harbor, and the fall of Manila less than one month later, Filipino and American troops under MacArthur's command strategically retreated and were eventually forced to surrender in April 1942. Seventy thousand Filipino and American POWs (sixty thousand Filipino troops and ten thousand American troops) were forced to undergo the infamous Bataan Death March. Only fifty thousand survived, with a few escaping into the jungle and the remainder dying from disease, starvation, beatings, and bayonet stab wounds. Fought mainly by poorly trained and ill-equipped soldiers suffering from tropical diseases and malnutrition, the Battle of Bataan was officially claimed to be one of buying time or stalling until America could rebuild its Pacific Fleet and send much-needed reinforcements. In actuality, America was still deciding on a war strategy and did not consider the Philippines to be of high military importance. In agreement with Britain, the United States was committed to Europe and the war against Germany and could not afford to fight on two fronts. Certainly, MacArthur believed that the future of the world lay with Asia, not Europe, and that the Philippines was "the key that turns the lock that opens the door to the mastery of the Pacific."[71] He could not, however, convince FDR that his inadequately trained Filipino Army (which he had commanded as field marshal since his retirement from the US army in 1937) could hold off a Japanese attack; nor could he convince them of the strategic importance of the archipelago. While the United States had a small contingent of troops in the islands as a sign to protest Japanese expansion, it was not yet committed to a war in Southeast Asia. Indeed, MacArthur spent the war fighting not only foreign enemies in the Asian theater of war but also his American enemies, namely rival commanders like Eisenhower and Hart, who questioned the importance of Asia and particularly the status of the Philippines.[72]

While not entirely covering up the historical facts of ill-prepared soldiers and their misgivings about MacArthur (soldiers popularly referred to him as "Dugout Doug"), *Bataan* is by no means a documentary film. In its initial scene, depicting the mass refugee flow of displaced Filipino civilians (particularly women and children) and wounded soldiers, it compresses its account by selecting out of the masses individual members of a single patrol. This pars pro toto construction allows the film to unfold its existential drama of love, nationhood, and death. Thirteen men, representing various ethnic, race, and class strata of American and

Filipino society, will come together to take a last stand. From the start, the film stresses that death is inevitable and represents the authentic achievement of the soldier fighting for freedom. The audience's knowledge of the outcome and the film's reiteration of it (opening close-up shot of the Japanese flag rising and the representation of the Japanese army as all powerful) ensure that *Bataan* is experienced as a catharsis. As in Greek tragedy, death and loss are not merely anticipated but experienced as war to achieve a purgatory effect in the viewer, distilling a purified and reawakened national soul.

Throughout the film, the hopelessness of the mission is foregrounded and is redeemed only by pathos-laden moments of emotional display as given in eulogies, confessions, and intimate letters. These confessional devices motivate the film's appeal to national sentiment and its imagined communal solidarity. This narrative of pathos and heroic death is coupled with a didactic narrative of war strategy. The accompanying narrative, though subordinated to the melodrama of existential-national heroism, is important in conveying an impression of battlefield and survivor strategies so as not to turn the genre into one of apocalypse and resignation.[73] The tension between the embrace of imminent death and the rational cunning required to escape from it creates the suspense of *Bataan* and of World War II combat films in general. It also allows the narrative to establish a Darwinian hierarchy of the survival of the fittest, eliminating the endorsed minorities one by one until the all-American white hero remains as the purest embodiment of the national soul. As Basinger notes, "after the loss of the leader, the minorities die first, and then the weak and the mentally sensitive."[74]

In spite of this Darwinian ending, minorities are strongly endorsed throughout the film and are not eliminated on account of an inherent flaw of race or character. The liberal imagination as set down by the demands of the OWI prevails and allows minorities to contribute within the framework of an American model of patriotism. *Bataan* is indeed remarkable in breaking with prevalent stereotypes of race. The African American soldier, Private Wesley Eeps, is not only an expert of technology (an engineer and demolition expert) but also studying ministry (see Figure 16). Upon the first death in the patrol, an important one since the commanding officer is killed, Eeps delivers a long eulogy and embodies both moral integrity and empathy. At several key points in the film, Eeps controls the narrative through point-of-view shots and close-ups. When he is not on screen, we continue to hear his comforting deep voice singing or humming the ragtime composer W. C. Handy's "St. Louis Blues." The Latino soldier is again linked to technology as a mechanic and owner of the patrol's only radio. In addition to being a connoisseur of American popular culture such as jazz, he also shows knowledge of Latin and is given a prominent death scene. Upon his death, his comrades twice spell out his name, R-A-M-I-R-E-Z, to ensure that it is properly printed on his cross. The Jewish

FIGURE 16. Tay Garnett's *Bataan* (1943) highlights an imaginary multiethnic combat unit, establishing a new film convention, contrary to the reality of a segregated US military during World War II.

character, nonstereotypically, is not depicted as an expert or what Sander Gilman calls the "smart Jew." Instead, he is a trustworthy and collegial fellow supporting all the men in the patrol, particularly the hero Sergeant Bill Dane, with his unshaken faith in their abilities. The Filipino characters, while treated with more ambivalence, are nevertheless recognized as Yankee allies—one is even named Yankee Salazar. Indeed, the film breaks with prevalent stereotypes of under- or overdeveloped intelligence, of disloyalty and double agendas usually attributed to minorities as nations within the nation as well as with the immorality attributed to them as potential corrupting forces in society.

While some stereotypes prevail, they are not singled out as flaws leading to their deaths. The Jewish soldier is stereotypically depicted as humorous and unfit for military service due to a "foot problem" but in the end dies a heroic death unrelated to his feet. The African American soldier is depicted bare-chested in the first half of the film, his body glistening with sweat and toil, evoking the bondage of slavery and the aura of a precivilized people. As one Filipino character reverts back to primitive wartime techniques, covering himself with only a loincloth and mud as camouflage and war paint, he is duly reprimanded by the sergeant for this precivilized behavior. From this point onward, the African American is never seen bare-chested but wears a long-sleeve shirt completely buttoned so as to stress his proper place in American civilization.

The treatment of the two Filipino characters is particularly interesting since it is more ambivalent than that of the other minorities. While clearly identified as American allies, they are mostly absent and appear unfit to fight modern technological warfare. They are not given prominent scenes of pathos other than in the initial opening shot of mass refugees. They are always spoken about and even quoted, but they do not speak for themselves. However, unlike the Japanese enemies, who are presented as fighting outside the rules of combat, they are given heroic qualities in order to distinguish them as American allies. In a crucial scene of recognition, this important difference between Asians is underscored when the young recruit is about to fire upon one of his Filipino allies after mistaking him, in spite of color difference, as Japanese. "Get the fog out of your eyes," his sergeant yells, also admonishing the American viewer at home to look more carefully, promoting thereby a new, more differentiated perception of Asian friends and enemies.

Bataan thus does not entirely abandon racial stereotyping, but reorients it toward a pluralist melting pot society that parallels OWI values. This liberal position also stresses a democratic leveling of class differences as given in the elite West Point commander voluntarily surrendering his command to the more experienced sergeant. As an exemplary racial and social democracy, the American and Filipino patrol represents in miniature the new liberal American credo that is now at stake in the war and about to be exported to Asia. As a morally and politically superior nation, the United States secures its right to legitimate intervention in what is perceived as the threat of a predemocratic Japanese imperialism. However, the mythmaking of democracy ironically places a double bind on America's internal affairs, forcing it to promote democracy within as well as beyond its national borders. While depicting events from a belated perspective with its revisionary transformation of defeat into success, *Bataan* narrates on another level a utopian vision of a nonracist and classless American society yet to be implemented. Rather curiously, the military figures in this respect as an avant-garde of ethnic and class relations.

This imagined narration of the military as a progressive institution of democracy is an important characteristic of World War II films, one that belies the military's long record of racism. Here it is instructive to turn to the rich military history of black Americans so as to better understand the implications of the combat genre's revisionary imaginings. Having participated in every American war and conflict with great distinction, black Americans prior to World War II generally viewed war and military duty as an opportunity to display to the national mainstream their patriotism and civic abilities. Several scholars, however, point to a reoccurring pattern in the national perception of black soldiers. During times of conflict, when manpower is needed, military and government officials (as well as the popular press) praise African American soldiers, often lavishly so, and vice versa, during peaceful periods, criticize and question them. At stake in these political debates was the status of blacks in the military, especially their promotion to the rank of commissioned officer. For example, in the post–Civil War or Indian War period (1869–1890), it became an established fact early on that black troops were well skilled in warfare and had high morale and regimental pride, "[boasting] among the lowest desertion and alcoholism rates."[75] In spite of racism (segregation, relegating blacks to warmer climates and to difficult and inferior assignments) the government at first treated its white and black troops uniformly in pay and in the distribution of weapons, equipment, horses, and so forth; however, once the western frontier was secured in the mid-1870s, black units came under heavy criticism, with authorities questioning their abilities and concluding they were unfit for military service.[76]

Similarly, in the Spanish-American War, the many war correspondents and "observers could not speak highly enough of the conduct of black soldiers."[77] It was claimed that the black 10th Cavalry even rescued Teddy Roosevelt and his Rough Riders during their famous charge of San Juan Hill. Rough Rider and future Secretary of the Navy Frank Knox wrote to his parents, "in justice to the colored race, I must say that I never saw braver men anywhere."[78] Roosevelt in particular embodies this vacillating attitude toward blacks, first speaking highly of black units in the press and citing them as "brave men, worthy of respect. . . . I don't think any rough rider . . . will ever forget the tie that binds us to the 9th and 10th Calvary."[79] Later he would dispute this claim in The Rough Riders, now alleging that he was forced to hold these same black troops at gunpoint as they attempted to flee to the rear of the line.[80] Here Roosevelt transforms the once highly praised soldiers into retreating minstrel stereotypes, who upon being threatened and exposed as cowards "flashed their white teeth at one another, as they broke into broad grins."[81] As Amy Kaplan observes, Roosevelt's change of heart and later hesitation to endorse black troops with his claim that they were "particularly dependent on their white officers" addresses not only white anxiety about black insurrection but also "the postwar debates about the viability of American imperialism and the fitness of nonwhites at home and abroad for self-government."[82]

In World War I this discrepancy in perception would come to a head, leading to a decline in relations between blacks and the military. Several black regiments served with distinguished combat records, but the most memorable was the 369th Infantry Regiment. Affectionately called the "hell-fighters" by the French, the regiment was the only American unit to receive over 170 citations for France's highest military order, the Croix de Guerre, for their extraordinary heroism under fire. It was also selected to lead the Allies in the march toward the Rhine.[83] Blatantly ignoring these and other distinguished honors received by black troops, military and government officials instead focused on the poor military record of the black 92nd Division, made up mainly of inadequately trained draftees led by white officers whose official policy was to scorn and humiliate black soldiers publicly.[84] Viewing blacks as ineffectual in combat due to the 92nd Division, the military after the war terminated black recruitment for several years and reduced existing black units to a minimum.[85] Their performance in World War I, military authorities concluded, established the long-held white suspicion of black combat inferiority.

In World War II, the Roosevelt administration grudgingly recruited blacks only after black communities increased pressure and the need for more manpower was established.[86] Assigned mainly to noncombat and menial service duties, black troops were not able to distinguish themselves as fighters as they had during earlier wars.[87] *Bataan*'s depiction of the heroic black soldier is consequently both unrealistic and realistic, staging once again the ambivalent drama of race relations in America. While *Bataan* breaks with film conventions in its positive stereotyping of minorities, it draws from the tradition of war narratives as mentioned earlier in its foregrounding of the patriotism and heroism of minorities in time of need. In World War II combat films, however, this race narrative would no longer follow the traditional black-white polarity of earlier war narratives. Thomas Edison's restaged documentary shorts on the Spanish- and Philippine-American Wars, for example, depict Cubans and Filipinos as black, using black actors to play their roles. *Bataan* radically alters this pattern and presents a more diffuse multiethnic and multiracial panorama, reflecting America's shifting alliances both at home and on the war front. This diffuse and diversified perspective of race makes it difficult to align patriotic sentiment with racial preference. In drumming up support for the war effort in Asia, internal differences of race are repressed so as to foreground a melodramatic narrative of a united America. The enemy's totalitarianism must be conquered by the national credo of democracy and cannot be questioned from within by actual ongoing domestic racial conflicts. The liberal imagination projects instead an idealistic vision of a desegregated military while denying the real political practices of racial apartheid and the fact that the military was not segregated until after World War II.

America's new role in Asia consequently involves a reorientation of color lines as *Bataan* tries to make clear to its audience. As dark-colored Asians, Filipinos upset the traditional American color spectrum of race, posing a visual problem to America's own history of racism and white supremacy. The admonition "Get the fog out of your eyes" can therefore also be read pedagogically as a warning against traditional racial profiling in terms of color. The relearning of color and racial alliances involves dissociation from colonial and racist discourses equating darker skin with barbarism and savagery as given in South Seas fantasy films. This perception is also depicted in *Bataan* with the juxtaposition of the Filipino soldier atavistically reverting to tribal warfare and the African American soldier displaying a Western technological attitude toward combat. From a perspective of racial prejudice, combat, with its disinhibition of human violence, pushes primitive races back into savagery and poses a threat to civilization. This violence, however, is contained by American civilization, which will bring liberation to both the residual savagery of the Philippines and the absolute savagery of Japanese imperialism, underscored by the brutal representation of Japanese warfare.

A crucial problem of American race discourse, as this reading of *Bataan* suggests, is its disregard for a multiethnic configuration of American nationhood with racial conflict staged in bipolar fashion, white versus black, white versus Asian, or white versus Hispanic. This binary treatment of race leads to the fragmentation of cross-ethnic solidarity and restores white supremacy in one form or another. *Back to Bataan*, released in 1945, while trying to do justice to the Philippines' struggle for sovereignty, treats the question of race once again in a neutral fashion and obscures *Bataan*'s earlier multicultural perspective. Indebted to film noir, *Back to Bataan* blurs the color boundaries between white Americans and dark-skinned Filipinos, leaving us with a monocultural image of combat troops. This neutralization of race may help to humanize Filipinos but poses the significant problem of cultural and ethnic assimilation to an implied American standard of whiteness. *Bataan*, conversely, even differentiates among white Americans stressing Jewish and Polish ethnicities as well as regional differences, thereby challenging a monocultural image of white American society. The American engagement in Asia, with its need to confront Orientalism, breaks open the ossified structures of race perception derived from an exclusive Eurocentric focus. Complicating this stance through a critique of inherited modes of perception engendered by Orientalism and Eurocentrism, *Bataan* presents a curious postmodern and multicultural image of America. The newly confronted question of Orientalism does not merely add another claim for ethnic recognition in America's landscape of diverse ethnicities. Meeting up with other prevalent discourses of race, Orientalism here enters into a multiethnic dynamic of competing and overlapping discourses on race, opening up the possibility to reconfigure the binary treatment of race into one concerned with interethnic definition and solidarity.

Released near the end of the war when America was more confident of victory, *Back to Bataan* is concerned not with heroic death and sacrifice but with liberation and consolidation of national interests. As with war narratives extolling African American soldiers at the beginning of wars and later withholding acknowledgment of sacrifice and heroism, *Back to Bataan* looks toward a postwar era and reveals a similar diminishment of race relations. Unlike *Bataan*, which revises past defeats (Pearl Harbor, Bataan) to sustain an uncertain present and project future victory, *Back to Bataan* is more confident of military success and therefore mainly concerned with the implementation of democracy both abroad and at home. The film's representation of race now retracts *Bataan*'s multicultural endorsement and becomes altogether schizophrenic in its simultaneous acceptance and rejection of Filipinos as American allies. The contradictions and inconsistencies of the earlier film, held together by its masculine celebration of war and love of nation, now resurface as competing ideologies. The liberal agenda of the OWI, which called for a stop on Hollywood's negative stereotyping of minorities so as to further a more democratic and pluralistic representation of society, is challenged by the anxiety of immigration and its concerns with purity of race and foreign contamination.

Robert G. Lee has discussed how anti-Asian representation has been used to create national myths in order to sustain the status quo in American racial hierarchy. Of particular importance here is Lee's analysis of the "yellow peril" and "model minority," stereotypes used at particular moments in American history to impede integration or to enforce assimilation, respectively.[88] According to Lee, the construction of the yellow peril myth grows out of national anxieties at the turn of the century concerned with the mass immigration of non-Anglo-Saxons, American imperialism, and global competition (represented in particular by the stunning rise and modernization of Japan). Especially, America's colonization of Hawaii and the Philippines was accompanied by the popular fear of mass inundation by brown- and yellow-skinned immigrants of degenerate races, demanding American citizenship and its privileges. Lee argues that these fears of naturalization and immigration created by America's adventures abroad were intimately related to that of the domestic "Negro problem" and mainstream anxieties about potential black rebellion and its challenge to white supremacy.

The Asian as "model minority" grows out of post–World War II America and is the liberal attempt to transform the unacceptable foreigner into an American via assimilation. The need to assimilate Asians, claims Lee, is motivated by several factors, the most important here being America's conflicts with communism and Asia, especially Red China, as well as the increasing militancy of American blacks and their refusal both to continue with the national practice of racial discrimination and to assimilate to white mainstream norms. Lee quotes Asian American writer Frank Chin to describe the situation: "Whites love us because we're not black."[89] What is significant about both the yellow peril and model minority myths is the triangular relationship in which Asian representation articulates white anxieties about black dissent.

In its representation of Filipinos, *Back to Bataan* projects an early prototype of the model minority myth but is also haunted by the early turn-of-the-century image of the yellow peril. Appearing on the one hand as patriotic allies willing to die for American ideals of democracy, Filipinos are likewise represented as social parasites who desire nothing more than immigration to the United States so as to sponge off of a benevolent democratic system. Starring opposite John Wayne as the Filipino Army Captain Andrés Bonifácio, Anthony Quinn figures as the exemplary model minority (see Figure 17). He is curiously represented as Asian by virtue of his Mexican ethnicity that nevertheless can pass for white when required as Quinn has starred as a white European Mediterranean in several films, most

FIGURE 17. Edward Dmytryk's *Back to Bataan* (1945) casts Anthony Quinn as Filipino Captain Bonifácio across from John Wayne's Colonel Madden.

notably Fellini's *La Strada* (1954) and the British drama *Zorba the Greek* (1964). As the grandson of the real-life venerated Filipino resistance leader of the same name, Quinn's character in *Back to Bataan* is that of a war-weary and resigned officer who gains strength from and whose patriotic legacy is redeemed by a renewed faith in American commitment and democracy. Remodeling himself after Colonel Madden (John Wayne), the initially reluctant Bonifácio increasingly displays the patriotic passion and responsible leadership of his teacher. The transformation of the Filipino captain into the decidedly white all-American image of John Wayne is made visually credible by the use of the light-skinned Quinn, who bears a slight but significant resemblance in looks, build, and masculinity to Wayne. In the character of Bonifácio, then, *Back to Bataan* projects a future vision of Philippine independence squarely based on assimilated American ideals in which Filipinos figure as model minorities worthy of sovereignty.

The counterpart to Quinn's character Bonifácio is Sergeant Biernesa, played by Filipino actor J. Alex Havier, who also starred in *Bataan* as the Filipino Scout aptly named Yankee Salazar. As the "authentic" Filipino, Biernesa figures as the dark foil to the white Bonifácio. As mentioned earlier, Filipino characters in *Bataan* are given prominence visually but ultimately remain silent, without the power of address or enunciation. In *Back to Bataan*, which bills itself as the story of Filipino resistance, Filipinos are represented more substantially as a psychologically complex people. Though a white actor plays the lead Filipino character, Asians are nevertheless used in several key roles and to represent the Filipino Army and guerilla fighters as well. Even Japanese enemies are given prominent close-ups and more character development. Sergeant Biernesa, Colonel Madden's omnipresent Filipino aide, appears usually at the side of the Wayne character ready to take orders and occasionally to offer advice and voice opinions. He fearlessly rescues Bonifácio during the Bataan Death March by passing as a Japanese soldier and also gives a rousing talk about the patriotic duties of Filipinos. Maximo (Ducky Louie), a young Filipino boy who befriends Madden, courageously gives his life to prevent the Japanese discovery of Madden's patrol, and Dalisay Delgado (Fely Franquelli), Bonifácio's glamorous fiancée, is a double agent who works for the Filipino resistance movement by posing as an informant for the Japanese.

However, in spite of or perhaps due to the strength and complexity of Asian representation, the film also cuts against its Filipino characters, raising the specter of the yellow peril. This transformation of the model minority into the inassimilable foreigner is seen particularly in the character of Sergeant Biernesa. He becomes pals with a white American hobo now serving military time as the patrol's cook, and it is through this association that the Filipino actor is intertwined with the myth of the yellow peril. In a significant scene occurring immediately after he has heroically rescued Bonifácio, Biernesa listens keenly to the vagabond describing the romantic life of train hopping across America. Dressed not in military uniform but as a Chaplinesque tramp, the hobo imagines a trip the two friends could take together:

BENDLE JACKSON (JOE): So we could spend the winter in Palm Beach.
BIERNESA: Doing what?
JACKSON: Um . . . taking it easy.
MISS BARNES: [interrupting] Have either of you seen Maximo?

BIERNESA: No Ma'am.

MISS BARNES: Or Jose Lapez, or Tomas Enaldo?

BIERNESA: No Ma'am.

JACKSON: Let's see. Now where were we?

BIERNESA: Taking it easy in Palm Beach, Florida, U.S.A.

JACKSON: Ah, yes. [Puffs on his cigarette] So we spend the winter in Florida. Then we hop a train—the streamliner mind you—nothing but the best for us.

BIERNESA: We still don't buy any ticket for this train?

JACKSON: Who buys tickets?

[CLOSE-UP OF BIERNESA, SMILING AND LOOKING OFF INTO THE DISTANCE WISTFULLY]

JACKSON: We hop off in New York in time for the opening ball game. We crash a few shows.

BIERNESA: Say, Joe?

JACKSON: Yes?

BIERNESA: When do we work?

JACKSON: [softly] Never.

BIERNESA: I sure am going to like the U.S.A.

The setting, a tropical night with twittering birds and palm trees, and the intimacy of the dialogue are reminiscent not of two soldiers in combat but rather of lovers sharing a fantasy. This rather curious scene works on several levels to discredit Asians. It introduces the fears of parasitic mass immigration and miscegenation associated with the yellow peril and also emasculates the Filipino soldier, calling into question through homoerotic allusion his former heroic act. Throughout the film, the techniques of film noir are further used to challenge Asian credibility. Low-key lighting, extreme high and low angles, and stock character types of the treacherous Asian femme fatale and wily Fu Manchu villains are deployed to create a sinister Asian underworld of shadows and murkiness. In the scene just outlined, the dark skin of Sergeant Biernesa is accentuated in a lengthy close-up of his face as the hobo's off-screen voice promises free train rides and ball games. Darkness is thus associated with freeloading, vagrancy, and indecency. Indeed, *Back to Bataan* visually conveys the sordidness and impropriety of race mixing and of Asians in general, turning against its own liberal agenda of the model minority and questioning finally its advocacy of Filipino self-governance and sovereignty.

As with *Bataan*, the ultimate contradiction in *Back to Bataan* lies in its effort to sell the liberation of the Philippines from Japanese colonization to the American audience as a morally just enterprise with images of John Wayne as the white leader of Western democracy (see Figure 18). Both films obscure America's own imperialistic suppression of Filipino sovereignty in the Philippine-American War some forty years ago and that the current war is also an attempt to recover

FIGURE 18. *Back to Bataan* (1945) depicts John Wayne in the role of Colonel Madden guiding the Filipino natives in their struggle for liberation.

its former colonial possessions. Indeed, in spite of the Philippines' eventual sovereignty in the post–World War II era, the United States would continue to have a strong economic and military presence there until recently, a hegemonic occupation described as soft colonialism. However, alongside all of these internal inconsistencies, a narrative of national interest emerges in World War II combat films in which a variety of ethnic groups take on a much more significant role than in previous eras of national crisis. While the liberal imagination in both films is shot through with contradictions concerning race perception and democratic participation in America, it nevertheless upholds a bold vision of interracial nationhood and challenges former melting pot narratives of an inherited or assimilated white Anglo-American identity.

By means of its Orientalism, relying on both positive and negative stereotyping of Asians, the combat genre curiously redirects racial struggle into a more complex multiethnic constellation that challenges traditional racial codes defining membership in America's national community. The role of Filipinos as dark Asians is of particular interest in that it does not allow Americans to bypass their color prejudices in seeking out allies in the Asian theater of war. Filipinos challenge the American color spectrum on both ends, fitting into neither a white nor a black binary code, that often asks new immigrants (Eastern European Jews, Irish, Italians, and more recently lighter skinned Asians) to redefine themselves as white so as to uphold America's racial hierarchy.

With the arrival of World War II Pacific combat film, then, fragments of a multicultural America appear on screen, foreshadowing an emerging reconfiguration of national identity. This new national imaginary as presented in the genre was indeed so powerful that it could not be dismantled after the war with a return to the status quo. In December 1945, the Navy passed an administrative order claiming that race or color was not to be considered in the administration of its personnel. Finally, after much political wrangling and agitation from groups such as the NAACP, the Urban League, and the Jewish War Veterans as well as the popular black press, President Truman signed in July 1948 Executive Order 9981, requiring equal opportunity in the military.[90] Within two decades, America would be forced to adapt its social reality to what appears in 1943 merely as cinematic illusion. *Bataan*'s utopian imaginings of a multicultural military would indeed become an actuality in the special limited and patriarchal context of the US military. However, multiculturalism and interracial solidarity remain an elusive ideal that the nation struggles to meet in spite of its advocacy of diversity.

John Ford's *They Were Expendable*, a combat film released after the end of World War II, in December 1945, is set on the eve of December 7, 1941, and revisits the humiliating American defeats suffered at Bataan and Corregidor but with the implicit knowledge of the eventual outcome of the war in the Pacific. This recapitulation allows Ford's film not only to restage World War II and thereby recant the earlier envisioned national utopia but also to break with the template of the patriotic combat film and move more boldly into the contemplative time image of post–World War II cinema. As such, the film, with its episodic intertwining of the everyday and unremarkable military duties (maintaining and cleaning the coral off a PT boat) along with its minor military missions, looks forward to Zinnemann's *From Here to Eternity* (1953), with its overall tedium of military life pre–December 7. Ford's work repositions the combat film's propaganda agenda and turns it into a docudrama with a high degree of verisimilitude, diminishing the utopian and multicultural overtures of the genre. Indeed, as critics have duly noted, Ford backpedals on his multicultural democratic utopia at the end of the war when it is time to implement it on the mainland.[91] *They Were Expendable* contains no roll call featuring a multicultural combat unit and offers only slight hints at diversity, which is now mostly defined in white ethnic terms that highlight its Irish American characters, namely Rusty Ryan (John Wayne), "Boats" Mulcahey, and "Slug" Mahan. Filipinos are depicted mostly in assisting and subservient functions and as a people protected by the US military. Surprisingly, the film makes a strong argument for the merit of women in World War II, something rarely seen in this masculine genre. The brief love interest of Rusty Ryan, namely Second Lieutenant Sandy Davyss (Donna Reed), is treated with multiple noirish close-ups and a focus on her toughness and capable professionalism rather than her sexuality. Davyss is shown during surgery in unflinching fashion assisting as an army nurse and reacts to the breakup of her relationship with Rusty due to his redeployment in an unsentimental and factual manner.

In contrast to this return to the racial status quo, Ford's grasp of the military genre reveals a stronger demystification of war than World War II propaganda films would have permitted. The film begins with a gorgeous display of luminescent white Navy dress uniforms that light up the screen. Upon the attack on Pearl Harbor, the lighting of the film switches radically to darker noirish colors and shows the Navy soldiers in tanned work uniforms. The film stresses that the initial idealistic luminescence of the featured PT squadron has to acquire its material body and substance in typical John Ford fashion through combat, death, and loss. The fleeting romantic encounter between Rusty and Sandy is similarly colored by war and shot during nighttime curfew hours in harsh noir style. This perspective also entails a critical look at the hierarchy of the military in which top brass like General MacArthur and the film's two heroic officers can flee the Philippines in safety, whereas the common enlisted men must stay behind, expecting imprisonment and death at the hands of the Japanese. In a scene where a young ensign delivers to the PT crew the congratulations of General MacArthur along with Silver Star decorations, he is simply ignored by the hardened crew, already wise to the hypocrisy of such military honors. The Japanese enemy is not depicted at all, turning the film into an ominous existential as well as national drama. In accordance with its dark title, the film wishes to praise the unsung heroes of war and position them for belated postwar rewards. Particularly, the Irish American community received eventually compensation for its wartime sacrifices and thrived in the postwar economy, gaining entrance into the mainstream with the election of John F. Kennedy as president in 1960. Incidentally, Kennedy served on a torpedo PT boat near the Solomon Islands in the Pacific theater. Similarly, white women gained wider access to job opportunities that would eventually lead to the more assertive women's movement of the 1960s. Racial minorities contributing to the war effort, however, would not reap these rewards immediately. Ronald Takaki notes in fact a retraction of opportunities for minorities in the US labor market: "For African Americans, men as well as women, World War II was a crossing, constituting what Robert C. Weaver of the Office of Production Management called 'more industrial diversification for Negroes than had occurred in the seventy-five preceding years.' At the end of the war, however, the defense industry contracted, and industrial opportunities for African Americans suddenly disappeared. Economic reconversion hurt black workers more than white workers. From July 1945 to April 1946, unemployment rates among blacks increased more than twice as much as among whites."[92] Nevertheless, the war left a dent in the armor of white exclusiveness, starting with the integration of the military in 1948 (Executive Order 9981) and the landmark decision *Brown v. Board of Education* (1954), which initiated the slow desegregation of schools and public institutions in the United States.

YELLOWFACE, ORIENTALISM, AND WORLD WAR II B FILMS

Less than two weeks after the Pearl Harbor attack, President Roosevelt appointed a coordinator of government films to establish a liaison with Hollywood and the government, leading to the creation of the OWI in June 1942. As Thomas Doherty argues, the government's unprecedented enlistment of Hollywood "as an active agent in the Second World War" is a turning point in American film history, signaling a change in the national perception of film.[93] Prior to the war, notes Doherty, "American movies were mainly considered an amusement or an investment."[94] However, during the war, films would be "recalibrated as a weapon of war" by the government, an acknowledgment of Hollywood's considerable ability to educate and persuade a national audience as well as accurately articulate its culture, politics, and values.[95]

Through a variety of strategic maneuvers, including the significant threat to halt film distribution to foreign markets, the OWI influenced and pressured the studios into a form of acceptance of its manual. This tacit censorship centered on two major goals of the OWI: to harness the potential of Hollywood as a government mouthpiece and to curb the blatant racism depicted in the shallow or grotesque representations of racial and ethnic Others, especially in popular B films. The OWI reviewed scripts of every major studio (with the exception of a stubborn Paramount, which nevertheless closely followed the manual) and consulted with powerful studio executives, pressuring them to change or discard objectionable material. Studios were often forced to reshoot scenes, and the OWI itself often rewrote key speeches. By fall of 1942, note Koppes and Black, the OWI had firm control over the industry "whether through script review or application of the manual."[96]

This control, however, pertained mainly to big-budget films. Indeed, the A-list World War II film followed for the most part the OWI manual, which represented a "comprehensive statement of OWI's vision of America, the war, and the world."[97] The OWI manual called for a prohibition on Hollywood's standard treatment of minorities who should now be depicted as productive citizens or resident immigrants ready to support the national cause. World War II, proclaimed the OWI manual, was "a people's war [that] everyone had a stake in, regardless of class, ethnic, or religious identification."[98] Furthering an anti-imperialist stance, the manual also emphasized that "the war was a people's struggle, not a national, class or race war."[99] Accordingly, studios were encouraged to "show democracy at work."[100] Thus prominent or A-list war/combat films such as *Bataan, Thirty Seconds over Tokyo,* and *Back to Bataan* depict imaginary democratic scenarios such as multicultural combat teams that were radically at odds with the everyday reality of a Jim Crow America. This section analyzes the rhetoric of race in representative A- and B-list World War II films, focusing on the example of yellowface. Typically, Hollywood's long-standing tradition of racial masquerade or mimicry as given especially in blackface and yellowface is most often associated with the social management and regulation of racial and ethnic Others; however, as critics have argued, mimicry's racist rhetoric is at bottom unstable and ambivalent, disrupting its own authority and calling into question the hierarchy of race and culture.

If A-list war films articulated the visionary ideals of nation and democracy, the B films of this genre reflected the national underbelly à la film noir, particularly America's continued problematic relation with the issue of race. The term "B picture" originally referred to a Hollywood film made during the Studio Era that was designed to fill the "lower half" of a double feature. A low-budget commercial product, a B film is typically a genre film (i.e., Western, gangster, sci-fi, horror, or thriller) filled with lesser-known B actors. As the foil to the prestige A picture, the B film is associated with inferior production, shocking plots, and lurid character portrayals. In the Depression Era, B film prevailed, making up approximately 75 percent of Hollywood's overall production.[101] While Westerns proved to be the most popular, horror, mystery, and thriller films also did well, including the well-liked Fu Manchu series. The latter, starring Boris Karloff or Warner Oland as the fiendish Oriental genius Dr. Fu Manchu, whose ambition is to take over the world, would help create the paradigmatic "yellow peril" Hollywood stereotype. With the start of World War II, studios rushed to use war as a sensational backdrop, especially in the various types of B film, depicting national enemies in grotesque and racist caricatures. B films such as Universal's *Menace of the Rising Sun* (1942)[102] and RKO's *Hitler's Children* (Edward Dmytryk, 1943) exploited the war, viscerally portraying America's foes, especially its Asian enemy Japan, in blatantly racist terms. To be sure, it is in the B film where the repressed unconscious of race returns to the surface, though not without its own censorship and distortion. The widespread practice of yellowface in B films, for example, stands out as a conspicuous feature in which the Asian Other can be at once represented and contained. World War II B films thus accommodate the fear of and fascination with the Asian Other without recourse to democratic models, revealing a brute stance of domination of what is perceived as a potentially rivaling and invasive civilization, the yellow peril. However, through its crude and primitive rhetoric, the B film ironically exposes the system of racial management concealed or glossed over in sophisticated A films.

Michael Rogin has provocatively argued that America's national culture is founded on the spiritual miscegenation of two American icons: Uncle Sam and the black mammy.[103] As the first popular form of American mass culture, blackface minstrelsy functioned to define norms of whiteness and nationhood. *The Jazz Singer* (1927), argues Rogin, depicts the national melodrama of assimilation in which a Jewish immigrant blacks up to become a legitimate white American. The widespread practice of Hollywood yellowface also performs a racial and national drama. Unlike blackface, however, its European predecessors have significantly shaped it through the extensive heritage of European Orientalism. Traditional European yellowface of the nineteenth and twentieth centuries as given in the high art forms of theater and opera typically depicted the Asian Other for Europeans who had never been in the presence of Asians. In the United States, yellowface, like blackface, was articulated via the popular art forms of vaudeville and low comedy, pursuing a different goal than that of a European aesthetic typification of exotic and fetishized Asians in faraway lands and colonies. Since Asian immigrants lived among Americans, their representation was not one of remoteness and mythical distance but spoke directly to the fears of the national collective. Fearsome images of miscegenation, rape, and labor market invasions were associated with Asians, especially Asian immigrants, so as to forestall their naturalization into legitimate citizens. Exclusionary labor and citizenship laws further kept Asian Americans at the periphery of society, similar to Jim Crow legislation that deprived African Americans of civil rights.[104] The fear of the yellow peril was intensified with the Japanese attack on Pearl Harbor, which was seen as "a stab in the back" bearing trademarks of so-called Asian wiliness and sneakiness.

The routine of yellowface becomes more complicated in the World War II era and does not simply result in the expected Orientalist representation of a hostile and base Asian enemy. Rather racial mimicry takes on the subtler tone of colonial management as described by Homi Bhabha: "If colonialism takes power in the name of history, it repeatedly exercises its authority through the figure of farce. . . . In this comic turn from the high ideals of colonial imagination to its low mimetic literary effects mimicry emerges as one of the most elusive and effective strategies of colonial power and knowledge."[105] Accordingly, as an extension of American World War II Orientalism and its colonial imagination, the discourse of mimicry becomes ripe with farcical and ironic elements, revealing what Bhabha calls the double vision of mimicry and mockery, in which the dominant power simultaneously asserts and disrupts its own authority. In World War II A film, the farce, namely a tone of exaggerated and nonrealistic high seriousness, presents itself in various images of democracy, particularly that of a multicultural combat team fighting side by side in spite of the reality of segregated armed forces and instituted racism in the form of Jim Crow laws.

Consider, for example, the famous roll-call scene from *Bataan* (1943; Tay Garnett, MGM), an A-list movie that film historian Jeanine Basinger refers to as the first seminal combat film.[106] A motley crew of thirteen men, representing not only the many branches of the armed forces but America's various ethnicities, races, religions, regions, and social classes, is assembled in Bataan to fight the Japanese. With characters ranging from an Irish American cook, a Latino American mechanic, a Jewish soldier, and a white naïve midwestern youth to an African American demolition expert, a Polish American engineer, two Filipino scouts/soldiers, and a white criminal, *Bataan* presents us with a cross-section of the United States and its territories. A similar scene of America as melting pot is found in the opening scene of *Guadalcanal Diary* (Lewis Seiler, 1943, Twentieth Century Fox) in which the men (a Mexican American, a Jewish soldier, a white tough guy from Brooklyn, an Irish American priest, etc.) are relaxing on ship before battle, talking, and singing. The Latino American soldier, Private Jesus "Soose" Alvarez (Anthony Quinn), rests his dark head against the chest of a blonde fair soldier while reminiscing about his senoritas at home. A version of international multiculturalism is found in *Thirty Seconds over Tokyo* (Mervyn LeRoy, 1944, MGM) when a group of Chinese children aiding the American raid of Tokyo (the historical Doolittle Raid) serenade the American soldiers with "The Star-Spangled Banner" sung in Chinese. In scenes such as these, the farce is obscured under the film's patriotic agenda of democracy in action. This agenda is stated clearly up front in the opening dedications of *Bataan* and *Guadalcanal Diary*. *Bataan* dedicates the film "to those immortal dead, who heroically stayed the wave of barbaric conquest," and *Guadalcanal Diary*, based on the memoirs of a war correspondent, refers to itself as "a new chapter in the history of America: by the correspondent who landed on Guadalcanal with the first detachment of U.S. Marines." Both films, revealing the close relation between combat film and newsreels, present their stories as realistic in spite of their imaginary scenarios of a multicultural combat team. Similarly, *Thirty Seconds over Tokyo* maintained realism by working and consulting with actual Doolittle raiders, including the captain, who is the hero of the story, and filming on location at the military base where the Doolittle raiders trained.

However, it is in the formulaic, low-budget B film that the discourse of the farce becomes significant not merely as hyperbolic and grotesque rhetoric but in its decisive treatment of the farce as farce. Unlike the A film's utopian and progressive agenda set forth in the democratic guidelines of the OWI, the B film does not approach the subject matter with the so-called ethical broad-minded belief in liberty and mass enlightenment. Instead, the genre takes a primitive approach, playing on mass anxiety and exhibiting a scopic fascination with the Asian Other. Two RKO B films, *Behind the Rising Sun* (Edward Dmytryk, 1943) and *First Yank into Tokyo* (Gordon Douglas, 1945), can be seen as paradigmatic of the B genre during wartime. Both films use the same lead B star, Tom Neal, who dresses up in yellowface to represent the Japanese enemy soldier. As a reflection of a repressed national psyche, these B films lay bare the imperialist ideologies and the anxieties that nourish them, which are for the most part concealed or glossed over in A-film productions. Both films accommodate the fascination with the Asian Other without recourse to democratic models. Comparing these two B films also allows us to see the unexpected turns and complexity in their drama of race relations. What is of interest here is the double bind of American World War II Orientalism that identifies its Oriental enemy as hostile to Occidental democracy, while attributing these self-same democratic values to its Oriental allies. At the core of this new American Orientalism lies an irresolvable tension between visionary ideals expressing on the one hand democratic sentiments, and on the other hand, the political policy that works to legitimate the war, the status quo with its racial hierarchy, and American expansion into the Far East.

The first film, *Behind the Rising Sun*, is an ambitious work directed by the young rising star Edward Dmytryk, who would later become known for his A-list films (*Crossfire, Back to Bataan, The Caine Mutiny, The Young Lions*). Released in August 1943, Dmytryk's controversial film boldly addresses an issue at the top of the OWI list, and like the sensational B film that started Dmytryk's career, *Hitler's Children* (1943), was meant to examine fascist culture and explain the nature of the enemy through his fascist mentality rather than racial character. Dmytryk claimed his purpose was to produce the first film to penetrate this isolated society of imperial Japan and show how the Japanese military, and not the Japanese people, went astray, as he was steadfastly opposed to any film that portrayed all Japanese as barbarians. The OWI, which had high hopes for Dmytryk's film, flatly refused to grant it an export license upon viewing the final cut, calling it "openly propagandistic."[107] *Rising Sun* employs two genre styles that are significant for our discussion: film noir and documentary or reportage. These two styles create the tension in the narrative, allowing elements of the B film to be expressed in A-film rhetoric. As is typical of war films, it opens with a statement claiming the veracity of its story and intersperses throughout its narrative documentary clips of Japanese society and the military's occupation in Manchuria. Narrated by a Japanese father (J. Carroll Naish in yellowface) grieving the death of his son, *Rising Sun* recounts how his once good and well-meaning son turns into a killer. The story begins with Taro (Tom Neal in yellowface) arriving home in Tokyo after graduating from Cornell (like his father) with high hopes of bringing American engineering technology and democracy to Japan. A high-ranking official in Japan, his father encourages him to enlist in the Japanese Army and in the course of the war Taro transforms into a cold-hearted murderer who looks on without much thought as Japanese soldiers in Manchuria stab babies, feed children opium, perform government-sanctioned rape, and torture American journalists, including women. While there are several sympathetic portrayals of the Japanese (the father, grandmother, and fiancée of the brutal son as well as Japanese liberals who are killed by the military), they are overshadowed by the more powerful scenes of killing, torture, and rape.

It is significant that the story, which explains Taro's irrational development into a murdering imperialist, is presented essentially in noir style with the father narrating throughout. Resembling the male victim who recalls his seduction and how he is lured in by the erotic exoticism of the femme fatale or spider woman, the father can only belatedly explain what happened to his son. And like the male tale of noir, it begins with greed, desire, narcissism, and vanity. It is not unusual for war films to use the noir style and reveal, like the femme fatale herself, a crisis in male domination. In noir films, strong males such as Humphrey Bogart characters (*The Maltese Falcon, The Big Sleep*) eventually put the femme fatale in her place. The spider woman consumes unlucky weaker male leads in *Double Indemnity, The Postman Always Rings Twice,* and *Sunset Boulevard.* A spy film such as John Huston's *Across the Pacific* (1942) similarly upholds male dominance and shifts the violence toward mostly other male agents such as Dr. Lorenz, who conspires with the Japanese and has the help of an American Japanese collaborator Joe Totsuiko (Victor Sen Yung). This A film starring Bogart does not shy away from controversial incriminating plots, which suggest possible American Japanese collaboration in the attack on Pearl Harbor and in a rare departure from Bogart's screen persona shows him mocking and patronizing the faulty English of the Japanese staff on the ship, thus slipping into the B genre.

The crisis of masculinity articulated in *Rising Sun* is compounded by the role of race as given in the yellowfacing of its three lead stars: the father, the son, and his fiancée. Revealing at once a masculine and racial crisis, yellowface becomes an attempt to master and dominate a threatening rival race. The practice of yellowface, the theatrical embodiment of the Asian Other, does not strive to give a close semblance of the enemy but is meant instead to manage this feared Other through the defensive strategy of identification and distortion. Makeup and appearance of the white actor in yellowface are deliberately improbable and grotesque to bring the enemy at once into closer contact with the American and ridicule him by making him appear merely as a diminished form of the American. Edward Said has discussed how Orientalism describes not the actual Orient but the Western imagination of the Orient, revealing finally a distorted version of the West itself. In yellowface, similarly, white Western physiognomy remains the norm and allows Asian features its expression only through the face of the West. As in noir films with its prolonged POV narrative, the spectator forms a sympathetic alliance with the father (particularly since he condemns Japan and his son at film's end); however, the tale itself occurs in the past with the crime already committed. The noir narration in the end disqualifies any kind of redemption for the Japanese, placing them beyond immediate reform. When the father commits ritual suicide at the end of his tale, the viewer understands that this act is the logical conclusion of a

FIGURE 19. Edward Dmytryk's B film *Behind the Rising Sun* (1943) sensationalizes the battle between East and West in a boxing match with an oversized Japanese fighter played in yellowface.

culture gone astray. In *Rising Sun*, off-screen but highly suggestive scenes of torture, rape, and murder add to the lurid and sensational treatment of Imperial Japan. Of interest here is the outlandish and memorable fight scene, a battle between two men representing the East and West, in which a gigantic Japanese judo/karate wrestler (played by Mike Mazurki in yellowface) competes against a slim and trim white American boxer (see Figure 19). The fantastic contest is a pure spectacle of strength and masculinity that cannot be taken seriously but presents itself simultaneously as a cathartic outlet for violence.

An ambitious B film that also uses A-film and OWI rhetoric, *Rising Sun* is strangely enough even more racist than the traditional B film. To be sure, audiences understand the conventions of B films as part of a populist, cathartic rhetoric based on passion and emotion rather than objective fact. The absurd plot and the grotesque representation of the enemy, not to mention low budgets, bad acting, and short deadlines are essential stylistic elements of the B film, which promises the masses titillation and a space to vent their hatred of the enemy and bond with fellow Americans. The traditional war B film does not disguise itself as anything more than a crude propaganda film. On the other hand, World War II A films, which grow out of reportage and documentary, tend to present their narratives as objective, historically truthful, and morally just. In addition, OWI guidelines force the repression of actual facts that damage America's claim to democracy. How does one, for instance, match up the liberal rhetoric of the OWI with the fact of Japanese American internment? Dmytryk's film, due to its use of B-film conventions, also does away with the positive elements of A film, namely the utopian envisioning of a radically democratic and multicultural America. In the end, *Rising Sun* puts forth only the negative aspects of both B- and A-film rhetoric.

In his A film *Back to Bataan* (1945), Dmytryk moves away from yellowfacing, instead using Anthony Quinn as the Filipino lead (Quinn's dark good looks were often used in Hollywood for the all-purpose ethnic, e.g., Chief Crazy Horse in *They Died with Their Boots On*, 1941; a Mexican American soldier in *Guadalcanal Diary*, 1943; a Spanish captain in the Spanish Civil War in *The Last Train from Madrid*, 1937). According to the *Los Angeles Daily News*, John Wayne insisted that his character Madden should play a secondary role to the Filipino lead. A Filipino actor, Alex Havier, was also used, playing a Filipino sergeant under Wayne's command, but he appears feminine and diminished in the presence of Wayne. Furthermore, he is associated with an American hobo whom he befriends in the course of the film as they together dream of riding boxcars, paying no fare, throughout the United States. Thus, while the film steers clear of yellowface, it still engages in Hollywood's practice of substituting ethnic actors with white actors and relegating ethnic actors to the function of a scenic backdrop.

First Yank into Tokyo (1945), directed by Gordon Douglas,[108] is a traditional B film that legitimates the dropping of atom bombs on Hiroshima and Nagasaki, with Tom Neal appearing once again in yellowface. In *First Yank* he is a handsome, white, all-American college football hero partially raised in Tokyo and thoroughly fluent in Japanese culture and language. Now a major in the US Army, he volunteers for a top-secret mission in which he must undergo irreversible plastic surgery to appear Japanese. His mission is to infiltrate a POW camp in Japan and obtain the formula of the atom bomb from one of America's top scientists held unknowingly by the Japanese, who believe him to be a refrigerator engineer. Neal's character volunteers for this sacrificial mission since he believes his fiancée, a head nurse stationed in Bataan, is dead. When he enters the camp disguised as a low-ranking Japanese soldier, he discovers not only that his fiancée is still alive but also that his old college roommate, a brilliant and brutal Japanese imperialist (Richard Loo), is running the camp. Moreover, this same ex-roommate has been making dangerous advances on his fiancée. Also important to the plot is the Korean ally Haan-Soo (Keye Luke), who parallels the Neal character and is disguised as a black-market Korean errand boy in order to subvert the Japanese and aid the Americans.

Complementing the outrageous and improbable storyline are the poor acting skills of Tom Neal, compounded by his grotesque yellowface makeup. Yellowfacing

FIGURE 20. The B film *First Yank into Tokyo* (1945) narrates the story of US spy Steve Ross undergoing irreversible plastic surgery (Tom Neal in yellowface) and sacrificing his love for nurse Drake (Barbara Hale).

in this more traditional B film unambiguously articulates hatred of the detested "Japs," reflecting the deep, unrepentant racism of America. The hero's facial surgery is irreversible, and he knows that his fiancée will never be able to love or marry him with his Asian facial features (see Figure 20). As such, the yellowfacing reveals the deep fear of contamination resulting from America's World War II campaign in the Far East. The fact that the film's hero, Major Steve Ross, cannot return from Japan and must sacrifice himself exposes the fear that America has forever been changed by its contact with Japan. Steve has been contaminated not merely by the surgery but by his early stay in Japan and by his Japanese college roommate, who later becomes the ruthless Japanese military leader responsible for kidnapping the scientist and his fiancée. The film's final image, an atomic explosion, using actual newsreel images of Japan's bombing, can thus be seen as an attempt to annihilate this unwanted relationship as well as stave off the outside world encroaching upon America.

At the same time, however, this form of Orientalism is juxtaposed against the representation of the Korean ally, Haan-Soo, who proves to be as brave and determined as the American hero. *First Yank* thus displays the double-sided and contradictory aspects of mimicry. Not only does the Korean character speak for himself (the role is not performed in yellowface), he is given significant screen time and gains in comparison to the American hero. Indeed, it is difficult to identify with Neal's character as a Japanese soldier due to his sheer inability to act. Conversely, the Korean Haan-Soo, played by actor Keye Luke, a Chinese American born in Canton and raised in Seattle, steals every scene in which he is present.[109] Similarly, in *First Yank*, the acting by the well-known and celebrated Asian American stars Richard Loo, Leonard Strong, and Benson Fong, who play glowering and villainous Japanese officers, further foregrounds the weakness of Neal's character. In particular, Richard Loo's Colonel Okanura, the college roommate turned rival lover, dominates the film in much the same manner as the femme fatale. Certainly depicting a stereotype, Colonel Okanura nevertheless holds the fascination of the spectator throughout the film and, as with the femme fatale, even death cannot diminish his vitality and power.

Michael Rogin has discussed how blackface in films such as *The Jazz Singer* plays a seminal role in defining whiteness and nationality. Yellowface performs a similar racial drama, allowing for the management and assimilation of the threatening Asian Other. At the same time, practices of mimicry, as Rogin has suggested, can be qualified through various conventions of film and acting. In the case of Al Jolson, the audience realizes that the portrayal is at once questionable and sympathetic. In *First Yank*, a similar balance is achieved between the Korean ally and the Japanese villains who counteract each other as well as the yellowfacing of the lead character. In addition, yellowfacing is partially neutralized through the convention of the villain itself, which is understood not in realistic but in fictive terms of the stereotype. In spite of their crude and grotesque representations, B films display a more realistic sense of race relations and performance, an absent component in A films' ideal utopia. It could be argued that more thoughtful war films should bring together the best of A- and B-film rhetoric, namely the ideals of a multicultural democracy balanced by more realistic depictions of race relations. And indeed, films of this sort become popular during the postwar period as seen in MGM's *Go for Broke!*, directed by Robert Pirosh (1951), Sam Fuller's *The Steel Helmet* (1951), and Mark Robson's *Home of the Brave* (1949).

As the visceral expression of a mass mentality, the World War II B film radically levels such ethical and lofty national ideals as set forth in A films such as *Bataan*, *Guadalcanal Diary*, and *Thirty Seconds over Tokyo*. With its emphasis on mass consumption, cheap entertainment, and surface-level expression, B film is the paradigmatic model for what Siegfried Kracauer calls the mass ornament with its aesthetics of distraction. Like the gaudy and ornate movie palaces of the early twentieth century that stimulate the senses "with such rapidity that there is no room left . . . for even the slightest contemplation,"[110] B film bombards viewers with clichéd plots, bad acting, sensational content, and outlandish and blatantly racist impersonations of ethnic and enemy Others. However, its one redeeming and most significant feature is that it radically challenges A film's paternalizing claims of cultural intervention as well as its unrealistic emancipatory vision. Kracauer states that the mass ornament with its "emphasis on the external has the advantage of being sincere."[111] In short, the mass ornament does not lie or adumbrate a given historical situation but simply reflects it in unmediated and crude fashion. "It is not externality," argues Kracauer, "that poses a threat to truth. Truth is only threatened by the naïve affirmation of cultural values that have become unreal."[112] In this context, B film exposes the real, if vulgar, underlying racial fears of American democracy. And if, as Kracauer claims, the mass ornament is an antidote to bourgeois fantasies, B film can be construed as the remedy to the A film's self-congratulatory liberal fantasies of a postracial and classless society.

In the A-list war film, mimicry is associated particularly with racial and ethnic minorities who assimilate to or mimic the dominant culture, hoping to gain acceptance and the promised accompanying rewards (i.e., social mobility, financial gain, middle-class compensations such as respectability). Films such as *Bataan* heavily promote this perspective in their depiction of the multicultural combat team, working for the common good of the nation. However, in the B film, the farcical mimicry of yellowface articulates the absolute inability of the Asian Other to assimilate. Yellowface thus mocks not simply the Asian Other but most significantly assimilationist and national rhetoric. It exposes the farce as farce in its abandonment of any serious national pretext, undermining official political and national agendas of benevolent intervention with their usual empty promises extended to minorities. Yellowface instead reveals the nation's desire to remain stubbornly provincial and shamelessly shallow, exposing selfish doubts and suspicion toward government authority demanding sacrifice for the sake of the elusive ideals of democracy and global power. The point of the argument here is not to revel in or enjoy the symptomatic racism of yellowface and mimicry but to show that A- and B-list film need to be placed in critical dialogue with one another. In doing so, we can begin to appreciate properly *Bataan*'s utopian image of a multicultural combat team as a yet-to-be-fulfilled historical project, a visual and historical ideal of national narration found in so many of the Pacific war films that the OWI approved.

3 ✿ POSTWAR HAWAII AND THE BIRTH OF THE MILITARY- INDUSTRIAL COMPLEX

The post–World War II era of Hawaii radically transforms the two dominant film genres with which Hollywood had approached Hawaii's annexed and incorporated islands during the first half the twentieth century, namely the South Seas fantasy film and the classic World War II combat film. The South Seas genre, with its white Christian missionary and colonial fantasies, legitimated the annexation of Hawaii under America's Manifest Destiny that made Hawaii subject to aggressive American economic expansion, development, and Christianization. As Emily S. Rosenberg comments on the early era of American expansionism, "At home, 'undercivilized' peoples were made to conform to Anglo-Saxon standards by many means, ranging from violence to educational persuasion. So, in dealing with foreigners, some believed that 'backward nations' could be brought into civilization only by means of force, while others sought to conquer the world peacefully, armed with sewing machines, Bibles, schools, or insights from the new social sciences. Whether the government would promote expansion by brutal domination or peaceful reform (or a mixture of the two) presented a tactical question within a broader consensus that accepted the necessity and ultimate benevolence of American expansion."[1] As a global economic and cultural institution, Hollywood played a significant role in asserting both American expansionism abroad and Anglo conformity at home. As the patriotic site for launching war propaganda films against Japanese imperial expansion in the Pacific, World War II Hawaii once again found itself deeply intertwined in the geopolitical interests of Hollywood's and America's cultural industry. In various

World War II films, Hawaii represented a new democratic multicultural society in Hollywood's imaginary, one that was held morally superior to mono-ethnic totalitarian nations such as Japan or Germany. This appropriation of Hawaii's multicultural landscape allowed the United States to promote a more unified national outlook in a time of war and also assert its own geopolitical claims in the embattled Pacific.

In the postwar era, the two genres of South Sea and multicultural combat film are updated in order to accommodate America's new role as a world leader. While some traditional South Seas films are still produced after 1945, their impact becomes less visible in an America that returns to its peacetime economic ambitions and wishes to maintain in many ways its prewar insular, white, racial and ethnic status quo in a changed postwar context. Instead, musicals set in exotic faraway Pacific locations, such as *The King and I* (1956), *South Pacific* (1958), and *Flower Drum Song* (1961), and romantic interracial melodramas, such as *The Teahouse of the August Moon* (1956), *Sayonara* (1957), and *The World of Suzie Wong* (1960), come to the fore. These Pacific film musicals usher in a new stage in which America seeks to expand its new global role in the Pacific Rim with films highlighting its newfound cosmopolitanism to audiences around the world. The work of nation building is transferred from its internal consolidation of territories and borders to a new level in which foreign diplomacy and military assertion of global American interests take center stage. As Christina Klein notes, the United States enters a new stage of Cold War Orientalism: "The global imaginary of containment offered a heroic model of education: it imagined the Cold War as a crusade against communism and invited the American people to join in. . . . The State Department's 'education for overseasmanship' encouraged Americans to 'look outward.' Directed to the world beyond the nation's borders, it represented the Cold War as an opportunity to forge intellectual and emotional bonds with the people of Asia and Africa."[2] In this changed geopolitical landscape, China, America's former ally, now turns into a communist foe whereas Japan emerges as the new partner. In addition to its overseas film exports, the State Department also organized music tours featuring African American jazz, mobilizing the cultural heritage of a minority still oppressed at home in order to highlight unique American cultural innovation abroad.[3]

The World War II multicultural combat films that represented a progressive American nationhood to global and domestic audiences are now frequently scaled back in their multicultural casting. Popular combat films such as *Sands of Iwo Jima* (1949), *Flying Leathernecks* (1951), *Force of Arms* (1951), *From Here to Eternity* (1953), *The Caine Mutiny* (1954), *Battle Cry* (1955), and *Bitter Victory* (1957) no longer represent the multicultural spectrum of the nation, featuring instead white mainstream protagonists. Apart from this regressive reconfiguration of the combat genre, the war film genre does not witness a significant decline in audience interest, as was the case with South Seas dramas. As Lary May observes, "previously combat films had declined in times of peace; the postwar films, including *Sands of Iwo Jima* (1949), *From Here to Eternity* (1953), and *Battle Cry* (1955), hearkened back to the 'good war' as a symbol of unity against a savage enemy."[4]

What initially looked like a return to peace and domestic affairs drawing down on the activity of war, escalated in fact to a new and more vigorous global assertion of power that requires the constant aid of newly emerging military technology. As May points out, "With the country still in a condition of war and the demand for unity informing politics, when conflict or problems arose the preferred solution was not through negotiation or compromise."[5] At the forefront of this new development stands the military-industrial complex, the effort to maintain military dominance and vigilance during peacetime. In his famous farewell speech from political office on January 17, 1961, President Dwight D. Eisenhower for the first time articulated his anxieties over an uncurbed military-industrial complex that he had seen being born during World War II as the supreme allied commander in the European war theater and had helped enlarge in the postwar era:

> This conjunction of an immense military establishment and a large arms industry is new in the American experience. The total influence—economic, political, even spiritual—is felt in every city, every State house, every office of the Federal government. We recognize the imperative need for this development. Yet we must not fail to comprehend its grave implications. Our toil, resources and livelihood are all involved; so is the very structure of our society. In the councils of government, we must guard against the acquisition of unwarranted influence, whether sought or unsought, by the military industrial complex. The potential for the disastrous rise of misplaced power exists and will persist.[6]

Eisenhower fears that the interests of the military complex will eventually pervert the nation's peaceful ambitions into one of a perpetual war economy facilitated by powerful lobbies of industrial branches that benefit from military contracts.

The beginning of the Cold War accelerates this development of remilitarization, since the United States now sees itself even more under the threat of a nuclear-armed Soviet Union with missile capabilities that can reach its continent within thirty minutes. Hollywood was quick to seize this opportunity and produced films that would agree with this new militant spirit. Indeed, according to May the postwar era witnesses an unusual expansion in violent and conflict oriented genres: "The rise of war films, westerns, and biblical epics corresponded to an unprecedented increase in films where violence provided the means to resolve central problems. . . . Formerly films that utilized violence to resolve problems predominated only in time of war."[7] Hollywood war film now has to accomplish the triple task of depicting past heroic battles, mourning its lost soldiers from World War II, and reasserting renewed military readiness in the face of potential conflicts. The transition from wartime to peacetime America thereby becomes blurred in many of these new war films. Films such as *From Here to Eternity* (Fred Zinnemann, 1953) reflect this disorientation and America's failed attempt to settle properly into a peacetime society. With the communist scare, peacetime takes on an even more paranoid dimension in *The Manchurian Candidate* (John Frankenheimer, 1962), a film that depicts the 1950s McCarthy era and the Korean War in hyperbolic terms. Both films deal with the Pacific, producing new and extreme variations of American Orientalism.

This chapter begins by looking at the prolonged arm of the military in American postwar cinema and the significance of Hawaii in the development of the military-industrial complex. Hawaii also repositions itself in the postwar era from a former agricultural industry into a modern mass tourist and service industry. While this economic development creates more prosperity and opportunity, leaving the South Seas plantation culture behind, it nevertheless allows structurally for only minor shifts in the redistribution of wealth held firmly by the white elites and the Big Five. A film like *Blue Hawaii* (Norman Taurog, 1961), as will be shown, still maintains the new state's subservient role, displaying the new configuration in which military and economic expansionist ambitions are hidden beneath the seemingly harmless surface structures of leisure and tourist culture. Crucial to the aesthetics of postwar film is the time image as defined by Gilles Deleuze.[8] Postwar film will feature the time image as a brake to the action image of combat film, shifting its focus instead on contemplative and morbid visions of war accompanied by death and meaninglessness. Fred Zinnemann's *From Here to Eternity* (1953) offers the most articulate version of the time image and its accompanying skepticism. Otto Preminger's *In Harm's Way* (1965) will eventually domesticate the time image and move it into the temporal zone of leisure culture with its playful aimlessness and hedonism. As such, the film alerts us that the battlefield in the postwar era comes in many new forms and cannot be restricted to the traditional boundaries separating private and public affairs, wartime and peacetime. The time image encodes the reality of the military-industrial complex, the perpetual war, in which peacetime is simply a state of military alertness for the next conflict. Hollywood will soften this image and serve it up in a leisure, romance, and entertainment format that is nevertheless deeply intertwined with military affairs.

FROM HERE TO ETERNITY: TIME, NATION, AND WAR

The action image of the fighting soldier changes in post–World War II films. According to Deleuze, World War II marks a paradigm shift in the cinema caused by a crisis in the action image, resulting in the time image coming to the fore. In postwar cinema, particularly in a war-ravaged Europe and Japan, movement and action become disconnected, resulting in the time image. Protagonists no longer act but become spectators to a world independent of them as seen in the characters of Italian neorealist films who sleepwalk through the narrative or in Yasuhiro Ozu's aloof static camera and its depiction of banal everyday events and conversations. The genre of traditional realism, as Deleuze explains, formerly bound to the "sensory-motor situations of the action-image," now enters a "purely optical space" in which the connection to reality is radically redefined: "The situation is not extended directly into action: it is no longer sensory-motor, as in realism, but primarily optical and of sound, invested by the senses, before action takes shape in it, and use or confronts its elements. Everything remains real in this neo-realism (whether it is film set or exteriors) but, between the reality of the setting and that of action, it is no longer a motor extension which is established, but rather a dreamlike connection through the intermediary of the liberated sense organs. It is as if the action floats in the situation, rather than bringing it to a conclusion or strengthening it."[9] While postwar combat films generally remain within the boundaries of the movement image, they do become contaminated with the style of new postwar realisms built on the time image. New elements such as retrospection and elegiac mood significantly slow down the action image and depict war, showing not so much the action of the battlefield, but loss and destruction. In short, war becomes more reflective and contemplative.

As Deleuze argues, the movement image, associated strongly with Hollywood's system of classical continuity editing with its rational structure and simultaneous occurrence of action and perception, dominates the first half of the twentieth century. The question here is how the action genre of war film fares in the second half of the twentieth century and the early twenty-first, which is dominated by a crisis of the action image in which action and reaction are unhinged, leading to the collapse of traditional sensory-motor situations. This venturing beyond the movement image into pure optic and sonic signs reflects above all the inability to comprehend and act upon the destruction of World War II. The distinctions between subjective and objective as well as past, present, and future begin to blur, resulting in the conversion of clearly marked spaces into fragmentary and dispersive time images: "A purely optical and sound situation does not extend into action, any more than it is induced by an action. It makes us grasp, it is supposed to make us grasp, something intolerable and unbearable. Not a brutality as nervous aggression, an exaggerated violence that can always be extracted from the sensory-motor relations in the action-image. Nor is it a matter of scenes of terror, although there are some-times corpses and blood. It is a matter of something too powerful, or too unjust, but sometimes also too beautiful, and which henceforth outstrips our sensory-motor capacities."[10] Deleuze describes the time image accordingly in its traumatic impact of war upon subjectivity and agency, exceeding its comprehensibility and rationality. For Deleuze, the time image reflects the radical doubt as expressed in European avant-garde cinema with its absence of clearly defined social agents or Japanese art house film (particularly Ozu) with its use of idle time and silence and lack of decisive action.[11] With its traditional action-centered image associated with imperialism and national ideology, American war films would appear to stand polar opposite to Deleuze's time image. Yet American war films since World War II, while still retaining a strong action image, have nevertheless been contaminated by the time image. As such, they provide the much-needed place, however tentative, within which to address and critically analyze the pure optic sign and its function as a temporal sign of irony and doubt.

In postwar combat films, action becomes decidedly more complex and dif-fused, transforming the image of war from the present activity of combat at a moment of extreme national crisis into an extended activity of and reflection on nation building that impacts upon the extended time of the nation and actively expresses its history and destiny. Whereas the wartime image of the soldier repre-sents an indivisible unity, the postwar movement image becomes discernible in its separate components of action, affection, and perception. Steven Spielberg's *Sav-ing Private Ryan* (1998), which returns to Benedict Anderson's question of patrio-tism and self-sacrifice, is an excellent example of how the postwar combat image has become contaminated by the time image, expressing a critical image of war that challenges the film's own lapses into sentimental representations of patriotism. Liquid and gaseous perception images in the battle scenes (particularly the notori-ous Omaha Beach sequence) are used not in association with the typical percep-tion of national enemies or allies but to perceive our own men under fire. Likewise, the close-up, associated with the affection image, is prominently used in combat scenes typically rendered in medium shots that capture the body in movement. This deliberate use of the close-up to depict action obstructs perception of the bat-tlefield as a whole, disorienting the spectator and emphasizing the soldier's frailty in the face of the enemy. The pure optical and sound images result in a simultane-ous inhibition and expansion of movement and a breaking down of action in time, articulating not the usual heroics but the pain and physical damage endured by the soldier's body. In short, the crisis of the action image in *Saving Private Ryan* reveals the profound powerlessness of the soldier in war, questioning the moral status of a nation that requires such a sacrifice.

Leading up to his grand achievement *From Here to Eternity*, which was awarded eight Oscars, Austrian exile director Fred Zinnemann similarly experimented with the time image in early postwar films such as *Act of Violence* (1948) and *The Men* (1950) and also in his famous Western *High Noon* (1952). The noir drama *Act of Violence* depicts former POW Joe Parkson (Robert Ryan) bent on avenging the deaths of his comrades in a Nazi prison camp. His CO, Frank Henley, as it turns out, informed the Nazis about a planned prison break with guarantees that his men would be spared punishment. The cynical Nazi officers trap and mortally maim the American soldiers with bayonets as they exit the tunnel, leaving them for dead. The sole survivor is Parkson, who walks away alive but with a recognizable limp, like a monstrous creation of war haunting the perpetrator of this crime in the postwar era. Henley is seemingly successful in the postwar building industry until he and his family are revisited by his nemesis Parkson. In order to protect his family, Henley is forced to abandon them, take shelter with a prostitute, hire a hit man under the influence of alcohol, and eventually sacrifice his life in order to prevent the planned assassination of Parkson and thereby reestablish military honor. He is given a second chance to revisit his betrayal, transforming it into a belated heroic death in atonement for the ten soldiers who lost their lives due to his actions.

Most of the film is shot in the noir setting of empty and abandoned streets of Los Angeles with Henley desperately trying to face up to his betrayal of his men. In one dreamlike and hallucinatory scene, Henley walks through an empty street tunnel, revisiting the tunnel of his desperate soldiers whom he had betrayed. The hiring of a hit man to resolve his dilemma also appears as rather nondecisive and takes place under the influence of alcohol in which career criminals push this option upon him. The film's settings are mostly psychological in nature, giving us an equivalent of Henley's state of mind as he flees through a maze of urban settings to avoid both his avenger and his own slow admission that self-interest had motivated his dubious deal with the Nazis. The film turns the action image of war upside down, converting it into a time image of endless torment, guilt, and regret. The successful transition from wartime into a postwar middle-class life—Henley is married and has one child—proves to be an illusion after all as war returns and finally engulfs the fearful commander in a belated heroic death. The noir genre, with its emphasis on corruption and disillusion, is a fitting expression for portraying the posttraumatic fallout of World War II with its mass casualties and unspeakable atrocities. In this respect, the film also forever closes off a return to a prewar and peacetime America, which can no longer be recovered in a dark, paralyzing, and traumatic postwar era.

John Auer's *Hell's Half Acre* (1954), a B-film noir drama set in Honolulu, similarly reflects the traumatic impact of war, as its hero, Chet Chester (Wendell Corey), abandons his former identity as a sailor who survives the attack on Pearl Harbor, declares himself dead, and descends into a life of crime. Keye Luke and Philip Ahn, formerly associated with the Charlie Chan franchise, feature prominently as chief of Honolulu's police and the film's main villain, respectively. When

Chester's wife visits from the mainland, he initially feigns amnesia but eventually leaves all his money to his son and sacrifices his life for the capture of Roger King (Ahn), his former partner in crime sought for multiple murders. Chester eventually dies the belated heroic death he missed when he survived the deadly attack on the battleship *Arizona*. The film's impressive noir cinematography takes viewers through Honolulu's infamous side of Chinatown, known as hell's half acre, and visually erects a maze of staircases, backdoors, and seedy establishments to convey the dead-end atmosphere of the postwar soldier, stuck in the city's time loop. The film also echoes Orientalist conventions of Chinatown noirs such as featured in Orson Welles's *The Lady from Shanghai* (1947) and Josef von Sternberg's *Macao* (1952) and *The Shanghai Gesture* (1941).

Zinnemann's *The Men* (1950), which features a young Marlon Brando in the lead role of a soldier having sustained a spinal injury, foregrounds postwar paralysis literally in a film set in a veteran's hospital housing paraplegic patients. A ward of soldiers in wheelchairs shows us an immobilized society stuck in the temporal loop of war. Although the film produces a predictable happy ending with the marriage of Ken (Brando) to his prewar fiancée Ellen (Theresa Wright), other members of the ward are not warranted this opportunity and remain trapped. Endless conversations among the patients, a constant focus on the ward, and tedious routines of physical rehabilitation once again create a claustrophobic time image in which no movement appears possible. This film finds echoes in Hitchcock's *Rear Window* (1954), where the photographer L. B. Jefferies, who had covered the war in the Pacific, ends up feeling trapped in an impending marriage and remains stuck in a wheelchair with two broken legs by the film's end. In Hitchcock's version of postwar paralysis, the hero has become an emasculated passive photographer and spectator yearning for the bygone days in which he rode in a jeep and wore combat boots. The postwar normalization in which women like Lisa (Grace Kelly) have forcefully entered the professional world appears to have no use for this last-frontiers generation. This changed context also becomes apparent in Zinnemann's Western *High Noon* (1952) where the pacifist Quaker wife Amy Kane (Grace Kelly) comes to the rescue of her aged and semiretired husband, helping him win the final duel in the film.

Zinnemann's *From Here to Eternity* (*FHTE*) complicates the time image of the war by adding several layers to a film that cannot be easily placed in a genre (noir, social problem, Western), as his three preceding films can. For one, the film does not address solely the individual fates of soldiers but also scrutinizes critically the entire institution of the military. In addition, by shooting on location at Honolulu's Schofield Barracks and depicting the time leading up to the attack on Pearl Harbor, Zinnemann sets the film at a time of national crisis akin to John Ford's *December 7th* documentary images of the Aloha Tower in the hours and minutes preceding the Pearl Harbor attack. However, as a World War II combat film made in the postwar era, *FHTE* departs from the agenda of typical World War II films and their messages of uplift, camaraderie, and political propaganda. Based on James Jones's 1951 best-selling novel and its scathing critique of the US Army, the film from the start proved difficult to produce in accordance with Hollywood's Hays Code, as the novel notoriously featured military corruption, violence, prostitution, sexually transmitted diseases, alcoholism, miscegenation, adultery, suicide, homosexuality, racism, homophobia, and murder as the established backdrop of the military subculture in prewar Hawaii.

Both Warner Brothers and Twentieth Century Fox showed a keen interest in producing *FHTE*, turning it down eventually due to the impossibility of retaining any of the novel's original intent and the Army's refusal to endorse the film. Columbia's president Harry Cohn eventually bought the rights and hired Jones himself to write the script. Unable to meet the task—"Jones explained that he could never lick the problem of how to have whore houses without having whore houses"[12]—Jones was replaced by Daniel Taradash, who turned the brothels into social clubs, tied together the novel's various subplots, and, with numerous rewrites and revisions, secured initial Army cooperation. Fred Zinnemann was hired to direct the film and he insisted, upon threat of quitting, that Army collaboration was essential to make the film realistic. Alterations and compromises were made so that Zinnemann was given access to film on location at Schofield Barracks and permission to employ soldiers as extras and use military consultants, dress, and equipment (guns and planes).[13]

Set in the months just prior to December 7, 1941, *FHTE* depicts the deadening monotony of the army during the prewar peacetime period with its aimless routine exercises (marching in circles, bugling) and leisure distractions (boxing competitions, billiards, drinking, social clubs/brothels, and women). When war finally arrives on that fateful Sunday morning at the film's close, it feels like a breath of fresh air cleaning out a rotten and stagnant environment and bringing a sense of national purpose to an absolutely lost and corrupt society. This society is depicted as exclusively white, and its mono-ethnic makeup stands in stark contrast to that of the novel, with its diverse ethnic characters such as the gay Jew Bloom, the Hawaiian Jimmy Kaliponi, the Native American Chief Choate, as well as Prewitt's local and mixed Asian Hawaiian girlfriend Violet Ogure. In addition, conversations in the novel frequently turn to cultural and racial prejudice and prompt Prewitt's defense of the "Negro" against such prejudicial remarks.[14] Though shot on location in Honolulu and other areas of Oahu, the film only occasionally depicts the island's local inhabitants, giving a false impression of Hawaii's racial and demographic makeup in which nonwhites outnumber whites by a three to one ratio. As Bailey and Farber note, Hawaii "is not a neutral environment" in terms of landscape, culture, and race. Hawaii, they argue, challenges the racialized, provincial outlook of white mainstream citizens of pre–civil rights America, shocking especially "white men [who] were suddenly made to feel that they were ones who were different": "Hawaii's population was a mixture of racial and ethnic groups unlike anywhere else in the U.S. In Hawaii, white Americans were not in the majority, and though racial and ethnic hierarchies undeniably existed, they differed from those on the mainland. In Hawaii, 'whiteness' was the not the natural condition. . . . Such a reversal of 'normality' was all the more disconcerting because it took place in what was, after all, America."[15] During Hawaii's bids for statehood in 1947, reservations about ethnic makeup led to rejection with a fear that its new members of Congress would advocate desegregation.

Whereas combat films made during the war stressed the multicultural makeup of American society to rally all members of the nation to do their patriotic duty and represent democracy, such diverse ethnic images quickly disappeared in postwar war films. A prewar romantic melodrama such as *Waikiki Wedding* (1937), with its own problematic depictions of Hawaiian native culture, could nevertheless depict realistic images of an Asian workforce, in particular an Asian secretary filmed in medium close-up during a phone conversation, speaking Standard English and dressed in the American norms for office workers. No such prominent realistic images can be found in *FHTE*, where brief excursions into Honolulu's Chinatown feature instead close-up images of two archaic-looking Chinese men dressed in traditional silk Chinese outfits, form-fitted garments with Mandarin collars, the *changshan*, and rounded black hats. These dated images of Honolulu's Chinese remind one more of the railroad workers of the pioneer era, also reminiscent of the Western genre, and are completely at odds with Honolulu's modern Western-styled Asian community. Elsewhere in the film a few natives are shown, mostly in the background, and sometimes incorrectly wearing aloha shirts, which were donned mostly by tourists and whites and became popular among locals only in the postwar period. Similarly, all other ethnic groups featured in combat films such as Jews, Hispanics, Filipinos, and African Americans (cf. *Bataan*) are now eclipsed and replaced by white ethnics. White soldiers now sing African American blues as they intone the "Re-enlistment Blues." Ethnic friction, if at all, is now mostly depicted among ethnic whites, between the sadistic Sergeant Judson (Ernest Borgnine) and Private Angelo Maggio (Frank Sinatra), and possibly between Sergeant Galovitch and Private Prewitt (Montgomery Clift).

Ironically, the film's radical deracialization of Hawaii resonated extremely well with mainstream audiences on the continent and possibly helped rally more support for Hawaii's renewed bid for statehood launched in 1954 with a signature campaign. This deracialization is accomplished via the popular tourist aloha shirt (see Figure 21), which stands in for the bleached-out identity of Hawaii, allowing white Americans a quasi-native position in the film and making Hawaii appear as a natural extension of the United States. Created in the early 1930s, the aloha shirt was especially popular among the American tourists and the upper classes, among whom it was associated with resort wear and leisure: "The major buyers of aloha shirts were tourists in Hawai'i (and eventually, in the prewar years, consumers on the U.S. mainland). Due to economic conditions, Hawai'i residents were focused on their need for work clothing: Hawai'i was still a plantation economy, with the bulk of the population primarily in the lower classes; only the upper classes could afford (or had the need for) clothing for leisure activities."[16] The shirt was made popular only in the immediate postwar era among local Hawaiian residents who were encouraged by various city resolutions pushed by the Honolulu Chamber of Commerce to wear aloha shirts to work during the hot summer months in order to benefit tourism and the Hawaiian fashion industry selling aloha attire, which included aloha shirts, *muumuus*, and resort wear. This promotion of aloha attire to benefit the garment and tourist industries was promoted throughout the postwar period with the institution of Aloha Week, Lei Day, and Aloha Fridays (the precursor to casual Friday), meeting the postwar craze of all things Hawaiian.[17] As DeSoto Brown and Linda Arthur claim, films such as *Naked Paradise* (1957) and *She Gods of Shark Reef* (1958) and especially A-list films such as *Big Jim McLain* (1952) and *FHTE* "spread the awareness of Aloha Shirts."[18] The 1950s were especially important to this promotion of all things Hawaiian with mainland clothing manufacturers entering the competition, culminating in Hawaii's successfully becoming the fiftieth state in 1959.[19]

Throughout *FHTE*, the soldiers wear aloha shirts when off duty and visiting "social clubs" and bars (e.g., New Congress Club, Kalakaua Inn). As Brown and Arthur note, however, though set in 1941, the film's famously featured shirts, rayon aloha shirts, "didn't actually exist when World War II began."[20] Thematically, the leisurely aloha shirts conflict with the uniforms worn during active duty, highlighting an army without resolve and unprepared for war. This lack of readiness is made specifically clear in the final scene where Prewitt is killed in his aloha shirt as he is trying to make his way back to the barracks in the wake of the Pearl Harbor attack. In terms of US territorial claims on Hawaii, however, the film betrays no such weakness of resolve. During peacetime American troops leisurely make themselves at home and in the absence of a strong Hawaiian visual presence appear to be the natural inhabitants. Once the war begins, the mainland's claim to Hawaii intensifies even more so as the American human sacrifice during the Pearl Harbor attack gives the soldiers killed a status of heroic martyrdom. This status eventually transforms into that of the military being the legitimate protector of Hawaii's independence from an apparent threat of Japanese occupation. Unlike Jones's highly critical novel, the film ends on a quick and unlikely overhaul of the Army's internal corruption. The corrupt Captain Dana Holmes, who runs his company as a boxing and gambling outfit, is duly court-martialed and quickly replaced by a new and kinder officer who cares for the troops.

FIGURE 21. Montgomery Clift as Private Prewitt out of step with military culture, sporting a leisurely aloha shirt in the company of Donna Reed as Alma at a "social club" in Fred Zinnemann's *From Here to Eternity* (1953).

In the film, Jones's attempt to use the caesura event of Pearl Harbor as the culmination of a catastrophe that already intrinsically announced itself within the moral decay of the Army is now transformed into the opposite and becomes the great patriotic moment in which all questions and criticism must cease. The film's tautological affirmation of the US presence in Hawaii nevertheless also demands its full recognition as a genuine US state, albeit at the expense of an unacknowledged act of colonialism. Similarly, in the 1952 film *Big Jim McLain*, starring John Wayne as a House Un-American Activities Committee investigator tracking down a communist conspiracy on the Hawaiian Islands, all the conspirators prove to be white Americans. America's paranoid fears are extended to Hawaii and hence make it ironically a true American territory. In Jones's novel, conversely, Hawaii is treated with more political realism but will eventually forever remain that first strange place.

Whereas Jones resented the idea of Hawaii as an island paradise, postwar American films set in Hawaii begin increasingly to convert racial Orientalism, of which the viewer sees some residual images in *FHTE*, into a more benign form of leisure and tourist Orientalism. The saloon piano music harking back to the pioneer days of Western expansion accordingly conflicts with the slide guitar of Hawaiian music emanating from a modern jukebox. In one scene, Maggio almost comes to blows with Judson, who is reluctant to stop his piano music, drowning out the Hawaiian music and ambience. The white hostesses at the social club, a sanitized stand-in for Hawaii's wartime prostitutes, appear against bamboo backdrops and beach furniture and are a more acceptable substitute for local women or "shack jobs" as they're called in Jones's novel. In the film, the hostesses wear flowers in their hair, presenting the islands with all their sexual allures and promises. Here it is interesting to note that the film follows the realism of America's racially segregated society, which made it imperative that white prostitutes would for the most part service the military stationed in Hawaii. Ultimately, the film remains ambiguous in its conversion of Hawaii into a legitimate US territory, shrinking away from the larger implications of Hawaii's multiculturalism that could challenge the racial hierarchy on the mainland.

The film's complex finale, with its multiple scenes, namely Maggio's death, Prewitt playing "Taps" in his memory, then proceeding to kill Maggio's torturer and going AWOL, and his return to the base upon the attack on Pearl Harbor to do his patriotic duty, only to be killed by friendly fire, also complicates the time image as it returns erratically to the action image. The time image is given both in its leisurely prewar form with Prewitt's aloha shirt recalling aimless hedonism and in its darker existential form of death when Prewitt performs the elegiac "Taps." One could interpret the ending as the redemptive beginning of war that sweeps away corruption, indecision, and lack of perspective. John Ford's films often combine wartime victory with darker images of death and sacrifice, restoring from within them a redemptive dimension. However, something more is at stake in a society that needs war to balance itself. Prewitt's death is not one of sacrifice but rather is marked by revenge for the meaningless death of his friend Maggio, beaten to death in an army brig, and ultimately does not contribute to the war effort. Instead, one can argue that the film represents the inauguration of the military-industrial complex that blurs the boundaries between peacetime and wartime, civil life and soldier life. Correspondingly, the time image can be seen as doubled, as one is dealing not only with the now slowed down temporality of the action image as given in Deleuze's notion of the time image but also with the high speed of the surprise attack on Pearl Harbor. Both time images convey meaninglessness and annihilation, leaving the film on a dark and nonaffirmative ending.

Paul Virilio views this new accelerated temporality as particularly indicative of the Cold War in which nuclear missile capabilities have changed the battlefield from one of space into one of time. The accelerated stealth capability for military strikes seen in the Pearl Harbor surprise attack now demands a constant military alertness

148   HOLLYWOOD'S HAWAII

to avert nuclear disaster in a postwar era. *FHTE*, while looking backward to this inaugural event, also looks forward in its depiction of a nation perpetually at war, during both peacetime and open conflict. The military barracks—coincidentally the main setting in *FHTE*—are according to Virilio merely the army quarters for temporary hibernation always ready to be awakened:

> Different systems for fortifying the national perimeter are only switches in the war's movement. . . . That is why one so often speaks of forts and blockhouses as so many alarms warning the hibernator: he needs to pass harmlessly from one continuum to another. That is difficult. This was attested to in 1940, the *lightning war* surprised sleeping beauty; since then all of the evolution in modern arms aims at avoiding this *surprise* (with the ICBM missile, equipped with a thermonuclear warhead, waking up in a matter of a few minutes). That is when the rupture point is reached between the two times of the military apparatus. On the one hand, the constant sophistication of arms tends to eliminate any possibility that sleeping beauty sleeps—she has too many bad dreams and sleeps with an eye cocked for danger. On the other hand, the theoretical adversary refuses the dichotomy "wartime/peacetime," just as he will refute through subversion and terrorism the dichotomy "civil/military."[21]

In John Ford and Gregg Toland's *December 7th*, Uncle Sam has spent a restless night only to have his worst nightmares confirmed in the blitz attack on Pearl Harbor. Similarly, as Jeanine Basinger claims, combat films are born in World War II and generally lead from the life in the barracks to that of the battlefield. Military alertness acquired during the training imports the mentality of war into civil life and its daily routines. The military-industrial complex thus takes its origin in a changed time continuum between peace and war, the state of emergency that in Virilio's words forever hovers above the nation: "The violence of speed has become both the location and the law, the world's destiny and its destination."[22]

Zinnemann insisted upon cooperating with the military in order to be allowed to shoot on location at Honolulu's Schofield Barracks. In his view, this joint enterprise would lend greater realism to the film. Ironically, the film betrays no local realism and probably could have been shot on studio back lots and the beaches of California. The iconic kissing scene at the beach, for example, shows no distinct geography of Oahu. Similarly, all backdrops reflect no actual settings of Honolulu, in contrast to Ford's *December 7th* with its distinct sight-seeing depictions of Diamond Head, Waikiki Beach, the Pali mountain range, and the Aloha Tower. What type of realism, then, did Zinnemann have in mind? Just as in the war machine, the realism in Zinnemann's film has shifted from space to time. The Schofield Barracks are used in the sense of remembrance, the site of December 7, now preserved as a time image of the nation under attack. Additional features of Hawaii are simply given stereotypically as costume (aloha shirts), soundtrack (Hawaiian music), and setting (bars with a few colorful natives to indicate they are not at the center of this national drama, unlike the barracks). Hawaii is accordingly fully incorporated into the time image of the nation as differences of location, race, culture, and ethnicity fade into the background, subsumed by the military and later war.

The only other important location in *FHTE* is its profane counterpart, namely the social clubs or thinly disguised houses of prostitution. As alternate barracks, they re-create a domestic heterosexual environment, albeit in its debased form of mere consumption of alcohol and implied sex. These decadent leisurely activities also spill over into the military routine and result in drunken brawls and adultery on Hawaii's beaches. In contrast to Jones, Zinnemann knew full well that censorship would simply fuel the viewer's imagination, which had been trained since the 1930s with enforcement of the Hays Code that resulted in classical Hollywood's distinct but recognizable style of omission and understatement. What is perhaps more important, however, is why in a time of impending war and national crisis such "alternate barracks" needed to be included in the film at all, especially if one wanted to accommodate censorship codes. Concerning melodrama, one could have simply relied on the film's complex love story with its married officers. However, this normative domestic realm is instead strongly subverted by adultery and infertility (due to gonorrhea) and reconstituted in its profane variation of the "whorehouse." In doing so, Jones's novel intended to criticize and satirize the decadence of military culture. While the film similarly engages some of this harsh critique, it also aims beyond this goal in its depiction of obscenity and military culture. Obscenity, in this sense, is not a lapse in morality but constitutes the very life of the soldier. The soldier forfeits the stable life of the bourgeois family and reverts atavistically to a life of primal instincts, one in which gambling, fighting, killing, and frequenting "whores" take center stage.

Prewitt, with his delicate and sensitive aesthetic nature, proves to be the misfit who falls in love with the prostitute, excels in bugling, and forgoes his natural talent in boxing. He is tragically unfit for military culture and duly killed at the film's end in his aloha shirt, though not without being awakened first to the violence slumbering within him. The film thus erects a world in which warfare and brutal masculinity become the norm, while giving a limited critique of military violence relegated to past practices. As Zinnemann states in a retrospective interview, "At the time that we made *From Here to Eternity*, the Army was absolutely sacred because of Korea and the victory in WWII. So one would have thought that to make a picture like *From Here to Eternity*, which was critical of what went on inside the Army, and what it did to individuals, would not be possible."²³ Since the film, however, elevates the life of the bar-racks to an existential condition, the military no longer figures as the true cul-prit but simply reflects in its corrupt institution the imperfection of the human condition. Unlike films such as Francis Ford Coppola's *Apocalypse Now* (1979) and Stanley Kubrick's *Full Metal Jacket* (1987), where the psychotic nature of warfare and military culture is shockingly exposed in Colonel Kurtz (Marlon Brando) and Private Lawrence (Vincent D'Onofrio), *FHTE* shies away from such a critical moment by invoking the national crisis of Pearl Harbor. Hence in spite of its occasional transgressive aspects, the film met with only minor concerns by the military and in its critical and popular success (eight Academy Awards) contributed to the rise of the military-industrial complex in the 1950s.

Similarly, an equally popular film, *The Caine Mutiny* (Edward Dmytryk, 1954), exposes administrative mediocrity and incompetence in the military (personi-fied by Lieutenant Commander Queeg; Humphrey Bogart) only to launch into an apologetic tirade against the main mutineer Keefer, in which his own attor-ney Greenwald accuses him of a fundamental disloyalty to the Navy. The film retracts its critique and ends on a call for patriotic loyalty even in the face of utter incompetence. Brian Neve links this surprise ending in Dmytryk's film to the director's own about-face cooperation with the House Un-American Activities Committee investigations in order to be removed from the Hollywood black-list: "*The Caine Mutiny* establishes a situation in which the audience supports the naval rebellion, but then the conclusion reverses the whole tone of the story and affirms the principle of obeying authority as a primary obligation."²⁴ "National security," as Neve points out, "undercuts the notion of a justified opposition to a tyrant."²⁵ The final exterior shots of Pearl Harbor reflect the overriding concern of national security as they show no longer the idyllic images associated with a prewar Hawaii but simply a heavily industrialized harbor with multiple cranes and loading docks, making the dominant military-industrial complex visible as such. Whereas John Ford and Gregg Toland present a mixture of idyllic and industrialized images of wartime Hawaii in their documentary *December 7th*, *The Caine Mutiny* forgoes Hawaii's tropical geography altogether and turns its mili-tary harbor into an industrial complex, serving as the backdrop for a white mili-tary drama in which the natives of Hawaii play no role whatsoever.

PROSTITUTION AND THE BIRTH OF THE MILITARY-INDUSTRIAL COMPLEX IN HAWAII

If one is to understand the military-industrial complex as a meeting and merg-ing of military interests and those of the private sector, its obscene birth can be located in Hawaii, for it is here where the military generated a massive sex indus-try for the benefit of its soldiers (see Figure 22). A musical war comedy such as

Pin Up Girl (H. Bruce Humberstone, 1944), starring Betty Grable, clearly hints at the use of women in wartime but does so largely in military terms in the film's elaborate closing scene consisting of lengthy drill formations with chorus girls sporting uniforms and rifles. The mass ornament conflates military service with the exhibition value of the woman's body, the pin up girl, into a form of national service. The pin up girl turned patriot serves, then, as sexual motivation and promised reward for men going to war. Films adumbrated this entertainment component and became a sponsor for the military-entertainment complex, a web of interests that combined recruitment and military interests with those of leisure culture.

With the commencement of war, the military began to generate on Honolulu's infamous Hotel Street a much more explicit and literal secondary industry of prostitution in new and unheard-of assembly-line fashion to accommodate the thousands of troops about to embark to and return from the Pacific theater. As Bailey and Farber point out, "Within months of the attack on Pearl Harbor, 30,000 and more soldiers, sailors, marines, and war workers killed time in the vice-district on any given day. Close to 250,000 men a month paid three dollars for three minutes of the only intimacy most were going to find in Honolulu."[26] With the principle of efficiency and temporal rationalization of labor process, the trade was performed in truly modern mass-production style: "The brothels were stripped down. They were devoid of sofas and comfortable chairs. No drinks were served, no entertainment was provided. The operation was assembly-line efficient."[27] Due to Jim Crow and racial segregation on the mainland, white prostitutes were brought to Hawaii to accommodate the equally racially segregated troops: "The 'sacrifice' of lower white-class women from the mainland had been a price the old elite had been willing to pay."[28] These white establishments provided additional work opportunities for Hawaiian locals in tertiary services such as cleaning rooms, selling leis and tourist paraphernalia, manning bar counters, shining shoes, and hawking watches and jewelry. While prostitution was officially outlawed, complex zoning and living restrictions were in place to maintain the trade and limit its impact on Hawaii's locals. During the war, local and military authorities shared jurisdiction in Hawaii, with the military giving much more leeway to prostitution.

Postwar film depictions of Hawaii's World War II sex industry, due to Hollywood's censorship codes, could not explicitly show its reality and instead resorted to sanitized images of dance bars and social clubs as seen in *FHTE*. Film audiences familiar with Jones's best-selling novel, wartime Hawaii, and Hollywood's censorship conventions, however, would easily recognize the real context in which the film cast the lives of young soldiers in Honolulu. Two films concerned with Honolulu sex work, *Miss Sadie Thompson* (1953) and *The Revolt of Mamie Stover* (1956), present this context in equally obscure fashion and dwell on a narrative stressing the return to family values. *Miss Sadie Thompson*, directed by Curtis Bernhardt

FIGURE 22. Historic photograph of sailors lining up on Honolulu's Hotel Street, with its assembly-line prostitution, during World War II. Courtesy of National Archives.

and starring Rita Hayworth, offers an updated version of *Sadie Thompson* (Raoul Walsh, 1928) and *Rain* (Lewis Milestone, 1932), which starred film icons Gloria Swanson and Joan Crawford. In this morality tale of a fallen woman on the mend, the powerful minister Davidson on a South Pacific island in the American Samoas outs Sadie as a former prostitute of Honolulu's Emerald Club. After her initial reluctance, he convinces her to return to San Francisco, where she faces a legal charge and must own up to her former life. However, on the night before her departure, Davidson attempts to rape Sadie and commits suicide thereafter. In the film's dubious depiction of an island festivity with hula dancing, the sexual appetites of Davidson are aroused and lead to his subsequent transgression. The original novella by W. Somerset Maugham and the adapted play version on which the film musical is based deal with the clash of an imagined premodern native culture of the South Seas and a Boston missionary's Puritan ethical values. *Miss Sadie Thompson*, although set in the post–World War II era, uses as location a remote and rural South Pacific setting to accommodate the illusion of a backward native culture. This choice inevitably leads to an unrealistic portrayal of the colonized and modernized South Pacific and establishes the presence of military and missionaries as paternalistic. The natives become a mere backdrop to the drama of the rehabilitation of a white prostitute. Davidson's hypocritical transgression and suicide frees Sadie from his religious clutches and allows her to make amends on her own terms by marrying Sergeant Phil O'Hara, who knows about her past and is willing to put it to rest. Though the film offers a three-dimensional Technicolor spectacle for Hayworth to highlight herself in musical numbers with her alluring sex appeal, it ultimately fulfills the conservative mandates of 1950s cinema, stressing the return to family values after years of military promiscuity. As Hitchcock's Lisa (Grace Kelly) similarly exhorts the war-hardened and obstinate bachelor L. B. Jefferies in *Rear Window* (1954), "Jeff, isn't it time you came home?"

The Revolt of Mamie Stover (1956), directed by Raoul Walsh, who had filmed the original silent version of *Sadie Thompson* in 1928, was shot on location in Hawaii and is set during the time before and after the attack on Pearl Harbor. The film's story is an adaptation of William Bradford Huie's 1951 novel of the same title that first appeared serially in the *American Mercury*. Buddy Adler, who had produced *FHTE*, sponsored Walsh's production, which can in many ways be seen as a parallel film. As with Jones's novel, Huie's graphic and explicit descriptions of wartime assembly-line prostitution in Hawaii once again could not be shown and were explained via the conceit of taxi dancing and private entertainment stalls. The sheer numerical quantity of serviced customers was shown with the device of copious rolls of fairground tickets with which the soldiers paid for dances and drinks. As Bailey and Farber note, "Each prostitute normally serviced about 100 men a day, at least twenty days out of every month."[29] Jane Russell in the lead role gives a convincing portrayal of Mamie as a modern, self-determined, and self-empowered woman who quickly learns to invest her hard-earned money in Hawaii real estate. While the film hints at eroticism in musical numbers and Hawaiian dance scenes, its main focus lies with the entrepreneurial and capitalist spirit of Mamie Stover, circumventing restrictions of location and movement in order to amass as much money as possible. Her accomplice is the reporter Jim Blair, with whom she has a secret affair but also business dealings. As Jim is drafted, she promises to stop her trade but is lured back by irresistible offers of profit. Jim returns unexpectedly, finds Mamie in the old "entertainment" establishment, and breaks the engagement with a lecture that money cannot be the ultimate pursuit of life. Mamie retorts that this advice applies only to people who have always had money. Enlightened partially by his words, she returns home to Mississippi and confesses to a police officer in San Francisco that she had made her fortune in Hawaii but lost it. This reference hints at the loss of Jim and prospective marriage and not the money per se. The film's ending thus stresses a return to civil society, pays respect to the desirable status of marriage, and retains the hard-earned money as the reward for Mamie's misguided but instinctively sound Protestant work ethic.

An extensively staged attack scene on the morning of December 7, involving many Hawaiian extras as the turning point in the film, becomes the inaugural moment for Mamie's entrepreneurial endeavors and her revolt. As she is physically beaten and disciplined off-screen by the establishment's bouncer Adkins for having violated a key rule by leaving the premise, the film cuts to the beginning of the

Japanese attack, when the panic of war erupts with locals evacuating their homes. Mamie is shown leaving the establishment relatively unscathed, using the distraction to leave the premises once again and purchase real estate from owners desperate to leave the islands. These scenes are shown in parallel shots, juxtaposing the attack scenes and Honolulu's population emerging on the street with Mamie's buying of real estate, constituting her own attack and revolt against patriarchal norms. The scenes stress movement and mobility, representing Mamie's own emerging socioeconomic mobility. In a curious reversal of the time image and its paralyzed male heroes in postwar films, Mamie fully embodies the action image. Later in the film, Mamie has a date with Jim at Waikiki Beach, another strictly forbidden location for women of the trade, and once again Adkins wishes to make trouble but the tables have turned. Jim is now in uniform and MPs come to his and Mamie's aid when a fight erupts with Adkins. The MPs teach Adkins a lesson, giving him a thorough beating and showing the audience that the military now rules the islands. In another surprise turn, the strict madam Bertha Parchman (played by Agnes Moorehead) holds on to Mamie as a financial asset and takes her side, dismissing the luckless Adkins from her services. Portrayed as a shrewd businesswoman, Bertha quickly understands that the military will protect her business interests and become her new clientele. Contrary to expectation, Mamie is shown not as a ruthless war profiteer but as a heroic woman who simply turns necessity into a virtue. In obscene but self-reliant fashion, she inaugurates Luce's American Century, converting both the military and prostitution into financial advantage.

In Huie's novel, which also describes the changes in wartime Honolulu in satirical fashion, the trade of the prostitute is equated with a form of military service for the nation: "In short, the traveling men emancipated Honolulu's whores from provincial exploitation. No longer were the whores to be regulated and exploited by the local fascists; they were now *fonctionaires*, as it were, of the Government of the United States. Naturally, all this national regulation made the whores feel patriotic. It nurtured their egos. They cheered at the flag-raising ceremony, tried to sing *The Star-Spangled Banner*, and recited the Pledge of Allegiance. They applauded lustily when Major Eldon P. Sumac, AUS, explained the New Deal to them and welcomed them into the crusade for a better world."[30] In addition to becoming a quasi-legitimate branch of the military, prostitution also ushers in a new economic mobility. At the lead of this development stands Mamie Stover, a bolder version of Rosie the Riveter, who is not content with merely manning a factory job:

> By the Spring of '43 Mamie had revolted against all the old restrictions except two. She had not yet married a serviceman, and she had not yet bought a home outside the restricted area. But on May first that year she formally completed her revolt by marrying Major Joseph Robert Albright, of the United States Air Force, and moving into a $40,000 home in Pacific Heights. Mamie cabled me the news

of the twin events. I was in London, and I remember reading the cable and thinking about it as I walked from the Dorchester Hotel over to Grosvenor Square.
Her marrying the major didn't surprise me—all over the world whores were marrying majors. But I was surprised that she had really invaded the Heights. I had
never believed that she'd find the courage to do it. Swimming at Waikiki, dining
at Wai Lee Chong's, buying a Cadillac, these were easy acts of defiance under the
circumstances. But to scale the Heights—to squeeze herself right in amongst the
old Anglo developers—I had never believed Mamie would dare it.[31]

While Huie stresses here the emancipation of women during wartime, he does
not mention a similar emancipation of the local Hawaiian population from
similar constraints of social and real estate zoning. In the film version, Jim Blair
occupies a house at the highest point, possibly at the top of Manoa Valley, overlooking the island from the colonial bird's-eye perspective. When the Hawaiian
natives emerge on the streets during the attack, the camera tracks their movements from the hilly terrain downward toward the city and eventually settles on
shots in which rural field workers hurriedly leave the plantations while being
strafed by Japanese warplanes from above. The visual geography places the white
American at the top of the island, a position to which Mamie aspires. The film
version does not grant Mamie this elevated perspective and never shows her
moving to Pacific Heights. Nor does the film allow Hawaiians a modern narrative of social mobility.

The sexual and gender politics in Walsh's film similarly reflects the contradictions of the postwar era in its depiction of wartime sexuality among the troops.
Marilyn Hegarty discusses the regulation of female sexuality during the World War
II era in which thousands of women, often termed "patriotutes," provided soldiers
with entertainment and other "morale-boosting services": "During the World
War II, women's bodies were nationalized and their sexuality militarized: women's
laboring and sexual bodies were, in a sense, drafted for the duration. The draft
called men to serve their country, and women likewise received their orders: to be
patriotic and support the war effort, in part by maintaining servicemen's morale."[32]
This paradox of enlisting women for quasi-military service while simultaneously
attempting to mark aspects of female sexuality as abnormal and diseased by equating it with venereal disease "created myriad problems, both institutional and individual."[33] Not only was this campaign, writes Hegarty, "complicated by deeply
embedded ideologies of the female and male sexuality and by issues of race, class,
and ethnicity,"[34] but it "also amplified ambiguous social attitudes toward women at
a time when serviceman had a 'male mystique' that valorized aggressive (hetero)
sexuality. Military policies, including sex education for servicemen, free contracep-
tives, prophylactic stations, and support of houses of prostitution, all recognized
and normalized male sexual needs and desires. The normality of women's sexual

desires was, however, silenced by the framing of female desire as a psychological problem or social pathology. The equation of female desire with deviance simultaneously oversexualized and desexualized many wartime women."[35] In *Mamie Stover*, the heroine's sexuality is never explicitly shown but remains confined to melodramatic kissing scenes with her love interest Jim Blair. Suggestive clubs and dancing serve as the cleaned-up stand-in for the business of sex conducted on Honolulu's Hotel Street. Conversely, the film depicts normative and marital sexuality among natives in derogatory fashion. During the attack scene, the film shows an overweight and unkempt Hawaiian family packing up their many children into a station wagon with a baby hanging off an almost bare-chested mother. Normative heterosexuality is both advanced in the case of white women and discredited for minorities where it may lead to excessive population growth or "breeding." Hegarty argues that such control of female sexuality "not only operated to mitigate women's wartime gains" but also had long-term consequences, impacting all women, but most of all black women, especially unmarried ones, who were marked as pathological and the antithesis of 1950s domestic and family culture.[36] Unfortunately, none of these films reflect in any way the social and cultural shake-up that the arrival of military and mass prostitution triggered in Hawaii. As Bailey and Farber point out, "Prostitutes had invaded every neighborhood. Hawaii's carefully calibrated social stratification was being mocked. Mainland whores, white women, were out in public, demonstrating daily how little white skin meant in the way of moral superiority or some sort of 'natural' right to lord it over the vast majority of Hawaii's people of darker hues. Already the hordes of working-class white soldiers, sailors, and war workers had damaged the racial equilibrium that gave stability to the island's ruling white families who had seemed indestructible for some forty years. Now the white prostitutes made further mockery of the whole racialist setup."[37] Bailey and Farber rightly argue that the old social order of postwar Hawaii would undergo radical changes due to the impact of military personnel and wartime prostitution that exposed the nineteenth-century missionary's claim of the moral superiority of white civilization as a complete fraud. However, with the new stronghold of the US military in Hawaii, it remained to be seen if Hawaii could ever truly shake off white rule in its postwar history where the military-industrial complex wove its tentacles around the islands in the form of land grab and various forms of subcontracting to mainland businesses that still define Hawaii's economy today.

BIG JIM MCLAIN: JOHN WAYNE AND THE IMPERIAL MILITARY BODY

The military-industrial complex takes on many different guises in its assumption that war is waged at all times and especially during times of peace. One such aspect is that of permanent vigilance expressed in the surveillance state, shielding national security from subversion and infiltration by a wily enemy. In a 1952 film concerning national security, Hawaii would reflect this new postwar outlook and serve as the strategic geography for new configurations in America's political climate, albeit no longer in the images and genre conventions of the war film as seen in *FHTE* and *The Caine Mutiny*. In an unlikely thriller scenario of a communist conspiracy bent on sabotaging the resupply of American warships engaged in the Pacific and the Korean War, labor unions in Pearl Harbor have apparently been undermined by subversive left-leaning elements on the islands. John Wayne, in the role of House Un-American Activities Committee (HUAC) investigator Jim McLain, emerges as the film's slightly powerless hero who can successfully bring a manslaughter case to justice—his partner Mal Baxter (James Arness) is drugged and accidentally killed—but ultimately fails to convict communist conspirators making ample use of their First Amendment rights. As with *FHTE* and *The Caine Mutiny*, national crisis and the concern for national security seem to have become permanent fixtures of American life. The film also reflects in thinly disguised manner the Hollywood purges of the late 1940s in which John Wayne had played a significant role as a conservative advocate of HUAC's agenda, promoting anti–organized labor sentiment and free-enterprise corporatism in the film industry. Apart from its dated, strongly biased, and convoluted plotline, the film nevertheless provides an interesting insight into the consolidation of America's military-industrial complex, evoking a nation now engaged in a permanent state of war run by government agents and military experts. As Lary May explains, "Films focusing on social reform did not disappear, but reform now was less the agency of citizens operating in the autonomous civic sphere than of experts aligned with the established institutions."[38] The deceptively leisurely looking Hawaii cannot conceal to the ex-Marine McLain that communist conspiracies and subversions hide underneath the façade of the respectable middle-class and its decorum. Ron Briley sums up the film's dubious legacy: "It is usually described as a period piece, representative of the anticommunist film genre, in which filmmakers, responding to Congressional inquiries regarding communist influence within the Hollywood community, attempted to demonstrate their Americanism by bashing communism and communists as a clear and present danger to American security and principles."[39] As such, the film rightfully appears as an inferior propaganda piece. However, made one and two years, respectively, prior to the films by Zinnemann and Dmytryk, *Big Jim McLain* engages Hawaii's location much more progressively, showing many unique locations of Honolulu and relying considerably on local actors and extras to create a more realistic atmosphere of Hawaii. As Luis I. Reyes indicates, the cast "was augmented by a score of Hawai'i residents in featured and bit parts and upwards of 500 islanders in atmosphere parts."[40] While many of the island images still show culturally conflicted assumptions about Hawaii's population, they also break with many outdated stereotypes stressing a premodern and preindustrial Hawaiian culture.

In contrast to its conservative political agenda advocating free enterprise as a fundamental American core value, the film also advances surprisingly progressive perspectives pertaining to Hawaii and its credibility and reliability as an American territory. The film can be seen as making a plea that Hawaii indeed is eligible for statehood since its native population is depicted as fully cooperative with the American authorities and the American way of life. Namaka, the former Japanese treasurer for the communists, for example, experiences a nervous breakdown due to a guilty conscience and returns to his Shinto traditions in penance for his wrong alliances before he is silenced in a mental hospital. His wife, having divorced him several years prior, disavows communism and serves as a nurse on the leper island Molokai to quarantine the diseased from the healthy populations. By means of these two characters, the Japanese are shown in activities of penance and atonement and hence once again appear as good citizens in a postwar climate of rapprochement between the United States and Japan. Conspicuous racist representations such as seen in the first version of *December 7th* (directed by Gregg Toland), in which Japanese Hawaiians in league with Shintoism are held responsible for the infiltration of the islands and their collaboration with Japan, have now been converted into the opposite and depict the islands' Japanese as morally conscious and cooperative individuals. In similar fashion, McLain receives the full support from the local authorities headed by the Honolulu chief of police, played by the real-life police chief, Dan Liu. In addition, all conspirators turn out to be white middle- or upper-middle-class citizens, working with white union leaders. The local Hawaiians and particularly the Asian population are depicted as model minorities steered and guided by mainland American experts. In addition to Dan Liu, the film includes local Hawaiian celebrities such as sportswriter Vernon McQueen, wrestling champions Lucky Simunovich and Sam Mokuahi, Hawaiian actress Soo Yong in the role of Mrs. Namaka, as well as local Hawaiian musicians.

The film strictly follows the new guidelines and precepts of the new Motion Picture Alliance for the Advancement of American Ideals, an organization Wayne helped found.[41] In contrast to communist atheism, the film shows respect toward religion and cultural traditions. Japanese Shintoism, for example, is shown as a legitimate religion and moral institution, unlike its depiction in *December 7th*. Another prominent example of this respect for cultural traditions in *Big Jim* is given in a performance of a traditional Hawaiian song sung in Hawaiian by the Singing Surfriders with a close-up of Hawaiian singer Rennie Brooks. However, progressive images of Hawaii are in the end contained and paired with regressive appropriations in which whites once again administer the islands. The song is introduced by a Hawaiian male choir and frames the white couple (Wayne and Olson) as natives, showing them to be intimately at home on the island. Although no words are exchanged during this scene, it is a forgone conclusion that the couple will marry. The white couple has appropriated Hawaiian folklore and marriage ceremonies, and the Hawaiian setting does all the speaking for them. After the formal dinner scene Wayne is shown in the de rigueur aloha shirt as he serves pineapple slices and advances his marriage proposal in a slightly comical reprise of Ringo Kid's manly and inarticulate proposal in *Stagecoach* (see Figure 23). Similarly, hula performances are desexualized and no longer fetishized and instead more innocently presented as cultural folklore, providing local flavor and tourist entertainment. Waikiki Beach is mostly reserved for white tourists—Hawaiian locals are only briefly shown in a work meeting near the beach—highlighted in a shot of John Wayne and Nancy Olson on an outrigger canoe heading toward Waikiki, framed by tourist surfers and Diamond Head in the background. While an equal respect is shown to all ethnic groups and social classes, a strict hierarchy remains in place with white elites at the top, native Hawaiians and Asian Hawaiians collectively working hard, and some whites such as the corrupt communists shown unfavorably or comically ridiculed like the debauched, aggressive, and loudmouthed woman Madge, a foil to the middle-class heroine and fiancée Nancy. Hawaii's ethnic groups are in this respect no longer denigrated as in Zinnemann's racialized depictions of Asians and Hawaiians or in Dmytryk's total invisibility of the local population but are instead both incorporated into the American mainstream and yet contained at the same time, living the promise of a model minority awaiting future rewards.

From a gender perspective, the film also appears to be progressively aligned with the new postwar ideals of private enterprise. Nancy studies to be a psychiatrist and at no point is seen threatening to the masculinity and social standing of McLain, who is perfectly fine with marrying a professional woman. It is rather Madge, depicted as a lower-class, loud-mouthed floozy, a dubious remnant from an earlier Hawaiian military leisure culture, who irritates McLain but never presents any seduction for him. Madge is appropriately shown to be living in the vicinity of Honolulu's Hotel Street, the city's once infamous red light district. She recalls John Wayne's earlier dubious romantic counterpart Bijou Blanche (Marlene Dietrich) in the Pacific comedy-melodrama *Seven Sinners* (Tay Garnett, 1940). In this earlier film, Wayne's character Dan, an officer in the Navy, falls for a woman of ill repute on a faraway Pacific US protectorate and wishes to marry her, not unlike Ringo Kid, who marries the prostitute with the heart of gold in *Stagecoach*. However, an extensive bar fight, the self-sacrifice of Bijou to forgo the marriage proposal, and words from his commanding officer finally bring him to his senses, as he realizes that he is ultimately married to the Navy and cannot ruin his prestigious family legacy and promising career for the chivalric cause of saving a fallen woman. By the 1950s, this military temptation of meeting loose women in various faraway ports, part of the recruiting strategy in earlier military films, no longer figures in the much

FIGURE 23. John Wayne in *Big Jim McLain* (1952) portraying McLain falling in love with psychologist Nancy Vallon (Nancy Olson) in Hawaii.

more rationalized world where military and economic interests join hands in the promotion of free enterprise and America's globally expanding markets.

Wake of the Red Witch (1948), a South Seas adventure and revenge melodrama directed by Edward Ludwig (director of *Big Jim McLain*), likewise stars John Wayne in the role of Captain Ralls in a prolonged feud with his European foil, shipping magnate Mayrant Ruysdaal Sidneye, over a woman, sea routes, pearls, and gold. While the film, set in the nineteenth-century South Pacific, features Polynesian natives and stars famous Hawaiian Olympic swimming champion Duke Kahanamoku as the head of a local tribe, their significance is ultimately minor for the film and reduced to clichéd ethnographic spectacle scenes such as tribal dancing and communal convocations. In contrast to classic South Seas fantasies, this film does not show any first encounters between Western and non-Western civilizations, but instead highlights white rule as an already established fact. Romance, be it between Wayne's Captain Ralls and Angelique or his first mate Sam Rosen and the racially mixed Teleia, takes a secondary role in this drama, mainly focused on mercantilism, savvy economic deal making, and bitter feuds over possessions. In the logic of Manifest Destiny, the islands are shown to belong properly to those who make better economic use of them, regardless of whether these activities fall outside the bounds of legality. As David Spurr defines its rhetoric of empire more stringently, "Faith in commercial expansion as a moral and even spiritual phenomenon is fundamental to the historical consciousness of a nation built on the principles of Manifest Destiny."[42] Accordingly, the film's ending disavows its harsh economic logic in a dark romantic closure, which reunites the star-crossed lovers Ralls and Angelique in death and secures the freedom of the younger couple from the tyranny of Sidneye, restoring a moral and spiritual dimension to commerce. In similar fashion, the film pits modern hands-on venture entrepreneurialism embodied by Wayne's heroic character against Old World clerical and obsequious rule represented by Sidneye. Ralls eventually meets his unfortunate yet necessary end as he secures the lost gold from the sunken Red Witch and becomes entrapped in the ship's cargo space, emerging in his death as the film's tragic and moral hero. The film's outdated portrayal of Polynesian culture is significantly updated and modernized in *Big Jim McLain*; however, the crude economic and imperial logic represented by Sidneye and Ralls remains and is merely sanitized as the practices of modern entrepreneurial business in *Big Jim McLain*.

Visually, *Big Jim McLain* owes some debt to John Ford and uses his former cinematographer Archie Stout in this quasi-documentary police procedural with reminiscences of *December 7th* and *The Battle of Midway*. Ponderous voice-over and patriotic military hymns frame the national significance of the presented investigation and a series of initial dissolve shots establish the military at the center of Hawaii's importance to the mainland. The film opens with a thunderstorm on the location of Daniel Webster's burial site in Marshfield, Massachusetts, and dissolves into a wide shot of the US Capitol, invoking Webster's legal and political career and citing him via voice-over as the spokesperson for the indivisible union. The camera quickly pans from a close-up of the Capitol to the entrance sign of the "Un-American Activities Hearing Room." Dissolving to the inside, it appears that HUAC is in the process of being mocked by the invocation of the constitutional rights on the part of its subpoenaed witnesses. John Wayne, shown in close-up, is called upon to head Operation Pineapple, tracking a communist conspiracy at the nation's periphery in Hawaii. On his flight to the islands, he is treated to some tourist aerial views of Molokai, Oahu, and Diamond Head, where, as the stewardess informs the passengers over the intercom, Captain Cook made first landfall and "discovered" the islands. Further highlights include Waikiki Beach with the Royal Hawaiian, Surfrider, and Moana hotels. Thus in a condensed few shots, the entire transformation of Hawaii into a modern tourist location is summed up without ever touching upon disputed aspects of sovereignty or colonial history. Upon landing, McLain and his partner are received with Hawaiian music, hula performances, and leis. In a series of quick establishing scenes, the agents finally arrive at Pearl Harbor, visit the USS *Arizona*, and drop leis on top of the sunken World War II battleship, which happens to be his partner's brother's grave. With both upbeat and elegiac patriotic music, the film evokes the Fordian ambivalence of nationalism with its gains and sacrifices. A bugle sounding out, the hoisting of the American flag, and a close-up of the *Arizona* commemorative plate invoke in serious fashion the national sacrifices of the entombed sailors, while close-ups of leis are shown floating on the water. Dissolves show the US flag and a cruising battleship before fading into the sign of the civilian authorities of the Honolulu Police Station, introducing McLain (see Figure 24) and Chief Dan Liu. The military framing of the film, indebted to the conventions of the combat film, will once again be invoked at the film's end, combining hula performances at the Navy dockyard and roll calls with close-ups of America's ethnically diverse fighting forces. However, apart from these World War II references, the film eventually settles into the thriller and occasional noir terrain of a civilian society where the enemy uses hidden political mobilization and subversive strategies.

The imperial body, which now claims Hawaii as a legitimate US territory, is invoked initially with the historical reference to Captain Cook, the "discoverer" of the islands, but then handed over to the powerful military body of the ex-Marine McLain, battle-hardened in the Pacific. Upon his arrival at the airport, McLain is preceded by rumors of his stunning physique and body, six-foot-four as the journalist Phil Briggs remarks. As Russell Meeuf points out, Wayne's physique in many ways constitutes his screen persona:

> More than a persona, John Wayne in the popular imagination is a body, a hard body whose intractability against the elements or his enemies provides the basis of his appeal. Although all stars are in one way or another defined by the representation of their bodies, Wayne's large yet graceful body with its unique swagger (think of Wayne effortlessly parting the herd of cattle in *Red River* [Howard Hawks, 1948] en route to his showdown with Montgomery Clift, or Wayne prowling the dusty streets in *Rio Bravo* [Howard Hawks, 1959]) expresses the key elements of his masculinity—his tenacity, his strength, his narrow moral code. Thus, the discourses surrounding Wayne in the fifties obsess over his massive frame and fluid movement, indicating the importance of Wayne's body to his stardom in contrast to other white, male stars of the period like Cary Grant or Jimmy Stewart.[43]

In fact, throughout the film, comments about McLain's body size, mentioned three times, remind the viewer of this embodiment of evolutionary physical superiority used to punch out effortlessly communists and other troublemakers. The Hawaiian body, while not denigrated as such, must clearly take a back seat to this superior-looking species of the white American conqueror. A carryover of Wayne's rugged individual Western characters, McLain's suited-up role as a government agent also points more to the constraints of clerical and domestic life of postwar America, as seen in his love interest Nancy studying

FIGURE 24. John Wayne leading up the investigation into communist subversion in *Big Jim McLain* (1952).

to become a psychiatrist. As Meeuf notes, Wayne's persona took on a darker side in the late combat film *Sands of Iwo Jima* (1949): "Wayne came to represent a dark vision of masculinity; it is here that he becomes the Cold Warrior/empire builder who rejects femininity and the nuclear family in favor of all-male spheres."[44] This battle-hardened body, however, since it cannot be reintegrated into American postwar society, must die at the end of the film like so many of Wayne's Western protagonists who have to return to the wilderness and cannot be domesticated.

In contrast, *Big Jim McLain* suggests a postwar climate of politics and war in which the heterosexual male hero must pursue marriage and establish a family. This film betrays anxiety that the viewer may no longer notice Wayne's imperial body hidden under a suit and the decorum of civility or the leisurely aloha shirt. The American military body has been converted into an administrative body, relying only on occasion on physical strength.[45] However, the audience needs to be reminded at all times that the white Western body is superior in the literal Darwinian sense to nonwhite and non-Western bodies. Other bodily performances of Hawaiian dances, including performances by children, and the ever-present marriage melodrama soften up Wayne's image and turn him into the figure of benevolent imperialism, emphasizing the nuclear family in 1950s America. All three bodies combined, namely the military body, the administrative body (McLain, his partner Mal Baxter, and the towering chief of police Dan Liu), and the communal body (Nancy, the Hawaiian performers), celebrate national unity and harmony against the body of communist infiltrators or an unruly and sexually aggressive woman (Madge). As James T. Campbell notes, "Befitting the exigencies of Cold War, the emphasis is less on individual valor than on teamwork, collective discipline, and the necessity of regimentation."[46]

The mass ornament of various cultural, military, and civilian bodies at the film's end illustrates this national orchestration of unity and empire. The benevolent view upheld by McLain and the authorities is underscored with the tolerance for mixed racial marriages seen in one scene (on a bohemian boathouse) and Wayne's knockout punch administered to a labor union worker stooping to racist remarks. Communists turn out to be racists with inferior size (Dr. Gelster is not even worthy of a punch) and are of European descent, speaking with foreign accents. Before turning to the final patriotic mass ornament at the Navy shipyard, the film offers likewise a neocolonial reinscription of Hawaiian authority as the HUAC's hearings now take place in Iolani Palace, once the home and governing body of the Hawaiian Kingdom but now serving the interests of the United States. The film, with its closing imperial gesture, makes a good case for the inevitability of Hawaiian statehood, since it has turned Hawaii into an all-American territory, reflecting its key interests with the merging of the private sector and the military, with its white government and military administrators having gone native (Wayne wearing the aloha shirt) and running the islands, and with the military owning large portions of this strategic stronghold against a perceived communist threat in the Pacific.

GO FOR BROKE! RESISTANCE, AMBIVALENCE, AND THE STRUGGLE FOR NATIONAL RECOGNITION

The postwar era also brings into clearer focus the persistent racial discrimination of America's apartheid society. Edward Dmytryk's noir thriller *Crossfire* (1947) draws attention to anti-Semitism in the military and ends with a pedagogic speech by the lead detective who notes that once the Irish and other American immigrant groups too suffered from discrimination. Curiously, the film in its indictment of discrimination completely brackets the topic of persistent racism against African Americans, only cautiously advancing an agenda of social reform and tolerance. Dmytryk, who still used yellowface and racist stereotypes of Japanese people in his B war film *Behind the Rising Sun* (1943), shows some modest growth but is not capable of delving deeper into the issue of racism. However, as Michael Rogin points out, "While the United States was defeating Nazism with a Jim Crow army, there was growing recognition that American Negrophobia was the counterpart of European anti-Semitism."[47] The 1949 film *Home of the Brave* (Mark Robson) effectively establishes these parallels on screen when a Jewish doctor treats an African American soldier suffering from a posttraumatic stress disorder. As Donald Bogle notes, the film connects the Pacific war experience directly to the American home front and the war against racism: "In the psychiatric sessions, it is revealed, however, that it was not the island experience alone that led to the soldier's disintegration. It is the American way of racism that has always forced the Mosses of the world 'outside the human race.'"[48] As with World War II combat film, this picture falsely depicts a desegregated unit, however now placing more emphasis on the vulnerable position of African Americans. The film documents the growing rise of civil rights issues and the pressure for a desegregated army. Rogin sketches out the political landscape that preceded the release of this film:

> A 1946 Army report proposing that an occasional Negro technician enter white units "where Negro personnel with special skills can be utilized to advantage as individuals" might have explained the black soldier's presence among whites, since he is brought in as the only surveyor. That report not only postdated the war, however, it was also never implemented. Civil rights forces pressed for military integration in the year before *Home* was filmed, and A. Philip Randolph and the NAACP threatened black draft resistance if the Army remained Jim Crow. When . . . Truman finally issued his executive order in 1948 looking toward military integration, the Army dragged its feet. It did not place black and white troops together until the Korean War.[49]

This diversification and complexity of the postwar movement image in the combat genre parallels America's political activity and its ambivalence as it moves from national insularity to wider global assertion and dominance. An analysis of an early post–World War II combat film, *Go for Broke!* (Robert Pirosh, 1951), released during the implementation of Truman's executive order to desegregate the army, illustrates this transformation of the war image. Made at a time of expansion in the Pacific, it transforms war into a Machiavellian political art form concerned not so much with the act of war or how war is waged but with the wagers of war, the political gambling involved in the maintenance and building of power. In *Go for Broke!* this new representation of war enacts the drama of a newly reconstructed postwar American identity that must now take into consideration its Asian citizens at home so as to build and maintain hegemony abroad. This A-list film is a curious hybrid between wartime combat film (the Korean War is being waged) with its unshaken adherence to American national doctrine while reflecting the expanding concerns of postwar America and its race war at home. In resorting to the myth of the Asian model minority, the film engages war on two fronts, legitimating at once in conservative fashion America's global hegemony and in liberal fashion a contained acceptance of minorities.

Go for Broke! depicts the story of the 442nd Regiment, an actual World War II combat team composed of nisei or Japanese American citizens, celebrated as one of the most decorated battalions of the war. The film adheres strongly to the established codes of the combat genre to represent the national image of the fighting soldier. The twist is that this national image now consists of a people who were once deemed national enemies and interned by the government. Ironically, however, the attempt to turn the image of the fighting American soldier into a fighting Japanese American soldier is not so difficult as it appears, especially when considering the liberal ethos of the combat genre with its adherence to FDR's and the Office of War Information's World War II policy on race: namely, the viewing of enemies, citizens, and allies according to political leanings and affiliations and not according to racial ancestry or cultural traditions (seeing the Japanese as fascist enemies, the Filipinos and Chinese as prodemocracy allies, African Americans as loyal citizens). Ahead of actual racial practices in many ways, the World War II combat genre and its radically democratic perspective imagined racial situations not possible in contemporary America. Segregated and racially biased armed forces had no place in this genre with its representation of war as essentially democratic, showing soldiers of all races/ethnicities, religions, and classes fighting side by side—even women were depicted as playing significant roles in wartime activities.

The credible image of a Japanese American fighting soldier, then, is not such an obstacle within the liberal legacy of the combat genre. What is an obstacle, however, is the film's ultimate goal, namely the representation of Japanese Americans as legitimate citizens. The film directly links this image of Japanese American citizens to fighting soldiers, collapsing the two images into one and creating a new postwar American identity, reflecting the nation's newly imagined transnational and multicultural perspective. Employing the didactic method of the combat genre with its close relation to other realist-based genres such as wartime documentary and newsreels that inform spectators about war, national enemies, and allies, the film now instructs spectators in the acceptance of a new group of American citizens. The first step in doing so is to foreground America as a country of different traditions, reversing the wartime combat presentation of American culture as essentially unified and homogenous. As a postwar film, *Go for Broke!* now focuses on various regional identities and their traditions, favorably comparing the Japanese American battalion to the all-American battalion from Texas. It is here where the film's depiction of Hawaii as "home" to Japanese Americans is significant, articulating a difference that adumbrates but does not challenge national identity. While the Texan battalion sings "The Eyes of Texas" and dances the two-step, the Hawaiian company sings Hawaiian chants, dances the hula, and plays the ukulele.

Though the film presents both mainland and Hawaiian Japanese Americans, it is the latter and their culture who are representative, revealing how identity and territory are related in this new identity. In the film's opening sequence, the audience follows the protagonist, Lieutenant Michael Grayson, a white Texan, newly assigned as commander of a Japanese American unit. As he drives into the training camp, he suspiciously eyes the troops, sneering at them and at his Japanese driver with condescension. Before the first troops appear, the viewer already hears Hawaiian ukulele music in the background. From Grayson's point of view, a small battalion of men is seen, performing not the expected military drills but Hawaiian dances and song (see Figure 25). One soldier-musician even sports a lei. The officer greets this spectacle with derision as it appears the soldiers are unfit for battle. As Dean Saranillio notes, "Japanese Americans are cinematically framed in the film in ways that highlight their small physical statures against larger white American soldiers like Grayson. Such juxtapositions made Japanese Americans palatable to a white American audience by rendering them unthreatening. . . . Their inability to perform what 'normal' soldiers are routinely able to do symbolically emasculates them."[50] However, combat fitness is not the only matter of importance in this postwar film; the ability to express authentically one's cultural sense of belonging is just as significant. In this sense, the dancing Hawaiian troops enlarge the performative action image of the combat genre to include the performance of cultural identity.

While in France and Italy, the combat team both fights and dances through the European landscape with the Hawaiian soldiers carrying ukuleles as well as guns.[51] In fact, the ukulele music provides a sort of musical backdrop to the war, revealing the role that art and culture play in America's expansion of global power. The opening sequence, then, depicts the transformation of war from an activity of combat into an aesthetics of war concerned with the wider symbolic realm of cultural power and expression. As Robert Eberwein has pointed out, war films, while frequently highlighting homosocial rituals of male bonding, also feature dance performances as communal or ethnic rituals. In *Guadalcanal Diary* (Lewis Seiler, 1943), for example, a dance scene below the battleship's deck features the character "Taxi dressed in semi-drag as an Hawaiian 'woman' dancing hula,"[52] before the tune changes showing Father Donnelly and Taxi dance to Irish music. In *Go for Broke!*, this ethnic cross-dressing reminiscent of minstrelsy is no longer needed, as Hawaiians themselves now own their performance. The film retroactively installs the goal of the double-V campaign in which the African American newspaper the *Pittsburgh Courier* asked in its editorial for a victory both abroad and at home.[53] And like the white officer Grayson who undergoes a change from a racist, provincial Texan to a cosmopolitan, nonracist American, the spectator experiences a similar transformation and becomes a knowledgeable citizen able to comprehend the significance of America's Pacific adventures. The key to this multicultural perspective, the film makes clear, is the acceptance of Japanese Americans as legitimate citizens. We also see the establishment of the perception image and its association with Grayson who watches his men as well as its co-relation to the action image associated with the performing Hawaiian soldiers. The correlation of these images, already broken down in its components, has significant consequences in the construction of national identity.

The film's foregrounding of Hawaii as the cultural home of Japanese Americans is as interesting as it is problematic. Hawaii is treated as equivalent to Texas, ignoring its status as a US territory that had been refused proper statehood along with its privileges of representation. This is not to mention the repressed history of Hawaii and its indigenous people, who were colonized by the United States for economic profit and military purposes. This metaphorical granting of quasi-statehood to Hawaii follows the logic of American war politics as expressed in FDR's address to Congress the day after Pearl Harbor was attacked: "The United States of America," Roosevelt announced, "was suddenly and deliberately attacked."[54] At this historical moment, Pearl Harbor, and by extension Hawaii, suddenly ceases to be a distant territorial outpost and is transformed into "America," providing a compelling and legitimate cause for war.

At the same time the designation of Hawaiian Japanese Americans as quasi-Americans or quasi-natives associates Japanese Americans with a home and cultural rootedness. What, however, do we make of mainland Japanese Americans (*katonks* as they are referred to in the film by the Hawaiian *kanakas* or *buddhaheads*) who live in places such as California, Montana, and Washington State with their long anti-Asian histories? The film touches on this issue tangentially via a letter from home describing the near lynching of a soldier's brother by white laborers, foregrounding the irony of war and minority status: why fight a war in the name of democracy abroad when one is not treated as a legitimate citizen at home? The

FIGURE 25. *Go for Broke!* (1951) features the famous Japanese Hawaiian 442nd Infantry Regiment, performing Hawaiian music and dance to stress cultural difference.

film cannot and does not attempt to answer this question but instead focuses on a model minority, the nisei of Hawaii, conveniently located in a peripheral region geographically and culturally removed from mainstream America. Furthermore, the blurring of Japanese Americans and Hawaiians allows for a problematic exoticism of Japanese Americans as innocent, outgoing, and carefree natives who require the tutelage of America.

This status of requiring the guidance and sponsorship of America parallels the situation in Asia: Japan is now a humble, defeated enemy and occupied by the United States with MacArthur as the supreme commander. Reduced by MacArthur to "a fourth-rate nation," Japan and its economy are being revived by the Korean War and American involvement; the Philippines is a neocolonial territory "liberated" by MacArthur in the war and granted independence; and Korea is threatened by America's former World War II allies but now enemies, China and Russia, requiring US troops, led by MacArthur as commander of UN forces in Korea. In America's new global constellation of nation building, Asians and Asian Americans play an instrumental role with the formerly perceived enemy from within the nation, the Japanese American, now serving as a bridge to Asia and its developing economic markets. The strategic expansion of America's interest and national allies requires some explanation at home where Asians are viewed as secondary citizens.

This explanation results in the refashioning of Japanese Americans into an exemplary minority. Indeed, *Go for Broke!* is one of the first films to employ the model minority myth, a construct designed during the Cold War to indicate the successful assimilation of Asian Americans. As Robert Lee has pointed out, however, this myth is concerned not so much with the inclusion of America's Asian citizens in the nation's social hierarchy but with the exclusion of African Americans with their collective refusal to assimilate and uphold a white status quo.[55] The growing demands of blacks for civil rights and the move toward militancy and other radical solutions by some only served to legitimate and spread the myth of Asian Americans as model citizens. In the film, this myth is stressed in the troops' knowledge of European culture and history. The irony of the scene is that a people generally presented in the combat genre as "barbarian Others" or "Japs" are now depicted not merely as the liberators of a European culture that has itself sunk into fascist barbarism but as its legitimate descendants. Japanese Americans, by virtue of their new Western national status, are now a part of Europe's two-thousand-year history reaching from biblical times to Alexander the Great, Caesar, Charlemagne, and Napoleon. Here, the image of the battlefield with its ancient Roman ruins is not simply that of a strategic point in warfare, as is often the case in combat films, but a historic setting and event that articulates the grand ambition of Western empire building that is now passed on to America.

Asian Americans, presented in the film as unfit to fight in the Pacific theater due to possible confusion with the "barbarian Other," become in the film legitimate defenders of Western Europe and its cultural tradition. However, while their superior intelligence (one soldier is a trained architect; others possess keen farming and economic skills and useful multilingual competence) qualifies Asian Americans as eligible heirs to European culture, it also makes them complicit with America's goals of global expansion. As a model minority, they are granted special status only on account of serving the nation's strategic interests. In this respect, they resemble the Jewish elites in the Austrian Habsburg Empire, perceived at once as staunch supporters of the empire and as a nation within a nation marked by dangerous intelligence and a hidden patois (Yiddish *mauscheln*). This crafty and wily Oriental intelligence is benevolently and comically disguised in the film as pragmatic "Yankee know-how," as seen particularly in the troops' outwitting of German spies through the use of Japanese in radio communication. However, it is also used against their own commanding officer, the racist Grayson, who is initially fooled by the term *bakatare* (stupid). This term is later made available as a shibboleth, a password, forcing the American Grayson to identify himself in the language of the enemy, Japanese. In the use of this password, the film projects an intercultural understanding where for once the American must speak the language of the Other. However, much of the film is careful to point out a hierarchy of language in which Standard English is ranked at the top of linguistic accomplishment. Japanese and German are depicted as languages of deception. Hawaiian creole or pidgin enhances the local color ambience of the 442nd Regiment but is not seen as a fit language when discussing European culture.

In the scene of the Roman ruin battlefield, for example, Hawaiian pidgin is juxtaposed to Standard English and serves as a reminder of an inferior unassimilated Asian American culture. Its speaker, Tommy, while depicted as an honest and good soldier, nevertheless remains naïve and childlike throughout the film, comically attached to a pig, which travels with him throughout the war and becomes the film's substitute for a romance. In rehabilitating Asian Americans from a prejudice of linguistic inferiority, the film stresses that Tommy is not the sole representative of his community and that other Asian Americans exhibit linguistic competence to an excessive degree. Not only are Asian Americans fluent in foreign languages (German in particular) and their local Hawaiian patois, but they also master Standard English and impressions of its regional dialects such as Texan. As a model minority, they possess the skills of multiple languages, yet do they really possess their own language? Unlike the dance scenes that stress the cultural authenticity of the performers, the variously displayed acts of linguistic competence raise doubts as to whether Asian Americans truly speak a native language or rather impersonate it. The film's philo-Oriental myth of model Asian citizens in the end must yield to the enunciatory power of Grayson and his racist Texan friend who pronounce the Asian troops for the time being as trustworthy co-citizens, a situation subject to change. Indeed, the use of Hawaiian pidgin as what Deleuze and Guattari have termed minor language, with its ability to undermine the major language and its sociocultural hierarchy, is prevented from being realized as an "authentic" language, unlike Hawaiian song and dance.[56] While the space of the nation allows for cultural and aesthetic variety, its language of power and administration remains rigidly English to protect the Anglo-American cultural heritage deemed to be superior and at the core of the nation's identity.

Similarly, at the level of the image, the film attempts to contain the crisis of the action image, which Deleuze notes is associated with the crisis of the American Dream. This rescue mission is done through the centering of the perception image. While the film assigns the action image to the American Asian soldiers, their commander is shown to be not simply a spectator but the bearer of the perception image, one who initially begins as a student of Asian American culture but quickly graduates only to become its judge. Likewise, the audience, which identifies with Grayson, also takes the position of judge, deciding the worthiness of Asian Americans as legitimate citizens. Action suffers under the burden of legitimacy, revealing the weakening of sensory-motor links. Associated with Standard English, perception is granted ultimate priority, thereby stabilizing and maintaining a traditional

Anglo-American identity as well as the American Dream. In this sense, minorities are used and deployed as catalytic images for America's interest in Asia under the pretext of being granted increased civil rights within the United States. However, this extension of civil rights rests solely upon the goodwill of the liberal American for whom minorities have to perform and demonstrate their exceptional merit and hence are transformed into token minorities.

Nevertheless, the film points to the great possibility of the combat genre and its Orientalism to imagine a radically democratic multicultural identity that breaks with the dominant American black/white racial perspective. Here it is interesting to note that the film has been successfully used by Japanese Americans and the people of Hawaii to promote statehood and, more recently, by the redress movement concerned with compensation for Japanese wartime internment. In spite of its ultimate maintenance of a white status quo, the film cannot entirely do away with the considerable potential of the combat image to articulate doubt and ambivalence, to challenge and imagine new national values. As with any wager, the outcome remains ultimately unpredictable. If *Go for Broke!* places its bet on a model minority in the service of national interest, the result, while ideologically predictable, still contains the possibility of the unexpected and the subversive. Once the Asian minority is introduced into the national polarity of black-and-white race relations, this binary order is eroded and calls for a nascent multicultural imaginary.

TECHNICOLOR, RACE, AND THE NEW SOUTH PACIFIC

With the advent of television and leisure culture in the 1950s, the film industry suffered significant setbacks in attendance. To retain its audiences, Hollywood began to push the color format, which until its full development in the late 1950s raised production costs considerably. Additional changes in format such 3D, Cinerama, widescreen, and seventy-millimeter super widescreen were also explored to create a viewing experience that differed strikingly from black-and-white television and served as an audience-draw akin to fairground attractions. As Peter Lev remarks, "One response of the Hollywood studios to the rapid audience loss of the late 1940s and the 1950s was to emphasize the motion picture's capacity for spectacle."[57] In response to the threat of leisure culture, Lev notes, films aspired to encode with on-location cinematography "the sights and sound of the United States and foreign lands" and relied on various spectacle genres such as the musical, the biblical epic, and "the exotic adventure film" to "stress the power of the image."[58] As an unforeseen byproduct, the increasing shift toward color production, 15 percent in the early 1950s and 50 percent by the mid-1950s,[59] also facilitated the exploration of a new film aesthetics that deviated from the classical Hollywood black-and-white style, which in many ways constituted the cinematic expression of a normative whiteness.

Since classical Hollywood cinema depended to a great degree on the look of the star and glamour, its cinematic forms had to convey this look via the system of three-point lighting. Overhead, key, and fill lighting contributed to a transcendental look borrowed from the European visual arts. White reflective surfaces such as white outfits, light-refracting jewelry, blond hair, and pale faces caked with white makeup proved ideal in reflecting light and producing a halo-like glow in close-ups. Josef von Sternberg perfected this look with Marlene Dietrich, installing the white star as the pinnacle of classical Hollywood cinema. As Richard Dyer observes, "The angelically glowing white woman is an extreme representation, precisely because it is an idealization. . . . The white woman as an angel was in these contexts both the symbol of white virtuousness and the last word in the claim that what made white special as a race was their non-physical, spiritual, indeed ethereal qualities."[60] Darker colors, by contrast, which absorb rather than reflect light, had little use in this classical lighting scheme that projected what Dyer calls metaphysical and spiritual qualities. As it turned out, the classical Hollywood style ideally matched and articulated America's Jim Crow segregation that was built on the supremacy of white Western civilization.

The switch to color film did not, of course, change the racially hierarchized landscape of Hollywood. However, it did allow for new aesthetic approaches that could do without white glamour images and instead foreground color in all its materiality and intensity as an alternative. Also, in an enlarged color spectrum, black simply did not mean the negation of white, as, for instance, in classic film noir where black and other shades of gray denote a culture of corruption, but could enter into many diverse relationships with other colors on the screen. Hollywood realized early on that tropical landscapes benefited from color film treatment, as the diversity of colors in tropical settings created an enticing spectacle effect and enhanced screen fantasy. Long before Hollywood started to think seriously about issues of race, the South Pacific proved a perfect match for color film. In 1938, for example, Dorothy Lamour's South Seas adventure film *Her Jungle Love* (George Archainbaud) was shot in the expensive Technicolor format a year prior to Victor Fleming's *The Wizard of Oz* and *Gone with the Wind*, which dazzled audiences with the new color technology. The film's cinematographer, Ray Rennahan, was considered one of the leading innovators in the development of the three-strip Technicolor process. *Her Jungle Love* depicts Bob Mitchell (Ray Milland) and his copilot marooned on a South Pacific island. While his partner explores the island separately, Mitchell meets up with the "Malayan" native Tura (Lamour) in a premodern jungle setting featuring green palms, a lion cub, a monkey tossing coconuts, and the exotic beauty Tura clad in a blue sarong dress with exotic print patterns. While Bob's white fiancée worries at home in a domestic bland setting, the film cuts back to a musical scene with Lamour singing a native lullaby song in an idyllic nature setting. The close-up highlights her Louisiana French Latin features, a stand-in for the Pacific

Islander, and presents her as an alternate exotic color ideal to the predominantly white world shown in a prior shot stressing whiteness with set and costume color. Further eyeline match cuts from Lamour's point of view focus on white water lilies, giving off the petal's pink hues and highlighting the yellow eyes at the flowers' center surrounded by vivid green foliage and blue water. Cuts to shots showing Lamour in red lipstick made to look natural draw further attention to color, stressing its innocent and natural beauty. While Hollywood clearly deploys the colonial stereotype of the noble savage, it also indirectly suggests an alternate aesthetics of color. At the end of the scene, the film cuts back to plain close-ups of black-and-white newspaper clippings, listing the two aviators as missing in the South Pacific.

Tura is subsequently introduced to the pleasures of Western culture such as a gramophone playing jazz music and also slowly acquires a decent command of English. The film merges Western technology and consumer entertainment with the colors of nature, creating a material rather than ethereal foundation for the screen image. In the unfolding farfetched adventure plot of the film, the Western-educated Malayan tyrant Kuasa blames "white devils" for having ruined his life. He wanted to marry an English girl once but was considered unfit: "Once a savage, always a savage." Kuasa admits to having kidnapped Tura, the child of his white beloved and her husband, raising her in revenge as a native on the island. In her captivity, Tura falls in love with one of the white adventurers visiting the island. The implausible happy ending between Bob and Tura, legitimate since Tura is shown to be white after all by the film's end, points to a prohibited cross-racial attraction stressed in the film's first part. The film blurs the boundary between race as a biological or cultural construct and also makes it clear that racial prejudice did play a significant role in the villain's alienation from civilization. In cinematic terms, the white world burdened by abstract concepts of civilization is abandoned for a more primordial and material world of color and fantasy. This temptation of color, however, as Hollywood quickly realized, had to be contained. Released one year later in 1939, *The Wizard of Oz* would likewise employ an alternative color aesthetics with Kansas represented in black and white and the fantastical Emerald City in color. Fleming's film stresses the reality principle by having Dorothy willingly return to the gray space of Kansas after having confronted her imaginary world and fears in color. Similarly, Fleming's spectacle *Gone with the Wind* (1939) projects the vivid hues of a bygone era, the plantation culture of the antebellum South, on screen. Its temperamental white heroine, whose name (Scarlett) also invokes color, likewise presents an excess that requires taming by reality.

In 1951, when color film was commercially more viable, Delmer Daves directed a Technicolor remake of the classic *Bird of Paradise* (1932) on location in Hawaii in order to cash in on the new color trend in Hollywood. Daves's vivid *Bird of Paradise* unfortunately could not fully deliver on its promises due to its remote nineteenth-century presentation of the South Seas, which came across as out-dated and unrealistic in a sobered post–World War II era. The film's cinematographer, Winton C. Hoch, known for his work on the John Ford classics *The Quiet Man*, *Mister Roberts*, and *Searchers*, appeared highly suitable for this color spectacle, which is mostly constrained by racist Hollywood conventions of casting and a script filled with outdated racial stereotypes. The film's opening claims that all customs presented had been carefully researched: "All native customs, rituals and dances shown in this film are based on those practiced by Polynesians during the last century." In addition, the film also makes a point of stressing that its locations are authentic: "This story was photographed in its entirety on the islands and waters of Hawaii, Oahu, and Kauai." This pseudo-documentary veracity supports the film's not so hidden racist message, namely that Hawaii, a Polynesian territory on the verge of statehood, appears forever inassimilable to Western norms and culture. Granted, the film depicts more authentic forms of Polynesian dances, involving many Hawaiian natives, but the framework of the film suggests a culture stuck in primitivism and not eligible as a legitimate member of a modern state. As Lenora Foerstel and Angela Gilliam point out in connection with the legacy of Margaret Mead, such popularized anthropology quickly erects stereotypes that fail to address the contemporary postwar conditions of the Pacific world: "To those who live there, the Pacific is certainly no paradise, not because they are constantly threatened by intertribal warfare, but because . . . these are islands where there is no work, some of which are used as nuclear testing zones and garbage cans and their inhabitants as nuclear guinea pigs, where old-style direct imperialism and settler colonialism still flourishes in places such as New Caledonia and French Polynesia, where the major sources of wealth everywhere (particularly minerals) are owned by foreign corporations, and where world financial institutions (particularly the IMF) increasingly determine what will be done with that wealth."[61] This gross simplification of contemporary political reality can certainly be seen in Daves's *Bird of Paradise*. However, it is also still quite apparent in the politically much more ambitious *South Pacific* (Joshua Logan, 1958) with its colorfully irradiated vistas of the South Pacific that belie the reality of the sixty-six atomic tests that the United States conducted between 1945 and 1958 in these remote regions and waters without any consideration for native inhabitants in nearby areas.

Mark Robson's realist drama *Return to Paradise* (1953) precedes *South Pacific* and brings back the race issues he had addressed in *Home of the Brave* (1949). Shot on location in Western Samoa with cinematographer Winton C. Hoch, this independently produced film did not succeed commercially but pointed to the possibility of a different representation of the South Pacific. The film departs in its opening from the myth of the "happy native" and describes the life on the island without joy due to restrictions by a Puritan missionary presence enforcing curfews and disallowing local music and dances. The film is set a decade before

World War II and depicts the white American drifter Morgan (Gary Cooper) being dropped ashore as a new freethinking and alternative spirit on an island stuck in an outdated nineteenth-century colonial and missionary administration. It is thus not the natives but the colonial administration that is shown as backward. Cooper's presence as the new American spirit of self-determination and freedom changes the island's outlook, leading to the inhabitants' revolt and the removal of the missionary villain Corbett from power. The film relies heavily on local extras who perform in several speaking roles and are not merely depicted as exotic background. Most significant, the film features an interracial kiss between Morgan's racially mixed daughter Turia, played by the Samoan Moira Walker, and a US Navy pilot. Falling outside of the American race paradigm, this kiss did not attract the same attention as Dorothy Dandridge's kiss in *Island in the Sun* (1957), often described as the first interracial kiss in Hollywood. The film ends more cautiously with Morgan protecting his daughter from a nonserious and fleeting relationship with a Navy pilot that would possibly not lead to marriage, allaying audience concerns over the issue of an interracial marriage. While the film strikingly differs from *Bird of Paradise* in its attempt to convey a more credible and realistic depiction of the South Pacific, the overall presence of the United States in Western Samoa, an island still under the administration of New Zealand during World War II, is neither examined nor questioned. Instead, the film points in utopian fashion to the promise of sovereignty (achieved in 1962) ushered in by the American spirit of democracy. The second part of the film conveniently rehabilitates the formerly tyrannical missionary Corbett and resolves all earlier contradictions in a happy harmony of civil life existing alongside religion. The film's initial bolder realism eventually succumbs to sentimentality and brackets important questions, especially that of US military expansion in the Pacific.

In stark contrast to Robson's realism, Joshua Logan's *South Pacific* pursues more the fantasy component of the South Seas, allowing the musical to dazzle with spectacle and color. In typical grand Hollywood fashion, the project's commercial appeal overrules any serious artistic concerns of representation. The film casts African American performer Juanita Hall in the hapless minstrel role of a Tonkinese woman from Vietnam (Bloody Mary), a role to which Hall brings great acting skills in spite of its stereotypical and racist format.[62] Bloody Mary eagerly wishes to marry off her daughter Liat to a young white American officer, Joseph Cable, making a mockery of her Asian capitalist outlook, portrayed as both greedy and immoral. In a parallel scenario of unfolding romance, the white American military nurse Ensign Nellie Furbush from Little Rock, Arkansas, falls in love with the French plantation owner, Emile DeBecque. Although DeBecque is a fugitive for a murder committed in France, he practically runs the island as the head of a large plantation, invoking the plantation system as a seemingly nonproblematic

and self-evident economic structure to which white Europeans are naturally entitled.[63] In stark contrast to *South Pacific* and released one year prior, Robert Ros-
sen's major box office hit *Island in the Sun* (1957) highlights the island's political
struggle for autonomy where its African Caribbean hero David Boyeur (Harry
Belafonte) challenges the plantation owner and murderer Maxwell Fleury (James
Mason) by running for political office. *Island in the Sun* further features on-screen
interracial romances but will forgo the happy ending of the hero's romance for
the sake of prioritizing the political struggle against the white oligarchy. In *South
Pacific*, conversely, DeBecque has two mixed children from a Polynesian woman
who has died a while back and is never shown on-screen. In addition, the struggle
for land ownership and democratic representation is entirely omitted and the film
focuses instead on the issue of racism with a view to US interests. Both Cable and
Furbush will eventually have to confront their racist prejudices when considering
marrying a Vietnamese spouse (Liat) or a French husband with two racially mixed
children. The plot twist conveniently turns Cable into a fallen war hero before he
has to reach a decision and pushes Nellie's enlightenment to the point that she is
willing to marry DeBecque and remain on the island, thereby circumventing any
prejudice she may face at home in Little Rock with her newly adopted children.

South Pacific opens with the documentary and ethnographic conventions of
National Geographic photo essays, depicting scantily dressed natives carrying
heavy logs and mothers followed by naked children. A few more scenic and idyllic shots of sea and landscapes and natives on canoes round out the first impressions and end on a glorious sunset photomontage. In the next shot, with a military
plane flying across the wide-open horizon, a new geopolitical reality is established
when Japanese artillery takes aim at the plane. As the young lieutenant Joseph
Cable approaches the Pacific island, the pilot points him to the modern nurses'
quarters as well as the barracks of the Seabees. The next shot cuts to a medium
close-up of Bloody Mary standing next to a canoe with a human skull attached to
its mast and a chain of teeth from predatory animals hanging from it. Though she
is a Tonkinese Vietnamese and dressed with an army jacket, Bloody Mary is established via these metonymic objects comically as a cannibal. The accompanying
song mocks her and informs us that "she is always chewing betel nuts and she don't
use pepsodent" and "her skin is soft like a baseball glove." For a film setting out
to challenge practices of racism, the minstrelsy treatment of Bloody Mary would
seem highly counterproductive. The subsequent parody of Luther Billis, a sailor,
treated to an equally comical and campy appearance, may perhaps aim to question
our perception of identity and look. Luther is reduced in his military masculinity
as he sports a boar's tooth bracelet, a necklace, chest tattoos, and a grass skirt he
has sewn himself along with other Seabees. The film draws conspicuous attention
to mismatched props and identity, foregrounding the construction of identity, a
topic later revisited in the film's critique of the social construction of racism in the

song "You've Got to Be Carefully Taught." Similarly, Bloody Mary does not appear as a passive and feminine stereotype of the Pacific but instead strikes a tough bargain, exhibiting a modern entrepreneurial outlook. Nevertheless, the initial jokes are built on traditions of minstrelsy and misogyny and undermine any true revelatory questioning of stereotypes. The film's larger contexts of plantation culture and colonial paternalism further discredit its liberal agenda, offering at best an education as to how a Jim Crow America should present itself in the company of a new postwar global society and avoid comparisons to the racism of the defeated fascist regimes. As a postwar propaganda vehicle, it stubbornly retains its provincialism and provides a Hollywood fare via comedy that wishes to have it both ways.

The film's color photography (by Leon Shamroy) thematically supports the new perspective on race, highlighting diversity rather than monochromatic whiteness; however, it also makes color a highly subjective phenomenon, allowing individual American military personnel practically to turn the islands into any fantasy mirage he or she desires. Bali Hai'i, the mysterious and forbidden island often shown in the background of the main island, promises with its rainbow colors a copious paradise of sex and innocence for the lonely Navy soldiers as well as an adventurous space of savagery appealing to Western civilizational superiority (see Figure 26). The protagonists' subjective experiences of love (Forbush, DeBecque) are supported by hallucinatory intensifications of color in various filtered POV shots, granting them a privileged space of fantasy and dream. When Bloody Mary is granted a similar hazy shot upon first meeting Joseph Cable, it is made to look obscene and comical with the older and unattractive woman showing an interest in the young and handsome white officer. Although she mispronounces his rank as "Lootellan" and shows him a shrunken head from Bali Hai'i, she cunningly explains the meaning of its name as "I am your special island" in her attempt to lure him to an encounter with her daughter Liat. Her siren song "Bali Hai'i" evokes the traditional South Seas fantasies of the sexually alluring islands where Cable will later meet Liat but also his death. During Cable's first meeting with Liat hazy shots prevail, inscribing the interracial romance as a deceptive mirage of Bali Hai'i. The film also clarifies Bloody Mary's interest in him as less sexual than socioeconomic in her attempt to land a good husband for her daughter, tainting the unfolding romance with economic calculation.

Finally, the lower class Navy soldiers cannot aspire to any subjective shots and must instead resort to more crude efforts of cross-dressing as a native woman (Luther Billis) to own their limited fantasy in comically dismissive fashion. Billis's USO performance as a native Polynesian woman is particularly troublesome, since the soldiers mock her as being ugly and old. While the color during this scene switches from a brightly lit stage to reverse wide shots of the military audience shown in a foreboding cold gray-blue tone, it appears that racist and sexist mockery is the only appropriate entertainment before the soldiers meet their uncertain fate in battle. Concerning the film's happy ending, Billis's Polynesian minstrel routine may also suggest that the mixed children are at least partially Western and hence more acceptable than pure natives. The film's so-called bold advances in challenging America's Jim Crow system appear as extremely compromised and credible only as sentimental lip service for reform. With its contradictory messages of both ridiculing and advocating emancipatory respect for Polynesian and Asian minorities, *South Pacific* reasserts white hegemony in its dazzling color format, meant ultimately to incorporate and subsume the foreign and the exotic in America's bid for world power.

The arrival of Joseph Cable and Luther Billis on Bali Hai'i shows both of them heavily bedecked with leis, cheered on by all natives, and paraded through a human aisle of welcome, ushering in the new white American rulers. The festival they attend features tribal dances and mixes liberally African and Asian traditions and costumes reminiscent of *King Kong*'s (1933) ethnographic confusion of Melanesians and Africans. Superficial lip service to America's spirit of reform concerning race becomes a legitimation for the colonization of the Pacific and perhaps should minimally allay the fears of nonwhite populations. The film, with its overpowering white colonial and American military screen presence on the Pacific island, bears out the geopolitical reality of the postwar era. As Christina Klein notes,

> In the years after 1945, the U.S. assumed control over virtually the entire Pacific. The U.S. already controlled Hawaii, Wake, Midway, Guam, and Samoa as a result of its first wave of Pacific expansion in the nineteenth century, and over the course of World War II established military bases on numerous other Pacific islands as it advanced upon Japan. As part of its occupation of Japan, the U.S. assumed control over the Japanese main islands. . . . It claimed near-total authority over Okinawa for an indefinite period of time and turned the island into a major military base. In 1946, the U.S. obtained 99-year leases in more than twenty bases in the Philippines. In 1947, it formalized its control over key islands within the Micronesian archipelagos of the Caroline, Marshall, and Mariana Islands (including the Bikini atoll on which it tested atomic bombs in 1946) when they became U.S. trust territories. These island bases complemented those that U.S. maintained on the Asian mainland: in China, until Chiang Kaishek's defeat in 1949, and in Korea, where U.S. forces occupied the southern half of the peninsula. As this expansion unfolded, U.S. policy-makers and journalists resurrected the nineteenth-century imperial idea of the Pacific as an "American lake."[64]

Klein identifies among Rodgers and Hammerstein's work a subcategory of Orientalist postwar musicals (*South Pacific, The King and I, Flower Drum Song*) produced and disseminated in an effort to convey cinematically America's new dominant role in the Pacific: "As articulators of 'America' at a time when the

FIGURE 26. The musical *South Pacific* (1958) features the seductive island of Bali Hai'i, a South Seas location where reality and imagination are blurred.

United States was assuming an ever-greater role in global affairs, Rodgers and Hammerstein also represented the nation around the world."[65] The film musical and the Broadway show *South Pacific*, according to Klein, pair an "anti-racist theme with one focusing on America's expansion in the Pacific."[66] However, as this discussion has tried to show, it is the latter rather than the former that prevails as the work's ultimate message. Even the highly lauded antiracist song "You've Got to Be Carefully Taught" clearly shows its limits by sentimentalizing racism, slavery, and colonial power as an expression of fear of the Other. As Klein summarizes the song's message sung by Nellie and Joe, "They are victims of a perverted pedagogy of 'hate and fear': as Southerners, and as Americans, they have been 'taught to be afraid' of 'people whose eyes are oddly made' and 'people whose skin is a different shade.'"[67] However, the self-serving reversal of the role of the aggressor into that of the victim undoes the song's serious claim and credibility. Beneath its self-legitimating and apologetic rhetoric, it betrays a will to power and domination rather than fear, one based on America's ideology of Manifest Destiny and its combined project of spreading capitalism and Christianity as the American version of European colonialism and Orientalism.

Emily Rosenberg's critical study *Spreading the American Dream* takes a similarly somber look at America's expansionism: "Entrapped in misapplied notions of nineteenth-century liberalism and myths of America's exceptional mission, Luce and other apologists for an American imperium only obscured understanding of the process by which Americans expanded their influence."[68] *South Pacific*, in its odd inclusion of a French plantation owner and the Vietnamese Tonkinese Bloody Mary and Liat, takes on overt political significance in the 1950s, when the United States steps up its military engagement in Vietnam, succeeding and replacing the defeated French colonial rulers in 1954. The brutal realities of the Korean and Vietnam Wars ultimately run counter to the film's Hollywood ending of family bliss, suggesting benignly that the "Cold War, as a struggle for allegiances, demands the skill of a parent, not a soldier."[69] The Pacific, as history has shown, instead becomes the bloody battlefield of proxy wars with communist China and Russia as well as a convenient testing ground for new military technology in America's attempt to secure and widen its global power. The film musical *South Pacific*, with its central romance and family dramas, fulfills in this respect a propaganda function of 1950s US military expansion by pushing political and cultural conflict to the periphery. Herbert Marcuse fittingly observes in his analysis of America's postwar culture that a culture of affluence is secured via peripheral military maintenance and violence: "War, too, is at the margin—it ravages only in the 'undeveloped countries.' Otherwise, peace reigns."[70] A more sinister reading of the film featuring both the plantation system and the military-industrial complex may suggest that the latter is the updated version of the former, with war economies generating the new affluence once produced by plantation economy.

BLUE HAWAII: LEISURE CULTURE AND THE MILITARY-INDUSTRIAL COMPLEX

Kathy Ferguson and Phyllis Turnbull capture in concise language the insidious conflation of military interests and civil society in Hawaii: "Everywhere you look in Hawai'i, you see the military. Yet in daily life relatively few people in Hawai'i actually see the military at all. It is hidden in plain sight."[71] *South Pacific*, for example, was shot on location on the tourist island of Kauai and simply looked to the unobservant bystander as yet another Hollywood set in Hawaii. The film itself, with its genre of the musical, disguises the role of the military and recasts the former World War II combat film as an entertainment product with songs and dance numbers. What harm could there be in such innocent pleasure? As Ferguson and Turnbull point out, camouflage becomes the contemporary rhetoric to hide how deeply embedded the military-industrial complex has become: "For something to be hidden it must be indiscernible, camouflaged, inconspicuously folded into the fabric of daily life. The key to this incompatibility is a series of narratives of naturalization and reassurance. The narratives of naturalization imbricate military institutions and discourses into daily life so that they become 'just the way things are.'"[72] In the course of Hawaii's history since its annexation, we see an intensification of its cinematic appropriation in military terms, even though some of the films may innocently point to the leisure culture of the South Pacific. The initial South Seas fantasies films mostly center upon a justification of Western presence in the Pacific such as missionaries promoting Christianity, traders harvesting pearls and other exotic commodities, and beachcombers seeking sexual distraction and escape from the constraints of civilization. With films such as *Flirtation Walk* (1934) and *Waikiki Wedding* (1937), the South Seas genre is updated in both military terms—the Pacific Fleet with its harbor in Honolulu—and industrial terms—the assembly-line pineapple canneries along-side modern mass-market advertising. The attack on Pearl Harbor gives rise to what Jeanine Basinger calls the new genre of the combat film. While this genre shows utopian and liberal views in its multicultural makeup of the tradition-ally segregated army, it also extends the range of the war film into the everyday. In contrast to the critical war films made in the wake of World War I, stressing violence of battlefields and futile mass slaughter, the combat film changes the agenda of war into one of sustained labor and effort toward final victory. As a consequence, battles occur only in the latter half of combat films, the first half reserved for the daily routines of training and preparation in military barracks. The focus on the home front that took center stage in World War I war films is now replaced by a war theater with no clear demarcation. War is everywhere and occurs all the time, making the activity of war permanent.

In the post–World War II era, Hollywood begins to implement this involve-ment of the military into everyday life by generating World War II comedies and musicals. John Ford and Mervyn LeRoy's *Mister Roberts* (1955) features the comedic cargo ship *Reluctant* operating in the rear of the Pacific Navy during World War II. Shot in Honolulu, it involved *South Pacific* director Joshua Logan and cinematographer Winton C. Hoch (*Bird of Paradise*, 1951; *Return to Paradise*, 1953). The film stars Henry Fonda as Lieutenant Roberts, desperate to see battle and using multiple ruses to escape his unexciting rear mission and secure a trans-fer onto a Navy destroyer deployed during the Battle of Okinawa. As his comic foil, Ensign Pulver (Jack Lemmon) spends his day in idle activities, naturalizing war as an everyday leisure routine. A plastic palm tree, a favorite of the unpopu-lar Captain Morton (James Cagney), serves as the appropriate prop aboard ship to bridge military service and leisure. John Huston's *Heaven Knows, Mr. Allison* (1957), shot in Trinidad but set in the South Pacific World War II theater, casts in more melodramatic fashion the encounter between a US Marine (Robert Mit-chum) and a Catholic nun (Deborah Kerr) stranded on a Pacific island having to negotiate daily survival and fight hostile Japanese invaders until their final res-cue by the US Navy. John Ford once again returns to the South Pacific with his romantic comedy *Donovan's Reef* (1963), shot in Kauai and starring John Wayne and Lee Marvin as two World War II Navy veterans and South Seas fantasy icon Dorothy Lamour (see Figure 27). Again extending the range of the military into the everyday, the film focuses on issues of racially mixed children, debate over an estate, and morality in general. The happy ending resolves all contradic-tions, giving the Boston heiress Amelia a new Polynesian half-sister Manulani, granddaughter of the island's last hereditary prince, a husband in Donovan (John Wayne), and possession of an even bigger estate now combining Donovan's shipping operation with her own estate via marriage. Lee Marvin's sanguine character Gilhooey comes into possession of his beloved bar and marries the South Seas icon Lamour, cast here as Miss Lafleur, but evoking memories of her past films. The appropriation of the South Pacific by the United States now appears as a natural domestic reality rather than an imperialist expansion into a region with contested claims. Boston, the home port of the nineteenth-century missionary and military incursions into the South Pacific, is now connected via marriage to its overseas possessions in the dynastic fashion of the old European empires, belittling the military conquest that secured these possessions.

In his discussion of leisure and everyday life, French sociologist Henri Lefebvre posits a strong link between work and leisure: "The so-called 'modern' man expects to find something in leisure which his work and his family or 'private' life do not provide. Where is his happiness to be found? He hardly knows, and does not even ask himself. In this way a 'world of leisure' tends to come into being entirely outside of the everyday realm, and so purely artificial that it borders on the ideal. But how can this pure artificiality be created without permanent reference to ordinary life, without the constantly renewed contrast that will embody this reference?"[73] In an alternate approach to the idealization of leisure in consumer culture, Lefebvre demands that we see work and leisure as closely connected: "We must therefore imagine a 'workleisure' unity, for this unity exists, and everyone tries to programme the amount of time at his disposal according to what his work is—and what it is not."[74] Leisure in this sense contributes to the socialization of labor, particularly when experienced as alienated: "We work to earn our leisure, and leisure has only one meaning: to get away from work. A vicious circle."[75] Leisure at best restores a "feeling of presence, towards nature and the life of the senses"[76] and thus temporarily suspends the alienation experienced in modern work routines. Francis Ford Coppola pushes this idea to its surreal extreme in *Apocalypse Now* (1979), where military service and combat are conducted alongside surfing on the beaches of Vietnam's Mekong Delta and waterskiing on the Nung River to the sound of the Rolling Stones' "Satisfaction." Similarly, Stanley Kubrick's *Full Metal Jacket* (1987) shows the Joker with a peace sign decorating his helmet and the Marines on a mop-up mission singing the tune of the "Mickey Mouse March." Both films critically reveal the intrinsic connection between consumer culture, leisurely and peaceful pursuits, and the harsher realities of imperialist war and expansionism.

Hollywood's turn to more leisurely depictions of Hawaii and the South Pacific in the 1960s after two intense decades with films connected to the war should consequently not deceive one into assuming a demilitarization of America's overseas interests. Instead, as the Vietnam War gears up and slowly spins out of control, a complementary leisure image of Hawaii and modern mass tourism begins to appear on American screens. The producers of *Blue Hawaii* (Norman Taurog, 1961) recruited renowned cinematographer Charles Lang Jr., who had worked under Billy Wilder in various romantic comedies (*A Foreign Affair*, 1948; *Sabrina*, 1954; *Some Like It Hot*, 1959), with the intent of rendering a photographic spectacle of island leisure culture. As a vehicle film for Elvis Presley, this comedic musical fuses seamlessly popular Hawaiian music and Elvis's own pop catalogue, as given, for example, in the song "Rock-a-Hula Baby." With its youthful appeal, *Blue Hawaii* lent Hawaii an updated image more closely connected to contemporary American pop culture, replacing the traditional ethnographic and folkloric soundscapes associated with the islands. By extension the film further appealed to a younger generation of mass tourists to make use of the newly launched and more affordable air travel on commercial jets between the continent and Hawaii that had started in 1960. To the superficial and innocent eye, the film serves simply as an advertisement vehicle for both Hawaii tourism and Elvis's music and film careers.

However, hidden in plain sight, the military frames the film as a narrative of successful discharge from service, returning the film's hero, Chad Gates (Elvis Presley), back to Hawaii where he will use logistic and entrepreneurial ingenuity to launch a new tourist service industry, "Gates to Hawaii," with his girlfriend, Maile Duval, who happens to be part native Hawaiian and part French (see Figure 28). The military presents itself here as a training facility for capitalist creativity and entrepreneurial leadership skills. Chad's achievement involves a generational conflict, pitting him against his parents who would want him to take over their Great Southern Hawaiian Fruit Company. The distortion of historical details is of interest here as well. Instead of depicting Chad as the son and heir of a typical New England family who owned the island's plantations, a historically incorrect southern family that had come from Atlanta to Hawaii is invoked. This distortion allows the film to connect Hawaii and southern plantation culture and discredit it with its comedic mockery of Chad's southern mother, Sara Lee Gates (Angela Lansbury), the strongest advocate for this outdated institution. Evoking Confederate General Robert E. Lee in her middle name, Sara Lee is strangely also related to Union General Matthew Polk and thus unites an America military history that was once divided. Her strong southern accent and outlook, seen especially in her condescending racist treatment of her Chinese servant Ping Pong (Tiki Hanalei), betray vestiges of the old South and is no longer shown as viable in contemporary Hawaii but still good for a few screen laughs built on the long tradition of Hollywood minstrelsy. Instead, Chad, who is close friends with local natives and eventually marries a mixed Hawaiian, points to a new outlook in which race and prejudice are seemingly a thing of the past. Compared to the more critical *Island in the Sun* (1957), this postracial outlook here is achieved practically without any effort or conflict of interest and blends well with the leisurely effortless tone of the film.

FIGURE 27. John Ford's *Donovan's Reef* (1963), starring John Wayne and Lee Marvin, revisits the South Pacific in more leisurely and comedic fashion.

The glaring contradiction here is the white actress Joan Blackman cast in reactionary Hollywood fashion as the mixed Hawaiian, making sure that Elvis's interracial kisses do not offend his southern fan base. Elvis, conversely, with his tanned skin and jet-black hair, is given an almost native look, adding further to the confusion. An additional historical distortion is that of Maile Duval's French origin. While the French had a strong presence in other parts of the South Pacific such as Tahiti, they had practically no presence in Hawaii. The film accomplishes here an evocation of South Seas fantasies that often starred mixed French Polynesians but may also, not unlike *South Pacific*, establish a tacit solidarity with the failed project of French colonialism in Indochina, a project the Americans inherited in their increased military engagement in Vietnam.

The film in its entirety advocates the new military values of racial desegregation, anticipated in World War II combat films and implemented under Eisenhower, and the rise of the mass tourist industry replacing the former plantation system in Hawaii. When faced with the military draft in 1958, Elvis feared for the continuity of his career and had two available options. The Pentagon was willing to permit Elvis to enter Special Services, which entailed basic training and subsequently required him to perform for free several times a year for the armed forces. His manager, Colonel Tom Parker, recommended against this choice, since it made Elvis look more like a draft dodger and would also lose him substantial income on his performances. He recommended the second choice of signing up for the full two-year service, which would make Elvis into an even bigger star, broaden his fan base, and turn him into an iconic national performer.[77] Elvis took his advice, spent two years in Germany, and cashed in on his experiences with the film *G.I. Blues* (Norman Taurog, 1960) after receiving a great welcome home party on TV hosted by Frank Sinatra, one that would tie him to the acting and singing legend who had relaunched his career with the military drama *FHTE*. While shooting *Blue Hawaii*, Elvis also helped raising funds for the USS *Arizona* Memorial with a benefit concert, endearing himself further to Hawaiians and the nation. A later live performance at the Honolulu International Center, *Aloha from Hawaii* (1973), broadcast globally via satellite to a billion viewers, added the final touches to Elvis's legendary commercially productive romance with Hawaii.

G.I. Blues, which precedes the three films Elvis made in Hawaii, establishes the absent backstory for *Blue Hawaii* as well as Elvis's own discharge from the army. *Blue Hawaii* opens with the usual tourist vistas of Waikiki but then cuts to more idyllic and depopulated montage shots of island and ocean scenery to drive home its imaginary nature as a consumer object to be possessed. This presentation recalls *South Pacific*'s Bali Hai'i, the island that calls out "I am your island." After the scenic introduction, we see Maile speeding in a red sports car along the roads of Oahu and eventually stopped by a Hawaiian police officer. When she tells him that she was in a hurry to pick up Chad from the airport after his military discharge, the officer immediately offers a police escort to the airport, as obviously every local Hawaiian seems to know of Chad and his military service. As we will later find out, Chad was not stationed in any critical zone, such as Vietnam or Korea, but in Europe where he had time to travel to Paris, Italy, and Austria and purchase a bikini for his girlfriend and a music box for her grandmother. To be sure, the film suggests Chad had himself a European vacation. At the airport, Waihila, played by Hilo Hattie, the comical Hawaiian hula dancer known from various film appearances, joins Maile and both welcome the returned hero, wearing his military uniform, with leis and a group of hula dancers. Chad quickly plots his escape with Maile to a remote beach corner with a traditional grass shack; Chad is so excited to be back in Hawaii that he runs into the ocean in full military attire. The focus is given to Chad's Army uniform as he swims with it in the ocean, making it amenable to leisure. Close-ups on their route to the beachfront show the couple playfully swapping Chad's military cap, blending seamlessly military and leisurely lifestyles. Back on shore, Chad proceeds to offer Maile the bikini purchased in Paris. As the couple returns to the ocean with Maile sporting her new bikini and Elvis his white swimming trunks, drawing attention to his tanned body, a clothesline with Chad's wet military uniform hanging from it frames the shot. The wardrobe and color of

FIGURE 28. Elvis Presley decommissioned from the army in *Blue Hawaii* (1961), trans-ferring his military background to the logistics of tourism.

celebrated costume designer Edith Head make a significant contribution to these scenes, as they naturalize the military, suppressing any traces of its violent purpose.

The bikini outfit brought by Chad for his girlfriend from Paris is of particular importance. Parisian engineer Louis Réard invented this two-piece swimwear for women in 1946, and Parisian fashion designer Jacques Helm modified it shortly thereafter. It was named after Bikini Atoll, the site for US nuclear testing until 1958, and was highly controversial due to its revealing nature. Teresia T. Keaiwa views the bikini in the context of the hidden exploits of the military in the Pacific as a device for amnesia, euphemistically recasting a shameful historical event as a garment of transparency and visibility: "The sexist dynamic the bikini performs—objectification through excessive visibility—inverts the colonial dynamics that have occurred during nuclear testing in the Pacific, objectification by rendering invisible. The bikini bathing suit manifests both a celebration and a forgetting of the nuclear power that strategically and materially marginalizes and erases the living history of Pacific Islanders."[78] As the flip side to the military presence in the Pacific, the bikini exults in leisure culture and purports to be entirely harmless, if not boldly feminist for the 1960s generation of women beginning to own their sexuality and bodies outside the constraints of traditional patriarchal norms. Film stars such as Ursula Andress and Brigitte Bardot would sport this piece of swimwear in provocative fashion in their films. *Blue Hawaii* proceeds more cautiously with Maile noting that her Hawaiian grandmother would be upset at her wearing the bikini. In the ocean, Maile loses her top, alerting viewers that this outfit is not yet ready for the American market. As the bikini top floats in the water, it is promptly retrieved by a dog and replaced with a shirt, which the dog dutifully brings to her when rescuing her from embarrassment. Although the film pulls back on the sexually exploitative look of the bikini, it also highlights its prurience. As a wet piece of floating garment, the bikini top further stands in metonymic relation to Chad's wet uniform hanging from the clothesline and connects it with its military origins, bringing the semantic chain of military, leisure, and consumerism full circle.

The predominant focus on the beach is on Chad going native. Enjoying the ocean, Chad is greeted from afar by his native friends riding in an outrigger canoe. The greeting involves a traditional call from a conch and a Hawaiian prayer chant (*pule*), and eventually lapses into a welcome song for the dear friend, namely Queen Liliuokalani's famous farewell song and Hawaii's unofficial state anthem "Aloha Oe." As Chad joins the local friends in the canoe, he becomes practically indistinguishable from them and looks deceptively native. Unlike Bing Crosby in *Waikiki Wedding* who was presented in a halo of white to offset him from the darker surrounding natives, the reverse is done in *Blue Hawaii* where the tanned Chad is visually assimilated and culturally absorbed by his native Hawaiian friends, cementing his birth right (although he was born in Atlanta) and legitimating his claim to the island. As with Crosby, whose "Hawaiian Wedding Song" and "Blue Hawaii" the musical borrows, Elvis will become the voice of the island, singing various well-known Hawaiian songs (e.g., "Aloha Oe") in Hawaiian alongside other pop songs and crossover songs into Latin and Caribbean beach music (see Figure 29). Chad masters these songs in Hawaiian, pidgin, and Standard English, tying Hawaii via various musical bridges to the continent. Similarly, Chad's local friends move effortlessly between these three languages/dialects, singing their songs in Hawaiian and ending (as a musical joke) in Standard English.

As was shown earlier, during World War II the military anticipated an early form of modern mass tourism when overseeing and indirectly sponsoring mass prostitution for its GIs in Hawaii. More gentrified entertainment such as hula shows and luaus also sponsored by the military were not yet marketed with the mass tourist strategies that they would take on in the 1960s.[79] The medium of Hollywood film, as given in Elvis's *Blue Hawaii* or *Gidget Goes Hawaiian* (Paul Wendkos, 1961), would eventually establish the mass appeal of Polynesian luaus and dance shows as part of the Hawaiian tourist package that the everyday or middle-class tourist could afford. *Blue Hawaii* ends on a large marriage tableau with Chad floating downriver on a raft with his bride surrounded by colorful and natively clad Hawaiians, recalling the glamour of plantation musicals such as Kern and Hammerstein's *Show Boat* (1951). This final scene would launch Hawaii's wedding industry, with tourist offices selling Blue Hawaii wedding packages on Kauai, a practice continuing today. In *Gidget Goes Hawaiian* this ceremonial and sacred aspect of marriage rites is altogether removed and Polynesian luaus and dances are simply part of the tourist fare along with sports activities involving the beach such as surfing, waterskiing, and sailing on a catamaran. *Paradise, Hawaiian Style* (1966), a type of sequel to Elvis's *Blue Hawaii*, similarly takes a strictly pragmatic commercial view of the islands with Rock Richards (Elvis Presley) and Hawaiian Danny Kohana (James Shigeta) becoming business partners in a tourist helicopter service. Danny is also shown in an interracial marriage with four mixed children who address Rock as "Uncle," reflecting the progressive outlook of the civil rights era. This film features at some length the Polynesian Cultural Center, with its theme park structures on the North Shore of Oahu that opened in 1963, providing a full immersion experience in Polynesian culture for tourists. The center is run by the Mormon branch of Brigham Young University in Hawaii, combining missionary and entrepreneurial interests. Jane Desmond notes critically that the Polynesian Cultural Center naïvely promotes the authenticity "of what are often residual modes of cultural practices in increasingly urbanized island communities."[80] *Blue Hawaii*, while occasionally reverting to traditional ceremonial Hawaiian lore, stresses its modern tourist economy with Maile working in a tourist office across the International Market on Waikiki Beach, featured in a significant scene. The International Market, which opened in 1957, fully admits to its commercial pursuits as a market for tourist souvenirs and all things Polynesian, in contrast to the Polynesian Cultural Center and its quasi-educational anthropological simulations of Pacific cultures. Chad Gates, expected to work for his father's pineapple plantation, rebels and eventually settles down with Maile to open his own Gates Tourist Office. The decommissioning of Chad from the military culminates in his newfound career in the mass tourist industry.

Otto Preminger's *In Harm's Way* (1965) is frequently characterized as a war epic due to its length and grand Pacific sea battle scenes at the film's end. Shot for the most part on various military installations in Hawaii such as Kaneohe's Marine Corps Air Station, Ford Island, Pearl Harbor, and Honolulu's red light district and Hell's Half Acre in Chinatown (arguably another military location of a different sort), Preminger's film strongly recalls the time image of Zinnemann's *FHTE* (1953) and its immobility of action. The film opens on the night of December 6, 1941, with a dazzling tracking shot of an officer's party, featuring a row of white, glowing Navy officer caps on a check-in desk, before craning into an overhead shot over a large, reflective swimming pool with officers in bright white uniforms and their dates, moving leisurely and gracefully about to jazz music. The social etiquette is broken when a young officer's wife, whose husband is away at sea, drunkenly performs a type of striptease, wrapping herself provocatively around a pole (see Figure 30). She eventually leaves the party with another officer and has sex on the beach, only to be killed in a car accident the next day as both of them rush back to the base in the wake of the Japanese attack on Pearl Harbor.

In a parallel scene Captain Rockwell Torrey (John Wayne) is shown on a heavy cruiser with an inept crew caught equally unaware by the Japanese attack. Aboard ship he is approached by Commander Paul Eddington (Kirk Douglas), who suddenly seems to awaken from his usual drunk disposition and exclaims in relief,

FIGURE 29. Elvis Presley going native, kicking sand, and hosting tourists in *Blue Hawaii* (1961).

"Ole Boy of Ages, we got ourselves another war, a gut-busting, Mother-loving Navy war." Torrey injures his arm and is subsequently demoted to desk duty for allowing his ship to be torpedoed by the Japanese. During his three-month convalescence, he befriends Navy Nurse Corps Lieutenant Maggie Haynes (Patricia Neal) and visits yet another exquisite officer party. Unlike *FHTE*, where the Japanese attack triggers a return to action, the Navy's post–December 7 routine appears in Preminger's film in an uninterrupted leisurely pace. The time image of doubt and immobility not only is transformed into the pursuit of leisure but also extends into the actual time of war. The film repeatedly shows large, formal and lavish dinner scenes for officers as they conduct military business on the side. Dating also takes up a considerable amount of time in wartime Hawaii, with officers portrayed as a socially privileged and entitled class, harking back to Stanley Kubrick's World War I satire *Paths of Glory* (1957), which mocks the socially aloof French high command. In its leisurely tone, the film also recalls in more muted fashion Kubrick's more absurdist and satirical portrayal of incompetent General "Buck" Turgidson (George C. Scott) in *Dr. Strangelove* (1964).

As Torrey, nicknamed "the Rock," is finally assigned for battle duty, he must consider separation from his newfound girlfriend, Navy Nurse Haynes. In an exchange between them, Haynes asks, "Will there be time for us out here?" Torrey responds, "We'll make time Maggie," prioritizing romance over the more pressing issue of war. Wartime action begins finally with a small operation trying to secure an airfield on a faraway and small Pacific island. Torrey is brought aboard to direct a military strategy in this operation and unofficially relieve the incompetent Vice Admiral Broderick. Torrey's op is called "Apple Pie," as he intends to launch a three-pronged attack on the island, slicing it up like a pie. Petty infighting between Broderick and Torrey's staff almost subverts the plan and shows the military as an administrative body driven by sheer careerism rather than strategic goals. The event that finally ruptures the leisurely pursuit of war is Commander Eddington's rape of Annalee, the fiancée of Torrey's estranged son Jere. The rape occurs on Hawaii's scenic Kaneohe Bay across from the landmark island Mokoli'i (locally known as Chinaman's Hat), now allowing violence to break through the veneer of leisure. In the aftermath of the sexual assault, Annalee commits suicide and leaves a note indicting the culprit. Before Eddington is brought to justice, he embarks on an unauthorized suicide reconnaissance mission, spots the Japanese fleet, and radios crucial information back to the base, meeting his end at the hands of a Japanese fighter squadron. The close-ups of Eddington performing these heroics prominently feature Annalee's scratches on his face, calling into doubt his actions. The final dismissal of Eddington's heroism is given by Torrey, who flatly rebuffs the enthusiastic recommendations that he receive a medal with a quiet but firm, "no recommendation." Using Eddington's information, Torrey launches a successful attack against the Japanese fleet and manages to repel them. Major naval battle scenes take up the final ten minutes of the film, that had shown hardly any military action, with the exception of the initial attack on Pearl Harbor. The film's combat framing at the beginning and the end is not meant as a buildup, as is usually the case in the combat genre. Rather it merely embeds the military's everyday pursuits within the frame of war. Administrative battles have taken the space of real battles that frequently occur off-screen. The film ends on Torrey's refusal to recommend Eddington for military valor, though without disclosing his true reason for doing so and thereby covering up Eddington's rape. The film's final close-up settles in on Nurse Haynes and refuses this close-up to John Wayne, starring in his last major war film. This significant shot can be seen as an acknowledgment of women's service in the war. More critically, the film links military violence directly with sexual violence against women, placing the hypermasculine military institution at odds with the institution of marriage as shown in frequent adultery and divorce among the officers' ranks, as well as rape. Military and domestic life, as the film suggests, are not compatible, and the final stable couple is produced only when Torrey retires. At the same time, the film shows that daily military life is accompanied by reckless hedonism and leisure, undermining the moral and national values it claims to protect.

The representation of war in 1960s cinema, as Preminger's film shows, is strongly inflected by modern leisure culture, with Hawaii as one of its central hubs.

FIGURE 30. Otto Preminger's *In Harm's Way* (1965) depicts a decadent military culture in World War II Hawaii.

The film also mentions Hawaii's role as a rest and recreation stop for the military going to and coming from war engagements. Hotels such as the Ilikai (1964) and the army's official recreation hotel Hale Koa (1975), on Fort DeRussy near Waikiki Beach, are notable locations for R&R stopovers. In a further twist to Hawaii's functional use for military purposes, it also provided in the mid-1960s training camps for tropical jungle warfare, simulating the terrain of Vietnam. When King Vidor had created lagoons artificially in 1931 for his film set of *Bird of Paradise* on Hawaii, he could not have foreseen that the army would follow in his footsteps by creating likewise an imaginary Pacific territory of Vietnam on the islands. As Simeon Man describes the training facility of Kara Village,

> From the mid- to late 1960s, Kara Village was the place where soldiers received their advance infantry training before going to war. It occupied the East Range of Schofield Barracks, distinguished from the rest of the army compound by make-shift huts, booby traps, and "Viet Cong insurgents," who more often than not were played by Native Hawaiian and Asian American GIs. Kara Village was a fiction of the US military imagination, a "native" place intended to mimic the sites of war an ocean away, to render the unfamiliar terrains of Southeast Asia knowable and actionable. As a laboratory of war making, it collapsed the distinction between Hawai'i and Vietnam and made them interchangeable sites of war.[81]

The stand-in performances of Native and Asian Hawaiians in Kara Village's simulated training terrain confer unto the participants the status of movie extras asked to portray the Vietcong enemy. The representation of Hawaii under military influence thereby becomes ambivalent, serving at once as a site of recreation and combat training, but also blurring the distinction between cinematic and factual reality. Hawaii in this ambivalent role offers the fullest expression of the military-industrial complex with its intersection of private and public interests, of war propaganda and its implementation in everyday routines.

In the postwar era, we have thus seen a transformation of central cultural stereotypes in the representation of Hawaii and the Pacific into the new rhetoric of what Christina Klein terms Cold War Orientalism, a combination of military power and diplomacy to build and enforce US global dominance. This new pragmatic Orientalism stands in stark contrast to World War II Orientalism with its utopian and visionary component of multiculturalism and nascent civil rights, the double victory campaign, as it was called in the African American community, with the hope of winning the war abroad and at home.[82] Instead, the postwar era was eager to resume the conservative status quo, urging women in the workforce to return to their former domestic life and minorities to assume their secondary positions in society. The new postwar Orientalism also promoted America's hegemonic dominance in the Pacific to stem against what Dwight Eisenhower called the domino effect of globally spreading Communism. Historically, however, the United States consolidated and strongly expanded its military role in the Pacific, with Hawaii playing a key role as the main naval port for the Pacific Fleet.

In a new reconfiguration of its strategic World War II role, Hawaii was slowly developed as a leisure site for mass tourism, economically aided by the new affluence of the late 1950s and significant advances in the technology of more affordable commercial airlines. The military-industrial complex with its World War II martial law management of the islands and their entertainment offered to enlisted servicemen, such as assembly-line prostitution, served as the profane vanguard for modern mass tourism.[83] The development of mass tourism occurred alongside Hawaii's new role as an R&R site for troops fighting in Korea or Vietnam. The postwar changes were also enhanced by a new emphasis on individualism and entrepreneurialism, marrying America's frontier spirit to that of capitalism. The GI Bill similarly tied military duty to promotion within the capitalist system by allowing soldiers to pursue college degrees sponsored by the military. For Hawaiians, however, these changes were not as radical. With the notable exception of the 442nd Regiment, few Hawaiians were allowed to serve in the army during World War II and hence could not pursue economic opportunities offered by the GI Bill. Instead, the plantation economy transformed into a tourist service industry and offered a new infrastructure of labor with locals manning low-paying jobs as gardeners, desk clerks, bellhops, waiting and kitchen staff, tour guides, cleaning crews, and other related services connected with the leisure industry. As Ferguson and Turnbull aptly put it, "Local men moved from agricultural work on the plantation to agricultural work on hotel grounds or to other out-of-sight work in the kitchens and similarly invisible spaces in tourism's social production."[84] Land ownership also experienced no significant redistribution but rather a rezoning to make beaches available for hotel complexes owned by mainland chains. "Productivity," as Ferguson and Turnbull note, was no longer measured in "metric tons and contiguous acres, but by its proximity to sandy beaches and clean bays."[85]

Blue Hawaii, for example, was shot in part on location in the wealthy district of Kahala, not far from the new real estate complex Hawaii Kai developed in 1959 on the former fishing grounds of Maunalua and Kuapa, which were dredged and artificially reshaped into a lagoon for the surrounding luxury condos and bungalows. American industrialist, steel magnate, and father of modern shipbuilding Henry J. Kaiser acquired the land from the Bishop estate, with the help of the military, which he had supplied with his liberty cargo ships and steel during World War II. Part of the military-industrial complex, Kaiser, with his military connections, was naturally offered preferential treatment in the development of postwar Hawaii. As Haunani-Kay Trask points out, the Bishop estate, set up to sponsor the Hawaiian Kamehameha schools, was dominated by a white majority of trustees with links to the military: "The Board of Trustees of the Bishop Estate, meanwhile, had read like a Who's Who of Hawai'i's rich and powerful since before the overthrow. All the contemporary trustees—Frank, Midkiff, Herbert Keppeler, Atherton Richards, Richard Lymari, and Hung Wo Ching—had direct or indirect ties to the Big Five, especially to Am Fac, a major developer of Estate lands. They were all Republicans, and three of them were former military men."[86] The political switch from Republican to Democratic, as Trask notes, also did not change the power structure originally set up by the Big Five in the nineteenth century: "As white-owned and white-managed sugar companies, they strengthened their power throughout the 20th century by intermarriage and interlocking directorates and by controlling the ruling Republican Party. When the Democrats came to power in 1954, they gradually replaced the Republicans in the partnership. But the alliance remained the same in its outlines: land use decisions for profit."[87] As was shown here similarly, the cinematic representation of Hawaii, whether motivated by Republicans such as John Wayne and Gary Cooper or more Democrat-leaning directors such as Joshua Logan and Mark Robson, remains stable in the colonial gaze to which Hawaii and the Pacific are subjected. Some nuances of representation may point to different perspectives in political outlooks, but the overall imperial perspective built on the legacy of Manifest Destiny and Henry Luce's updated notion of the American Century was never questioned. The Pacific was and remains, in the ideology of these films, a territory or state that belongs to the United States and hence is subservient to its interests, strategic, political, and economic.

4 ✿ CONCLUSION

The New Cultural Amnesia in Contemporary Cinema and Television

The romantic comedy *50 First Dates* (2004), set in Oahu, centers on Lucy Whitmore (Drew Barrymore), who suffers from severe short-term memory loss and amnesia, being wooed anew daily by the persistent island playboy and marine biologist Henry Roth (Adam Sandler). As such, the comedy appears to offer typical Hollywood fare of a complicated love plot combined with situational humor. In its progressive liberal outlook, the film superficially shows sensitivity toward disability (although it makes fun of other disabilities such as lisping and obesity) and turns Hawaii, via Henry Roth's job at Sea Life Park, into an ecological sanctuary of the twenty-first century (although most sea life is caged in). The question remains why Hawaii was chosen at all for this romantic plot, which could have been set anywhere. Little of the actual life of Oahu is shown on-screen, and Hawaiian culture is ridiculed in the minstrel performance of Rob Schneider in the role of Ula, a marijuana-smoking, uneducated, pidgin-talking lazy Hawaiian with a protruding belly, shark scar, and glass eye, married to an unattractive native woman with five children. In the tradition of the plantation genre, playful and beloved native children and adults humor and serve the white cast. In addition, the staff of the restaurant, at which Lucy spends her days, has made it their special mission to protect her, making her life their center in a gesture of *ohana* and aloha spirit that turns them into semblances of plantation mammies and caretakers.

The film, with its disturbing race and ethnic hierarchy, elevates the white American Henry Roth (named after the famous Jewish immigrant writer) and Lucy Whitmore against the native Hawaiians, as well as against the initially ridiculed and ambiguously gendered Russian immigrant marine park assistant Alexa (in one gross-out scene a sick whale blows vomit on her). Surprisingly, the film drew nothing but positive criticism at the time of its release, with occasional unease about the newly emerging gross-out humor in romantic comedies. A. O. Scott in the *New York Times* calls the film an "impressively daring romantic comedy."[1] Roger Ebert in the *Chicago Sun-Times* notes, "As entertainment it's ingratiating and lovable."[2] With its focus on a white female lead in the position of vulnerability and victimization, the film calls for chivalric protection and solidarity and transforms the playboy Roth into a caring lover, a conversion that was somehow made possible by the benevolent spirit of Hawaiian island life. The romantic drama lures the viewer into sentimental identification with white suffering and illness at the expense or forgetfulness of its Hawaiian characters. As such, the film performs the amnesia with which its main heroine is afflicted, allowing viewers to forget the burden of history and conflict that once also characterized the relations between the United States and Hawaii. As with the film's device of the videotape that stabilizes the condition of memory loss for Lucy, the film itself normalizes American history and allows for its white protagonists to move forward in an unencumbered fashion. The burden of history, in a film where history has come to an end and starts forever anew, is thereby redeemed in the magical fashion of a Hawaiian fantasy. The film ends appropriately in Alaska as yet another ecological sanctuary to which the main protagonists can escape. As the forty-ninth and fiftieth states, Alaska and Hawaii bring the film's national focus (fifty dates) full circle, providing the utopian horizon for a happy ending. The valuable task of a twenty-first-century ecological outlook is connected to the chivalric task of protecting and entertaining the film's white heroine and for the white couple to own their world anew every day in a space where the burden of history and conflict is absent and disability becomes magical.

The film's positive reception coincides with a time of post-9/11 awareness of the United States' precarious role as the world's leading superpower and increasing internal demographic changes and emerging multicultural discourses that can be seen as a threat to the racial status quo built on the legacy of white supremacy. In the wake of this hyperawareness of history and guilt accumulated during the formation of the American empire, amnesia offers the cure for an overburdened white consciousness and resets history to ground zero.[3] The film follows in this sense the format of the 1970s TV show *Fantasy Island*, also filmed in Hawaii, which allows its various and mostly white characters to fulfill their secret dreams during each episode. It also harks back to South Seas fantasies that provided in the face of economic depression during the 1930s a fantasy escape to islands of abundance where Western economic worries were nonexistent. The present-day use of Hawaii similarly fulfills a function of fantasy escape and a withdrawal into family plots in order to forget larger pressing historical and political contexts. It is therefore not surprising that contemporary Hawaiian and traditional Polynesian cultures are only minimally featured in these films, since they have become simply a tourist backdrop for white melodramas.

Forgetting Sarah Marshall (2008) features a post-breakup melodrama with its white characters vacationing in Hawaii and sorting out their messy romantic lives. British comedian Russell Brand corners the attention during musical cameos, traditionally reserved for Hawaiian performers. *Just Go with It* (2011) involves another Hawaiian vacation in which a plastic surgeon (Adam Sandler) asks his assistant to pose as his estranged wife (Jennifer Anniston) in his effort to win back his girlfriend. *Soul Surfer* (2011) offers a melodramatic comeback story of a young girl seriously injured in a shark attack with a predominant focus on her white family. The film's plot recalls the comeback story of surfer Anne Marie Chadwick (Kate Bosworth) with encouragement from real-life white Hawaiian surfer Keala Kennelly in *Blue Crush* (2002). In line with these Anglo-normative scenarios, *50 First Dates* produces two white couples at the film's end, namely Lucy and Henry, as well as her brother and European immigrant Alexa. Risky cross-cultural romances, once featured in South Seas fantasies, are now entirely absent not because of prohibition but because they would interfere with the narcissistic fantasy withdrawal into the comfort zone of white melodrama. In this new functionalization of Hawaii, the island is thoroughly American and has become the home turf for mainland drama. Recalling perhaps globalization and its accompanying woes, Hawaii's diverse multicultural life is deliberately omitted in these romantic comedies and melodramas.[4]

With comedy and melodrama, we witness an increase of amnesia in the evolution of Pacific films since the 1960s. Hawaii's leisure industry is defined not only by its beautiful beaches and oceanic environment but also by its ability to make tourists forget its location as the "first strange place" and domesticate it instead as the untroubled space of the American home away from home. It will be helpful here to retrace the steps of this development that have led to the intensification of historical amnesia, making it Hawaii's latest tourist commodity. Concerning the representation of Hawaii's exemplary multicultural landscape, this new development comes with a diminishment of this utopian horizon and settles instead on US isolationism and provincialism or a naïve notion of a postracial society that is apparently already in place. This approach implies that films present Hawaii as basically white and negate the demographic fact of an Asian and Hawaiian majority population versus the roughly 24 percent of white inhabitants.

RACE, LAND, AND PROPERTY

With the rapid economic development of Hawaii since achieving statehood in 1959, questions concerning the legitimate ownership of the land would once again have to be addressed in the new context of emerging national debates on race and civil rights. The aggressive expansion of Hawaii's mass tourism showed a blatant disregard for the local population and native Hawaiians with mainland-based construction companies building hotels, leisure centers, golf courses, artificial beachfronts, lagoons, and high-rise complexes that stood in stark contrast to Oahu's island topology. Contributing to this construction boom, the military likewise launched and promoted the invasive construction of several highways and tunnels to connect its various bases. The profit shares from all these projects stayed mostly within the hands of the white elites, cutting in here or there some emerging elites among Japanese and Chinese Hawaiians. However, for most of Hawaii's local population these changes produced little economic improvement and instead were often accompanied with forceful dislocation from areas to be developed, a problem that continues today and underlies, along with the high costs of rent and real estate, Hawaii's acute crisis of homelessness, the highest in the nation.

Haunani-Kay Trask locates the birth of the modern Hawaiian movement in the Kalama Valley protest of 1971, with nonviolent protestors arrested for trespassing on private property in their attempt to block new construction and protect the land rights of the local population: "Land claims first appeared, as in Kalama Valley, as community-based assertions for the preservation of agricultural land against resort and subdivision use. By the mid 1970s, these claims had broadened to cover military-controlled lands and trust lands specifically set aside for Hawaiians by the U.S. Congress but used by non-beneficiaries. Justification for these claims had also expanded. In the beginning of the decade, the rallying cry was 'land for local people, not tourists.'"[5] Trask claims that these initial struggles over land use were more "akin to the American Indian Movement than to the Black Civil Rights Movement" with the issue of race being articulated only at a later stage: "Many of the issues in the struggle—e.g., class divisions between Hawaiians, racial divisions between *haole* (whites) and people of color, the prior claims of local people against mainland in-migrants—were to grow in significance in later years."[6] In the American lens of filmic Hawaii, conversely, these same issues would be raised in the 1963 film *Diamond Head* (Guy Green) but presented with a reverse emphasis on race to accommodate the mainland debates on civil rights.

Diamond Head was filmed on location in the sparsely populated town of Hanalei, Kauai, showing none of the construction explosion in Oahu. When the film visits the location of Honolulu briefly, it restricts itself to bars, lobbies, and Waikiki beachfront with no visible signs of intensifying mass tourism. The actual drama is said to take place in the new state as shown by a title insert "Hawaii, 1959" on the Big Island, featuring the large estate of Richard "King" Howland (Charlton Heston), his name evoking the absolute rule of the *haole*. The opening wide shot of the film features King in a Western outfit traversing the land on a white stallion and some modern agricultural equipment operated by locals. These shots evoke plantation culture and cast King in the role of the overseer on horse. The many subsequent wide shots of verdant natural landscapes with horses and cattle are reminiscent of Westerns and also recall the tradition of the paniolo, the Hawaiian cowboy. The unfolding narrative presents a struggle over the inheritance of this land complicated by interracial marriage and romance. At the same time, Howland wants to run for political office as a first Hawaiian senator, which ties his private life to the perception of a wider public.

Howland's sister Sloane returns to the estate with her native Hawaiian childhood friend, Paul Kahana, played by white teen idol James Darren (who also starred in *Gidget Goes Hawaiian*), whom she wishes to marry, to the dismay of her racist brother. For the viewer, race is represented in tactile fashion when Sloane is first shown in close-up and a brown hand moves from off-screen toward Sloane's face, caressing it. This shot anticipates a similar shot in the famous interracial marriage drama *Guess Who's Coming to Dinner* (1967), when Joey's white hand reaches from the left into the screen and places a white daisy onto John's ear (Sidney Poitier shown in a side profile close-up). *Diamond Head* proceeds in less gentile fashion as the camera then cuts to an overhead shot, showing Sloane resting on top of Paul and him touching and caressing her body and chest covered by a white dress and insinuating a censored interracial sexual encounter. When confronted with his sister's marriage plans, Howland, whose own son and wife are no longer alive, insists he will not have someone of mixed race inherit his estate Manoalani. As the owner of a twenty-million-dollar estate, he explains to his sister that her plan is out of the question: "We've been on these islands for over a hundred years but we never mixed our blood." Ironically, King himself has an Asian mistress by the name of Mai Chen, played by the French Vietnamese actress France Nuyen, who had starred as Liat in *South Pacific*. In a series of plot complications, Paul Kahana meets his death at the hand of King when he steps in a fight between Mai Chen's brother and King during his engagement party and is accidentally stabbed and killed. In a further complication, Mai Chen is pregnant with King's child, delivers a son, and dies during childbirth. King initially disowns the child and reclaims him as his legitimate son only after some soul searching while riding furiously through the forest and swamps. He returns with his white horse, now entirely soiled and caked with mud and rushes to the bedroom, only to find an empty house and crib, as his sister Sloane, now dating Dr. Dean Kahana, Paul's half-brother from a mixed-race marriage, intermittently adopts the child.

In true soap opera style, the civil rights drama of the film, with its many racial complications and turns, eventually drowns out the connected question of property and land ownership. The film culminates in the late moral awakening of King, who finally accepts his mixed-race child. One should note that the child is mixed of white and Asian descent and is unlike the offspring from the aborted marriage of Sloane. Had Sloane's marriage to Paul Kahana been realized, her child would have been of white and native Hawaiian descent, coming closer to the mainland equivalent of a mixed African American child. Sloane instead will marry the *hapa haoli* (half-white) half-brother Dean Kahana, who is a medical doctor in contrast to his deceased native Hawaiian brother Paul, who, while having had a top college education, appears aimless. Mei Chen's brother, the Asian male, for which the film likewise has little constructive use, is similarly depicted as economically drifting and trying to shake down King over his affair with his sister. In the film's cautious progressive agenda, interracial marriage is encouraged between Asian females and whites or white females and half-Hawaiians, mirroring the many mixed-race romance films of the late 1950s, dealing with the fallout of mixed overseas military children. Ultimately, however, pure Hawaiian or Chinese Hawaiian males are not suitable marriage material in this deceptive drama that condemns racism but subtly preserves its hierarchies with some concessions. The brownface performance by James Darren as Paul Kahana and Aline McMahon as Paul and Dean's Hawaiian mother Kapiolani Kahana leaves no doubt about the film's limited interest in progressive issues. Her two husbands are either deceased or not around, leaving King as the true patriarch of the island. The sentimental ending coaxes the viewer to believe that it was Howland's land to give in the first place and obscures a century of intense settler colonialism and expropriation by white US citizens who came as immigrants to Hawaii.

By the film's end, the question of land ownership is completely sidelined and gives way to a race melodrama in which Heston emerges as the belated white hero cured of his racism. The question of his twenty-million-dollar estate, however, is indefinitely postponed. By implication, it is ultimately King's land to give and brings his project of settler colonialism full circle without any further critical investigation as to why he should own this land or represent Hawaii as a senator.

The discussion of postwar films about the Pacific and Hawaii also benefits when these films are brought into association with newly emerging films set in the Far East. The flurry of films documenting American and Asian rapprochement in the late 1950s and early 1960s can be seen as updated versions of South Pacific films, highlighting the new geopolitical interests of the United States in Asia. Films such as *Love Is a Many-Splendored Thing*, *The Teahouse of the August Moon*, *Sayonara*, *The World of Suzie Wong*, and *Flower Drum Song* parallel topics found in South Pacific films such as *South Pacific*, *Blue Hawaii*, and *Diamond Head* and may even render the Pacific genre obsolete due to increasing direct engagement with various Asian countries and cultures. In a brief recourse to some of these films, I explore how they share some key rhetorical agendas about civil rights and the discourse of race in America.

Christina Klein suggests that a historic shift from racialization to ethnicity in American culture set the stage for a more liberal multicultural landscape in the war and postwar era: "In the 1930s and 1940s the racial formation of people of color within the U.S. began to change as racialization gave way to ethnicization. . . . During WWII, official and unofficial propagandists celebrated America as racially, religiously, and culturally diverse nation, and in the process they transformed the ethnic immigrant from a marginal figure into the prototypical American. . . . As a democratic nation of immigrants, the reasoning went, America alone possessed the ideals and the experiences to lead a multiracial world of independent nations in which imperialism had lost all legitimacy."[7] While such an assessment certainly reflects the new rhetoric in cultural discourse, the ongoing practices concerning race and imperialism were less progressive in nature. Rather, the political and cultural discourse changes to a disingenuous format in which US policy and rhetoric, for the purposes of imperial expansion, present themselves as liberal abroad while retaining the status quo at home. In a series of interracial romance films set in the Far East, a subtle double code fools the foreign viewer into comprehending America as the progressive new world leader, while indicating to the domestic viewer that the racial status quo will be safely maintained at home. Gina Marchetti traces this deceptive rhetoric in two films (*Love Is a Many-Splendored Thing*, 1955; *The World of Suzie Wong*, 1960) set in Hong Kong, an ideal location for US foreign propaganda in the Far East: "This is a cold-war Hong Kong—poised between post-1949 Chinese communism and the decay of the British Empire. As such, it provides an ideal place for America to assert and legitimate its presence in Asia as an 'enlightened' Western power opposed to British colonialism and promising a neocolonial prosperity in the face of socialist leveling."[8] The films, as Marchetti points out, insert the United States into the geopolitical landscape of the Far East as the new progressive power. However, these films rely heavily on conservative stereotypes of passive and pliant Asian women, who are eventually domesticated and abandon their active career as medical doctor or prostitute to serve in the traditional role of wife or mother, setting back the clock for US feminism at home.[9]

Similarly, one might add, strong reservations about the viability of interracial romance remains. In *Love Is a Many-Splendored Thing* the foreign correspondent Mark Elliott (William Holden) conveniently dies in the Korean conflict, leaving Dr. Han Suyin (played in yellowface by Jennifer Jones) a widow with the comfort of a homeless Chinese child, whom she adopts from the streets of Hong Kong. In *The World of Suzie Wong* an unlikely happy ending between a prostitute (Nancy Kwan) and a bohemian painter (William Holden) gives an upbeat note to the tragic death of her secret son during a flood, a potential child for the couple who would have made them a family. The film figuratively aborts this child twice, as he is not Robert Lomax's biological child, and ensures that US audiences remain undisturbed by the possibility of an interracial romance with mixed offspring. In *Sayonara* (1957), set in postwar Tokyo, an interracial relationship succeeds against all obstacles between Major Gruver (Marlon Brando), decorated hero and son of a general, and Hana-Ogi, a renowned dancer and theater actor, whereas similar relationships with the lower class airman Joe Kelly and his spouse Katsumi lead to double suicide or are grotesquely dismissed in the case of Gruver's intended bride Eilleen and her Japanese lover Nakamura, a Kabuki performer played by Ricardo

Montalbán in yellowface. What appears as the triumph of love is granted only to a male member of the white elite, while women and members of the lower class are met with the reality principle of the actual racial practices prevalent in the United States. These romance scenarios are in the end firmly rooted in the socioeconomic realities of property, career, and ownership. Eilleen's legacy as a general's daughter is not to be wasted on a foreigner, Joe and Katsuma were never meant to stray from the flock and fraternize, and even Major Gruver's relationship is shown as an exception and produces no offspring.

The film *Flower Drum Song* (1961), another Rodgers and Hammerstein postwar integration musical, steers clear of interracial romance but offers a more progressive outlook on Asian American culture. As Klein explains, "It created a cultural space in which Asian Americans could be publicly embraced as 'real' Americans."[10] With its all-Asian cast and depiction of San Francisco's Chinatown as a thoroughly American and acculturated space, the film challenges the stereotype of Asians as the non-Western and inassimilable Other. While the casting of the San Francisco's Chinese community invariably mixes Chinese American (Jack Soo), Japanese Hawaiian (James Shigeta), Japanese (Miyoshi Umeki), binational Eurasian (Nancy Kwan), and Puerto Rican (Juanita Hall) actors, it avoids yellowface, with the exception of Juanita Hall's toned-down performance, featuring an all-Asian cast for minor roles and extras. Asian Americans are given for the first time a significant screen presence as a community, akin to films like Vidor's *Hallelujah* (1929) and Preminger's *Carmen Jones* (1954), with their all–African American cast. The character of Linda Low (Nancy Kwan) receives a significant mirror treatment in one scene, giving her the sexual desirability usually reserved for white stars (e.g., Marilyn Monroe) and practically always denied to African American actresses until recently. As Nancy Kwan's image is multiplied in three separate bedroom mirror images, she is shown wearing different outfits, empowering her also as a modern female consumer. The film ends on two modern marriages of choice in contrast to the initial arranged marriage that temporarily creates two unhappy couples. The illegal immigrant Lei Mi, sporting an outdated Chinese queue, is successfully married off and modernized and becomes a legitimate American, critiquing mildly the low quotas for Asian immigration. Nevertheless, with the presentation of the emerging Asian model minority, fluent in all things American, the question of segregation is never really tackled directly. Instead, the community appears to exist as Americans living in a ghettoized parallel society (Chinatown) with no contact or intersection with other Americans other than in the form of media and consumer culture. In addition, in its elevation of the Chinese community, the film obscures the historical violence against Asian Americans on the West Coast, such as the Chinese Exclusion Act of 1882, the various immigration restrictions for Asians in the 1920s, and the internment of Japanese Americans during World War II.

What at first may appear as a cultural opening in the fabric of America is quickly managed in these films, as was the case with postwar Hawaii and its representation in cinema. Uncomfortable questions about race, discrimination, property, and lack of entitlements are not directly broached. The films suffer from creating a model minority and do not convey a nuanced depiction of the diversity of Asian cultures, something that is also rarely seen in films about Hawaii's diverse population, with Hollywood resorting to shorthand versions where one Asian community becomes the stand-in for all Asian Americans. The connection of ethnicity and nationality (e.g., Chinese, Filipino, Korean, Japanese) is thereby racialized into the homogeneous group of Asians. Contrary to Klein's optimistic assessment that ethnicity has fully supplanted race in postwar discourse, Hollywood still heavily relies on racial notions in its depiction of minorities, even if its overt racism from the past is now more muted and less recognizable.

Perhaps a benefit with films set in Hawaii is their inevitable connection to the question of land grab and expansion of territories, something obscured in the mentioned films about Asia and Asian Americans that focus more on the possibility of bridging racial and cultural differences. In a final example concerning race, sovereignty, and property, consider the recent films *The Descendants* (2011) and *Princess Kaiulani* (2009). These films can be seen as more updated and critical attempts to understand Hawaiian history, unlike their epic forebears in the 1960s based on novels by James Michener. The 1966 film epic *Hawaii* (George Roy Hill), while critically pointing to the emotional severity of its Calvinist hero, Reverend Abner Hale, hailing from Yale Divinity School, in the end affirms the inevitable Christianization of Hawaii by New England missionaries. The mass deaths of Hawaiians due to imported diseases are depicted as tragic but ultimately represented as a part of the Christian deity's unfathomable designs for Hawaii and its future to be shepherded by white missionaries and Christian civilization. The film comes with many offensive first-contact stereotypes such as ethnographic nudity, sexual promiscuity, incest, and the hoisting of the obese queen Alii Nui Malama (Jocelyne LaGarde) like cattle onto the ship arriving from New England. Hawaii is fictively framed as a matriarchy rather than a patriarchy, from within which women eventually rebelled against the many *kapus* (taboos) placed upon them and their practices. This historical distortion along with its emasculated male characters portrays Hawaii as weak and susceptible to colonization. The account of history remains highly eclectic and specifically sets Abner's mission apart from the land grab that started with New England missionaries. Although Jerusha (Julie Andrews), Abner's wife, criticizes her husband's arrogance and inhumanity shortly before her death, it only leaves us with a more humbled and chastened Abner at the end, dismayed at the new generation of missionaries who wish to turn the missionary agenda in Hawaii into an economically self-supporting system. Considering that the descendants of the first New England missionaries eventually became the ruling Big Five oligarchy of

Hawaii, this representation of their modest early advances is a gross understatement. With its European lead actors Max von Sydow (Abner Hale) and Julie Andrews (Jerusha), the film further removes its account from any direct connection to US imperialism.

The 1970 sequel *The Hawaiians* (Tom Gries) stars Charlton Heston as Whip Hoxworth, who is married to Hawaiian royalty (Geraldine Chaplin as Purity). As a descendant from the Hale missionary family, he uses the inherited family fortune, while cynically denouncing it as "85,000 acres of nothing," to build the Hawaiian pineapple industry with the help of Chinese indentured labor. The Protestant and capitalist logic that land properly belongs to those who increase its value works to the advantage of the land owner, with water wells providing him with much-needed irrigation for his plantation project. Once again disease, this time leprosy, strikes, sending Hoxworth's faithful servants Mun Ki (Mako) and Nyuk Tsin (Tina Chen) to Molokai for permanent quarantine while Hoxworth's Hawaiian wife descends into melancholy madness and retreats into a Hawaiian commune on the seaside. The film ends on the historical plague in Honolulu's Chinatown, destroying Nyuk Tsin's family fortune after she has miraculously returned from Molokai. Her daughter's marriage to Hoxworth's son seals not only a lifelong friendship but also a business deal between two enterprising communities, namely the Asian model minority and the white American settlers. Hawaiians, as displayed in a short scene in which Queen Liliuokalani asks for the beheading of American traitors plotting against her, are not up to the modernity of capitalist enterprise and have written themselves out of history. In curious narratives colored by the concept of biological and social Darwinism, the stronger white species prevails in both films, installing itself as the rightful owner of Hawaii. While the two films show some remaining concern with race as the earlier discussed social problem films (e.g., the opening scene of *The Hawaiians* depicts the condition of Chinese imported labor on what looks like a slave ship), they now project a restorative vision of US expansionism justified by a deterministic reading of history with its falling and rising civilizations.

In their more critical engagement with Hawaii's annexation and occupation, contemporary films such as *Princess Kaiulani* and *The Descendants* conversely address the overlooked or repressed question of land rights. *Princess Kaiulani* revisits the struggle of asserting independence and avoiding annexation in the final days of the Hawaiian Kingdom. *The Descendants* looks toward the future of a Hawaii trying to curb the ever-growing expansion of the tourist and construction industries and return the islands to an ecological balance. As melodramas with a more specific focus on Hawaii's history, they show more genuine involvement with this history and attempt to avoid an amnesiac escape from it, as was initially discussed with contemporary romantic comedies. *Princess Kaiulani* focuses on the forgotten historical heiress to the throne of the Hawaiian Kingdom during the tumultuous events of the kingdom's overthrow. A majority of scenes are shot during the golden hour, giving Hawaii an autumnal ambience of warmth that history will soon obliterate. Modernization is indicated not necessarily as a hostile element, since the Hawaiian royals are shown in contemporary Victorian fashion, hula dances are performed in long gowns and evoke a spiritual rather than a sexual element, and finally Iolani Palace is lit by the young princess in 1886 as the first palace in the world operating on electricity. The ceremony is interrupted by the Annexation Club, run by Lorrin Thurston and Sanford Dole, grandchildren of New England missionaries, seeking to overthrow King Kalakaua. A putsch is averted, and the young princess is sent abroad for schooling in Scotland, the native home of her father. During this stay the princess is met with racism and cultural arrogance at her school and public events but also affection and love in the Scottish home where she resides. While this biopic takes the usual liberties by not following the exact details of Princess Kaiulani's life, it allows in Hollywood fashion of melodrama to develop her full psychology of choices concerning love and politics.

Engaged to the son of her guardian, she discovers that news of the overthrow of her aunt Queen Liliuokalani had been withheld from her and therefore decides to return to the United States and eventually Hawaii to come to the rescue of her people. In the United States, she manages the delicate diplomatic task of intervening with President Cleveland for the restoration of Hawaii's sovereignty and also wins the heart of the American press. Unfortunately, Cleveland's favorable view is short-lived, since he vacates his office for the incoming President McKinley, who sets a much more aggressive imperialist agenda and supports the annexation of Hawaii. The film, perhaps needlessly so, frames Thurston into the true villain and makes Sanford, the first governor of Hawaii, a more moderate advocate of democracy to be extended to Hawaiian citizens. With voting restrictions for women until the 1920s and Asian immigrants until the 1930s, Hawaii's white voting majority practically allows it to run the islands' affairs under the cover of democracy. The film, in many ways a costume drama with a strong kinship to its British genre and its non-critical view of the aristocracy, nevertheless frankly addresses the unlawful annexation of Hawaii, never fully acknowledged in Hollywood films up to the release of this film. This admission in a popular film follows sixteen years after President Clinton's official apology to Hawaii in 1993 and remains unique.

The Descendants, directed by the Indie filmmaker Alexander Payne, picks up the question of amnesia featured in *50 First Dates* but with the seriousness it deserves in relation to Hawaii's history. The film, based on the novel of Kaui Hart Hemmings, stays close to a perspective of Hawaii seen through the critical eyes of a Hawaiian author, surpassing by far the usual entertainment fare of Hollywood. It opens with the comatose Joane King, wife of Matt King, being regularly visited by her husband in the hospital after an accident during a boating race. Matt King's plea "wake up," as the film will show, will have to be applied to him as well, namely his obliviousness in his private life to the extramarital affair of his wife and in his public life with his neglect of his Hawaiian ancestry and the accompanying moral obligations to the Hawaiian community. His ancestry is established early in the film through voice-over, providing necessary information about his wealth and status in Hawaii. Close-ups of two family portraits highlight his great-great-grandparents who entered a mixed marriage between one of the last princesses related to King Kamehameha and a white banker, son of a New England missionary family. This combination of power and land brings the King family into wealth and the possession of valuable land leases that are about to expire under a new law that prohibits the transfer of these rights in perpetuity. The film's trajectory in its double narrative seeks a solution to both public and private concerns. Although many reviewers on the mainland simply mistook the film for a melodrama with dysfunctional family members (it is a convention in independent films to not convey harmonious images of this institution), the film stresses on numerous occasions its public concern with the legacy of Hawaii and its possessions passed down among the *haole* elites. To underscore this topic, the film opens in medias res, with the near and eventual fatal accident, demystifying Hawaii as the tourist paradise. Establishing shots of Honolulu taken from an elevated position show Diamond Head, the city's trademark tourist site, crowded into the background by skyscrapers and Highway 1 cutting through a maze of buildings. Little of the original nature paradise is visible, as the next shot cuts to a multilane traffic jam usually associated with Los Angeles. The city appears as unattractive, overdeveloped, modern urban real estate. Matt King himself turns out to be a real estate lawyer, and the secret affair of his wife involves another real estate agent, Speer, whose sign is prominently shown in close-up before we meet the actual character. Speculation on the part of King suggests that Speer, who would benefit largely from the sale of the King estate, may have even dated King's wife to wield some influence on this decision. In Kauai, where King visits his extended family to reach a final decision, we once again see numerous tourist developments such as resorts and golf clubs. King himself is shown in a T-shirt of the Outrigger Club, an exclusive escape for the island's elite on the outskirts of Waikiki, which he regularly frequents. A final display of family pictures also shows that the interracial marriage that built the family's fortune is from then on basically a legacy of white couples, keeping the estate in the hands of the white elites. King's cousins are shocked to hear when he refuses to sign the handover documents from which everyone stands to make a considerable profit. At this point, however, woken up to the dysfunctionality within his family, King develops moral qualms about the exploitative use of the land trust that Hawaii bestowed on his family. The film ends on a gesture of sacrifice with King returning the lease to the original ownership of Hawaii. The utopian, and slightly artificial, happy ending stresses the ecological sanctity of Hawaii's Pacific islands to be preserved for posterity. Hawaii's land, as the film suggests, should no longer be subjected to real

estate speculation and development for pure profit. As with *Diamond Head*, however, it remains the decision of the white land owner (90 percent white) to rededi-
cate its purpose, thereby turning him into an ecological philanthropist. The casting
of Clooney, known for his liberal activism, deceptively obscures a more realistic
depiction of the issue of land ownership and subsumes it under the sentimentality
of the white liberal savior and ecologist. Casting Clooney as mixed Hawaiian further adds a layer of appropriation whereby representation and voice of Hawaiians
seamlessly pass into white ownership.

The ending, unfortunately, also does not reflect the current aggressive development on Oahu, Maui, and Kauai, with an additional eye to the formerly prohibited island of Molokai, as the leper colony fades out. Not surprisingly, in its visit
to Hawaii, *Anthony Bourdain: Parts Unknown* (season 5, episode 7, 2015), an exotic
food TV show documenting various global cuisines, had a brief stopover in Molokai and met local residents who were formerly part of Hawaiian nativist protests
against construction. Contemporary TV shows such as *Hawaii Life* (2013–present)
advertise affordable real estate for more affluent mainland middle-class families in
many areas of Hawaii. The formerly elite real estate market on Maui, boasting such
clients as the late George Harrison, Eric Clapton, and Oprah Winfrey, has been
expanded and extends now to average mainland buyers at the exclusion of poorer
Hawaiians. In doing so, this real estate reality show further promotes the economic
dispossession of Hawaii's native population by presenting the island to a mass market of US buyers and highest bidders.

THE MILITARY-ENTERTAINMENT COMPLEX REVISITED

With the release of *The Manchurian Candidate* (1962), based on Richard Con-
don's 1959 novel, the reality of US strategic and neocolonial interests in the
Pacific ranging as far as Korea, Vietnam, and the Philippines was no longer
political news but had become the subject of a satirical spy thriller mocking Cold
War paranoia. The film's highly implausible plot, the capture of American soldiers in Korea, their subsequent brainwashing in Manchuria by a team of Russian and Chinese communists, and the final creation of a communist assassin
steered by his own mother as his American handler, was the stuff of B-list material.[11] However, it was presented in Frankenheimer's film with A-list production
value, heightening the film's enormous popularity as an entertainment product.
Once directly subservient to the interests of military propaganda, Hollywood
had finally emancipated itself from its patriotic service and instead turned the
country's military agenda into a product of pure entertainment. This is not to say
that its films no longer contributed to US geopolitical interests. Rather, direct
propaganda was now substituted with entertainment and an inbuilt amnesia co-
opting audiences into silent complicity. In his essay on "Spectacle as Amnesia

in Imperial Politics," Michael Rogin comments on the increased conversion of World War II, the good war, into a vision of justified US postwar imperialism ending in spectacle: "First, the good war established the military industrial state as the basis for both domestic welfare and foreign policy. Second, it made covert operations at home and abroad an integral part of the state. Third, it drew the political parties together behind an interventionist bipartisan foreign policy. . . . Fourth, the good war's popularity linked the mass public to the structures of power. . . . Finally, World War II celebrated the undercover struggle of good against evil and thereby prepared the way for the covert spectacle."[12] As Rogin points out, the consolidation of the military-industrial complex occurs on several levels by coordinating expansionist interests of geopolitical and global importance. The military global mission of the United States is thereby naturalized and becomes, as a not so "covert spectacle," an integral part of the fabric of American society and culture, especially in its forms of leisure and entertainment. This seismic shift from presenting the military-industrial complex as a necessary substratum of US capitalism toward a presentation of politics as consumer entertainment product, a spectacle, inaugurated in the 1960s an entirely new paradigm of the military-entertainment complex. The joint business and government interest of Hollywood in war films originally began during World War I and intensified during World War II. However, political topics could not be presented in the form of pure entertainment until the 1960s, when Hollywood's censorship relaxed and affluence facilitated a consumer perspective on every aspect of American life, including politics. In responding to the implementation of the military-industrial state, films like *Blue Hawaii* (Norman Taurog, 1961) and *Dr. Strangelove* (Stanley Kubrick, 1964) push the leisure aspects of military life each in its own way, hence normalizing its existence.

This leisurely approach to national interests comes with a high degree of consumer self-awareness and presents political and military movie plots and characters as recognizable Hollywood stereotypes for the pleasure of the audience. The Asian communist villain Dr. Yen Lo in *Manchurian Candidate*, built on the tradition of the wily Fu Manchu, no longer carries the same racist resonance, as Khigh Diegh's performance is highly entertaining, providing a likeable Oriental villain in tongue-in-cheek fashion, not unlike the cardboard villains in the James Bond series. Diegh's acclaimed performance led to his return in the popular TV series *Hawaii Five-0* as the beloved and ever elusive Chinese spy master and villain Wo Fat who presented Detective McGarrett, much like Sherlock Holmes's Dr. Moriarty, with puzzling and intriguing plots that could never reach a conclusive ending or result in McGarrett or Wo Fat's ultimate victory. In the recent relaunch of this acclaimed TV series, Wo Fat is physically disfigured during an explosion and eventually killed by McGarrett, betraying a deeper sense of insecurity about geopolitical dominance in the Pacific and the world. Conversely, during the 1960s the

United States, more fully secure with its global dominance, could take a leisurely view of its Cold War enemies and aggrandize them hyperbolically into entertaining supervillains. Oddly enough, this type of over-the-top presentation gave Asian characters for the first time screen appeal in terms of pure entertainment rather than as a problem group or model minority. This development was foreshadowed in various B-list crime films of the 1940s (*Mr. Moto, Mr. Wong*) and in the detective series *Charlie Chan*, albeit more in the terms of the racial restrictions prevalent in Hollywood at that time. Kigh Diegh's Anglo-Egyptian-Sudanese ancestry made him look credibly like an Oriental villain, even though his Asian appearance is simply one of stereotypical coincidence.

Hawaii Five-0, a CBS police procedural that ran from 1968 to 1980, making it the longest running TV series at the time, surpassed only by *Law & Order* in 2003, is indebted to the international spy drama and found in its Honolulu setting a perfect microcosm for global drama. While a majority of episodes do not involve international incidents and instead focus on various forms of local crime such as gang activities, kidnapping, or a psychotic Vietnam vet on the loose, to name a few, the demographic makeup of Hawaii, which is strongly featured in this series, makes it an early example of global television. With casting that featured next to the two white lead detectives Steve McGarrett and "Danno" Williams a regular cast of Hawaiians and Polynesians, such as detectives Chin Ho (Kam Fong; Chinese Hawaiian), Kono (Zulu; native Hawaiian), Ben (Al Harrington; American Samoan), Duke (Hermann Wedemeyer; native Hawaiian), and forensic expert Cheng Fo (Harry Endo; Japanese Hawaiian), this show projected a remarkable portrait of Hawaii and its diverse population. In addition, guest stars apart from Wo Fat (Kigh Diegh) included numerous actors from Hawaii in repeat roles such as Moe Keale (Truck Kealoha), Kwan Hi Lim (Tosaki), Tommy Fujiwara (Charlie Ling), Danny Kamekona (Nick), Seth Sakai (Batai), and Douglas Mossmann (Frank). While reflecting realistically the prevailing political hierarchy with two white lead detectives and a white governor at the top of the administration, *Hawaii Five-0* as a multicultural show was unprecedented in US television history with its scope of ethnic characters. For local flavor, Hawaiian actors mostly spoke in Hawaiian-accented English, a hybrid of Standard English and pidgin English, which also set the show linguistically apart from mainstream television. On-location shooting with excellent cinematography also permitted viewers a vicarious visitor status to the islands. Finally, guest appearances from famous mainland stars helped make the show one of the most popular crimes series in US history, establishing a version of a successfully assimilated Hawaii as central to current events on the mainland.

Beneath the show's progressive agenda of multiculturalism, a more pragmatic geopolitical interest aligned the series with some of the more conservative ideals of the time. During the height of the Vietnam War, when Hawaii served as a major R&R center and naval base, the islands' incorporation was held up as the successful expansion of US democracy in the Pacific, making it once again a gateway to the Far East. The show, with its law and order emphasis, upholds the US Navy and Coast Guard in numerous episodes, the notion of a free democratic society in episodes involving communist China and its espionage plots, and a regulation of minorities with model character versus nonmodel behavior (gangs, crime, etc.). The overall impression of the show is that of the military-industrial complex spreading deep into the fabric of society with the help of Hawaii's special police force, though without the paranoia of a surveillance state. Once again, a military-entertainment complex makes police activity appear as exciting and fair, especially during a time when the political fallout over the Vietnam War created a more divisive society on the mainland, with police often suppressing free speech and antiwar demonstrations. Instead, the show mostly gives us a utopian image of politics in paradise. The series even accommodates in some episodes the demands of the Hawaiian nativist movement as a legitimate cause deserving to be heard though not yet ready for implementation in the near future. The sympathy for Hawaiians and their diverse ethnic populations ultimately disarms the critical viewer, since such a depiction of minorities had not been seen before.

In stark contrast, the reboot of the series in 2010 eliminates much of the Hawaiian diversity and involves viewers mostly in a white melodramatic crime drama. The casting is by far more inauthentic if not indifferent to Hawaii, as two Korean American actors who are not from Hawaii take on the roles of Chin Ho, the Hawaiian Chinese detective, and Kono Kalakaua (presumably Hawaiian but cast as visibly Korean). Native Hawaiians are now recast in minstrel form as loveable, obese operators of a shrimp vending van, namely Kamekona (Taylor Wiley) and his brother, who are the only characters speaking a Hawaiian-accented English. The many action and chase scenes of the new series do not necessarily add to the local flavor of Hawaii but instead appear borrowed from Hollywood action films. The militarism of the police, with additional SWAT teams, is amped up and conveys an island under siege, mostly reminding viewers of the post-9/11 mainland rather than the more peaceful setting of Hawaii. McGarrett now comes with a distinct military past as a former Marine with Special Forces training, and Danno Williams is a cop transplanted from urban New Jersey. This alteration of the series may well be necessary in the current climate of militarism, when mainland police forces have become heavily militarized in their training and equipment. The multicultural aspect of Hawaii is all but eliminated in this new show, where the mainland has appropriated the islands for its own purposes. It is not surprising that in present films set in Hawaii, white actors such as George Clooney (*The Descendants*) and Emma Stone (*Aloha*) can be effortlessly cast as Hawaiian or part Hawaiian, allowing them to go native, since no Hawaiian identifiers are necessary in a seemingly white-dominated on-screen Hawaii. In reality whites remain a minority in Hawaii, making up only 24 percent of the overall population.

The military aspects of Hawaii were further developed in the hit series *Magnum, P.I.* (1980–1988) written by Donald Bellisario, the creator of the current mainland hit series *NCIS*, with its exclusive focus on the military security apparatus. Similarly, *Magnum, P.I.* gives its main characters a military past, with former Vietnam veterans and Marines (Theodore Calvin, Rick Wright) trying to make a civil career on Oahu, stressing again the leisurely aspect of postmilitary life. T. C., cast as an African American vet, runs a helicopter charter service and his fellow white soldier Rick Wright manages a bar. Private investigator Magnum meanwhile secures a bohemian lifestyle in the guesthouse of a two-hundred-acre beachfront estate, Robin's Nest, owned by the famous writer Robin Masters, who is permanently absent and abroad on frequent travels. The ex-British Army officer Jonathan Quayle Higgins III, a pedantic military man, manages the large estate and serves as a comic foil to Magnum, a man of leisure and ladies, driving Masters's red Ferrari and wearing a Rolex watch. Magnum is in many ways an updated version of the beachcomber, whereas Higgins recalls Hawaii's pre-American past via the British Empire still featured on the Hawaii flag. Higgins marks at the same time a shift toward global Anglo-dominance, which is mocked by Magnum but also inherited as legacy and legitimation of the American presence in Hawaii. The show, with its emphasis on leisure culture and tourism, reflects an unencumbered post-Vietnam era before the onset of Reaganomics and its intense professionalization of all aspects of life. Magnum appears more as a throwback to the 1960s, although his military past has made him a successful investigator. The mostly unused beachfront property of Masters establishes the incorporation of Hawaii as mere financial equity that shows no organic link to social and cultural life on Oahu. Although the show still features multicultural aspects of Hawaii, these are significantly diminished in comparison to *Hawaii Five-0*. Location shots often occur on the exclusive properties of the white elite (such as the King Kamehameha Club run by Rick) and show little of daily life other than in the form of tourism, making the islands more the property of the mainland tourists than its local population.

The hit television series *Lost* (2004–2010), shot on Oahu, brings a new creative approach to the islands. Hawaii as a location remains an anonymous Pacific island akin to the popular comedic TV show *Gilligan's Island* (1965–1967). However, in contrast to the all-white TV comedy, *Lost* features the Pacific as meeting place of global cultures hailing from Australia, Korea, Iraq, France, the United Kingdom, and the United States, where its multinational plane-wrecked survivors struggle to escape what turns out to be a parallel global universe. Highlighting Hawaii's legacy as a global multicultural nexus point, the series variously combines survivalist primitivism, military technology, geological and scientific experimentation, corporate scheming and corruption, as well as elements of science fiction, mysticism, and popular philosophy. The show resembles the format of the US reality TV show *Survivor* (2000–present) as it places its characters into basic biological and anthropological problem-solving situations of securing food, building a community, and protecting its future. However, by making the show a multicultural meeting point, it also highlights twenty-first-century challenges of global coexistence. Hawaii and its Pacific ambience are now reinterpreted from a former South Seas paradise into a natural oceanic sanctuary, stressing sustainability and ecological balance.

As an example of a more regressive appropriation of Hawaii, the TV reality show *Dog the Bounty Hunter* (2004–2012), shot and set on Hawaii, turns natives into bounty money with an admixture of benevolent Christian missionary spirit. The show converts the prison-industrial complex into pure television entertainment and focuses on petty Hawaiian criminals who have missed court dates or skipped bail. Unlike the more graphic series *Cops* (1990–present), this show takes viewers to Hawaii's tourist settings and also makes a few arrests along the way. The show is consciously coded as Hawaiian with Duane "Dog" Chapman shown in his Da Kine Bail Bonds office on Queen Emma Street, not far from the historical former Police Headquarters of Honolulu. Dog's white wife Beth frequently engages in conversation with locals and has mastered Hawaiian pidgin, scolding them on occasion not to "give her stinkeye." His son Leland sports Polynesian tattoos and also has mastered mixed martial arts. On the part of the criminals, the most common violations include drug offenses and ensuing avoidance of court dates. In a typical episode, native Hawaiians, down on their luck, are hunted and captured by Dog and his crew, invoking their motto "no ice in paradise," in various raids across Honolulu's and other neighborhoods. While initially advertised as dangerous and potentially violent, the profiled criminals turn out to be practically harmless and figure as examples of social and economic marginalization rather than seasoned career criminals. Dog, who takes on the persona of a well-meaning missionary, advises his captured criminals to smash their crack pipes, consider the impact of their behavior on their family, and reenter a path of reform, though not without some melodramatic tears on the part of the delinquents and some joint group prayers by the criminals and the bounty hunters fortifying their resolve.

Sociologically, the show provides insight into the poorer sections of mostly native and mixed Hawaiians on Oahu, Maui, and the Big Island. However, the show refuses to address the socioeconomic context of its "criminals on the run" and instead approaches it with old-fashioned Protestant ideals of individual conduct and responsibility. As a 2010 study of the Justice Policy Institute from the University of Hawai'i shows, native Hawaiians are disproportionately represented with greater numbers of arrests, prison sentences, and prison and probation terms, drawing comparison with Native Americans and inner-city African Americans on the mainland.[13] Concerning drug offenses, the report notes, "Native Hawaiians do not use drugs at drastically different rates than other races or ethnicities, but go to prison for drug offenses more often than other races or ethnicities."[14] The show, with its criminal profiling of native Hawaiians, contributes thereby to a cover-up of the socioeconomic fallout of Hawaii's colonization and idealizes in the figure of Dog the white missionary, uplifting natives who have lost their way. Meanwhile, occasional glimpses of Dog's spacious residence in the pricy neighborhood of Kahala highlight his anointed status as a white guardian of morality and family values (even though Dog did a five-year jail stretch as an accomplice in a first-degree murder in his earlier years). Dog's own criminal past is used to promote the possibility of redemption, softening the show into an endearing neocolonial Christian spectacle of reform. Although Dog claims that he has Native American ancestors and wears shell-ornamented and bleached hair extensions, enhancing his messianic look, the show simply combines the prison- and military-security-industrial complex into a form of profitable entertainment at the expense of native Hawaiians. For mainland viewers, the show also reinforces stereotypes of darker ethnicities being more prone to criminal activities, affirming mainland racism as universal fact. In an age clamoring for media attention, the show ironically was well received in Hawaii, and Dog was frequently honored at various charity events of local schools for being an outstanding citizen in his fight against drugs, promoting the rehabilitation of criminals.

In recent years, Hawaii has been the location for many films that mostly make use of its natural setting and studio facilities but have no connection to Hawaii thematically. The island, once substituted by LA studio back lots, is now itself a back lot for various non-Hawaiian locations. Notable films that have used Hawaii's scenic location include *Jurassic World* (2015), *Big Eyes* (2014), *Godzilla* (2014), *Battleship* (2012), *Avatar* (2009), *2012* (2009), *Tropic Thunder* (2008), *Snakes on a Plane* (2006), *Punch-Drunk Love* (2002), and the *Jurassic Park* trilogy (1993, 1997, 2001). Though thematically concentrating on World War II Hawaii, Michael Bay's romantic war epic *Pearl Harbor* (2001) made little use of Hawaii's location and was filmed for the most part in California and the United Kingdom. Its predominantly white cast (Ben Affleck, Josh Hartnett, Kate Beckinsale) further removes the film from Hawaii and turns it into a mainland melodrama. Historical obliviousness serves the film's purpose of turning its drama into a late example of the good war, fought by the greatest generation. The attack on Pearl Harbor is misrepresented in Bay's film in the usual fashion as an attack against US territory and not a preemptive strike directed against a legitimate military target. Moreover, no Hawaiian victims are shown, no mention of Japanese internment is made, nor is any reference given to immediately imposed martial law restricting all movements for Hawaiians and allowing the military to take over all administrative affairs of Hawaii. Instead, the film's focus on loss and casualties restricts itself exclusively to US military personnel. As such, the film resonated well in a post-9/11 environment with the nation once again under attack. In most of these films, one notes a contemporary concern with ecology, though predominantly represented in apocalyptic and dystopian terms of war and ecological disaster. As a marine and nature sanctuary, Hawaii is and will be used in the foreseeable future as a Hollywood stand-in for dramas involving global culture, sustainability, and ecological balance.

Aloha (Cameron Crowe, 2015) presents in this new mode an ecologically inflected military-industrial complex fusing Hawaii's ecological outlook with US military concerns. Casting of blonde Emma Stone as one-quarter Hawaiian drew criticism but works predictably within the Hollywood logic of profit, using popular white stars as focalizing draws for film audiences. This business strategy also explains the casting in *The Descendants of* star George Clooney rather than a more credible and part-Hawaiian actor such as David Strathairn, who, though known, usually does not carry entire films. To this date, Dwayne "The Rock" Johnson, of Samoan and African Canadian ancestry, is the only Pacific film star with wide recognition value; however, his many comedic, action, and sci-fi roles do not touch upon the Pacific, with the exception of the adventure sci-fi comedy *Journey 2: The Mysterious Island* (2012), filmed on Oahu's Waimea Bay but narratively set in Palau.

Set in contemporary Hawaii, *Aloha* often appears forced and artificial in its attempt to give Hawaii a more realistic and recognizable representation from a Hawaiian point of view. Emma Stone, for example, as Captain Allison Ng, sings with a Hawaiian group of musicians Gabby Pahinui's slack guitar classic "Waimanalo Blues" as one of her favorite tunes, but does so unconvincingly. Mitchell, the white son of retired Brian Gilcrest's (Bradley Cooper) former girlfriend Tracy (Rachel McAdams), turns out to be a "Hawaiian myth buff" and decorates his room with the flag of the Hawaiian nationalist movement. Gilcrest's daughter Grace comes to melodramatic awareness during a hula dance class that Brian, her mother's former boyfriend, is indeed her biological father. This scene is shot with many medium close-ups of her dancing the hula, placing other Hawaiian class members out of the frame. Apart from such obvious Hollywood distortions, however, the film does address political claims for sovereignty by the Hawaiian nationalist movement and features a cameo of Bumpy Kanahele, Hawaiian nationalist leader and head of Nation of Hawai'i. His T-shirt, filmed front and back and stating "Hawaiian By Birth—American By Force," is nevertheless undermined as he is shown to be close friends with Gilcrest and admires the military in general, while asserting that Hawaii is "under occupation." Since the nationalist movement's flag, presented by him to Gilcrest, is shown in a final shot in the children's bedroom of the Hawaiian myth buff Mitchell, to whom it has been bequeathed, the film further suggests that this movement is at best in its infancy and thereby belittles its seriousness. Other cameos of Hawaiian musicians are likewise used in exploitative fashion to evoke the usual atmosphere of local Hawaiian cookouts and luaus accompanied by Hawaiian music.

As a new feature, the film portrays the military and military contractors cooperating closely with native Hawaiians, seemingly respecting their customs and lands.

Brian Gilcrest retired from the military and, now a contractor, oversees a traditional Hawaiian blessing for a pedestrian gate on a former Hawaiian burial ground
on Hickam Field and secures Hawaiian participation in exchange for two mountains and cell phone service. This ludicrous plot device allows the film to introduce
Emma Stone's part-Hawaiian character Allison Ng, who in turn will introduce
Brian as a local liaison to King Kanahele, the Hawaiian nationalist leader. Gilcrest
is at the same hired by billionaire Carson Welch (Bill Murray), who intends to
install a communications satellite to aid six poor Pacific Rim countries. Later this
claim is found out to be an outright lie, forcing Brian and the military to sabotage
its concealed weaponized nuclear capability, causing the satellite to explode. Predictably the romantic comedy ends in the production of two couples (Brian and
Allison and the restored marriage of Tracy and her husband Woody) as well as the
blessing of the gate, ridiculously suggesting that the military preserves balance on
Hawaii and protects the islands from ruthless private businessmen.

The film's opening montage made up of video and documentary footage introduces its major thematic strands of military technology in conflict with Hawaii's
peaceful and ecological outlook. Hawaiian cultural icons (Duke Kahanamoku,
Queen Liliuokalani), dancers, wartime images, and King Kamehameha parades
alternate with historic footage of rocket launches, drones, and other reconnaissance technology. Ironically and unintentionally the montage also captures the
military-entertainment complex, as it intercuts space and rocket technology footage with leisure footage from Hawaii, showing the two as intimately connected. As
Brian Gilcrest lands at Hickam Field, Hawaiian dance ceremonies alternate with
military ceremonials such as "Taps." Later in the film, Captain Ng claims, "This
is not the military of old, . . . this is the new." She invokes the Outer Space Peace
Treaty of 1967 and promises the Hawaiian king that the military "will not put weapons above these sacred skies." This promise tacitly overlooks that Hawaii is already
militarized to its teeth with many nuclear-powered carriers and nuclear submarines patrolling the Pacific. As Haunani-Kay Trask, Hawaiian activist-scholar and
staunch defender of Hawaiian independence, summarizes the facts that the film all
too obviously ignores,

On O'ahu, the capital of our state and the most densely populated island, the
military controls 25% of the land area. Statewide, the combined U.S. armed forces
have 21 installations, 26 housing complexes, eight training areas, and 19 miscel-
laneous bases and operating sites. Beyond O'ahu, Hawai'i is the linchpin of the
U.S. military strategy in the Asia-Pacific region. It is home to the largest portage
of nuclear-fueled ships and submarines in the world. These ships are received,
cleaned, and refashioned at Pearl Harbor, where workers are called "sponges"
because of their high absorption of radiation during cleaning. Regionally, Hawai'i
is the forward basing point for the U.S. military in the Pacific. The Seventh Fleet,

which patrols the world from the Pacific to the coast of Africa, is stationed at Pearl Harbor. . . . This kind of "peaceful violence" results in land confiscations, contamination of our plants, animals, and our peoples, and the transformation of our archipelago into a poisonous war zone. Additionally, many of the lands taken by the military are legally reserved lands for Hawaiians. In the southern and eastern Pacific, U.S. military violence has taken the form of nuclear testing in the Marshall Islands, the dumping of nuclear waste on Christmas Island, the siting of electronic facilities vital to nuclear war, and construction of air bases with nuclear capabilities, including airborne delivery of weapons. To the east of Hawai'i, in the Marianas Islands and Guam, there are airbases with nuclear capabilities. The violence of nuclearization and militarization associated with nuclear testing in the Marshall Islands includes the detonation of over 66 bombs. We must all remember that the world's first hydrogen bomb was tested on Bikini Island.[15]

The film's utopian narrative of demilitarization remains one of wishful thinking and does little to change the status quo of Hawaii in its spurious narrative, where the military checks the island's safety against rogue corporate interests. The film is divided in its message by trying to give more voice to Hawaii and at the same time defending the major interest group, the military, that has kept Hawaii under occupation. In a shot sequence interspersed with the final credits of the film, King Kanahele ceremonially reburies ancestor bones relocated from the Hickam gate together with Gilcrest on Hawaiian land and hands him a volcano stone. The old Hawaiian flag is shown upside down, with the British part of the flag in the lower left corner, a further reminder of the kingdom's hostile annexation and its state of occupation. Unfortunately, with the film framing the military as the guardian of stability, these scenes mostly constitute lip service for liberal-minded audiences.

With the rebalancing of US military power in the Pacific, starting under the Obama administration in 2012, strong military and strategic interests in Hawaii have in fact increased. As the United States gradually disengages from the unstable regions of the Near and Middle East, it has turned its view toward the large, profitable markets of China and India, while also protecting its older interests in Japan, South Korea, and Taiwan. Crowe's film *Aloha*, which involves the military much more significantly than recent films about Hawaii (*50 First Dates*, *Forgetting Sarah Marshall*, *The Descendants*) reflects the new remilitarization of the Pacific but seeks to tame its reality with a discourse of ecology, one of Hawaii's latest cultural exports. The Disney animation film *Lilo & Stitch* (2002) similarly imagines that a misguided military genetic experiment producing the monster Stitch will eventually be corrected, once Stitch escapes to Hawaii. Stitch, programmed to cause chaos, meets his true match in the unruly Hawaiian girl Lilo, Hawaii's peaceful land and seascape, and its contagious *ohana* spirit. They transform Stitch to a degree that he becomes civilized and finally settles down in Hawaii, adopted by Lilo and her sister Nani. To the tune of Elvis songs that curiously represent Hawaii, this Disney film combines Hawaiian family dysfunctionality (Lilo is raised by her sister Nani) with an out-of-control military technology, only to balance it into a peaceful harmony of restored family values. In turning to the discourse of ecology, both *Lilo & Stitch* and *Aloha* find new narrative formulas to naturalize the inevitable US claim on Hawaii in the face of its recently increased military role in the Pacific.

In our concluding examination of contemporary films and television programs about Hawaii, it has become apparent that two diametrically opposed themes dominate in the on-screen representation of the Pacific, namely amnesia and militarization. The former is rooted in escapist fantasy and white melodrama, negating any historical accountability of the United States toward its quasi-colony of Hawaii. Instead, Hawaii figures as a wholesome ecosystem that restores broken relationships or induces new romances. Its natural and oceanic habitats remind viewers that a belief in ecological balance and sustainability will correct all problems, even those that the films steadfastly refuse to address such as race, property, and political representation. The white coded liberal universe that sees Hawaii as a home away from home appears benevolent but gives little voice to those inhabitants who have been socioeconomically displaced by settler colonialism, tourism, real estate prices, and cost of living. In contrast to these fantasy escape scenarios, films with a dose of realism view Hawaii as a battleground for global conflicts and the maintenance of geopolitical dominance via military power. The necessary remilitarization of Pacific culture is made palatable to audiences via thriller and action plots, providing lowbrow entertainment rather than high-minded political seriousness. Once again, the reality of contemporary Hawaii and the Pacific falls through the cracks in such scenarios that indulge in the ever-growing enlargement of the military-industrial-entertainment complex.

As was also shown throughout our discussion, Hollywood does not take its task of filming the Pacific lightly, relying on some of the best directors, writers, and cinematographers in the industry. Its cinematic distortions of representation have been achieved with considerable film aesthetics, ranging from spectacular nature and oceanic scenes to underwater and color photography, complex editing, the creation of new genres such as the South Seas fantasy, the combat film, and battlefield documentary, as well as the use of classical Hollywood conventions of melodrama and musicals to highlight the work of nation building. In addition, the industry's top stars have been involved in this enterprise to convey the Pacific's full incorporation into the imaginary space of Hollywood drama. While contemporary audiences may be dismayed at some of the racist stereotyping and disavow these films as mere Hollywood products, audiences of the past received them favorably and saw them as an extension of the mainland's imaginary space. This systematic conceptualization of the representation of the Pacific continues today with new technological and aesthetic developments to promote its appropriation. As such these films and television programs also provide a map to the ideological concerns that help build the edifice of the United States.

Hollywood films about Hawaii and the Pacific betray a colonial and imperial mind at work and give insight into the structures of power that have governed and still govern the United States today. Hawaii and the Pacific appear in this sense as a symptom pointing to the nation's repeated attempts at self-portrayal. To what extent the South Pacific is a space of leisure or military conflict remains forever undecidable as Hollywood preserves the structural ambiguity of its symbolic universe, making it a form of entertainment rather than political discourse. It is in this fashion that it interposes itself between representation and consumption as a form of mediation. Cinematically mediated images of the South Pacific and Hawaii purposely compromise and co-opt this region in order to serve as the continuing playground for the fantasy production of the United States.

NOTES

INTRODUCTION

1   King Vidor, *A Tree Is a Tree* (New York: Harcourt Brace, 1953), 196. See also Raymond F. Betts, who discusses this anecdote with regard to the artificiality of South Seas films in "The Illusionary Island: Hollywood's Pacific Place," *East-West Film Journal* 5, no. 2 (July 1991): 30–46, 35.

2   Gilles Deleuze, *Cinema 1: The Movement-Image*, trans. Hugh Tomlinson and Barbara Habberjam (Minneapolis: University of Minnesota Press, 1986), 148.

3   Ibid., 148.

4   Wheeler Winston Dixon, *Visions of Paradise: Images of Eden in the Cinema* (New Brunswick, NJ: Rutgers University Press, 2006), 22.

5   Slavoj Žižek, *The Plague of Fantasies* (London: Verso, 1997), 98.

6   Paul Virilio, *War and Cinema: The Logistics of Perception*, trans. Patrick Camiller (London: Verso, 1989), 3.

7   Kathy E. Ferguson and Phyllis Turnbull, *Oh, Say Can You See? The Semiotics of the Military in Hawai'i* (Minneapolis: University of Minnesota Press, 1999), xiii.

8   Henry R. Luce, "The American Century," reprinted in *Diplomatic History* 23, no. 2 (Spring 1999): 159–171, 167.

9   Public Law 103-150 (November 23, 1993), S.J. Res. 19.

10 See Taylor Kate Brown, "Aloha to the US: Is Hawai'i an Occupied Nation?," *BBC News Magazine*, November 2, 2015. Brown writes, "Williamson Chang, a professor of law at University of Hawai'i, is one of those Hawaiians. He argues under international law, one country can only annex another by treaty—a document which both parties sign. This is how the entire rest of the US was formed—the Louisiana Purchase, the treaties with Native American tribes, the addition of the Republic of Texas. Anything else—including what happened in Hawai'i—is an occupation, Chang says." The Hawaiian Independence Day (November 28), in fact, celebrates the 1843 formal recognition of Hawaii's kingdom by France and Great Britain as an independent and sovereign nation.

11 Beth Bailey and David Farber, *The First Strange Place: Race and Sex in World War II Hawaii* (Baltimore: Johns Hopkins University Press, 1992).

12 Lisa G. Corrin, "Mining the Museum: Artists Look at Museums, Museums Look at Themselves," in *Mining the Museum: An Installation by Fred Wilson*, ed. Lisa G. Corrin (New York: New Press, 1994), 8.

13 Ibid., 8.

CHAPTER 1   THE SOUTH PACIFIC AND
HAWAII ON SCREEN

1   William Kennedy Laurie Dixon largely developed the Kinetoscope, a peephole device for viewing motion pictures, between 1888 and 1892 in Edison's laboratory.

2   Sanford B. Dole was a cousin of James Dole, who founded the Hawaiian Pineapple Company in 1901, which took its origins with Castle and Cooke's company in 1851 that invested in Hawaii's sugarcane industry and was known as one of the Big Five companies running Hawaii's agricultural industries.

3   Virilio, *War and Cinema*, 15.

4   Miriam Hansen, *Babel & Babylon: Spectatorship in American Silent Film* (Cambridge, MA: Harvard University Press, 1991), 61.

5   Judith Mayne, *Private Novels, Public Films* (Athens: University of Georgia Press, 1988), 73.

6   While Hawaiian dance and music culture was performed and shown at the World's Columbian Exposition in Chicago (1893) and various other international exhibitions thereafter with a similar emphasis on imperial acquisitions, these exhibits did not reach mass audiences in the entire country, as was the case with cinema. A popular but fairly exclusive Hawaiian Room at the Hotel Lexington in wartime New York would similarly offer hula shows that the average citizen could watch in movies at a much more affordable price. See Adria L. Imada, *Aloha America: Hula Circuits through the U.S. Empire* (Durham, NC: Duke University Press, 2012).

7   Hansen, *Babel & Babylon*, 78.

8   Charles Musser, *The Emergence of Cinema: The American Screen to 1907* (Berkeley: University of California Press, 1990), 109.

9   Richard Abel, *Encyclopedia of Early Cinema* (New York: Routledge, 2005), 487.

10   *Kanakas Diving for Money, no. 2* (June 22, 1898), Library of Congress. Diving for money and off piers remains a popular pastime in Hawaii today.

11   *Boys Diving, Honolulu*, H16361, American Mutoscope & Biograph Company, April 10, 1902, filmed August 1, 1901, in Honolulu, HI.

12   *Cutting Sugar Cane*, H18040, American Mutoscope & Biograph Company, May 23, 1902, 16 mm.

13   *Loading Sugar Cane*, H21496, American Mutoscope & Biograph Company, September 5, 1902.

14   Ferguson and Turnbull, *Oh, Say Can You See?*, 6.

15   Ibid., 34.

16   Ruth M. Tabrah, *Hawaii: A History* (New York: Norton, 1984), 82.

17   See "About Us/History" at www.outriggercanoeclub.com.

18   Stephen Greenblatt, *Marvelous Possessions: The Wonder of the New World* (Chicago: University of Chicago Press, 1991), 57.

19   Musser, *Emergence of Cinema*, 152.

20   This film no longer exists in print. *Aloha Oe* was produced by Thomas H. Ince, a one-time partner of D. W. Griffith who built his own studio in Culver City, which would eventually become the home of MGM.

21   Jeffrey Geiger, *Facing the Pacific: Polynesia and the U.S. Imperial Imagination* (Honolulu: University of Hawai'i Press, 2007), 40. For a full account of early voyager and settler violence, see Geiger's chapter "The Garden and the Wilderness," 18–73.

22   Poster reprint in Lowell Angell, *Theatres of Hawai'i* (Charleston, SC: Arcadia, 2011), 22.

23   Gary Y. Okihiro, *Pineapple Culture: A History of the Tropical and Temperate Zones* (Berkeley: University of California Press, 2009), 18.

24   Hansen, *Babel & Babylon*, 64.

25   Ibid., 64.

26   Ibid., 81.

27   Michael Rogin, *Blackface, White Noise: Jewish Immigrants in the Hollywood Melting Pot* (Berkeley: University of California Press, 1996), 76.

28   Ibid., 90.

29   Hansen, *Babel & Babylon*, 81.

30   Betts, "Illusionary Island," 31, 46. Betts's cited source is the text of a special program for the film's premiere; "White Shadows in the South Seas" folder, Theatre Arts Library, University of California, Los Angeles (46).

31   Ibid., 30.

32   *Moana's* staged indigenous and premodern population, as Francis Flaherty, wife of the director, notes in a journal "had in many cases traveled abroad, gone to missionary schools, spoke English and drove cars." Quoted in Geiger, *Facing the Pacific*, 144.

33   Dixon, *Visions of Paradise*, 28.

34   This film, unfortunately, no longer exists in print. Its plot is based on a racialized rescue narrative. Lorna, the daughter of Madge and Captain Blackbird, is promised by a corrupt white trader, now living with Madge, to the native leader Waki for marriage. She is saved from this indignity in a last-minute rescue. Walsh had also starred in Griffith's *Birth of a Nation* and came of age as a filmmaker under Griffith's influence and racist views.

35   Rogin, *Blackface, White Noise*, 91.

36   Hernan Vera and Andrew Gordon, "Sincere Fictions of the White Self in the American Cinema," in *Classic Hollywood, Classic Whiteness*, ed. Daniel Bernardi (Minneapolis: University of Minnesota Press, 2001), 273.

37   Rogin, *Blackface, White Noise*, 148–149.

38   Marsha Orgeron, "Making *It* in Hollywood: Clara Bow, Fandom, and Consumer Culture," *Cinema Journal* 42, no. 4 (Summer 2003): 76–97, 76.

39   Ibid., 78.

40   Similarly, the career of Fleming was on the rise. Fleming had started out in the photographic section in World War I, served as chief photographer for President Wilson at the Versailles Conference, and acquired his early skills in cinematography as assistant to D. W. Griffith.

41   Hansen, *Babel & Babylon*, 71.

42   Ibid., 71.

43   Rogin, *Blackface, White Noise*, 73.

44   Walter Benjamin, "The Work of Art in the Age of Mechanical Reproduction," in *Illuminations*, ed. Hannah Arendt, trans. Harry Zohn (New York: Schocken, 1968), 225.

45   Adrienne L. Kaeppler, "Acculturation in Hawaiian Dance," *Yearbook of the International Folk Music Council* 4 (1972): 38–46, 38–39.

46   Ibid., 42.

47   Jane C. Desmond, *Staging Tourism: Bodies on Display from Waikiki to Sea World* (Chicago: University of Chicago Press, 1999), 39.

48   Ibid., 40.

49   Richard Dyer, *Stars* (London: BFI, 1998), 57.

50   Hansen, *Babel & Babylon*, 116.

51   See Okihiro, *Pineapple Culture*, 60.

52   Cited in ibid., 18.

53   Ibid., 102.

54   Ibid., 102.

55   Ibid., 103.

56   Ibid., 103.

57   Ibid., 106, 108.

58   Ibid., 117.

59   Glenn K. S. Man, "Hollywood Images of the Pacific," *East-West Film Journal* 5, no. 2 (1991): 16–30, 27.

60   This poem was first published in 1899 in the popular American magazine *McClure* with the subtitle "The United States and the Philippines Islands."

61   Sofia Ortega also plays the minor character of Mahumahu in Vidor's *Bird of Paradise*.

62   Mordaunt Hall, in his *New York Times* review of *Rain* (October 13, 1932), takes issue with the film's strong criticism of the religious fanaticism embodied by Davidson: "He walks as if he had spent years as a private in the Prussian Army, and in a sequence the usually sagacious Mr. Milestone has him repeat the Lord's Prayer four times." At the same time, the review does not mention anything about its provocative interracial family, the close-up ethnographic depiction of native fishermen discovering Davidson's body, or the overall problematic representation of natives, as an incorporated people and territory, as backdrop in the film. The concern with correct representation is instead simply applied to white characters and the ruling colonizing elites such as the raving and raping missionary or what Hall views as the too weakly depicted "lovelorn hero" Sergeant O'Hara. This review is indicative of the persistent racial bias of the period, with no concern for the fate of America's colonies and their people. The Hollywood production code enforced in 1934 would further make sure that white supremacy, with its systematic disenfranchisement of minorities of color, would also be maintained on the screen.

63   It is also interesting to note that Jewish actors could not play Jewish characters in lead roles and instead had to play other ethnicities in blackface (e.g., Al Jolson's conflicted role of the Jewish blackface performer in *The Jazz Singer* with the Swedish Warner Oland playing the Cantor Rabinowitz) or yellowface (Paul Muni and Luise Rainer in *The Good Earth*) or in makeup and costume as in the Italian gangster roles played by Muni and Edward G. Robinson.

64   Daniel Bernardi, "Introduction," in Bernardi, *Classic Hollywood, Classic Whiteness*, xi–xxvi, xvi.

65   Yunte Huang, *Charlie Chan: The Untold Story of the Honorable Detective and His Rendezvous with American History* (New York: Norton, 2010), 183.

66   Ibid., 183.

67   On occasion, the Chan series will surprise viewers with utopian shots of multiethnic representation. For example, *Charlie Chan at the Race Track* (1936) features initially a multiethnic Asian and Hawaiian cast at Honolulu's Police Department. Only as Chan leaves for the mainland does the series revert to its usual pairing of Chan (Warner Oland) with his son Lee (Keye Luke) and a black minstrelsy sidekick surrounded by a corrupt white upper class. In this respect, the opening shots of Honolulu's multiethnic

and democratically depicted police unit can be seen as depicting a utopian counter-world to corruption, white privilege, and racism.

68   All biographical information concerning Apana is from Huang, *Charlie Chan.*

69   Ibid., 250–251.

70   Ibid., 250.

71   Siegfried Kracauer, "The Mass Ornament," in *The Mass Ornament: Weimar Essays,* ed. and trans. Thomas Y. Levin (Cambridge, MA: Harvard University Press, 1995), 75–86, 75–76; the essay originally appeared in its German version in 1927. Here I am greatly indebted to Miriam Hansen, who first introduced me to the writings of Kracauer and the Frankfurt school critics.

72   Ibid., 76.

73   Ibid., 76.

74   Patricia Mellencamp, "*Gold Diggers of 1933*: Containing Social Turmoil—Containing Women," in *Hollywood Musicals: The Film Reader,* ed. Steven Cohan (New York: Routledge, 2006), 65–76, 68.

75   Ibid., 66.

76   Martin Rubin, "Busby Berkeley and the Backstage Musical," in Cohan, *Hollywood Musicals,* 53–61, 59.

77   Due to various scandals in the 1920s involving popular Hollywood stars, especially the Fatty Arbuckle case, in which the actor stood trial for the rape and accidental death of actress Virginia Rappe, Hollywood faced nationwide criticism and calls for federal censorship from major political, civic, temperance, and religious organizations. Fearful of government censorship, the major Hollywood studios formed the Motion Picture Producers and Distributors of America (MPPDA) in 1922 as a public relations office that would address such scandals, improve Hollywood's image, and ensure the financial health of the industry. Studio heads hired Will H. Hays, former chairman of the Republican National Committee and US postmaster general. Backed by religious organizations, especially leaders of the Catholic Church, the Production Code, popularly known as the Hays Code, was drafted in 1929, adapted by Hays in 1930, and strictly enforced beginning in 1934 under the administration of Joseph Breen. The code greatly impacted the content and style of Hollywood films, especially those made between 1934 and the late 1950s. The code was a set of moral guidelines, outlining what was and was not suitable content for public audiences. It was, as Richard Maltby writes, "a corporate statement of policy about the appropriate content of entertainment cinema and acknowledged the possible influence of movies on the morals and conduct of those who saw them" (46). See Tino Balio, ed., *Grand Design: Hollywood as a Modern Business Enterprise, 1930–1939* (Berkeley: University of California Press, 1993), especially Richard Maltby's chapter 3, "The Production Code and the Hays Office," 37–72. The code had a list of items not to be shown on-screen, including miscegenation, childbirth, sexual perversions, nudity and the sex organs of children, ridicule of the clergy, profanity, illegal drugs, rape or assault, the use of firearms, and sympathy toward criminals. Due to postwar culture and the advent of television, the code was seen as outdated and weakened after the late 1950s. It was only minimally enforced and eventually replaced in 1968 by the MPAA film rating system.

78   Keeler was also married to Al Jolson and would later star across from him in the musical *Go into Your Dance* (1935).

79   Kracauer, "Mass Ornament," 78.

80   Andre Sennwald, "Flirtation Walk, or Life among the Cadets at the Strand," *New York Times*, November 29, 1934.

81   Benjamin, "Work of Art," 241.

82   Adria L. Imada, "Hawaiians on Tour: Hula Circuits through the American Empire," *American Quarterly* 56, no. 1 (March 2004): 111–149, 114.

83   Ibid., 111.

84   Okihiro, *Pineapple Culture*, 116–117.

85   Hannah Arendt, *Imperialism: Part Two of the Origins of Totalitarianism* (New York: Harcourt Brace Jovanovich, 1968), 6.

86   Ibid., 11–14.

87   Okihiro, *Pineapple Culture*, 153.

88   Ibid., 153–154.

89   DeSoto Brown, "Beautiful, Romantic Hawaii: How the Fantasy Image Came to Be," *Journal of Decorative and Propaganda Arts* 20 (1994): 254–271, 268.

90   Okihiro, *Pineapple Culture*, 148.

91   Carol J. Clover, "Dancin' in the Rain," in Cohan, *Hollywood Musicals*, 157–173, 162.

92   See, for example, *The Barricade* (1921), where Jakob Solomon adopts the son of his deceased Irish business partner Michael Brennan. The film depicts Robert Brennan's upward social mobility with him leaving the Lower East Side and his Jewish family and friends behind who had helped him to regain his social footing. Similarly, Victor Fleming's *Abie's Irish Rose* (1928) offers an interethnic marriage melodrama between the Jewish Abie Levy and the Irish Rosemary Murphy, much to the initial consternation of their parents who consent upon the birth of twin babies.

93   The fourteen-part film serial *Robinson Crusoe of Clipper Island* (Republic Pictures, 1936) anticipates the espionage plot of *Hawaii Calls*. The story centers upon an attempt to derail and sabotage the technological advances of Dirigible Aviation in the Pacific. It stars Native American actor Mala in the lead role of Polynesian US intelligence agent Ray Mala alongside Princess Melani (Mamo Clark) and his Irish and British friends McGlaurie and Tupper. Though the film is a B production, its inclusive casting makes it stand out as one of the more liberal South Seas productions of the 1930s.

94   Thomas Mitchell, who is of Irish American descent, starred in famous films such as John Ford's *Stagecoach* (1939) and *Hurricane* (1937; nominated for Oscar), Fleming's *Gone with the Wind* (1939), Capra's *It's a Wonderful Life* (1946), and Hawks's *Only Angels Have Wings* (1939). Apart from James Cagney, mostly cast in gangster roles, Mitchell stands out as the most prominent male Irish American screen actor of his time.

95   Victor Mature is considered one of the first Italian American actors receiving larger screen presence with the exception of the Italian Rudolph Valentino who dominated the silver screen in the 1920s.

96   Amy Kaplan, *The Anarchy of Empire in the Making of U.S. Culture* (Cambridge, MA: Harvard University Press, 2002), 96.

97   As Dixon notes, "The Edenic cinema offers us glimpses of life free from strife, rich and meaningful, devoid of pain and privation. Indeed, these films offer the viewer a moment out of time, in which audience and cast members alike can partake of a vision of personal freedom and safety, a zone of privilege and protection that transcends the demands of daily existence." See Dixon, *Vision of Paradise*, 8.

98   Emily S. Rosenberg, *Spreading the American Dream: Economic and Cultural Expansionism 1890–1945* (New York: Hill & Wang, 1982), chap. 2, "Capitalists, Christians, Cowboys," 14–38.

99   Ibid., 54.

CHAPTER 2   WORLD WAR II HAWAII

1   Luce, "American Century," 167.

2   Ibid., 168–169, emphasis original.

3   Ibid., 166.

4   Ibid., 170.

5   Kinley Brauer, "Manifest Destiny Revisited," *Diplomatic History* 23, no. 2 (Spring 1999): 379–384, 379.

6   Michael H. Hunt, "East Asia in Henry Luce's 'American Century,'" *Diplomatic History* 23, no. 2 (Spring 1999): 321–353, 323.

7   See David Spurr, *The Rhetoric of Empire: Colonial Discourse in Journalism, Travel Writing, and Imperial Administration* (Durham, NC: Duke University Press, 1993), 118–120. Spurr discusses how Manifest Destiny in the vein of Henry Luce is still used in America's perspective of the Third World as depicted in the 1981 *Time* magazine article "American Renewal," reviewing Ronald Reagan's first presidential term.

8   Edward Said, *Orientalism* (New York: Vintage Books, 1979). See also Edward Said, *Culture and Imperialism* (New York: Knopf, 1993).

9   See Alexander Lyon Macfie, *Orientalism* (London: Longman, 2002) for a discussion of the various positions on Orientalism as well as refinements and critiques of Said's arguments.

10   Deborah Gewertz and Frederick Errington, "We Think Therefore We Are?," in *Cultures of U.S. Imperialism*, ed. Amy Kaplan and Donald Pease (Durham, NC: Duke University Press, 1993), 635–655.

11   Gary Okihiro, "When and Where I Enter," in *Asian American Studies: A Reader*, ed. Jean Yu-Wen Shen Wu and Min Song (New Brunswick, NJ: Rutgers University Press, 2000), 3–20.

12   See Lisa Lowe, *Immigrant Acts: On Asian American Cultural Politics* (Durham, NC: Duke University Press, 1996).

13   See Fatimah Tobing Rony, "*King Kong* and the Monster in Ethnographic Cinema," in *Critical Visions in Film Theory*, ed. Timothy Corrigan et al. (Boston: Bedford/St. Martin's, 2011), 840–859, 851.

14   Haunani-Kay Trask, *From a Native Daughter: Colonialism and Sovereignty in Hawai'i*, rev. ed. (Honolulu: University of Hawai'i Press, 1999), 17.

15   An earlier and more limited version of these reflections on John Ford and Henry Luce appeared originally as "John Ford's Vernacular Orientalism and Wartime Hawaii," *Quarterly Review of Film and Video* 26, no. 4 (August 2009): 293–310. My stance on Ford has since become more nuanced, as will become evident with the broader discussion of his films in this chapter.

16   Said, *Orientalism*, 167.

17   Ibid., 240.

18   Ella Shohat and Robert Stam, *Unthinking Eurocentrism: Multiculturalism and the Media* (London: Routledge, 1994), 113. In this otherwise perceptive study, the US role in the

Pacific, Hawaii, and Asia is not adequately discussed and thereby obscures in its Euro-centric focus US global expansion via this geopolitical region.

19   See Graham Cassano's "'The Last of the World's Afflicted Race That Believe in Free-dom': Race, Colonial Whiteness, and Imperialism in John Ford and Dudley Nichol's *The Hurricane* (1937)," *Journal of American Studies* 44 (2010): 117–136. While my dis-cussion pays closer attention to cinematic details, I basically agree with Cassano's assessment of the film: "I argue that *The Hurricane* offers a fundamental critique of European imperialism, and imperial 'whiteness.' At the same time, the energies for that critique come from a paradoxically 'progressive' orientalism that represents South Seas 'natives' as inherently wild and independent" (117). However, Cassano ignores the important convention of family in cinema, which is rarely granted to minorities. Ford's film expends great effort to place the Tahitian family at the center of the film, and hence deemphasizes ethnographic stereotypes of non-Western and wildly pro-miscuous tribal structures attributed to Polynesians.

20   Glenn Man points out that some structural difference is preserved in the film's ending, since natives are not fully given the treatment of a complex psychology: "Even as the film criticizes De Laage as representative of the repressiveness of civilized culture, it privileges him, reflecting the dominant ideology which proclaims that the West-erner can be both loving and sensual as well as sophisticated and principled. Mean-while, the natives remain pure in passion and sensuality, but simple and childlike." Man, "Hollywood Images of the Pacific," 22.

21   Joseph McBride, *Searching for John Ford* (New York: St. Martin's, 2001), 383–384.

22   Dan Ford, *Pappy: The Life of John Ford* (New York: Da Capo Press, 1998), 180.

23   Kit Parker Films, *December 7th: The Movie* ("*Banned for 50 Years by the U.S. Govern-ment*"), released 1991.

24   *December 7th*, dir. John Ford and Greg Toland (Navy/Field Photo, 1943). Unless oth-erwise stated, all discussions of the film refer to John Ford's edited version.

25   Field Photo proposal, quoted in McBride, *Searching for John Ford*, 354.

26   See website of the Japanese Cultural Center of Hawaii, http://hawaiiinternment.org/untold-story/untold-story.

27   McBride, *Searching for John Ford*, 384.

28   Franklin D. Roosevelt, "Infamy Speech," University of Oklahoma, College of Law, US Historical Documents, http://www.law.ou.edu/hist/infamy.html.

29   Here it is interesting to note that prior to the war Hawaii had applied for and been denied statehood twenty times.

30   Quoted in Bailey and Farber, *First Strange Place*, 140.

31   Ibid., 29.

32   Ibid., 17–18.

33   Geoffrey M. White and Jane Yi, "*December 7th*: Race and Nation in Wartime Docu-mentary," in Bernardi, *Classic Hollywood, Classic Whiteness*, 301–338, 304.

34   Ibid., 304–305.

35   Bailey and Farber, *First Strange Place*, 21–22.

36   Ibid., 22–23.

37   Bernardi, "Introduction," xiv–xv.

38   Doris "Dorie" Miller was the first African American to be awarded the Navy Cross. A mess attendant, third class, assigned to the USS *West Virginia*, Miller was honored for aiding the ship's captain and then manning, without previous training, an antiair-craft machine gun on the morning of December 7, 1941. Miller later died during the

war and was awarded posthumously the Purple Heart; the American Defense Service Medal, Fleet Clasp; the Asiatic-Pacific Campaign Medal; and the World War II Victory Medal.

39 Takashi Fujitani, "*Go for Broke,* the Movie: Japanese American Soldiers in U.S. National, Military, and Racial Discourses," in *Perilous Memories: The Asia-Pacific War(s),* ed. Takashi Fujitani, Geoffrey White, and Lisa Yoneyama (Durham, NC: Duke University Press, 2001), 239–266, 242.

40 Kracauer, "Mass Ornament," 77.

41 Moreover, the planes depicted here are American Dauntless bombers practicing military maneuvers interspersed with actual footage of Japanese Mitsubishi Zeros in flight.

42 Luce, "American Century," 159.

43 Ibid., 159.

44 See Homi Bhabha, "DissemiNation: Time, Narrative and the Margins of the Modern Nation," in *The Location of Culture* (London: Routledge), 139–170.

45 Benedict Anderson, *Imagined Communities: Reflections on the Origin and Spread of Nationalism* (London: Verso, 1983), 1–7.

46 Ibid., 1–7.

47 Kracauer, "Mass Ornament," 77.

48 Anderson, *Imagined Communities,* 9.

49 See Ferguson and Turnbull, *Oh, Say Can You See?* Ferguson and Turnbull compellingly discuss the overwhelming presence of the military in Hawaii, showing how it has normalized its presence (becoming virtually invisible) and obscured other legitimate forms of discourse, especially "those practiced by the indigenous people of Hawai'i, the descendents of contract laborers and other immigrant groups, feminists, [and] environmentalists" (xiv).

50 McBride, *Searching for John Ford,* 358.

51 Ibid., 335.

52 *The Battle of Midway,* dir. John Ford (Navy/Field Photo, 1942).

53 In order to prevent rivalry between the various military services, Ford strategically gave the Navy, the Marines, and Air Force equal representation in the film.

54 Clayton Koppes and Gregory Black, "What to Show the World: The Office of War Information and Hollywood, 1942–1945," *Journal of American History* 64 (1977): 87–105.

55 Lowe, *Immigrant Acts,* 1–36. See also Robert G. Lee's *Orientals: Asian Americans in Popular Culture* (Philadelphia: Temple University Press, 1999).

56 Lowe, *Immigrant Acts,* 5.

57 Ibid., 7–8.

58 Ronald Takaki, *Strangers from a Different Shore: A History of Asian Americans* (New York: Penguin, 1989), 357.

59 Here it is instructive to compare America's filmic treatment of its German and Italian enemies to that of the Japanese and Japanese Americans. Even as the United States learned about their horrific crimes against humanity in the implementation of the Final Solution, Germans were as a rule represented on screen as a misguided people whose corruption was due to their fascist leaders. Conversely, Japanese were usually depicted as innately evil.

60 According to Thomas Doherty, *Projections of War: Hollywood, American Culture and World War II* (New York: Columbia University Press, 1993), Hollywood's new

representation of minorities in World War II films had a profound social impact: "The sight and celebration of the heretofore invisible or lampooned granted a cinematic validation—and impetus—to a civil rights revolution in the making" (5).

61   Clayton Koppes and Gregory Black, *Hollywood Goes to War: How Politics, Profits and Propaganda Shaped WWII Movies* (New York: Free Press, 1987), 56.

62   Ibid., 57–58.

63   Ibid., 65.

64   Koppes and Black, "What to Show the World," 91.

65   See Koppes and Black, *Hollywood Goes to War* and "What to Show the World." According to Koppes and Black, the manual was widely distributed throughout Hollywood and welcomed especially by writers, who as a group tended to be more liberal and politically active.

66   Koppes and Black, "What to Show the World," 95. See also Doherty's *Projections of War*, where he points to Hollywood's desire to imitate and rival Nazi Germany's powerful propaganda machine, particularly as presented in the films of Leni Riefenstahl.

67   An early discussion of mine on this topic appeared as "War and Orientalism in Hollywood Combat Film," *Quarterly Review of Film and Video* 21, no. 4 (October–December 2004): 327–338.

68   Jeanine Basinger, *The World War II Combat Film: Anatomy of a Genre* (New York: Columbia University Press, 1986), 37. Basinger's work is indispensable in discussing combat as well as war films in general, laying out the evolution of the combat genre and its relation to history, technology, and the film industry.

69   Ibid., 24.

70   *Bataan*, dir. Tay Garnett (MGM, 1943).

71   Douglas MacArthur, quoted in Geoffrey Perret, *Old Soldiers Never Die: The Life of Douglas MacArthur* (Holbrook, MA: Adams Media, 1996), 26.

72   MacArthur, who claimed to be and was perceived as an expert on the Orient and its way of life, is of utmost importance in a study of World War II Orientalism, but my chapter here can deal with MacArthur only tangentially. A master at garnering and manipulating public opinion, MacArthur staked his entire career on his belief in the Orient's significance to America. His role in the war and in postwar Japan as the supreme commander of the occupation forces cannot be understood without careful consideration of his unique perspective of Asia.

73   We see the complete breakdown of this didactic aspect in many Vietnam films with their portrayal of war and imperialism as a social pathology.

74   Basinger, *World War II Combat Film*, 57.

75   Gerald W. Patton, *War and Race: The Black Officer in the American Military* (Westport, CT: Greenwood, 1981), 5.

76   Marvin Fletcher, *The Black Soldier and Officer in the U.S. Army 1891–1917* (Columbia: University of Missouri Press, 1974), 22–23.

77   Ibid., 36–37.

78   Frank Knox, quoted in Jack D. Foner, *Blacks and the Military in American History* (New York: Praeger, 1974), 77.

79   Theodore Roosevelt, quoted in ibid., 81.

80   Theodore Roosevelt, *The Rough Riders* (1899; repr., Lincoln: University of Nebraska Press, 1998), 144–145.

81   Ibid., 145.

82   Amy Kaplan, "Black and Blue on San Juan Hill," in Kaplan and Pease, *Cultures of U.S. Imperialism*, 219–236. Kaplan's excellent chapter discusses Roosevelt's narrative of the charge up San Juan Hill, one "which retrenches along racial lines" (221). The conflict in Roosevelt's narrative, she claims, occurs not so much between the American and the Spanish but between the white American and black American troops, who are forced to intermingle and fight side by side. Roosevelt's racist degradation of black American troops is part of the nation's larger imperial project that not only expands the empire abroad but also promises to reunify the nation, healing the Civil War wounds between the North and South and calling its legacy, the Reconstruction (and thereby black civil rights), into question. The black troops raise the threats of black rebellion and national self-representation, claims Kaplan, and resonate with those of the Cuban revolutionaries fighting for independence. Here it is interesting to compare Roosevelt's representation of black troops to that of Griffith in *Birth of a Nation*, where a divided country comes together in its common realization of blacks' unworthiness as American citizens.

83   David Levering Lewis, *When Harlem Was in Vogue* (Oxford: Oxford University Press, 1979), 3–4.

84   Richard J. Stillman, *Integration of the Negro in the U.S. Armed Forces* (New York: Praeger, 1968), 18–21.

85   Ibid., 19.

86   Roosevelt issued an executive order in December 1943 that instituted the acceptance of blacks on an equal basis into the military.

87   In spite of these overwhelming barriers, however, a small percentage of black soldiers still managed to see combat and win impressive military honors. See Stillman, *Integration of the Negro*, 25–26, and his description of the 99th Fighter Squadron, the 92nd Division, and the Navy stewards' branch.

88   Lee, *Orientals*, 106–144 and 145–179.

89   Ibid., 145.

90   Stillman, *Integration of the Negro*, 39–40.

91   See, for example, Michael Dempsey's perceptive essay "John Ford: A Reassessment," *Film Quarterly* 28, no. 4 (Summer 1975): 2–15. In contrast to Dempsey, I argue that Ford's incomplete advances in the depiction of a multicultural America cannot be judged and dismissed by contemporary standards but must be seen in the historical context in which such advances provided necessary breaks in the dominant white cultural discourse. Dempsey's essay is impressive, however, in that it offers an early critical evaluation of race in Ford's work, largely ignored by the many fans of his cinema.

92   Ronald Takaki, *Double Victory: A Multicultural History of America in World War II* (New York: Little, Brown, 2000), 49.

93   Doherty, *Projections of War*, 5.

94   Ibid., 5.

95   Ibid., 5.

96   Koppes and Black, *Hollywood Goes to War*, 95.

97   Ibid., 65.

98   Ibid., 67.

99   Koppes and Black, "What to Show the World," 95.

100   Koppes and Black, *Hollywood Goes to War*, 67.

101   Brian Taves, "The B Film: Hollywood's Other Half," in Balio, *Grand Design*, 313. According to Taves, 50 percent of films produced in the 1930s by major Hollywood studios (Big 8) can be classified as B films. Combined with smaller studios (Poverty

Row), the output of B films in the decade climbed to 75 percent, or a little over four thousand films.

102   *Menace of the Rising Sun*, producers Thomas Mead and Joseph O'Brian (Universal Pictures, 1942).

103   Rogin, *Blackface, White Noise*, 3–18.

104   See Lowe, *Immigrant Acts*, 1–36.

105   Bhabha, *Location of Culture*, 85.

106   Jeanine Basinger, *The World War II Combat Film* (Middletown, CT: Wesleyan University Press, 2003), 56–57.

107   Koppes and Black, *Hollywood Goes to War*, 275.

108   Douglas had also directed the comedy shorts *Spanky and Our Gang* during the 1930s and the feature film *General Spanky* (1936), with its minstrelsy performances, particularly those of Buckwheat (Billie Thomas) and Alfalfa (Carl Switzer).

109   Keye Luke was very well known in Hollywood for his bit parts since he starred in many film and TV shows that required Asian characters. Luke appeared as the "Number One Son" of Warner Oland's Charlie Chan. On television, he starred as Kato, the sidekick of the Green Hornet, and later in his career as Master Po, the venerable teacher of the Shaolin priest played by David Carradine, on the popular *Kung Fu* series. Luke also had numerous guest appearances on *M*A*S*H*, *Hawaii Five-0*, *T. J. Hooker*, and *Miami Vice*.

110   Kracauer, "Cult of Distraction," in Levin, *Mass Ornament*, 326.

111   Ibid., 326.

112   Ibid., 326.

CHAPTER 3   POSTWAR HAWAII AND THE BIRTH OF THE MILITARY-INDUSTRIAL COMPLEX

1   Rosenberg, *Spreading the American Dream*, 42.

2   Christina Klein, *Cold War Orientalism: Asia in the Middlebrow Imagination, 1945–1961* (Berkeley: University of California Press, 2003), 23.

3   See Penny M. von Eschen, *Satchmo Blows Up the World: Jazz Ambassadors Play the Cold War* (Cambridge, MA: Harvard University Press, 2006).

4   Lary May, *The Big Tomorrow: Hollywood and the Politics of the American Way* (Chicago: University of Chicago Press, 2000), 206.

5   Ibid., 207.

6   Dwight D. Eisenhower, "Farewell Address, January 17, 1961," in James Ledbetter, *Unwarranted Influence: Dwight D. Eisenhower and the Military-Industrial Complex* (New Haven, CT: Yale University Press, 2011), 211–220, 215–216.

7   May, *Big Tomorrow*, 206.

8   I would like to dedicate this chapter to the late Angel Medina, who introduced me to the philosophical concept of temporality and Deleuze's time image in many hours of discussion.

9   Gilles Deleuze, *Cinema 2: The Time Image*, trans. Hugh Tomlinson and Robert Galeta (Minneapolis: University of Minnesota Press, 1989), 4.

10   Ibid., 18.

11   Ibid., 15–16.

12   Cited in Lawrence H. Suid, *Guts and Glory: The Making of the American Military Image in Film* (Lexington: University Press of Kentucky, 2002), 145.

13 For the production history of *From Here to Eternity*, see Suid, *Guts and Glory*, 142–152.

14 See Charles I. Glicksberg, "Racial Attitudes in *From Here to Eternity*," *Phylon* (1940–1956) 14, no. 4 (1953): 384–389. Glicksberg argues that the novel, via its revolutionary character Prewitt, tries to confront racial prejudice with Prewitt, frequently rejecting the racial prejudices of his peers.

15 Bailey and Farber, *First Strange Place*, 22–23.

16 DeSoto Brown and Linda Arthur, *The Art of the Aloha Shirt* (Waipahu: Island Heritage, 2008), 36.

17 Ibid., 48–49.

18 Ibid., 61–62.

19 Ibid., 56–57.

20 Ibid., 62.

21 Paul Virilio, "Military Space," in *The Paul Virilio Reader*, ed. James der Derian (Oxford: Blackwell, 1998), 28.

22 Paul Virilio, "The State of Emergency," in der Derian, *Paul Virilio Reader*, 57.

23 Brian Neve and Fred Zinnemann, "A Past Master of His Craft: An Interview with Fred Zinnemann," *Cineaste* 23, no. 1 (1997): 15–19, 17–18.

24 Brian Neve, "HUAC, the Blacklist, and the Decline of Social Cinema," in Lev, *History of the American Cinema. The Fifties*, 77.

25 Ibid., 77.

26 Bailey and Farber, *First Strange Place*, 95.

27 Ibid., 102.

28 Ibid., 130.

29 Ibid., 100.

30 William Bradford Huie, "The Revolt of Mamie Stover: Part III of a New Novel," *American Mercury*, April 1951, 492–507, 494.

31 Ibid., 507.

32 Marilyn E. Hegarty, *Victory Girls, Khaki Wackies, and Patriotutes: The Regulation of Female Sexuality during World War II* (New York: New York University Press, 2008), 7.

33 Ibid., 158.

34 Ibid., 156.

35 Ibid., 158.

36 Ibid., 162.

37 Bailey and Farber, *First Strange Place*, 120.

38 May, *Big Tomorrow*, 204.

39 Ron Briley, "John Wayne and *Big Jim McLain* (1952): The Duke's Cold War Legacy," *Film & History* 31, no. 1 (2001): 28–33, 28.

40 Luis I. Reyes, *Made in Paradise: Hollywood's Films of Hawai'i and the South Seas* (Honolulu: Mutual Publishing, 1995), 70.

41 May, *Big Tomorrow*, 203.

42 Spurr, *Rhetoric of Empire*, 119.

43 Russell Meeuf, "John Wayne as 'Supercrip': Disabled Bodies and the Construction of 'Hard' Masculinity in *The Wings of Eagles*," *Cinema Journal* 48, no. 2 (Winter 2009): 88–113, 91–92.

44 Ibid., 92.

45 John Ford's biopic *The Wings of Eagles* (1957) in similar fashion depicts the disabled hero Frank Spig Wead (John Wayne) who enlists in the navy after the attack on Pearl Harbor and provides brilliant logistic help from the desk for the war effort. Thus, the

definition of the military body has now widened from the physically fit fighting body to that of the administrative soldier or expert. Once Wead's logistic innovation of the jeep resupplying larger carriers with planes shows its effects, he returns from the war theater into the fold of his family, resolving finally a melodramatic struggle waging throughout the film, as he is torn between his military and family duties.

46 James T. Campbell, "Print the Legend: John Wayne and Postwar American Culture," *Reviews in American History* 28, no. 3 (September 2000): 465–477, 472.

47 Michael Rogin, "Home of the Brave," in *The War Film*, ed. Robert Eberwein (New Brunswick, NJ: Rutgers University Press, 2006), 82.

48 Donald Bogle, *Toms, Coons, Mulattoes, Mammies & Bucks: An Interpretive History of Blacks in American Films* (New York: Continuum, 1991), 144.

49 Rogin, "Home of the Brave," 83.

50 Dean Itsuji Saranillio, "Colliding Histories," *Journal of Asian American Studies* 13, no. 3 (October 2010): 283–309, 294.

51 It is interesting to note that hula and military duty are directly conflated rather than presented in the image of "imperial hospitality" where female Hawaiian hula dancers entertain the troops. See Adria L. Imada, "The Army Learns to Luau: Imperial Hospitality and Military Photography in Hawai'i," *Contemporary Pacific* 20, no. 2 (Fall 2008): 328–361, 332.

52 Robert Eberwein, "Sexuality and Masculinity in World War II Combat Films," in *Masculinity: Bodies, Movies, Culture*, ed. Peter Lehman (London: Routledge, 2001), 149–166, 156.

53 See the *Pittsburgh Courier*, February 14, 1942: "Last week, without any public announcement or fanfare, the editors of *The Courier* introduced its war slogan—a double 'V' for a double victory to colored America."

54 Roosevelt, "Infamy Speech."

55 See Lee, *Orientals*, 145.

56 See Gilles Deleuze and Felix Guattari, *Kafka: Toward a Minor Literature*, trans. Dana Polan (Minneapolis: University of Minnesota Press, 1986). Particularly the chapter "What Is a Minor Literature?" (16–28) explores at length the strategic possibilities for Kafka to steer through a complex linguistic landscape involving German, the official administrative language of the empire, Czech, the national language of a politically oppressed region within the Habsburg Empire, and Yiddish, the language of diasporic Jewish culture.

57 Peter Lev, "Technology and Spectacle," in Lev, *History of the American Cinema. The Fifties*, 107.

58 Ibid., 107.

59 Ibid., 108.

60 Richard Dyer, *White* (London: Routledge, 1997), 127.

61 Lenora Foerstel and Angela Gilliam, "Foreword," in *Confronting the Margaret Mead Legacy: Scholarship, Empire, and the South Pacific* (Philadelphia: Temple University Press, 1994), xiii.

62 Juanita Hall, of African American and Irish descent, became the first African American woman to receive a Tony Award for her Broadway performance in *South Pacific*. In spite of this success, she was generally cast in very stereotypical roles such as a West Indian brothel keeper in Harold Arlen's musical *House of Flowers* (1954), a Chinese American marriage broker in Rodgers and Hammerstein's *Flower Drum Song* (1958), and in the minstrel role of Bloody Mary in the film version of *South Pacific*. The

implied subtext in this film situates her somewhere between a sly businesswoman and a pimp with echoes of a savage sorceress casting a spell upon Joe Cable.

63   The film follows here in the tradition of the plantation genre, discussed earlier in films such as *Waikiki Wedding* and *Honolulu*, a genre that seeks to extend the racial hierarchies of the Old South by depicting the plantation system in benign and sentimental terms, obscuring its legacy in slavery and colonial domination. In *South Pacific* it serves the purpose of advocating the new American benevolent imperialism and Orientalism and likewise obscures the military practices that secure global dominance.

64   Klein, *Cold War Orientalism*, 163.

65   Ibid., 160.

66   Ibid., 162.

67   Ibid., 162.

68   Rosenberg, *Spreading the American Dream*, 229.

69   Klein, *Cold War Orientalism*, 165.

70   Herbert Marcuse, *One-Dimensional Man: Studies in the Ideology of Advanced Industrial Society* (Boston: Beacon, 1964), 84.

71   Ferguson and Turnbull, *Oh, Say Can You See?*, xiii.

72   Ibid., xiii.

73   Henri Lefebvre, *The Critique of Everyday Life*, vol. 1, trans. John Moore (1947; London: Verso, 1991), 34.

74   Ibid., 30.

75   Ibid., 40.

76   Ibid., 40–41.

77   Allana Nash, *The Colonel: The Extraordinary Story of Colonel Tom Parker and Elvis Presley* (New York: Simon & Schuster, 2003), 174–180.

78   Teresia T. Keaiwa, "bikinis and other s/pacific n/oceans," *Contemporary Pacific* 6, no. 1 (Spring 1994): 87–109, 87.

79   See Imada, "Army Learns to Luau," 332–335.

80   Desmond, *Staging Tourism*, 171.

81   Simeon Man, "Aloha, Vietnam: Race and Empire in Hawai'i's Vietnam War," *American Quarterly* 67, no. 4 (December 2015): 1085–1108, 1085.

82   See Henry Louis Gates Jr., "What Was Black America's Double War?," *Root*, May 24, 2013.

83   As Bailey and Farber note in *First Strange Place*, the military's active involvement with mass prostitution was inspired by epidemiological reasons and the effort to manage and control the spread of venereal diseases. In addition, various zoning laws enforced by the military were meant to suppress protest from Hawaii's local populations against such a massive expansion of prostitution, which was outlawed in the territory.

84   Ferguson and Turnbull, *Oh, Say Can You See?*, 39.

85   Ibid., 40.

86   Haunani-Kay Trask, "The Birth of the Modern Hawaiian Movement: Kalama Valley, O'ahu," *Hawaiian Journal of History* 21 (1987): 126–153, 129–130.

87   Ibid., 130.

CHAPTER 4   CONCLUSION

1   A. O. Scott, "*50 First Dates* (2004): Film Review: A Love That's Forever, if Only for a Day," *New York Times*, February 13, 2004.

2   Roger Ebert, "*50 First Dates* Review," *Chicago Sun-Times*, February 13, 2004.

3   Francis Fukuyama's *The End of History and the Last Man* (1992; repr., New York: Simon & Schuster, 2006), with its controversial claim that the historical evolution of mankind has ended in Western liberal democracy, anticipates the new amnesia and indulgence in white matters.

4   In the 1990s, a focus on Hawaiian diversity was still possible in films, though guided by a mainland model culture. For example, *Race in the Sun* (1996), starring Halle Berry and James Belushi, shows more ethnic diversity but casts Hawaiian school kids as misfits in need of mainland inspiration and tutelage provided by the new science teacher Sandra Beecher (Halle Berry).

5   Trask, "Birth of the Modern Hawaiian Movement," 126.

6   Ibid., 126–127.

7   Klein, *Cold War Orientalism*, 224.

8   Gina Marchetti, *Romance and the "Yellow Peril": Race, Sex, and Discursive Strategies in Hollywood Fiction* (Berkeley: University of California Press, 1993), 110.

9   Ibid., 111–113.

10   Klein, *Cold War Orientalism*, 230.

11   See Charles Young, "Missing Action: POW Films, Brainwashing and the Korean War, 1954–1968," in *Hollywood and War: The Film Reader*, ed. J. David Slocum (London: Routledge, 2006), 207–223. Young discusses the very real fear of the government and the nation that American Korean War POWs had been brainwashed and collaborated with the enemy.

12   Michael Rogin, "'Make My Day!' Spectacle as Amnesia in Imperial Politics," in Slocum, *Hollywood and War*, 81–87, 81.

13   "The Disparate Treatment of Native Hawaiians in the Criminal Justice System" (Justice Policy Institute, University of Hawai'i at Manoa, 2010), 10–13.

14   Ibid., 12.

15   Haunani-Kay Trask, "The Color of Violence," *Social Justice* 31, no. 4 (2004): 8–16, 12.

SELECTED BIBLIOGRAPHY

Abel, Richard. *Encyclopedia of Early Cinema*. New York: Routledge, 2005.

Anderson, Benedict. *Imagined Communities: Reflections on the Origin and Spread of Nationalism*. London: Verso, 1983.

Angell, Lowell. *Theatres of Hawai'i*. Charleston, SC: Arcadia, 2011.

Arendt, Hannah. *Imperialism: Part Two of the Origins of Totalitarianism*. New York: Harcourt Brace Jovanovich, 1968.

Asahina, Robert. *Just Americans: How Japanese Won a War at Home and Abroad*. New York: Gotham Books, 2006.

Bailey, Beth, and David Farber. *The First Strange Place: Race and Sex in World War II Hawaii*. Baltimore: Johns Hopkins University Press, 1992.

Balio, Tino, ed. *Grand Design: Hollywood as a Modern Business Enterprise, 1930–1939*. History of the American Cinema, no. 5. Berkeley: University of California Press, 1995.

Basinger, Jeanine. *The World War II Combat Film*. Middletown, CT: Wesleyan University Press, 2003.

———. *The World War II Combat Film: Anatomy of a Genre*. New York: Columbia University Press, 1986.

Bayoumi, Mustafa, and Andrew Rubin, eds. *The Edward Said Reader*. New York: Vintage, 2000.

Beckwith, Martha. *Hawaiian Mythology*. Honolulu: University of Hawai'i Press, 1976.

Belton, John, ed. *Movies and Mass Culture*. New Brunswick, NJ: Rutgers University Press, 1996.

Beltrán, Mary, and Camilla Fojas, eds. *Mixed Race Hollywood*. New York: New York University Press, 2008.

Benjamin, Walter. "The Work of Art in the Age of Mechanical Reproduction." In *Illuminations*, edited by Hannah Arendt, translated by Harry Zohn, 217–251. New York: Schocken, 1968.

Bernardi, Daniel, ed. *Classic Hollywood, Classic Whiteness*. Minneapolis: University of Minnesota Press, 2001.

———. "Introduction." In Bernardi, *Classic Hollywood, Classic Whiteness*, xiii–xxvi.

———. "Introduction: Race and the Emergence of U.S. Cinema." In *The Birth of Whiteness: Race and the Emergence of U.S. Cinema*, edited by Daniel Bernardi, 1–11. New Brunswick, NJ: Rutgers University Press, 1996.

———, ed. *The Persistence of Whiteness: Race and Contemporary Hollywood Cinema*. London: Routledge, 2007.

Betts, Raymond F. "The Illusionary Island: Hollywood's Pacific Place." *East-West Film Journal* 5, no. 2 (July 1991): 30–46.

Bhabha, Homi. *The Location of Culture*. London: Routledge, 1994.

Bogdanovich, Peter. *John Ford*. Rev. ed. Berkeley: University of California Press, 1978.

Bogle, Donald. *Toms, Coons, Mulattoes, Mammies & Bucks: An Interpretive History of Blacks in American Films*. New York: Continuum, 1991.

Brauer, Kinley. "Manifest Destiny Revisited." *Diplomatic History* 23, no. 2 (Spring 1999): 379–384.

Briley, Ron. "John Wayne and *Big Jim McLain* (1952): The Duke's Cold War Legacy." *Film & History* 31, no. 1 (2001): 28–33.

Bronfen, Elisabeth. *Specters of War: Hollywood's Engagement with Military Conflict.* New Brunswick, NJ: Rutgers University Press, 2012.

Brown, DeSoto. "Beautiful, Romantic Hawaii: How the Fantasy Image Came to Be." *Journal of Decorative and Propaganda Arts* 20 (1994): 254–271.

Brown, DeSoto, and Linda Arthur. *The Art of the Aloha Shirt.* Waipahu: Island Heritage, 2008.

Brown, Taylor Kate. "Aloha to the US: Is Hawai'i an Occupied Nation?" *BBC News Magazine,* November 2, 2015.

Buck, Elizabeth. *Paradise Remade: The Politics of Culture and History of Hawai'i.* Philadelphia: Temple University Press, 1993.

Buruma, Ian, and Avishai Margalit, eds. *Occidentalism: The West in the Eyes of the Enemies.* New York: Penguin, 2004.

Campbell, James T. "Print the Legend: John Wayne and Postwar American Culture." *Reviews in American History* 28, no. 3 (September 2000): 465–477.

Cassano, Graham. "'The Last of the World's Afflicted Race That Believe in Freedom': Race, Colonial Whiteness, and Imperialism in John Ford and Dudley Nichol's *The Hurricane* (1937)." *Journal of American Studies* 44 (2010): 117–136.

Chambers, John Whiteclay, and David Culbert, eds. *World War II: Film and History.* Oxford: Oxford University Press, 1996.

Chapman, James. *War and Film.* London: Reaktion Books, 2008.

Chow, Rey. *The Protestant Ethnic & the Spirit of Capitalism.* New York: Columbia University Press, 2002.

Clarke, Thurston. *Pearl Harbor Ghosts: December 7, 1941—The Day That Still Haunts the Nation.* New York: Ballantine Books, 2001.

Clover, Carol J. "Dancin' in the Rain." In Cohan, *Hollywood Musicals,* 157–173.

Cohan, Steven, ed. *Hollywood Musicals: The Film Reader.* New York: Routledge, 2006.

Cooper, George, and Gavan Daws. *Land and Power in Hawaii: The Democratic Years.* Honolulu: Benchmark Books, 1985.

Corrin, Lisa G. "Mining the Museum: Artists Look at Museums, Museums Look at Themselves." In *Mining the Museum: An Installation by Fred Wilson,* edited by Lisa G. Corrin, 1–22. New York: New Press, 1994.

Courtney, Susan. *Hollywood Fantasies of Miscegenation: Spectacular Narratives of Gender and Race, 1903–1967.* Princeton, NJ: Princeton University Press, 2005.

Cripps, Thomas. *Making Movies Black: The Hollywood Message Movie from World War II to the Civil Rights Era.* Oxford: Oxford University Press, 1993.

DeBauche, Leslie Midkiff. *Reel Patriotism: The Movies and World War I.* Madison: University of Wisconsin Press, 1997.

Deleuze, Gilles. *Cinema 1: The Movement-Image.* Translated by Hugh Tomlinson and Barbara Habberjam. Minneapolis: University of Minnesota Press, 1986.

———. *Cinema 2: The Time Image.* Translated by Hugh Tomlinson and Robert Galeta. Minneapolis: University of Minnesota Press, 1989.

Deleuze, Gilles, and Felix Guattari. *Kafka: Toward a Minor Literature.* Translated by Dana Polan. Minneapolis: University of Minnesota Press, 1986.

Dempsey, Michael. "John Ford: A Reassessment." *Film Quarterly* 28, no. 4 (Summer 1975): 2–15.

der Derian, James, ed. *The Paul Virilio Reader.* Oxford: Blackwell, 1998.

Desmond, Jane C. *Staging Tourism: Bodies on Display from Waikiki to Sea World*. Chicago: University of Chicago Press, 1999.

Dixon, Wheeler Winston, ed. *American Cinema of the 1940s: Themes and Variations*. New Brunswick, NJ: Rutgers University Press, 2005.

———. *A Short History of Film*. New Brunswick, NJ: Rutgers University Press, 2013.

———. *Visions of Paradise: Images of Eden in the Cinema*. New Brunswick, NJ: Rutgers University Press, 2006.

Doherty, Thomas. *Projections of War: Hollywood, American Culture and World War II*. New York: Columbia University Press, 1993.

Dombrowski, Nicole Ann. *Women and War in the Twentieth Century*. London: Routledge, 2004.

Dougherty, Michael. *To Steal a Kingdom: Probing Hawaiian History*. Waimanalo, HI: Island Style Press, 1992.

Dower, John W. *War without Mercy: Race & Power in the Pacific War*. New York: Pantheon Books, 1986.

Dye, Bob, ed. *Hawai'i Chronicles III: World War Two in Hawai'i*. Honolulu: University of Hawai'i Press, 2000.

Dyer, Richard. *Stars*. London: BFI, 1998.

———. *White: Essays on Race and Culture*. London: Routledge, 1997.

Ebert, Roger. "*50 First Dates* Review." *Chicago Sun-Times*, February 13, 2004.

Eberwein, Robert. *The Hollywood War Film*. Oxford: Blackwell, 2010.

———. "Sexuality and Masculinity in World War II Combat Films." In *Masculinity: Bodies, Movies, Culture*, edited by Peter Lehman, 149–166. London: Routledge, 2001.

———, ed. *The War Film*. New Brunswick, NJ: Rutgers University Press, 2006.

Eisenhower, Dwight D. "Farewell Address, January 17, 1961." In Ledbetter, *Unwarranted Influence*, 211–220.

Eschen, Penny M. von. *Satchmo Blows Up the World: Jazz Ambassadors Play the Cold War*. Cambridge, MA: Harvard University Press, 2006.

Ferguson, Kathy E., and Phyllis Turnbull. *Oh, Say Can You See? The Semiotics of the Military in Hawai'i*. Minneapolis: University of Minnesota Press, 1999.

Fischer, Lucy, ed. *American Cinema of the 1920s: Themes and Variations*. New Brunswick, NJ: Rutgers University Press, 2009.

Fletcher, Marvin. *The Black Soldier and Officer in the U.S. Army 1891–1917*. Columbia: University of Missouri Press, 1974.

Foerstel, Lenora, and Angela Gilliam. *Confronting the Margaret Mead Legacy: Scholarship, Empire, and the South Pacific*. Philadelphia: Temple University Press, 1994.

Foner, Jack D. *Blacks and the Military in American History*. New York: Praeger, 1974.

Ford, Dan. *Pappy: The Life of John Ford*. New York: Da Capo Press, 1998.

Fujitani, Takashi. "*Go for Broke*, the Movie: Japanese American Soldiers in U.S. National, Military, and Racial Discourses." In *Perilous Memories: The Asia-Pacific War(s)*, edited by Takashi Fujitani, Geoffrey White, and Lisa Yoneyama, 239–266. Durham, NC: Duke University Press, 2001.

Fukuyama, Francis. *The End of History and the Last Man*. 1992. Reprint, New York: Simon & Schuster, 2006.

Gates, Henry Louis, Jr. "What Was Black America's Double War?" *Root*, May 24, 2013.

Gaudreault, Andre, ed. *American Cinema 1890–1909: Themes and Variations*. New Brunswick, NJ: Rutgers University Press, 2009.

Geiger, Jeffrey. *Facing the Pacific: Polynesia and the U.S. Imperial Imagination.* Honolulu: University of Hawai'i Press, 2007.

Gewertz, Deborah, and Frederick Errington. "We Think Therefore We Are?" In Kaplan and Pease, *Cultures of U.S. Imperialism,* 635–655.

Ginneken, Jaap Van. *Screening Difference: How Hollywood's Blockbuster Films Imagine Race, Ethnicity, and Culture.* Plymouth, UK: Rowman & Littlefield, 2007.

Glicksberg, Charles I. "Racial Attitudes in *From Here to Eternity.*" *Phylon* (1940–1956) 14, no. 4 (1953): 384–389.

Grant, Barry Keith, ed. *American Cinema of the 1960s: Themes and Variations.* New Brunswick, NJ: Rutgers University Press, 2008.

Greenblatt, Stephen. *Marvelous Possessions: The Wonder of the New World.* Chicago: University of Chicago Press, 1991.

Hall, Mordaunt. "Review of *Rain.*" *New York Times,* October 13, 1932.

Hansen, Miriam. *Babel & Babylon: Spectatorship in American Silent Film.* Cambridge, MA: Harvard University Press, 1991.

Hark, Ina Rae, ed. *American Cinema of the 1930s: Themes and Variations.* New Brunswick, NJ: Rutgers University Press, 2007.

Hegarty, Marilyn E. *Victory Girls, Khaki Wackies, and Patriotutes: The Regulation of Female Sexuality during World War II.* New York: New York University Press, 2008.

Heimann, Jim, ed. *Hula: Vintage Hawaiian Graphics.* Cologne: Taschen, 2003.

Hemmings, Kaui Hart. *The Descendants.* London: Vintage Books, 2009.

Hoopes, Roy. *When the Stars Went to War: Hollywood and World War II.* New York: Random House, 1994.

Huang, Yunte. *Charlie Chan: The Untold Story of the Honorable Detective and His Rendezvous with American History.* New York: Norton, 2010.

Huie, William Bradford. "The Revolt of Mamie Stover: Part III of a New Novel." *American Mercury,* April 1951, 492–507.

Hunt, Michael H. "East Asia in Henry Luce's 'American Century.'" *Diplomatic History* 23, no. 2 (Spring 1999): 321–353.

Imada, Adria L. *Aloha America: Hula Circuits through the U.S. Empire.* Durham, NC: Duke University Press, 2012.

———. "The Army Learns to Luau: Imperial Hospitality and Military Photography in Hawai'i." *Contemporary Pacific* 20, no. 2 (Fall 2008): 328–361.

———. "Hawaiians on Tour: Hula Circuits through the American Empire." *American Quarterly* 56, no. 1 (March 2004): 111–149.

Jacobson, Matthew Frye, and Gaspar González. *What Have They Built You to Do? The Manchurian Candidate and Cold War America.* Minneapolis: University of Minnesota Press, 2006.

Kaeppler, Adrienne L. "Acculturation in Hawaiian Dance." *Yearbook of the International Folk Music Council* 4 (1972): 38–46.

Kaplan, Amy. *The Anarchy of Empire in the Making of U.S. Culture.* Cambridge, MA: Harvard University Press, 2002.

———. "Black and Blue on San Juan Hill." In Kaplan and Pease, *Cultures of U.S. Imperialism,* 219–236.

Kaplan, Amy, and Donald Pease, eds. *Cultures of U.S. Imperialism.* Durham, NC: Duke University Press, 1993.

Keaiwa, Teresia T. "bikinis and other s/pacific n/oceans." *Contemporary Pacific* 6, no. 1 (Spring 1994): 87–109.

Keil, Charlie, and Ben Singer, eds. *American Cinema of the 1910s: Themes and Variations.* New Brunswick, NJ: Rutgers University Press, 2009.

Kelly, Mary Pat. *Proudly We Served: The Men of the USS Mason.* Annapolis, MD: Naval Institute Press, 1995.

Klein, Christina. *Cold War Orientalism: Asia in the Middlebrow Imagination, 1945–1961.* Berkeley: University of California Press, 2003.

Konzett, Delia Malia Caparoso. "War and Orientalism in Hollywood Combat Film." *Quarterly Review of Film and Video* 21, no. 4 (October–December 2004): 327–338.

Koppes, Clayton, and Gregory Black. *Hollywood Goes to War: How Politics, Profits and Propaganda Shaped WWII Movies.* New York: Free Press, 1987.

———. "What to Show the World: The Office of War Information and Hollywood, 1942–1945." *Journal of American History* 64 (1977): 87–105.

Kracauer, Siegfried. "Cult of Distraction." In Levin, *Mass Ornament*, 323–328.

———. "The Mass Ornament." In Levin, *Mass Ornament*, 75–86.

Ledbetter, James. *Unwarranted Influence: Dwight D. Eisenhower and the Military-Industrial Complex.* New Haven, CT: Yale University Press, 2011.

Lee, Robert G. *Orientals: Asian Americans in Popular Culture.* Philadelphia: Temple University Press, 1999.

Lefebvre, Henri. *The Critique of Everyday Life.* Vol. 1. Translated by John Moore. 1947. London: Verso, 1991.

Lev, Peter, ed. *History of the American Cinema. The Fifties: Transforming the Screen.* Berkeley: University of California Press, 2003.

———. "Technology and Spectacle." In Lev, *History of the American Cinema. The Fifties*, 107–125. Berkeley: University of California Press, 2003.

Levin, Thomas Y., ed. and trans. *The Mass Ornament: Weimar Essays.* Cambridge, MA: Harvard University Press, 1995.

Lewis, David Levering. *When Harlem Was in Vogue.* Oxford: Oxford University Press, 1979.

Liliuokalani. *Hawaii's Story by Hawaii's Queen.* Honolulu: Mutual Publishing, 1990.

Lowe, Lisa. *Immigrant Acts: On Asian American Cultural Politics.* Durham, NC: Duke University Press, 1996.

Luce, Henry R. "The American Century." Reprinted in *Diplomatic History* 23, no. 2 (Spring 1999): 159–171.

Macfie, Alexander Lyon. *Orientalism.* London: Longman, 2002.

———, ed. *Orientalism: A Reader.* New York: New York University Press, 2000.

Maltby, Richard. "The Production Code and the Hays Office." In Balio, *Grand Design*, 37–72.

Man, Glenn K. S. "Hollywood Images of the Pacific." *East-West Film Journal* 5, no. 2 (1991): 16–30.

Man, Simeon. "Aloha, Vietnam: Race and Empire in Hawai'i's Vietnam War." *American Quarterly* 67, no. 4 (December 2015): 1085–1108.

Marchetti, Gina. *Romance and the "Yellow Peril": Race, Sex, and Discursive Strategies in Hollywood Fiction.* Berkeley: University of California Press, 1993.

Marcuse, Herbert. *One-Dimensional Man: Studies in the Ideology of Advanced Industrial Society.* Boston: Beacon, 1964.

Matelski, Marilyn J., and Nancy Lynch Street, eds. *War and Film in America: Historical and Critical Essays.* London: McFarland, 2003.

May, Lary. *The Big Tomorrow: Hollywood and the Politics of the American Way.* Chicago: University of Chicago Press, 2000.

Mayne, Judith. *Private Novels, Public Films.* Athens: University of Georgia Press, 1988.

Mayo, Mike. *War Movies: Classic Conflict on Film.* Farmington Hills, MI: Visible Ink Press, 1999.

McBride, Joseph. *Searching for John Ford.* New York: St. Martin's, 2001.

McClintock, Anne. *Imperial Leather: Race, Gender and Sexuality in the Colonial Conquest.* London: Routledge, 1995.

Medina, Angel. *Reflection, Time and the Novel: Toward a Communicative Theory of Literature.* London: Routledge, 1979.

Meeuf, Russell. "John Wayne as 'Supercrip': Disabled Bodies and the Construction of 'Hard' Masculinity in *The Wings of Eagles.*" *Cinema Journal* 48, no. 2 (Winter 2009): 88–113.

Mellencamp, Patricia. "*Gold Diggers of 1933*: Containing Social Turmoil—Containing Women." In Cohan, *Hollywood Musicals*, 65–76.

Melzer, Arthur M., Jerry Weinberger, and M. Richard Zinman, eds. *Multiculturalism and American Democracy.* Kansas: University of Kansas Press, 1998.

Michener, James A. *Hawaii.* New York: Ballantine Books, 1959.

———. *Tales of the South Pacific.* New York: Macmillan, 1974.

Mintz, Steven, and Randy Roberts, eds. *Hollywood's America: United States History through Its Films.* New York: Brandywine Press, 1993.

Monaco, Paul. *History of the American Cinema. The Sixties: 1960–1969.* New York: Scribner, 2001.

Musser, Charles. *The Emergence of Cinema: The American Screen to 1907.* Berkeley: University of California Press, 1990.

Nash, Allana. *The Colonel: The Extraordinary Story of Colonel Tom Parker and Elvis Presley.* New York: Simon & Schuster, 2003.

Neve, Brian. "HUAC, the Blacklist, and the Decline of Social Cinema." In Lev, *History of the American Cinema. The Fifties*, 65–86.

Neve, Brian, and Fred Zinnemann. "A Past Master of His Craft: An Interview with Fred Zinnemann." *Cineaste* 23, no. 1 (1997): 15–19.

Okihiro, Gary Y. *The Columbia Guide to Asian American History.* New York: Columbia University Press, 2001.

———. *Island World: A History of Hawai'i and the United States.* Berkeley: University of California Press, 2008.

———. *Margins and Mainstreams: Asians in American History and Culture.* Seattle: University of Washington Press, 1994.

———. *Pineapple Culture: A History of the Tropical and Temperate Zones.* Berkeley: University of California Press, 2009.

———. "When and Where I Enter." In *Asian American Studies: A Reader*, edited by Jean Yu-Wen Shen Wu and Min Song, 3–20. New Brunswick, NJ: Rutgers University Press, 2000.

Orgeron, Marsha. "Making *It* in Hollywood: Clara Bow, Fandom, and Consumer Culture." *Cinema Journal* 42, no. 4 (Summer 2003): 76–97.

Patton, Gerald W. *War and Race: The Black Officer in the American Military.* Westport, CT: Greenwood, 1981.

Perret, Geoffrey. *Old Soldiers Never Die: The Life of Douglas MacArthur.* Holbrook, MA: Adams Media, 1996.

Pomerance, Murray, ed. *American Cinema of the 1950s: Themes and Variations.* New Brunswick, NJ: Rutgers University Press, 2005.

Redhead, Steve, ed. *The Paul Virilio Reader.* New York: Columbia University Press, 2004.

Reyes, Luis I. *Made in Paradise: Hollywood's Films of Hawai'i and the South Seas.* Honolulu: Mutual Publishing, 1995.

Rhodes, Karen. *Booking Hawaii Five-O: An Episode Guide and Critical History of the 1968–1980 Television Detective Series*. London: McFarland, 1997.

Robin, Ron. *Enclaves of America: The Rhetoric of American Political Architecture Abroad, 1900–1965*. Princeton, NJ: Princeton University Press, 1992.

Rogin, Michael. *Blackface, White Noise: Jewish Immigrants in the Hollywood Melting Pot*. Berkeley: University of California Press, 1996.

———. "Home of the Brave." In Eberwein, *War Film*, 82–89.

———. "'Make My Day!' Spectacle as Amnesia in Imperial Politics." In Slocum, *Hollywood and War*, 81–87.

Rony, Fatimah Tobing. "*King Kong* and the Monster in Ethnographic Cinema." In *Critical Visions in Film Theory*, edited by Timothy Corrigan et al., 840–859. Boston: Bedford/St. Martin's, 2011.

Roosevelt, Franklin D. "Infamy Speech." University of Oklahoma, College of Law, US Historical Documents. http://www.law.ou.edu/hist/infamy.html.

Roosevelt, Theodore. *The Rough Riders*. 1899. Reprint, Lincoln: University of Nebraska Press, 1998.

Rosenberg, Emily S. *Spreading the American Dream: Economic and Cultural Expansionism 1890–1945*. New York: Hill & Wang, 1982.

Rubin, Martin. "Busby Berkeley and the Backstage Musical." In Cohan, *Hollywood Musicals*, 53–61.

Said, Edward. *Culture and Imperialism*. New York: Knopf, 1993.

———. *Orientalism*. New York: Vintage Books, 1979.

———. *Representations of the Intellectual*. New York: Vintage, 1996.

Saranillio, Dean Itsuji. "Colliding Histories." *Journal of Asian American Studies* 13, no. 3 (October 2010): 283–309.

Schatz, Thomas. *History of the American Cinema. Boom and Bust: American Cinema in the 1940s*. Berkeley: University of California Press, 1997.

Schmitt, Robert C. *Hawaii in the Movies, 1898–1959*. Honolulu: University of Hawai'i Press, 1990.

Scott, A. O. "*50 First Dates* (2004): Film Review: A Love That's Forever, if Only for a Day." *New York Times*, February 13, 2004.

Sennwald, Andre. "Flirtation Walk, or Life among the Cadets at the Strand." *New York Times*, November 29, 1934.

Shohat, Ella, and Robert Stam. *Unthinking Eurocentrism: Multiculturalism and the Media*. London: Routledge, 1994.

Silva, Noenoe K. *Aloha Betrayed: Native Hawaiian Resistance to American Colonialism*. Durham, NC: Duke University Press, 2004.

Slocum, J. David, ed. *Hollywood and War: The Film Reader*. London: Routledge, 2006.

Spurr, David. *The Rhetoric of Empire: Colonial Discourse in Journalism, Travel Writing, and Imperial Administration*. Durham, NC: Duke University Press, 1993.

Stannard, David E. *Honor Killing: How the Infamous "Massie Affair" Transformed Hawai'i*. London: Penguin, 2005.

Stillman, Richard J. *Integration of the Negro in the U.S. Armed Forces*. New York: Praeger, 1968.

Sturdevant, Saundra Pollock, and Brenda Stoltzfus. *Let the Good Times Roll: Prostitution and the U.S. Military in Asia*. New York: New Press, 1992.

Suid, Lawrence H. *Guts and Glory: The Making of the American Military Image in Film*. Lexington: University Press of Kentucky, 2002.

Tabrah, Ruth M. *Hawaii: A History*. New York: Norton, 1984.

Takaki, Ronald. *A Different Mirror: A History of Multicultural America.* Boston: Little, Brown, 1993.

————. *Double Victory: A Multicultural History of America in World War II.* New York: Little, Brown, 2000.

————. *Pau Hana: Plantation Life and Labor in Hawaii, 1835–1920.* Honolulu: University of Hawai'i Press, 1983.

————. *Strangers from a Different Shore: A History of Asian Americans.* New York: Penguin, 1989.

Tasker, Yvonne. *Soldier's Stories: Military Women in Cinema and Television since World War II.* Durham, NC: Duke University Press, 2011.

Taves, Brian. "The B Film: Hollywood's Other Half." In Balio, *Grand Design,* 313–350.

Taylor, Charles. *Multiculturalism.* Edited by Amy Gutman. Princeton, NJ: Princeton University Press, 1994.

Thelen, David, and Frederick E. Hoxie, eds. *Discovering America: Essays on the Search for an Identity.* Chicago: University of Illinois Press, 1994.

Trask, Haunani-Kay. "The Birth of the Modern Hawaiian Movement: Kalama Valley, O'ahu." *Hawaiian Journal of History* 21 (1987): 126–153.

————. "The Color of Violence." *Social Justice* 31, no. 4 (2004): 8–16.

————. *From a Native Daughter: Colonialism and Sovereignty in Hawai'i.* Rev. ed. Honolulu: University of Hawai'i Press, 1999.

Turse, Nick. *The Complex: How the Military Invades Our Everyday Lives.* London: Faber & Faber, 2008.

Twain, Mark. *Letters from Hawaii.* 1866. Reprint, Honolulu: University of Hawai'i Press, 1975.

————. *Roughing It in the Sandwich Islands: Hawaii in the 1860s.* 1872. Reprint, Honolulu: Mutual Publishing, 1990.

Vera, Hernan, and Andrew Gordon, "Sincere Fictions of the White Self in the American Cinema." In Bernardi, *Classic Hollywood, Classic Whiteness,* xi–xxvi.

Vidor, King. *A Tree Is a Tree.* New York: Harcourt Brace, 1953.

Virilio, Paul. *Art and Fear.* Translated by Julie Rose. New York: Continuum, 2006.

————. *Desert Screen: War at the Speed of Light.* Translated by Michael Degener. New York: Continuum, 2002.

————. "Military Space." In der Derian, *Paul Virilio Reader,* 22–28.

————. "The State of Emergency." In der Derian, *Paul Virilio Reader,* 46–57.

————. *War and Cinema: The Logistics of Perception.* Translated by Patrick Camiller. London: Verso, 1989.

Virilio, Paul, and Sylvere Lotringer. *Pure War.* Translated by Mark Polizotti. New York: Semiotext(e), 1983.

White, Geoffrey M., and Jane Yi. "*December 7th*: Race and Nation in Wartime Documentary." In Bernardi, *Classic Hollywood, Classic Whiteness,* 301–338.

Wilson, Rob. *Reimagining the American Pacific.* Durham, NC: Duke University Press, 2000.

Wood, Houston. *Displacing Natives: The Rhetorical Production of Hawai'i.* Lanham, MD: Rowman & Littlefield, 1999.

Yellin, Emily. *Our Mothers' War: American Women at Home and at the Front during World War II.* New York: Free Press, 2004.

Young, Charles. "Missing Action: POW Films, Brainwashing and the Korean War, 1954–1968." In Slocum, *Hollywood and War,* 207–223.

Young, Robert. *Colonial Desire: Hybridity in Theory, Culture, and Race.* London: Routledge, 1995.

————. *White Mythologies: Writing History and the West.* London: Routledge, 1990.

Žižek, Slavoj. *The Plague of Fantasies.* London: Verso, 1997.

INDEX

ABOUT THE AUTHOR

DELIA MALIA CAPROSO KONZETT is an associate professor of English and cinema studies at the University of New Hampshire. She holds a PhD from the University of Chicago, has taught in film programs at Yale University and NYU Tisch School of the Arts, and is the author of *Ethnic Modernisms: Yezierska, Hurston, Rhys, and the Aesthetics of Dislocation.* Her publications in numerous film and literary journals cover a variety of topics and contexts on representations of race in film and literature.